GETTING STARTED IN FORENSIC PSYCHOLOGY PRACTICE

How to Create a Forensic Specialty in Your Mental Health Practice

Eric G. Mart

Chris E. Stout, Series Editor

WILEY

John Wiley & Sons, Inc.

Library of Congress Cataloging-in-Publication Data:

Mart, Eric G.
    Getting started in forensic psychology practice : how to create a forensic
specialty in your mental health practice / by Eric G. Mart.
        p.   cm. — (Getting started series)
    Includes bibliographical references and index.
    ISBN-13: 978-0-471-75313-1 (pbk.)
    ISBN-10: 0-471-75313-0 (pbk.)
    1. Forensic psychology.   2. Forensic psychology—Practice.   I. Title.   II.
RA1148.M29   2006
614'.15–dc22
                                                    2006007383

Printed in the United States of America.

10 9 8 7 6 5 4 3 2 1

To my parents, Clyde and Maureen Mart,
and my other parents, John and Ardis McCallion

Contents

CONTENTS

Series Preface

As the behavioral health care marketplace grows more challenging, providers are finding it necessary to develop smarter business tactics in order to be successful. We are faced with shifting payment structures, increasing competition, complex funding mechanisms, the bankruptcy of many managed care agencies, and growing malpractice liability risks, all against a backdrop of layoffs and dwindling economic resources. It is times like these that make Wiley's *Getting Started* series of books all the more important.

Many individuals studying in the mental health professions graduate with no idea of how to go about starting their own mental health practice. Alternatively, there are many health practitioners who wish to shift the focus of their current practice into other areas. The *Getting Started* series of books provides the information, ideas, tools, and strategies providers need to enable their practices to evolve and thrive in any circumstance. This series works to break down the ingredients of a successful mental health practice into more manageable components, and thus more achievable components. It is my goal to bring readers the best of the best in the *Getting Started* series in an effort to help them start, maintain, and expand their successful mental health practice.

The *Getting Started* series is not discipline specific. It is meant for all levels of behavioral health care students, as well as providers—

undergraduate students, and professionals in all the fields of behavioral health care. Current books include *Getting Started in Personal and Executive Coaching* and *Getting Started in Private Practice*, and now *Getting Started in Forensic Psychology Practice*. Other titles will focus on various mental health disciplines including group practice and marriage and family practice, as well as topics such as integrating technology with your mental health services.

Successful practice in any area or specialty takes work; there are no overnight successes. But being successful is quite doable. This series provides the organizing methods most of us never learned in graduate or medical school training, or that were available only by hiring one's own consultant. You will learn what works and what doesn't work without having to make costly missteps first.

Is establishing or growing your practice going to be difficult? To a degree, the likely answer is yes. Of course, it will take some work, but it will likely be well worth the effort. I hope you find the *Getting Started* series to be a helpful set of tools in achieving your professional goals.

Chris E. Stout
Series Editor

Acknowledgments

Thanks to my colleagues of the Psylaw-L and American Board of Forensic Psychology Listservs for their comments and the benefit of their experience. I am also grateful to Chris Stout for his input on this project. Finally, I wish to thank the baristas at Borders in Concord, New Hampshire, for keeping me well supplied with espresso during the writing of this book.

Eric G. Mart

Introduction

General mental health practice has become more difficult for practitioners with each passing year. Psychologists and other mental health practitioners are being pressured professionally and economically by a number of forces. Managed care has made things much harder with its reduced coverage for clients and almost complete neglect of diagnostic testing. There are increased demands for paperwork and a general interference with the process of therapy, which many therapists find exasperating. Reimbursement rates have declined as well, while overhead has increased. In addition, general lack of funding for mental health treatment has limited primary prevention efforts, so clients are often more distressed and more difficult to treat when they are finally seen by a therapist.

In the face of increasing frustration and decreasing satisfaction with general psychotherapy practice, many mental health professionals have begun to consider new approaches to their work, such as managed-care-free practices and personal and professional coaching. Forensic psychology practice is an area that has many advantages:

It is managed-care-free.
It is more lucrative than general psychotherapy practice.
It is intellectually challenging.

It is an expanding area of practice.
It covers a wide range of subspecialties.
Demand for services is high.

This book was written to help mental health professionals at different points in their training and careers to discover how to begin the process of entering this exciting area of practice. My goal was to provide practical information about a number of important topics, including:

How clinical and forensic practice differ.
How to decide if forensic practice is for you.
Subspecialty areas of forensic practice.
Becoming competent in this area.
Marketing your practice.
Risk management.
How to perform forensic assessments.
Testifying in court.

This book is designed to be helpful to graduate students who are considering moving into forensic practice after licensure, newly licensed clinicians who wish to specialize in this area, practicing clinicians who wish to add some forensic work to their clinical practices, and those who want to take the plunge and work in this area full-time. I have tried to provide information about what is really important to know on a practical, nuts-and-bolts level to allow you to start working in this rapidly developing area of psychology. Of course, a successful entry into this area will require study, supervision, networking, and a good deal of hard work. That being said, I am certain that *Getting Started in Forensic Psychology Practice* will help you to take your first steps toward success in this area.

What Is Forensic Psychology?

WHAT YOU WILL LEARN:

The Meaning of "Forensic"

Areas of Forensic Practice

Criminal Law–Related Practice

Offender Assessment and Treatment

Forensic Work with Children and Families

Juvenile Delinquency

People invariably respond in one of two ways when told that someone is a forensic psychologist or other forensic mental health practitioner. Those who know the word "forensic" only in association with television shows like *CSI* (or if they are a bit older, *Quincy*) look confused. They wonder why a mental health professional would work with dead people, since the dead would seem like a population unreceptive to psychotherapy. The second group, which is larger, says something like "Oh, that must be fascinating!" Unfortunately, most of the people in the second group don't really know what most forensic mental health practitioners actually do, either, although they know that most of their clients are among the living. Forensic mental health practice is a hot area because of the media exposure that has been a by-product of the public's interest in high-profile crimes and trials as well as the coverage provided by Court TV, *Forensic Files*, and the 24-hour cable news shows that highlight the forensic sciences as they relate to crime investigation. In addition, shows like *Law and Order*, *CSI*, *Profiler*, and other programs of that type have lent a certain glamour to this line of work. As a result, forensic psychology and justice studies programs are increasingly popular at colleges and universities, and established graduate schools are scrambling to offer forensic specializations. Unfortunately, few people have any real idea of what forensic mental health practitioners actually do in their day-to-day work. Whereas there are forensic psychologists who specialize in crime scene analysis and criminal profiling, the bulk of forensic work is performed in areas less known to the public but in their way every bit as interesting. This chapter provides an overview of where forensic psychologists fit into the legal system and the many different areas in which forensic psychologists work.

THE MEANING OF "FORENSIC"

Many people think that the word "forensic" means something in some way related to murders or to the dead. In fact, the word "forensic" is derived from the Latin word *forensis*, which means of or pertaining to the forum, which was where the courts of law were situated in Roman times. Consequently, it makes sense that forensic psychology involves matters that are in some way associated with the courts and legal decisions. Such matters may be criminal, civil, or administrative, as will be discussed in greater detail, but matters are forensic in nature to the extent that they provide information to the courts and assist the decision maker (a judge, a jury, an administrator, or whoever else is responsible for making a legal decision). Forensic specialists are involved in the courts to help the decision maker (generally referred to as the finder of fact) with technical information that a layperson would not be reasonably expected to know. To quote Federal Rule of Evidence 702, experts can testify "if scientific, technical or otherwise specialized knowledge will assist the trier of fact to understand the evidence or to determine a fact in issue."

It is also important to understand that there is a difference between being what is called a "witness of fact" or lay witness and an expert witness. A lay witness is an individual who observed something that has a direct impact on the case. For example, someone might turn a corner and witness a mugging. Under the rules of evidence, that person testifying as a lay witness could tell the judge and jury in a trial what he saw and heard and perhaps identify the assailant and victim. But because he is not testifying as an expert, he would not be able to provide the court with his thoughts about the likelihood that the blows he saw the assailant direct against the victim were the likely cause of the victim's injuries or whether the victim was likely to have suffered post-traumatic stress as a result of the attack, or provide any other opinion that would require specialized experience, training, or education.

It should be understood that mental health professionals, along with medical pathologists and crime scene investigators, are not the only forensic specialists. Anyone who has specialized knowledge about a specific subject at issue in a legal proceeding can be a forensic expert by virtue of training and/or experience. For example, let's imagine that someone is unlucky enough to die of food poisoning after buying and eating a hot dog from a New York City street vendor. The plaintiff's lawyer may allege that the poisoning occurred because the owner of the hot dog cart did not follow generally established procedures regarding sanitation and maintenance of the cart in question. The average member of a jury would not be expected to know very much about how such carts are supposed to be maintained. In such a case, the plaintiff's lawyer might enlist the services of a hot dog cart expert, perhaps someone who owned a company that ran a large number of hot dog carts across Chicago and who was responsible for developing standards of maintenance and sanitation for these hot dog carts. This individual would have many years of experience in this line of work and know a great deal about how a hot dog cart should be kept in good repair and how food poisoning can be averted. In such a case, the court hearing the case could decide that this individual was qualified to provide expert testimony on this subject to help the jury decide whether the owner of the cart that caused the fatal food poisoning was negligent or the poisoning was an unfortunate or unforeseeable accident. In such a case, the owner of the Chicago hot dog cart company would now be a forensic hot dog cart specialist.

Also, depending on how common such cases of food poisoning were, this newly minted hot dog cart expert might find himself in demand, particularly if his testimony was well received by the jury. Lawyers involved in similar lawsuits might discuss the expert, and he might start receiving referrals to testify in similar cases around the country. Lawyers might fly him in to testify in cases around the country, and it could even happen that he might make more money testifying than selling hot dogs. He could keep the hot dog business going and do the expert testimony as a sideline, or he might even become a full-time expert witness.

If this sounds farfetched, it isn't. Just as an example, when automobile tires are put on rims and inflated, they have a nasty tendency to explode with enough force to break bones and in some cases kill the mechanics who do this work. It happens often enough that there are lawyers who handle nothing but tire-related cases, and forensic tire experts who spend their days investigating such cases and testifying in the associated lawsuits. Forensic mental health practice in its basic elements is no different from forensic automotive tire practice—or, for that matter, forensic hot dog cart practice. They all have the same basic elements in that they provide the fact finder with specialized information not readily known to the layperson and that they are qualified to do so by virtue of their specialized training and experience.

AREAS OF FORENSIC PRACTICE

The past 20 years have seen a burgeoning of areas in which mental health professionals have been qualified—that is, allowed by the court to testify as expert witnesses. In this chapter we discuss several of these areas of forensic expertise, some of which overlap.

CRIMINAL LAW–RELATED PRACTICE

Forensic mental health practice is by definition related to the legal system, and much of the legal system is concerned with criminal law. Some forensic psychologists practice entirely in this arena while others

4

work in both criminal and noncriminal areas. This section describes some of the more common areas of criminal-related forensic practice.

Assessment of Criminal Competencies. Courts often require assessment of various criminal competencies such as competence to stand trial, competence to waive Miranda rights, competence to confess, competence to plead guilty, and competence to be executed.

These areas of assessment exist because of certain constitutional and legal rights that are guaranteed to defendants in criminal cases. In order for someone accused of a criminal offense to stand trial, the individual must have a reasonable understanding of the trial process and grasp enough of what is going on to assist a lawyer in putting together and presenting a defense. The basic idea of the right to be competent to stand trial dates back to early English common law and was originally applied to individuals who literally could not answer the charges against them because they were deaf or mute. It was thought that it was fundamentally unfair to put people on trial when they could not defend themselves or follow what was being said in their trials. In some cases, the court attempted to assess whether the individual was truly unable to communicate ("mute by visitation of God") or willfully refusing to speak ("mute of malice"). If the latter, the accused was sometimes compelled to speak through the expedient of placing increasingly heavy weights on their bodies until they either decided to become more communicative or expired.

Today, there are cases in which individuals charged with crimes clearly do not have the ability to understand the trial process; examples would be individuals with severe retardation, brain damage, or incapacitating mental illness. However, many persons with milder degrees of these problems may have the ability to understand enough regarding the adjudicatory process to be considered competent to stand trial, and sometimes it is not immediately clear if such individuals have the requisite abilities and comprehension. In such cases, psychologists are typically called by the court to assess the individual and assist the court in determining whether the accused is competent to stand trial.

There are areas of practice that are closely associated with competence to stand trial. For example, defendants in criminal cases are sometimes assessed to determine whether they have the necessary understanding of the legal process to waive their Miranda rights when arrested. These rights, which most people know by heart from watching crime shows on television, include the right to remain silent and the

5

right to consult with a lawyer before being questioned or to have the lawyer present while they are being questioned by the police. They are also entitled to have a lawyer appointed for them free of charge if they do not have the resources to hire their own attorney. Defendants can waive these rights, but they have to do so in a voluntary and knowing manner. In some cases, the extent to which defendants who made statements to the police after receiving Miranda warnings understood the implications of what they were doing is questioned. In such cases, psychologists may be utilized to help determine whether the defendants had an adequate grasp of the warnings they received.

Some of the other competencies mentioned earlier have been subsumed under general competence to stand trial since the United States Supreme Court decided the case of *Godinez v. Moran* in 1993. In this case the court ruled that competence to represent oneself in a criminal trial or plead guilty was essentially no more difficult than general competence to stand trial, and that no higher standard was required for these competencies. This has left open the question of whether psychologists performing competency evaluation should routinely include these other areas of competence in their assessments, and this issue is still being worked out in court cases and in the professional literature. It should be understood that the standard for competence to stand trial is not high, and that it is not necessary to have the same level of understanding of the legal process as that held by lawyers; otherwise, lawyers would not be needed.

One specialized area of competence assessment is competence to be executed. This may seem bizarre; how competent does someone need to be to be put to death? However, it is a principle of the law in this area that an individual cannot be put to death if he or she does not understand the implications of the sentence—for example, whether they understand why they are being executed and the finality of death. Psychologist experts are utilized by the court to assess the defendant's understanding of the issues involved in standing trial, as well as the probable cause of any deficits observed and the likelihood that the defendant can be restored to competence in a reasonable length of time. Performing evaluations in this area of practice requires an understanding of the legal standards that govern the finding of competence and incompetence in the jurisdiction in which the psychologist practices as well as good interviewing and diagnostic/testing skills.

The Insanity Defense. The insanity defense is a contentious area of forensic practice for a number of reasons. First, it tends to be unpopular with the public because of a widespread belief that it is commonly used to allow the guilty to escape their just punishment. In fact, it is rarely used and even more rarely successful. A second reason is that the legal standards for finding an individual not guilty by reason of insanity have differed over time and continue to differ by jurisdiction. A few states no longer allow the insanity defense, and some also allow a verdict of "guilty but insane." Generally speaking, in order to be found to be legally insane, individuals must either not know that what they were doing was wrong (for example, attacking a roommate with a shoe under the misapprehension that the roommate is actually a giant cockroach) or be unable to control their actions (an individual with a seizure disorder striking someone with his hand while in the throes of a grand mal seizure). In some states, the person's actions must be the direct result of a mental disease or defect, and some states do not include the inability to control actions as part of the legal definition of insanity.

Finally, there is a clear subjective element in the assessment of legal insanity, which is also referred to as mental state at time of offense (MSTO) or not guilty by reason of insanity (NGRI). It should be understood that to be convicted of a crime, defendants have to be exercising their free will in order to purposely do harm. For example, an individual who flails his arms while having a seizure and hits someone in the nose would not be found guilty of assault, because he had no conscious awareness of his actions and no intent to do harm. This malicious intent is referred to in the law as *mens rea*, which means guilty mind. A finding of NGRI means that the court decided that the defendant did not have the necessary mental state to be found criminally liable for his actions. Psychologists provide evaluations in NGRI cases in order to assist the court in determining whether defendants knew that what they were doing was wrong or were able to control their actions at the time the crimes were committed.

This is an example of a major difference between clinical and forensic assessment. In clinical assessment, the mental health professional generally tries to determine the client's diagnosis for purposes of treatment planning, and the time frame for the diagnosis is generally thought of in terms of months or years. In an NGRI assessment, the professional's task is to provide the court with information about the defendant's mental state at the time the crime was committed. This requires a knowledge of the law governing this issue in the expert's jurisdiction, as well as knowledge of best practices in the field to make this determination.

Mitigation/Diminished Capacity. This is an area of practice that has some similarities to NGRI assessment, but with a different focus. In criminal cases, there are two general types of defense: exculpating and mitigating. In an exculpatory defense, the defendant basically says, through his or her attorney, "I didn't commit the crime." The defendant tries to demonstrate that they could not have robbed the bank because they were out of town or didn't assault the victim because they were defending themselves, or they provide other evidence that clears them of the crimes with which they are charged. In mitigation/diminished capacity, the defendant admits that he/she committed the crime, but tries to show that there were extenuating circumstances. In diminished capacity, defendants attempt to show that while not legally insane (NGRI) when committing the crimes, their mental states contributed to their actions. For example, an individual who is otherwise law-abiding may attempt to commit so-called suicide by cop by brandishing a weapon at a police officer. In such a case, the psychologist may perform an evaluation to provide the judge or jury with information that either supports or undermines the defendant's claim of diminished capacity. Mitigation defenses are generally offered in the sentencing phase of a criminal trial and are used to try to convince the court that the defendant should be treated more leniently than would be the case if there were no mitigatory factors.

False/Disputed Confessions. This is a relatively new area of forensic practice. The recent interest in this area is related in large part to the widespread use of DNA testing in criminal cases. The use of DNA testing has resulted in large numbers of individuals who were found guilty of crimes being exonerated and released from jail. Surprisingly, a substantial percentage of those who were falsely convicted actually confessed to the crime at some point before their conviction. There had already been a good deal of debate in the professional literature about whether police interrogation techniques could produce false confessions, but with the advent of the use of DNA evidence, it became clear that false confessions occurred with some frequency. Psychologists working in this area use specialized techniques to determine whether a defendant has specific characteristics that would make him or her more vulnerable than the average defendant to falsely confessing under the pressure of police interrogations.

Eyewitness Identification/Police Lineups. Eyewitness testimony is probably the first area in which psychologists were allowed by the courts to testify. A century ago, experimental psychologist Hugo Munsterberg performed research on human memory and perception. He provided testimony in courts about how the memories of witnesses could be inaccurate. Today, psychologists frequently provide testimony about how eyewitnesses can unintentionally misidentify defendants, and also offer information to the court about how memory is affected by different circumstances. A specialized subarea in this general realm of expert testimony involves police lineups and photo arrays. In lineups, a suspect, along with other uninvolved individuals (called foils), is viewed by a victim or witness through a two-way mirror. In a photo array, the same process occurs through the use of photographs. Psychologists have performed research and discovered that witnesses' identifications in these procedures can be influenced and made more inaccurate if proper procedures are not utilized by law enforcement. Common errors include implying that the criminal is definitely present, asking the witness about the suspect while not asking about the foils, or otherwise indicating the police officer's hunch about the identity of the alleged perpetrator. Psychologists can review the research on the subjects of lineups and photo arrays and also evaluate the actual circumstances of a particular instance in which these techniques were used.

OFFENDER ASSESSMENT AND TREATMENT

This area is obviously related to criminal forensic work, but it is given its own section because the focus is slightly different from criminal work per se. In addition, it is a rapidly growing area that covers a great deal of ground, although the overlap with criminal forensic work is evident.

Sexual Offender Assessment and Treatment. Sexual offender assessment and treatment has been a growth area in forensic practice for several decades. This growth has been driven by a number of trends, one of which has been an increasing awareness of sexual crimes in American society. As victims have become more willing to come forward, there has been a corresponding increase in prosecutions and convictions of sexual offenders. Sexual offenders now make up a large portion of the prison and probation/parole population, and this has put increasing pressure on the criminal justice system to do something to cope with this population. Two aspects of the system's response to this problem have involved psychologists. First, there is an ongoing effort by the legal system to try to differentiate between those sexual offenders who pose a great risk of recidivism (repeat offending) and those who are at lower risk and can be safely maintained in the community. The other part of this response is to utilize sexual offender treatment to lower the risk of recidivism for convicted offenders.

Another trend that has increased demand for the services of psychologists in relation to this population has been the adoption of sexual predator commitment laws in a number of states. Since the early 1990s states have passed laws that allow for the civil commitment and continued confinement of sexual offenders past the end of their criminal sentences. These offenders are deemed appropriate for civil commitment if the court finds that they pose a high risk for recidivism. In 1997 the U.S. Supreme Court upheld these types of laws in the case of *Kansas v. Hendricks*. In these cases, psychologists are called upon to assess the risk of sexual reoffense of convicted sexual offenders as they near the end of their criminal sentences. In addition, most of these sexual predator laws require the committed individuals to receive treatment while confined as a way of possibly decreasing the risk they pose if released.

Psychologists may become involved in this area of practice in a number of ways. They may be called on by both the prosecution and the defense in criminal cases to assess the recidivism risk of convicted sexual offenders in the sentencing phase of their trials. To do this, psychologists utilize a wide range of techniques and instruments that have been shown to have some predictive validity in determining risk. In some cases, these experts may utilize psychophysiological methods such as the plethysmograph (which directly measures sexual arousal to deviant stimuli) and the polygraph (more commonly known as the lie detector). These experts also employ tests that are predictive of general criminal recidivism and other tests that are specific to sexual offenders. It should be noted that these types of assessments are designed to measure recidivism risk for individuals who have been convicted of a sexual offense. They are not designed to be used to determine whether someone accused of a sexual offense is guilty or is the kind of person who would be likely to commit such an offense. These questions are for the judge or jury to decide, and there is nothing in the scientific literature that supports the ability of even the most experienced of experts to make such judgments accurately. Further, most courts will not admit such testimony in these types of cases.

The treatment of sexual offenders is another area in which the services and expertise of psychologists are utilized. Almost every city and town of any size in the United States has at least one sexual offender treatment program, and many have more than one. Therapists working in this area of practice generally run groups utilizing a combination of cognitive-behavioral and relapse-prevention techniques to help offenders develop empathy for their victims, understand their offense pattern, and manage deviant impulses. Group process is thought by many offender therapists to increase the efficacy of therapy, but some offenders are seen individually or in both individual and group therapy. Psychologists working in this area often work closely with probation and parole officers to monitor the progress and behavior of group members. It should be noted that while there has been a good deal of research to support the accuracy of sexual offender risk assessment, the research on the efficacy of sexual offender treatment is much more equivocal. However, despite the lack of support for the effectiveness of this type of treatment, it is undeniable that there is great demand for this type of service.

Domestic Violence Assessment and Treatment. As with sexual offenses, there has been an increasing consciousness of the prevalence and harmfulness of domestic violence in our society. The roles of psychologists in this area in many ways parallel those involved with sexual offenders. In some cases, forensic experts are called on to assess for recidivism risk in those convicted of domestic violence. And, as with sexual offenders, many of those convicted of domestic violence are ordered into domestic violence treatment programs and anger management groups. There is an ongoing demand for these services, although, as with sexual offender treatment, the efficacy of these interventions is open to debate.

Substance Abuse Assessment and Treatment. Substance abuse is a huge societal problem that shows few signs of abating. A large percentage of crimes are committed while the offender is under the influence of some type of psychoactive substance. Drugs and alcohol are contributing factors in a wide range of crimes, and in cases of possession and sale, they are the basis of the charged offense. Drug and alcohol use is often an issue in divorce and child custody/visitation. For these reasons, the skills of psychologists in the area of substance abuse are frequently utilized by the legal system. Forensic practitioners may become involved in performing assessments of those involved in the criminal justice system who have substance abuse problems for purposes of treatment planning. They may also work with persons convicted of drunk driving who require court-ordered assessment to determine the nature of and seriousness of their problem and also to provide court-ordered aftercare. Assessments may be ordered by the court when substance abuse becomes an issue in divorce or visitation cases. As with other forms of offender treatment, a psychologist must be prepared to work with probation/parole officers or guardians *ad litem* (lawyers or clinicians appointed by the court to protect the interests of a dependent person such as a child in a divorce) to report on a client's level of cooperation and progress in therapy.

FORENSIC WORK WITH CHILDREN AND FAMILIES

Mental health experts do many kinds of forensic work in relation to children and families. Along with criminal forensic work, this is one of the largest areas in which psychologists provide services to the courts and to clients who are involved with the legal system, either criminally or civilly. This is another area in which there is a certain amount of overlap with criminal forensic work, since some types of cases such as those dealing with child abuse can be dealt with either civilly, criminally, or both.

Child Custody and Visitation. Since approximately half of all marriages end in divorce, it is an unfortunate fact that there are many children who are affected by the dissolution of their families. Even though most divorces are reasonably amicable and the majority of child custody issues are settled by agreement of the parties, given the large number of divorces in a large country, even a small proportion of disputes over custody and visitation will produce a large number of cases. Problems arising from custody and visitation disputes are so common that some psychologists work only in this area. One important function for psychologists in this area is providing custody assessments for divorce courts. When parents cannot agree on custody and visitation arrangements, the court must step in and decide that matter. Such evaluations are complex and involve interviewing parents and children; psychological testing; contacts with collateral sources such as teachers, neighbors, and babysitters; as well as observations of the family members interacting. Psychologists use the data they elicit in these assessments to assist the court in developing a custody and visitation schedule that is in the best interests of the family's children under the circumstances. Assessments may also be requested when the court has provided orders for custody and visitation but the parties continue to have disputes about visits, child support, school choices, and other matters such as religious education. Assessments may also be required when a substantial change in circumstances requires the court to revisit custody and visitation. One example of this is when the parent with primary physical custody seeks to move out of the area. In such cases, courts must grapple with difficult issues, such as whether the additional income that may be provided by the better job a parent may be able to take by moving outweighs the impact on the children of having to leave their community and having less regular contact with the noncustodial parent; the insights of psychologists play an important role in the court's decision.

Psychologists may also become involved in custody and visitation issues in the role of mediator. There is a movement in the courts to encourage people to work out their child custody–related issues outside of court, using neutral lawyers and psychologists to work with the parties and develop agreements that both sides can live with. In some states, some type of predivorce mediation is mandated, and this creates practice opportunities for psychologists. A related role is that of visitation or parenting coordinator. Individuals working in this area are placed by the court in a role in which parents bring their visitation- and parenting-related disputes to them before going to court. The parenting coordinator listens to the concerns of both parents and then makes a decision about the best course of action. While the parents do not give up their rights to take disputes to court, it is made clear that the court will give great weight to the decisions of the parenting coordinator, and this often keeps the issues out of the courtroom.

Finally, some psychologists become involved in divorce-related issues by serving as court-ordered therapists to divorcing families — children or parents. This role is somewhat different from that of the traditional therapist in that the court-ordered therapist may be required to provide information to the court through either written reports or direct communication to the guardian ad litem or the judge. Clearly, such therapy is not as confidential as traditional therapy, and the demands for documentation are more stringent than is usual in other types of therapy.

13

Child Abuse (Emotional, Physical, and Sexual). Unfortunately, emotional, physical, and sexual child abuse is far too common in our society. Psychologists play many roles in this area of forensic practice. In some cases, they may be called on to assess allegations of child abuse. This often involves interviewing the alleged victim using specialized techniques designed to elicit an accurate and complete account of the child's experiences while minimizing the use of methods of questioning that have the potential to reduce the accuracy of the child's account. In some cases, abuse allegations may be assessed using a comprehensive methodology that includes interviews with parents who may be suspected of perpetrating child abuse, psychological testing, and the collection of information from other sources. As with the assessment of sexual offenders, it must be understood that no test or technique can prove that a particular child has or has not been abused; as a consequence, the evaluator's role in such cases is that of using his or her expertise to gather information that can assist the court in making decisions about the presence or absence of abuse.

Psychologists may also perform evaluations to determine the risk of recidivism of child abuse if the abuser is a family member. Such evaluations can help with treatment planning for an abusive parent to reduce the risk of further abuse of a child, or to gauge whether such treatment is likely to be effective.

Termination of Parental Rights. In some cases, children who have been abused or neglected by their parents are removed from their homes and taken into the care of the state. When this occurs, most states must make a good-faith attempt to provide services and support in order to reunify the family, if possible. At the same time, the federal government and many states have recognized that in some cases these efforts have little chance of success, or that such steps will probably not be effective in a reasonable amount of time. There are statutes that specify that if the risk of further abuse or the inability to maintain a family that is supportive to healthy child development is likely to persist, then termination of parental rights (TPR) must be considered. Termination of parental rights is an extremely serious decision and not one that is to be undertaken lightly. It has been likened to the death penalty of family law, because when the parental rights are terminated, the parents lose all standing with regard to their offspring. The children can be adopted, and the natural parents cease to be parents in any sense but biological. They receive no visits or news of the children, who may move far away and never see their birth parents again. This step occurs in a relatively small proportion of child abuse and neglect cases, and courts generally require some type of evaluation by one or more psychologists to help determine whether TPR is in the best interests of the children. TPR evaluations are fundamentally different from custody evaluations because of the way the psycholegal issues are framed. Custody evaluations are performed in large part to determine which parent can best meet the children's needs and can be thought of as a parenting contest. TPRs are not meant to determine, for example, whether children removed from their homes are better cared for by the foster parents than by the natural parents. These evaluations are designed to inform the court as to whether the birth parents are likely to be able to become adequate caretakers of their children, and are not meant to provide a comparison between the parents and the foster parents.

Psychologists performing such evaluations must painstakingly review the records and history of the family, speak to those who have worked with the family, and observe the children with their parents. These techniques are often combined with psychological testing and extensive interviewing of the parents and children to help the court determine whether TPR is in the best interests of the children and whether the parents' deficits as caretakers can be remedied.

JUVENILE DELINQUENCY

While there is some overlap with forensic work with children and families, forensic work with juvenile delinquents is a distinct area of practice for which the services of psychologists are in demand. It should be understood that the justice system for delinquents has a different purpose than the adult criminal justice system. Adult criminals are sentenced to accomplish three specific purposes: incapacitation (preventing them from committing further crimes), rehabilitation, and punishment. The juvenile justice system leaves out the punishment component as a guiding purpose, although it is undeniable that some interventions for juveniles are experienced by the youths as aversive. The goal of the system is to safeguard society from the actions of criminally oriented youths while emphasizing educational and psychotherapeutic interventions. Psychologists are utilized in the juvenile justice system in a number of ways.

15

Sentencing/Dispositional Assessments. Because of the rehabilitative focus of the juvenile justice system, many judges make it a practice to obtain assessments of children and adolescents before deciding what interventions, restrictions, and placements to order. Assessments may include evaluation of the juvenile's intellectual and educational status, neuropsychological assessment to rule out/in information-processing deficits or problems with executive functioning, and techniques to determine whether specific psychological disorders are present. This information is utilized along with other data to decide whether a particular juvenile can be sent home with probation and counseling or requires some type of residential placement.

Transfer to Criminal Court. A related type of assessment can be ordered when a juvenile commits a serious crime and the possibility of trying the defendant as an adult is considered. Most jurisdictions have statutes that provide guidelines for what criteria should be considered in making this decision. The criteria often include factors such as the seriousness of the crime alleged, the maturity and sophistication of the minor, the probability of rehabilitation in the juvenile correction system if the adolescent is found guilty, and the risk of criminal recidivism. Psychologists conduct evaluations and provide testimony in these proceedings, which are sometimes referred to as juvenile certification hearings.

Juvenile Competence/Miranda Waiver. While juvenile law is governed by different standards from criminal law for adults, certain standards cut across both areas. Juveniles must be competent to stand trial, just like adult defendants. In some states, there are different and generally looser standards for juvenile competence than those for adults, while in others the standards are the same. In the same way, when juveniles are questioned by the authorities, they must have their Miranda rights read to them and explained. And, just as with adults, their decision to waive their rights must be voluntary and knowing. The psychologist may be called upon to assess a juvenile's understanding of the trial process and/or the extent to which he/she was cognizant of his/her rights and was capable of a reasoned decision about making a statement of confession when questioned.

Court-Ordered Treatment. Many psychologists provide therapy for juveniles who are before the court due to delinquency. There is a demand for professionals who are willing to work with this challenging population, which many therapists prefer to avoid. Some develop particular areas of specialty, such as therapy with juvenile sexual offenders, fire setters, drug abusers, and those with conduct disorder or oppositional defiant disorder. These populations have a wide variety of associated comorbid disorders such as attention deficit/hyperactivity disorder (ADHD), depression, or anxiety, and many have trauma-related symptoms caused by maltreatment and neglect. Consequently, those working with these populations should have a firm grounding in developmental psychology and child and adolescent psychopathology along with specific knowledge and training in therapeutic techniques tailored to these specific types of problems.

Is Forensic Practice for You?

All areas of mental health practice require practitioners to have certain characteristics and abilities if they are to be successful in their work. A certain level of intellectual ability is an obvious requirement; to some extent, the need for an advanced degree serves as a rough screening process for this requirement. A certain amount of communication skill is necessary, as is empathy, self-confidence, and specialized knowledge. But forensic mental health work presents special challenges and is most emphatically not for everyone. The qualities that make someone a good therapist, consultant, personal coach, or clinical diagnostician will not necessarily make a good forensic mental health expert. There is a certain amount of overlap, but also a great deal of divergence in roles, skills, and personalities. This chapter discusses some of these issues with the aim of helping you decide if working in this specialty area is for you.

Clinical Versus Forensic Practice

One of the most obvious ways that forensic mental health practice is different from clinical practice is the purpose of the practitioner's work. Forensic practice takes place in a different world from clinical practice, and it is a world where the rules are not set by mental health professionals. The rules for the forensic mental health practitioner and the purpose of his/her work are set by lawyers and judges, not by the dictates of the best interests of the client. Forensic practitioners are playing a different game by a different set of rules than they are used to, and this can be a real shock to the neophyte.

Consider the situation of the psychotherapist in private practice. Private psychotherapists have many advantages in their role that are often not considered. For example, they start out in a one-up situation to their clients. Clients come to the therapist because they have a problem that they have concluded that they cannot fully deal with on their own. Because of this, they have talked to their physicians, their friends, and others to find a therapist with a reputation for being skilled at dealing with problems similar to theirs. In most cases, they come to the therapist's office with the hope and expectation that the therapist can help them with their problem in a way they have not been able to themselves.

Therapists also control the physical environment in a way that enhances their stature in the eyes of the client. They have their diplomas and certificates on the walls of their office, attesting to their education and years of experience. The chairs in the consulting room are arranged in the way the therapist finds most comfortable and most conducive to having the kind of conversation that he/she feels is most helpful to the client. Some therapists sit at a 45-degree angle to the client, while others may sit directly facing the client or talk to the client across a desk. Some therapists have a number of seats and let clients choose where they sit, while others direct them to a particular chair. The therapist can decorate the office in the style that is congruent with his/her approach to psychotherapy; some have sleek, modern furniture and accessories and others go for a warmer, friendlier style, with knickknacks and pictures drawn by children on the walls.

Psychotherapists also set many of the rules of engagement for their relationships with their clients. They decide whether to use a 45-, 50-, or 60-minute hour in their work. In psychotherapy, therapists have much more control than clients regarding how much they reveal about themselves. They may attempt to be the blank slate recommended by some schools of therapy, or they may self-disclose to the client, believing that this is a good way to develop a psychotherapeutic alliance. At the same time, the client is urged, with methods more or less subtle, to reveal as much about their thoughts, feelings, and behavior as possible. Consequently, even though some clients can be quite challenging, the work of the private psychotherapist takes place on terrain that is at least familiar, and in many ways is controlled by the therapist.

Now consider the work of a forensic psychologist. Whether the forensic psychologist is performing an evaluation of competence to stand trial, a child custody assessment, or a sexual offender risk assessment, the basic referral questions are for the most part determined by the court. For example, while the forensic psychologist has a certain amount of freedom in determining how to go about his/her evaluation, the competence to stand trial assessment is governed by the standards of the courts in that jurisdiction (whether the client has a factual and rational understanding of the process of standing trial, whether the client can consult with an attorney with a reasonable degree of rational understanding, and, in some areas, whether any observed deficits are caused by a mental disease or defect). On a very basic level, it does not matter what the psychologist thinks competence is; it is what the court thinks that matters. As a result, the psychologist enters the court in a one-down situation just by the nature of his/her role, which is to assist the court.

Incompatibility of Therapeutic and Forensic Roles

But before psychologists even enter the courtroom, there are important differences in the way they play their professional role. These differences have been clearly described in Stuart Greenberg and Daniel Shuman's article "Irreconcilable Conflict between Therapeutic and Forensic Roles" (1997). This article should be essential reading for anyone considering undertaking forensic work and also for clinicians who may be drawn into court through no fault of their own.

Further, these distinctions are important because psychotherapists may not understand the distinction between these roles and may be tempted to provide forensic testimony about a patient in a misguided attempt to assist the patient in cases such as child custody and personal injury. This can happen, for example, when a client involved in a personal injury case that involves allegations of posttraumatic stress disorder (PTSD) is treated for the presenting problem by a therapist. After six months of counseling sessions, the therapist may be asked to go to court to provide testimony that the client has been diagnosed with PTSD, that the client has symptoms consistent with this disorder, and that the likely cause of the PTSD was the negligence of the defendant in the case. As Greenberg and Shuman point out, such testimony is problematic for number of reasons. One of the most obvious is that nearly all therapists use as their point of departure in diagnosis and treatment the account of the client. The client comes to the office claiming to be depressed because her husband is a brutal alcoholic who terrorizes the family when intoxicated. The therapist accepts this account more or less uncritically and bases subsequent psychotherapeutic interventions on this untested hypothesis. This is fine for psychotherapy, but forensic evaluators are required to use the hypothesis testing model and to pursue and develop all reasonable explanations for alleged or observed symptoms, including symptom exaggeration and malingering. It would be unusual and probably inappropriate for therapists to enter into a psychotherapeutic relationship with the client from a stance of skepticism and hypothesis testing.

This is only one of the differences between the role of the forensic evaluator and the role of the psychotherapist noted by Greenberg and Shuman. The authors point out 10 essential differences between these roles. The first of these is that for the psychotherapist, the patient/

litigant is his/her client, whereas for the forensic evaluator, the attorney who requested the assessment is the client. The idea that the person sitting in the consulting room is not the client is very alien to those who have worked exclusively in psychotherapeutic roles and can be quite difficult to get used to. In the same way, the relationship between psychotherapist and client is governed by therapist-patient privileges and protections such as confidentiality, while the relationship between the forensic evaluator and his/her client (the lawyer) is governed by a different set of rules, which include attorney-client and attorney work product privilege. Both sets of rules offer a degree of protection against disclosure of confidential material, but there are important differences between the two sets of rules that must be clearly understood when moving from clinical to forensic work or vice versa.

Another important difference noted by Greenberg and Shuman is that the general attitude of the therapist toward the client is supportive, accepting, and empathic, while that of the forensic evaluator is neutral, objective, and detached. For those making the transition between clinical and forensic work, this can be a major obstacle. Psychotherapists spend their careers developing their empathy as well as their joining skills in order to be better able to provide psychotherapy to their patients. It can be very difficult to move from that position to one in which little that the client says is taken at face value. A forensic psychologist told me about a case involving allegations of child abuse by the child's grandparents that were raised by the biological father. A number of prior investigators, including the local child protection agency, had investigated the case in some depth and come to the conclusion that there was no evidence that the grandparents were anything but loving with their grandson. When the father spoke to the forensic psychologist he asked him with some agitation, "What can I say to make you believe me?" The psychologist paused for a moment and explained that there was nothing that the father could say that would make him believe him or not believe him, since it was not his job to be a human lie detector. He did point out that if the father had evidence that there had been any type of abuse he could investigate the facts of the case. This stance with regard to clients by forensic mental health providers may seem hardhearted to those used to clinical work, but it is an essential element of the forensic role that must be mastered.

Greenberg and Shuman point out a number of other important

differences in the roles of the forensic evaluator and the psychotherapist. One of these is the fact that different skill sets and competencies are needed in each role. Psychotherapists need to have current knowledge and training on the best way to provide psychotherapeutic interventions for the particular conditions and problems with which their clients present. In contrast, forensic evaluators need to be skilled and knowledgeable in the assessment of the particular psycholegal problem (criminal competency, civil competency, child custody, sexual offender risk assessment, etc.) that is the issue in the case. One example of this is the need for forensic evaluators to be knowledgeable about the assessment of dissimulation and malingering, which is less important for psychotherapists and clinical evaluators. When there is no underlying legal issue, it would be unusual for a client to come to a psychotherapist and describe symptoms of anxiety and depression that do not actually exist (although such things can occur with clients with factitious disorders). The situation is very different when external circumstances raise the stakes, such as when there is contested child custody or the possibility of a large monetary settlement in a personal injury case. In such cases, it is quite common for individuals to present with all types of emotional problems and cognitive deficits that have no basis in reality. The dynamics of the two situations create a need for a different set of assessment skills.

There are other important differences in the roles of the forensic evaluator and the clinician that are pointed out by Shuman and Greenberg. For example, the amount and control of structure in each relationship is very different. Traditionally, psychotherapists allow the agenda of the session to be set in large part by the client. This may vary in degree depending on the orientation of the therapist, from the unstructured free-association techniques utilized by psychodynamically oriented therapists to the more highly structured sessions that are commonly used by those who are more behaviorally oriented. But in either case, the general agenda and priorities for the session are determined by the client. In contrast, the forensic evaluator for the most part determines the structure of the evaluative session, determining what tests to give and what questions to ask in order to develop information relevant to the issue at hand. Another difference is the degree to which the relationship of the psychotherapist and the forensic evaluator with the client is adversarial in nature. The role of the psychotherapist is to be supportive and helpful to the client. Although the conclusions of the forensic evaluator may ultimately be helpful to the client, they may also be distinctively unhelpful, for example, when the evaluator determines that the client has a high likelihood of sexually violent reoffending and because of this conclusion the client is sentenced to civil commitment under violent predator laws.

The Greenberg and Shuman article makes it clear that while many of the actions performed by psychotherapists, clinical evaluators, and forensic mental health professionals overlap, there are important differences in the way forensic professionals operate due to the differing demands of the legal terrain in which they work. To be able to appreciate these differences and, more importantly, to orient one's practice around them is fundamental to successful forensic practice. If you pursued a career in mental health because of a desire to be helpful to individuals, the skepticism, interpersonal distance, and lack of a sense of alliance between yourself and your clients so necessary in forensic work will seem alien and at times a bit inhuman. But the purpose of forensic mental health practice is to assist the workings of the justice system rather than any one individual, although such work may be helpful to individuals. For example, a criminal defendant who receives a lighter sentence because an assessment you do provides the court with information that is used in a diminished capacity defense may be pleased with the outcome. In contrast, when information you provide to the court in a child custody matter contributes to a decision that the child's mother will have primary physical custody rather than the joint physical custody that the father requested, that father is likely to feel that your assessment has been not only unhelpful but damaging to himself and to his child. Most psychotherapists want people to cooperate and get along, and this is generally an appropriate stance to take in psychotherapeutic work. In the same way, many therapists do not like to point the finger of blame at any one individual in a relationship or family, seeing it as counterproductive. But as a forensic mental health professional, such an approach would be inappropriate and counterproductive. In many areas of forensic practice, the court wants just such information: who did what to whom and who is responsible for observed problems. Making the transition from one mind-set to another can be very challenging for the professional wishing to make a transition from clinical and psychotherapeutic work to forensic practice.

DIFFERENCES BETWEEN THERAPEUTIC AND EVALUATIVE ROLES

Therapist Role	Forensic Evaluator Role
The client is the patient/litigant.	The client is the attorney and/or court.
Therapist-patient privilege governs disclosure.	Attorney-client privilege governs disclosure until the evaluator becomes a witness.
Attitude toward client is supportive, empathic, and accepting.	Attitude toward subject is neutral, objective, and detached.
Competence is required in therapy techniques for treatment of the client's impairment.	Competence is required in forensic evaluation techniques relevant to the legal claim; familiarity with the law is required as it applies to that issue.
Evaluation and hypothesis testing are related to the purposes of therapy.	Evaluation and hypothesis testing are related to the legal issue at hand.
Information is drawn mostly from the client with little external scrutiny.	Litigant information is critically scrutinized and supplemented by collateral sources of information.
Therapy is mostly patient-structured, less structured than forensic assessment.	Forensic assessment is evaluator-structured, more structured than therapy.
Therapy is a helping process, rarely adversarial.	Forensic assessment probes for information the litigant prefers not to divulge.
Goal is to benefit the patient.	Goal is to assist the trier of fact (judge or jury).
Basis of therapy is the therapeutic alliance; critical and legally damaging judgments by the therapist could undermine the alliance.	Evaluative purpose of the forensic interview is known in advance by the subject; critical judgments by the forensic examiner are less likely to cause lasting distress in the client.

THREAT, SAFETY, AND GENERAL UNPLEASANTNESS

There are other aspects of the forensic psychologist's role that differ from the role of the psychotherapist. One of these is that some of the clients they will evaluate can be obnoxious, unpleasant, or potentially dangerous. While this can also be the case with the clinical population, it is much more common in forensic practice. Depending on what area of forensic practice you decide to enter, you may be called upon to assess (and therefore spend considerable time up close and personal with) murderers, child molesters, individuals with very unpleasant paraphilias, as well as people who assault their domestic partners and/or their children. This can bring up any number of issues for the aspiring psychologist. First, some of the accounts the psychologist will be told or will read about in record reviews will be profoundly disturbing and difficult to process. For example, as part of a personal injury suit or defense consultation, the psychologist may be called on to view videotapes of small children describing in agonizing detail how they were molested, or listen to PTSD victims recount how they were treated with unspeakable cruelty for years. It can be extremely difficult to control one's visceral and fundamentally human reactions to exposure to such material, and it can also be difficult to remain objective. In the same way, discussing the details of aberrant sexual behavior with an offender can be disturbing and embarrassing at first, and some psychologists never become comfortable dealing with these matters.

A related concern that arises from the population with whom forensic psychologists work is the issue of personal safety and the chance of being assaulted. Again, although this can occur in clinical practice, it is much more likely if one's practice is loaded with psychopaths, violent criminals, rapists, and batterers. But it should be noted that even if you work with less obviously dangerous clients, such as custody litigants or guardianship cases, the chance of physical assault still exists. Steps can be taken to minimize this risk (and are discussed in Chapter 5), but many mental health professionals are understandably concerned about their personal safety while doing forensic work. It is also the case that some clients, while not overtly physically threatening, will attempt to intimidate the psychologist through an overbearing manner, veiled threats, or verbal challenges. This is very different from the type of relationship mental health professionals have with their clients once a therapeutic alliance has been established. Many mental health professionals are understandably reluctant to practice in an atmosphere so charged with conflict and possible physical harm.

CLIENT DECEPTIVENESS

In the same way, forensic psychologists often deal with clients who, to varying degrees, are not straightforward and honest in the way they present themselves and their accounts of events leading to the assessment. Again, while clients seen in clinical practice may often take some time to tell the therapist what is really going on in their lives, or present their versions of events in a self-serving manner, deception in some form is the rule rather than the exception for psychologists in their forensic work. It can be very disconcerting to interview clients who have been convicted of physically abusing their children and have them tell you that the charge was an isolated incident when you have already read the case file and know that they have five previously founded charges of such abuse and that they actually admitted under oath to this behavior as part of a consent decree with the court. It is also not uncommon to have forensic clients produce invalid, fake good MMPI-2, MCMI-3, and other objective test profiles, even though you have discussed with them the importance of being straightforward in their approach to the instruments, explained that faking good answers would be detected and would almost certainly hurt their case. Such behavior, while understandable in the context of the clients' experiences and understanding of their situations, is extremely frustrating and can make psychologists feel as though they are having their intelligence insulted by their clients.

THE HOSTILE ENVIRONMENT

The environment in which the forensic professional works can also be a source of stress. Evaluations and therapy may generally be performed in the office, but it is also the case that there may be a need to evaluate clients in jails, prisons, youth detention centers, state psychiatric hospitals, and developmental centers. The problems associated with going into such settings can range from mere inconvenience to highly frustrating and sometimes frightening situations. Inconveniences include the difficulty of scheduling appointments; every institution has its own policy for this and may require a letter from the attorney requesting your services, a call from that attorney, copies of your curriculum vitae (CV) and license, and who knows what else. Worse, these policies can change from visit to visit so that what was sufficient last time around now does not get you through the door. You may call the shift commander at the jail to make your appointment and be told that you need to talk to the medical department, and then be told by the head nurse that you need to make arrangements with the shift commander. Finally, having gotten this confusion settled and been given a time and date for your assessment, you may show up on time at the jail only to find that nobody told the person at the front desk that you were coming, and that none of the people you talked to on the phone are working that day. Or you may find that only one hour has been allotted for your assessment when you were told you could have three hours, or find out that the room they reserved for you has no table, or be told that you can see the client but you have to leave your psychological tests in your car. Once in the room, you may discover that you forgot some of your protocols or that you brought only one pen and it doesn't work. The room may be freezing or stifling, or may resound like an echo chamber. You may need to use the bathroom two hours into the assessment and have to do a great deal of explaining and persuading before you can convince a guard to escort you there. And, getting out is sometimes as difficult as getting in. You can easily find yourself locked into the testing room for 30 minutes to an hour, wondering if the officer in the control booth even knows you are there, and wondering how long it would take for them to find you if the client had strangled you on impulse.

Once back in your office, your problems are not over. There is often considerable time pressure to get your report done and to the court, and it may be necessary to work late or on weekends to keep up with the workload. Also, forensic mental health practice is fundamentally different from many other businesses in terms of time pressure. For example, if the owner of a restaurant closes it down and takes a week's vacation, he will not make any money while the restaurant is closed, but business will then resume at a normal pace. The forensic mental health professional may take some time off, but many of the assessments that were not done during the break will be waiting when he/she comes back to the office, increasing work pressure. Lawyers often make things worse by neglecting to tell you that you are needed in court that week or waiting until the day before a report is due (never having told you that they needed it right away) to call and ask where it is. This would not be so bad if the matters involved were not so serious, but it is often the case that parents may not see their children for several more months, or a man may have to stay in jail until the matter is rescheduled, so it becomes necessary to frantically rearrange your schedule to accommodate this latest crisis.

GOING TO COURT

Let's assume that despite all these obstacles you have managed to complete your report in a timely manner and send it to the lawyer who has retained your services. If the lawyer decides that your report is helpful to the client, the lawyer may ask you to testify at trial. Scheduling can be difficult, since the courts have their own way of arranging their dockets, which does not necessarily take the preferences or availability of the mental health expert into account. Also, trials are often rescheduled despite the fact that you have blocked off half a day for your testimony. It also sometimes happens that you may drive an hour to court, arrive at the appropriate time, and find that because some other cases went longer than their allotted time periods or because the judge inexplicably decided to go through the process of listening to someone plead guilty instead of getting on with your case, you are not reached on that day. The lawyer who called you to testify asks you to come back the next morning, despite the fact that you have a full schedule the following day. Since it is already five o'clock and the office manager has gone home, it won't be easy to contact those individuals coming in for evaluation or therapy on the following day. Perhaps you can double back to your office and try to change your schedule, but this can involve additional driving and getting home very late after a day that has already been quite stressful. Sometimes the lawyer can get a continuance of the trial, but not always. There are no hard-and-fast rules for dealing with these types of situations, which can come up with surprising frequency in forensic practice.

But despite all these obstacles, your day in court finally arrives. After all the anticipation and worry that led up to this moment, you are called to the stand by the lawyer who retained you. You are sworn in and take the stand, arranging your file so that your curriculum vitae, report, raw data, and all of the documents you reviewed are in some type of order and you can get to them without too much shuffling of papers. The next step is getting qualified as an expert, a process known as voir dire (meaning to "speak the truth"). The lawyer who retained you goes over your curriculum vitae with you and tries to impress the court through your answers with the many ways that your education, training, postdoctoral internships, publications (if you have any), presentations, attendance at professional workshops, and memberships in professional organizations all make you eminently qualified to do the kind of evaluation you have done in this case. After making his pitch, the lawyer you are working with asks the court to qualify you as an expert in the relevant area and then sits down.

The other lawyer now gets the opportunity to show that you know nothing about what you are doing and should not be qualified to provide therapy to a dachshund, let alone testify in this case. This can be

30

particularly stressful for mental health professionals who have not been through this process; while patients may challenge your expertise and credentials on occasion, they tend not to do it in an organized manner, relentlessly, and in public. The opposing attorney may attempt to raise questions about the quality of your graduate program, whether you ever took course work related to this specific issue (despite the fact that there were no such courses back in 1985 when you received your degree), and whether you have ever been sued for malpractice or had a complaint filed against you with the local board of registry. Depending on the situation, he/she may ask ridiculously overspecific questions regarding what percentage of your practice actually involves evaluating left-handed, redheaded dyslexics in order to show that you actually lack the qualifications to be doing the type of assessment you did with this particular individual. Lawyers vary in what kinds of questions they are willing to ask and range from fair, reasonably relevant queries to the lowest cheap shots imaginable, and you have to be prepared to deal with the whole range.

Courts generally will qualify well-trained experts and you do not have to be renowned in your field to be considered sufficiently qualified. Despite this, there are occasions when a judge, for good or questionable reasons, will decide that your qualifications are deficient and simply dismiss you from the case. This can be very bruising to the ego, since it goes directly to the expert's sense of him- or herself as a competent individual, but it is something that you have to be prepared to handle if you are going to work in the forensic arena. The direct examination is generally not too stressful, since if the lawyers you are working with know what they are doing, they will have discussed your testimony in some detail with you prior to going to court. Consequently, direct examination questions are often softballs gently lobbed in your direction that provide you with the opportunity to present your results in a manner that explains your conclusions in the most advantageous manner and also in a way that supports the point that the lawyer wants to make through your testimony.

Now it is opposing counsel's turn. Even the most experienced expert witness experiences a little anxiety when opposing counsel stands up, greets you pleasantly ("Good morning, doctor. I just have a few questions for you."), and starts in on the cross-examination. The cross-examination is designed to undermine everything about your testimony, and that includes your objectivity, methodology, the relationship between your data and your conclusions, and anything else they can think of that might undermine you in the eyes of the judge or jury. This book is not intended as a guide to coping with cross-examination, and there are plenty of excellent books on the market that deal with just this subject in great detail. However, there are many time-honored methods of using cross-examination to confuse, fluster, annoy, and otherwise rattle experts. One common technique is to ask the expert, "How much were you paid for your opinion in this case?" with the purpose of suggesting that the expert is simply a hired gun who will say whatever he/she is paid to say. The correct reply to this question is to state, "I am paid for my time, not for my opinion." Another cross-examination technique is to ask the expert something like "Now, doctor, psychology/psychiatry/social work is as much art as science, isn't it?" in order to suggest that the results of the expert's work are basically just opinions and that anyone can have an opinion. Additional tactics include reading off long lists of people the expert did not speak to, tests not given, questions not asked, and the like in order to suggest to the judge or jury that the expert was either selective in his/her data collection or didn't do a thorough job. This can be particularly galling since while on the stand and being cross-examined experts are not generally allowed to explain why they made the choices they did in their approach to their assessment. Additionally, during cross-examination attorneys will often as part of the question subtly or not so subtly incorrectly restate something that the expert said during direct testimony. In the same way, they may read a sentence or two from the expert's report or deposition transcript out of context. This requires the expert to be vigilant and sometimes forceful in not allowing lawyers to put words in their mouths and to be assertive in a way that clinical work seldom requires.

It also must be understood that all of this takes place in public. Most court proceedings are open to spectators and in some cases to the media if the case has a high profile. When working with a therapy client, there may be the occasional session that goes badly, but at least any mistakes that are made do not end up on the evening news. One of the most common fears that people have is that of public speaking, and mental health professionals can generally get through their whole career without having to give a public presentation. For the forensic mental health professional, the ability to present oneself while in a public and adversarial situation is one of the most important aspects of the job. Even if the professional is comfortable speaking to groups, it must be kept in mind that there is a world of difference between speaking to a group of sympathetic colleagues at a workshop put on for the state psychological association and being cross-examined by a highly trained attorney whose goal is to make you look like a fool, in a room full of jurors, bailiffs, attorneys, and spectators, not to mention the judge.

And one of the worst parts of all of this is that sometimes the criticisms raised by opposing counsel during cross-examination are at least partly true. Forensic mental health professionals are no more infallible than anyone else. They occasionally misscore protocols, leave out important pieces of data, misconstrue things that are said to them, and make a host of other errors. Frankly, no assessment is ever perfect. There are always more people to talk to, more tests that could have been given, better ways of asking questions, and more data to be collected. However, in the real world there comes a point when the expert simply has to finish the assessment, which would otherwise go on forever. As a consequence, there is always some deficiency that can be pointed out in the work of the mental health professional, and it can be difficult and stressful to admit this publicly. Doing so is very different from having a sympathetic colleague point out a problem with a report in a clinical case conference.

All of these drawbacks are not meant to scare off individuals who are considering moving into forensic work. Every branch of mental health practice has its advantages and disadvantages; the question is whether your personality and skills match well with the demands of forensic work. The skill sets for clinical work and forensic work overlap to some degree, but differ enough that there are many excellent clinicians and psychotherapists who either have no wish to take on forensic roles or would find the role far too stressful and adversarial for their tastes. This is perfectly understandable, and neither role is superior to the other. The question arises when someone early in his/her career is contemplating working in the forensic arena or when an experienced clinician decides to branch out into forensic work. It is at that point that the decision must be made as to whether one has the desire, abilities, and temperament to succeed in this area.

ATTRIBUTES REQUIRED FOR FORENSIC PRACTICE

So, how do you determine whether forensic mental health practice is for you? As part of preparing to write this book, I surveyed a sample of forensic psychologists using an online questionnaire regarding the extent to which they found particular qualities and attributes important or unimportant to the practice of forensic psychology. The survey was not designed to be particularly scientific; it was used to get a sense of what other professional forensic psychologists thought were the most important qualities and abilities necessary to do the job well. I discovered that their views on this subject were fairly close to my own, and there were no real surprises. These are the five most important qualities that the 38 forensic psychologists thought were required to succeed in their field.

INTELLIGENCE

Intelligence was the highest-rated quality in the survey, with 76 percent of the sample rating that quality very important and 24 percent rating it important. Nobody rated it lower than that. This is not surprising, since having a high level of intellectual ability helps in practically every endeavor. Clearly, the more intelligent you are, the more you can learn about forensic psychology. More intelligent practitioners will be able to interpret data in a more sophisticated manner, keep more hypotheses in mind as they analyze test results, and explain their conclusions more clearly than those who are less intelligent. However, you almost never find an unintelligent Ph.D. or Psy.D. psychologist just because the process of getting through college, getting accepted to graduate school, obtaining the doctorate, and passing the license examination means that you must be reasonably intelligent. One of my professors once told me that whereas he did not think that scores on the national psychology licensing examination really predicted anything important such as clinical skill, diagnostic acumen, or financial success, he felt that the exam did serve an important purpose in weeding out the real yahoos.

However, there are areas of psychology in which being a bit more intelligent than the average run of your colleagues is a real advantage, and forensic psychology is one of those areas. This is not to suggest that practitioners in other areas are less intelligent; I can personally attest to the fact that I have met plenty of school, counseling, and clinical practitioners who probably have higher IQs than I have, and who certainly have a better grasp of the more technical aspects of the field. However, some areas of psychological practice do not place the same demands for analysis and mental agility on the practitioner as does forensic work. For example, I began my career as a school psychologist working in the New York City schools. I liked the work and it was fun to be part of the life of the school community. The problem was that all I was supposed to do was to administer IQ and achievement tests, and a couple of projective tests and write up the reports. There comes a point in that kind of job where you have quickly become good enough; if you were twice as good it would make no difference, because the system that employs you has no need for any additional information. If the world's greatest school psychologist had taken the job instead of me, the result would be the same even though he would have forgotten more about the Wechsler tests than I ever learned; all the administrators wanted were the verbal, performance, and full-scale IQ scores.

Forensic psychology is much more intellectually demanding than many areas of practice for a number of reasons. The questions being investigated are often complex; for example, how do you determine if someone who is now deceased had the requisite mental abilities to make changes to his will just two weeks before he died? There is the fact that other psychologists and attorneys will seek to find any weakness or error in your methods and as a consequence will go over your file and report with a fine-tooth comb. There is also a need for fast thinking, as you will be asked questions on the witness stand for which you have not prepared and you will have to come up with a rational response immediately.

Unfortunately, there is not a great deal any of us can do about our level of intellectual ability. Some people are lucky and are blessed with exceptional intellectual skills, while others are less gifted, and our raw brainpower is not likely to change. This is not to suggest that you have to be a genius to be a forensic psychologist, but it is necessary to do an objective appraisal of your own abilities before you embark on a career change to this area. Also, it is important to point out that hard work and study can go a long way. Many forensic psychologists do superior work by virtue of being very familiar with the literature, methodical in their approach, and careful in their choice of methodology. In the movie *Once Upon a Time in Mexico*, the character played by Willem Dafoe is taking piano lessons from a private teacher. The piano teacher tells him that if your heart is pure, the music will simply flow out of you. Willem Dafoe asks him what happens if your heart is not pure. The piano teacher grins and tells him (changing the wording slightly to protect the reader), "Then you have to practice like a son of a gun." The same is true of forensic practice; if you didn't have perfect Graduate Record Examination (GRE) scores and were not the valedictorian of your graduating class, be prepared to work very hard at your craft.

At the same time, if the field is for you, such work will not be onerous and will often be interesting and stimulating.

SCIENTIFIC APPROACH

The second most highly ranked attribute in my survey was a scientific approach. It is common to hear psychologists who work primarily as therapists described their work as a mix of science and art. And who would argue the point? The human mind is highly complex and those studying it have the added drawback of having to use the organ being investigated to do the investigation. Psychotherapy is full of ambiguities and complex issues, with every one of the issues in a case having an impact on every other issue. The work of better therapists is informed by research, but they use their own instincts, insights, guesses, and hunches as much as or more than they use empirical data. Sometimes clients get better as a result of therapists' understanding of the problems and skilled interventions, but at least as often they improve because of nonspecific effects such as empathy, the relationship with the therapist, or just many hours of venting to a good listener. It could hardly be otherwise. Practicing psychotherapists are generally not in a position to run large-scale experiments using matched client samples, nontreatment control groups, and carefully defined treatment protocols. As a consequence, although most psychologists who work as psychotherapists learned about the scientific method and empiricism in graduate school, and may even have done a bit of research when they were forced to for their dissertations, it is not really necessary for them to bring a great deal of scientific rigor to their work on a daily basis.

Things are very different in the practice of forensic psychology. As has been mentioned before, the work of a forensic psychologist comes under a great deal of scrutiny by courts and lawyers to ensure that it is as scientific as it can practically be. The best example of this can be seen in the application of the Daubert standard. It must be understood that prior to 1993, the presentation of scientific evidence in courts was governed by the case of *Frye v. United States* (1923). The Frye standard, as it was called, stated that scientific testimony was admissible only when the particular theory or technique was generally accepted in the field within which it originated. Under the Frye standard, the presiding judge had a great deal of latitude in deciding whether a particular theory was generally accepted by the scientific community as evidenced by the number of academic papers on the subject, the common usage of tests or techniques, or other evidence that suggested that the theory was now part of the scientific field's accepted repertoire. To use an example from psychology, the Wechsler IQ tests could be admitted because they had been in wide use in psychology for decades in one form or another, had hundreds of scholarly articles written about them, and were shown in surveys to be some of the most popular tests used by psychologists in the course of their work. In contrast, Mart's Thematic Tea Leaf Test (which I just this minute made up) has been used by only one practitioner, has no research regarding the technique whatsoever, and has not even been heard of by any psychologists other than the originator, let alone actually adopted for use. For these reasons, it is unlikely that Mart's Thematic Tea Leaf Test would pass the Frye test for admissibility in court as a scientific technique.

There were many problems with the Frye test, including the vagueness of its criterion, the huge amount of discretion it gave to individual judges, and the ambiguity about when a particular technique crossed the line from unscientific to scientific. The situation was greatly changed in 1993 when the United States Supreme Court altered the definition of scientific testimony in the case of *Daubert v. Merrell Dow Pharmaceuticals*. In this landmark case, the court ruled that evidence would be admitted as scientific only after it was scrutinized in the light of four criteria. These include:

1. The extent to which the reliability and validity of the evidence has been tested, or even if it is possible to conduct such a test.
2. The extent to which the evidence has been subjected to peer review and commentary.
3. Whether the evidence has been reviewed sufficiently to permit an estimate of the potential rate of error, and if so whether that rate of error is justified in the context of the case.
4. The degree of acceptance of the evidence in the relevant field.

As can be seen from these criteria, the Daubert decision tightened up the definition of what constitutes scientific evidence in the federal courts. And not only in the federal courts; many states have adopted their own versions of the Daubert standard and made similar changes in their rules of evidence. Now it is not sufficient to simply walk into court and tell the judge that you received your doctorate from a very prestigious school of psychology and that you have developed your theories about criminal behavior based on your 20 years working in this field. You will have to go further and demonstrate that the tests, techniques, and theories that you relied on in doing your forensic assessment meet the four Daubert criteria. The first step toward being able to do this would be having the ability to understand the implications of these criteria and answer questions put to you about them. For example, if you gave the House-Tree-Person drawing test as a way of determining whether someone was a psychopath, you would have to know the extent to which that technique has established reliability and validity both generally and for diagnosing psychopathy. You would also have to be familiar with the literature on the subject to be able to inform the judge of the extent of peer review of this application of the technique. Assuming the technique has any validity for assessing this aspect of personality, you would have to know the test's rate of false positive and false negative diagnosis when used in this matter; how many normal people does it label psychopathic and how many psychopaths does it misidentify as normal? Further, if the test's detection of true positives and true negatives is only 65 percent and it is being used in sentencing for a capital crime, can the use of a test with such tepid utility be justified when the stakes are so high? Obviously, the answers will vary depending on the technique or theory, but if you want to work successfully in forensic psychology you have to at least be able to formulate these questions and articulate the answers.

This is just one example of the type of scrutiny courts will place on your work if you decide to enter the forensic arena. Now, it should be understood that some states are Frye states and others are Daubert states, but in any jurisdiction there will be some standard of scientific reliability against which your work will be measured. Also, not all types of courts utilize such strict rules of evidence. Generally, neither Daubert nor Frye applies in matters such as juvenile delinquency, divorce, and child custody and less serious crimes that are dealt with in district courts. However, even though the judges in these other courts are not held to the strict rules of evidence, their decisions about what scientific testimony to admit and what to exclude are generally informed by these rules. The difference is that in courts where the strict rules of evidence do not apply, objections to the scientific basis of expert testimony are dealt with through the cross-examination of the expert by opposing counsel rather than through simply having the testimony ruled inadmissible by the court. In such situations, when an attorney objects to expert testimony on the basis of its lack of scientific reliability, judges will often reply that such objections "go to the weight of the testimony and not to the admissibility," which is the court's way of saying that you may testify as to your opinion but that doesn't mean that the court is going to take it very seriously. So even in more informal proceedings, it is no longer the case that a forensic psychologist can simply offer testimony that is not backed up by some scientific reasoning and expect not to meet with spirited resistance.

The need to be scientific in one's approach to testimony does not mean that only those psychologists who conduct large-scale research at major universities are qualified to provide expert testimony. It is not really necessary that a forensic psychologist ever do a piece of hard research or publish a single peer-reviewed article (although doing so can be extremely helpful). There are many highly successful forensic psychologists who neither research nor publish. It is necessary to know enough statistics and methodology to be an effective and critical consumer of science, so that it is possible to have an informed idea about what theories, tests, and methodologies have regional support and acceptance and which are less well-established or even questionable. Additionally, it is important to bring a critical, hypothesis-testing mind-set to your professional work and study. You should be able to have a sense of when claims for a particular assessment technique sound too good to be true or when another expert is making categorical statements about the efficacy of some form of offender treatment that do not appear to be borne out by the data. As previously mentioned, this can be accomplished by reading books by well-known experts in particular areas of forensic practice that survey the literature, by reading journals and articles, and by attending continued education programs in your areas of forensic practice. Approaching forensic work with a scientific mind-set need not be burdensome or excessively challenging, and if you like this kind of work it can be stimulating. But such an attitude is absolutely necessary, and if one neglects the scientific approach to forensic work, it will inevitably lead to dissatisfied clients, embarrassing cross-examinations, and ultimately a lack of success in this field.

WILLINGNESS TO BECOME KNOWLEDGEABLE ABOUT THE RELEVANT LITERATURE

This third most highly rated quality may sound like something that all mental health professionals should be willing to do, and to some extent this is correct. Psychotherapists working with clients with obsessive-compulsive disorder, eating disorders, post-traumatic stress disorder, or any other type of problem should be knowledgeable about recent developments in these areas and should follow the literature on the subjects specifically and psychotherapy generally. To do less is probably unethical, and certainly does not serve the interests of one's clients. At the same time, there is a fair amount of literature that suggests that much of what works in psychotherapy is related to nonspecific factors such as the personality of the therapist. Deep knowledge of the research on the cognitive-behavioral treatment of phobias and fidelity to a specific treatment protocol may have less to do with positive outcomes in therapy than these nonspecific factors. Additionally, the work of the psychotherapist is not subjected to a great deal of scrutiny, and as long as the client feels he/she is being helped it is unlikely that any problem will arise if the psychotherapist has not been reading journals or attending workshops related to the client's specific problem. Also, psychotherapy generally is not a rapidly developing field where standards of treatment change from month to month. Certainly, there have been developments in the treatments of specific disorders and anyone working with these populations should be aware of any improvements in technique or approach. But the general approach to psychotherapy, whatever one's theoretical orientation, does not change dramatically over a period of months.

The same cannot be said about forensic psychology. Because forensic psychology exists at the interface between law and behavioral science, the rules of the game can change rapidly when new legal decisions are handed down by the courts. For example, in *Atkins v. Virginia* (2002) the U.S. Supreme Court ruled that it is unconstitutional to put a mentally retarded individual to death because doing so constitutes cruel and unusual punishment. Whatever one thinks of this ruling, it had an immediate effect on any forensic psychologist who performs sentencing evaluations in capital cases. Prior to the Atkins ruling, the fact that an individual was or was not mentally retarded had no direct impact on whether the person should be sentenced to death. A competent forensic psychologist evaluating such an individual would almost certainly assess intellectual ability through psychological testing, collateral interviews, and record review because an individual's intellectual status could have a mitigatory effect on the jury's decision to impose the death penalty and instead recommend a sentence of life imprisonment without the possibility of parole. But on the day that the Atkins decision was handed down, everything changed for forensic psychologists doing such evaluations in states that utilize the death penalty. Determining whether an individual is or is not mentally retarded went from being one fact to be considered by the jury to an essential issue that could literally mean the difference between life and death. Suddenly, the courts were filled with requests for assessments of mental retardation for individuals currently on trial for capital offenses. Not only that, but every competent lawyer with a client on death row was now indicating to the court that the client needed an immediate assessment to determine their intellectual status vis-à-vis Atkins.

The problems of new developments raised by Atkins did not stop with mere requests for intellectual assessment of those potentially facing capital punishment. There was a flurry of publications, which continues to this day, regarding all sorts of theoretical and practical issues raised by the Atkins decision. Some of these involve the definition of mental retardation. Some organizations involved in developmental disabilities set the IQ cutoff at 70, while others use 75 as the upper limit. Since there are many more people with IQs of 75 than 70, this definitional difference could have an impact on hundreds or thousands of individuals now on death row or who eventually may come to be considered for capital punishment. Then there is the issue of the standard error of measurement. With some IQ tests it can be three or four points, whereas with other tests the standard error of measurement can be much higher. What is the forensic psychologist involved in an Atkins case to tell a jury about an individual with an IQ of 71? Even with the best IQ tests that 71 could actually fall between 68 and 74; does such an individual meet the IQ cutoff criterion for execution? How about somebody whose full-scale IQ has varied over the years from 65 at age 12, to 69 at age 16, to 76 at 22 when he committed premeditated murder? Or the individual whose full-scale IQ is 69 and meets the IQ criteria for mental retardation, but a closer examination of the scores shows a verbal IQ of 62 and a performance IQ of 79? And do multiple administrations of IQ tests actually cause practice effect and so-called IQ creep so that gradually increasing scores are not really a valid reflection of the defendant's actual intellectual potential?

In the same way, low IQ is not the only criterion for a diagnosis of mental retardation. The individual so diagnosed must have equally low adaptive behavior, and the diagnosis must be made before the age of 18. Think of the problems these issues raise for the forensic psychologist doing such an assessment. What if the defendant lived in a poor district that gave social promotions (the practice of passing children into the next grade so they could stay with their peers) and did not have much of a special-education program so that it is unlikely that the defendant would ever have been diagnosed as mentally retarded even if he had been? Or what if the defendant dropped out of school at age 12 and began a life of menial labor and crime? Does the forensic psychologist take the position that even though the individual gives every sign of mental retardation, by definition he cannot be because it was never diagnosed in the defendant's minority, even though such fidelity to the *Diagnostic and Statistical Manual* (4th ed. text revision (DSM-IV-TR)) might contribute to a man losing his life? Or should the forensic psychologist be more flexible and do a retrospective analysis of all the information available to supply the historical component of the diagnosis? If so, how accurate is the forensic psychologist's estimate likely to be? And how accurate are the various adaptive behavior scales utilized in making this diagnosis? How strong are the interrater reliability and the predictive validity of each test?

Another example of the same type of thing occurred in 1993 in the case of *Godinez v. Moran*, which was also decided by the United States Supreme Court. The issue of competence to stand trial was briefly described in the "Areas of Forensic Practice" section in Chapter 1. Put simply, in order to be competent to stand trial a defendant has to have a factual and rational understanding of the issues involved in standing trial as well as a reasonable degree of ability to assist an attorney in putting on a defense. At the same time, many states have had special hearings to determine other issues such as whether a defendant understands the issues involved in deciding to go forward without a lawyer or in determining whether to plead guilty. Some states have treated these latter issues as separate competencies, while others have lumped them together with competence to stand trial in general. This issue finally came to a head when the *Godinez* case was brought before the Supreme Court to decide this issue once and for all. Justice Clarence Thomas, writing for the court, provided an analysis that made the ruling clear that competency to waive counsel and to plead guilty are not separate and more difficult competencies than general competence to stand trial, since defendants in a normal trial make decisions about whether or not to testify, which witnesses to call, what to tell their attorneys about their actions, and a host of other matters that the court felt were just as complex as decisions to waive counsel or plead guilty.

Unfortunately, the court did not provide any guidance for what forensic psychologists were supposed to do about how to perform their competency assessments now that all of these new competencies were lumped in with the issues that originally had formed the entirety of competence to stand trial assessments. On the one hand, psychologists could simply ignore the issues of waiver of counsel and pleading guilty and simply give their standard competence to stand trial assessment. This would make sense if they felt that the Supreme Court ruling meant that if a defendant were determined to be competent or not competent, the individual's status with regard to waiver of counsel and pleading guilty would automatically be the same, since the court had made clear that this is so. Unfortunately, there is substantial disagreement among psychologists as to whether this is actually the case. After all, just because the Supreme Court justices think that these competencies are the same does not make it so; to paraphrase the nineteenth-century French neurologist Jean-Martin Charcot, theory is good but it doesn't prevent things from being true, and there is a developing body of scientific evidence to suggest that the Supreme Court may have gotten this one wrong.

On the other hand, forensic psychologists performing competency assessments might decide that the most prudent course of action would be to expand their standard battery of questions and tasks to include specific questions about waiving counsel and pleading guilty, since one interpretation of the Supreme Court ruling could be that these issues are now subsumed as part of competency generally and should be assessed. The ambiguity left by the Supreme Court in this case leaves forensic psychologists to try to find defensible positions based on their understanding of this complicated psycholegal issue.

But it is important to note that these types of examples are not simply interesting in the abstract. If you choose to testify in such cases, you can be sure that your views on nearly all of these issues will be carefully scrutinized and you will be cross-examined on them by experienced attorneys. Not only that, but the attorneys may hire psychological consultants whom you never see who will go over every aspect of your report and your data to find even the slightest ambiguities, inaccuracies, or other potential weaknesses. Opposing counsel, whether prosecutor or defense attorney, will almost certainly hire the best and most highly credentialed opposing expert he/she can find to present these criticisms in open court. And one of the most common methods used to attack an expert's credibility is the learned treatise technique. In the learned treatise technique, the opposing attorney presents the expert witness with a variety of articles and books written by experts in the field who appear to be presenting an opinion contrary to that presented by the expert witness. The expert witness is generally questioned about a particular book and asked if the book is considered authoritative in the field of psychology. If the expert agrees that it is, the treatise is then used by way of contrast to the opinion just expressed by the expert on the stand. Now, there are many excellent books on how to cope with lawyers' cross-examination techniques, and this is not the place to go into an elaborate discussion of how to answer these types of questions in court without appearing evasive. But it is absolutely necessary to be familiar with the major books and current research on the subject about which you are testifying. You have to be ready to go back to your texts and also to perform a PsychLit search just make sure that some important article has not been published in the month that has elapsed between the time you evaluated the defendant and when you finally took the stand. If you are unwilling or unable to develop this type of command of the relevant literature in the area of forensic psychology in which you are considering practicing, you should probably reconsider your wish to work in this specialty area.

INVESTIGATORY ABILITY

This attribute was deemed to be very important by 63 percent of my forensic psychologist sample, and important by another 34 percent. This attribute relates to a number of abilities and attributes that are involved in the forensic psychologist's need to get to the bottom of a problem. One important component of this is the ability to suspend judgment while gathering data in an assessment. It is a natural human tendency to come to a conclusion, consciously or unconsciously, before all the data have been collected. But as Sherlock Holmes said, "It is a capital mistake to theorize before you have all the evidence. It biases the judgment." This tendency to come to a premature conclusion has been termed confirmatory bias. Bad investigators often draw their conclusions before they have examined all the data. Once this has occurred, they tend to take note of facts that support their conclusions and neglect those that contradict their theories. Confirmatory bias is seen in many professions; police refer to the tendency to focus on a suspect early in the investigation and ignore other possibilities as tunnel vision. Medical doctors have a saying about this problem in diagnosis: "You look for what you know, and you find what you look for."

Because this is such a natural tendency, as a forensic psychologist you must constantly guard against this problem using a number of strategies. The first is to consciously remind yourself not to jump to conclusions. There is a tendency to become more confident in your abilities as time goes on and this is generally justified. Many of my colleagues have told me that in initial therapy sessions, they can generally figure out the basis of a client's problems and their diagnosis in the first 15 minutes. They may be right, but in forensic assessment it is very important to treat your own conclusions with healthy skepticism and ask yourself, over and over, about your basis for reaching a particular conclusion. I am often reminded of a scene in the movie *The Long Riders* in which David Carradine played the outlaw Cole Younger of the Jesse James gang. The gang has just ridden out of town after robbing a bank, and they are waiting for a boat to ferry them across a river. Cole, with his brother, is keeping a lookout for the posse pursuing them. When his brother asks when he thinks the posse will get there, Cole replies that they will not be coming; they will ride a couple of miles out of town, get tired, and go home. His brother, puzzled, asks why they are still keeping watch, and Cole Younger smiles and replies, "Because every once in a while I'm wrong." The ability to be self-critical is not universal, and even those who have it must constantly guard against complacence.

Forensic psychologists also use what are known as debiasing strategies to guard against confirmatory bias. There are a number of ways to structure your approach to assessment that help minimize bias. One of these is to use a hypothesis testing approach. In this approach, the forensic psychologist looks at the problem and generates every reasonable hypothesis that could possibly apply. Take, for example, a case of alleged child sexual abuse. In any such case, there are a number of obvious hypotheses that can be formulated even before the specifics of the allegation are known. These include:

1. The child's statements about the abuse are an accurate reflection of what actually occurred.
2. Some of what the child says about the abuse is accurate, but other elements are inaccurate.

3. The child's statements are accurate but misdirected (names Uncle Bob when it was actually Uncle Fred).
4. The child's statements are inaccurate and are an artifact of poor interviewing techniques including leading questions, coercive questions, repeated questions, and repeated interviews.
5. The child is making false statements to accomplish a recognizable goal (for example, getting a disliked stepfather out of the family home).

Having generated these hypotheses, the forensic evaluator carefully collects and examines all available data to see which of these hypotheses most likely reflects the reality of the case. It is important to generate hypotheses, because if you neglect one or more logical possibilities, it is unlikely that you will ask the kind of questions that will confirm or disconfirm that possibility.

Another debiasing strategy is to use multiple sources of data. This might involve record review, collateral interviews, a mental status examination, clinical interviews, and objective testing. If these disparate sources of data converge, there is an excellent chance your hypothesis is correct. But if they do not, you need to explore further to resolve any apparent contradictions. For example, I might interview one individual and decide that he seems normal enough and is not exhibiting any severe psychopathology. I then administer the MMPI-2 and find that the individual has produced a valid protocol with clinical elevations of the Schizophrenia, Mania, and Depression scales. Given the contradiction between my clinical impressions and the results of testing, I now have to do more investigation to resolve the matter. Could I be interviewing a very troubled individual on a particularly good day? Did I neglect to ask the right questions? These questions must be resolved before you can come to any firm conclusions about diagnosis. The data you derive from your mental status examination may comport well with the client's psychiatric records and the results of the MMPI-2. This kind of cross-checking provides support for your conclusions. Objective tests such as the MMPI-2, the PAI, and others of this type are particularly helpful in this regard because they are, just as the name suggests, objective. While a particular client may make a bad impression on you for good or bad reasons, the MMPI-2 has no capacity for developing irrational prejudices. If the Depression scale on a particular client's protocol is elevated, it is because the client endorsed, with no input from you, a relatively large number of items related to feeling and acting depressed; the clinician had nothing to do with this elevation.

The noted forensic psychologist Reid Meloy has suggested a report format in which, in his summary, he lists each of his diagnostic conclusions and then enumerates the data from the assessment that support each conclusion. A clinician using this approach might state that he or she is diagnosing a client with schizophrenia because:

1. The client was hospitalized three times in the past five years and was discharged each time with a diagnosis of undifferentiated schizophrenia.
2. The records indicate that the client responds well to antipsychotic medication and rapidly decompensates when he is noncompliant with his medication regimen.
3. The client admitted that he hears voices that tell him to do bad things, and he appeared to be responding to voices during the clinical interview.
4. The results of objective testing are consistent with a diagnosis of schizophrenia.

Whatever strategies the forensic psychologist utilizes to remain as objective as possible, the important thing is to approach each case and assessment with the same attitude that a good detective or forensic pathologist brings to his/her job. This involves suspending judgment, continuing to ask questions and develop alternative hypotheses, and proceeding in a methodical manner. If you are the kind of person who places a great deal of importance on your hunches, guesses, and intuitions, it is possible that forensic work is not for you.

DIAGNOSTIC ABILITY

The need for accurate psychodiagnosis is in no way limited to forensic psychologists. Since good treatment follows from good diagnosis, the ability to accurately diagnose is essential for clinical, counseling, and school psychologists as well as forensic practitioners. However, excellent psychodiagnostic skills are the sine qua non of forensic practice for a number of reasons. Accurate diagnosis is required to answer many of the referral questions asked of forensic psychologists. Consider, for example, a defendant whose lawyer has decided to use an insanity defense in a case of simple assault. The psycholegal issue, depending on where you are, is whether the defendant understood the wrongfulness of his/her actions and was able to form the requisite criminal intent. In some jurisdictions another issue may be whether the defendant was able to prevent him/herself from committing the crime. Interestingly, New Hampshire, where I mainly practice, is the only state in the country that uses a different standard for a finding of legal insanity, which is that the defendant's actions were the product of his/her mental defect or disease.

Now, if we utilize the previously mentioned Grisso five-step model, we can see that the first step in such an assessment is functional; we have to collect data that either supports a conclusion that the defendant did not understand the wrongfulness of his/her actions (the defendant was hitting you on the head with a shoe, but truly believed that you were a giant cockroach) or provides evidence that he/she did know that what he/she was doing was wrong. If we decide that the former conclusion is the case, the next step is the causal component. In this part of the model, we need to provide information to the court that explains why the defendant was acting in a particular way. A number of conditions can cause serious breakdowns in reality testing, and it is essential that we be able to explain the defendant's actions. Was she suffering from a transient postpartum psychosis? Is he floridly psychotic? Did he recently suffer a serious head injury? Or what if he is only saying that he thought the victim was a cockroach and is pretending that he is psychotic? How would you rule malingering in or out? There are techniques that can be used to assess each of these possibilities. Some of these are common to other branches of applied psychology and some are specialized forensic techniques, but it is important to be knowledgeable about the applications and limitations of all of these techniques if you are going to be able to effectively address this component of the referral question.

A solid grasp of the DSM-IV-TR and its system of multiaxial diagnosis is also important. It is not always the case that a full five-axis diagnosis is required in a forensic case, but it is important to be able to apply the system accurately when required. It can be very damaging to your testimony in cross-examination to have a thoughtful attorney (sometimes with the help of a forensic psychologist who does not even appear in court) point out that you have diagnosed a defendant with

Bipolar II but that the criteria you cite to support the diagnosis do not match up with the official diagnostic criteria from the DSM-IV-TR. It is also helpful to be knowledgeable about this diagnostic system, because you may be the one called upon to critique the diagnostic assessment of another psychologist.

Whereas there are any number of accepted approaches to psychodiagnosis, good diagnostic skills are indispensable to the aspiring forensic psychologist. The ability to apply them in a forensic context is a related but separate skill that will be discussed in Chapter 6, but a basic foundation of diagnostic ability is an essential element that must be acquired and continually honed.

A THICK SKIN

A thick skin (which I define as the ability to absorb criticism, constructive or otherwise, without undue emotional upset) was rated as very important to forensic psychologists by 47 percent of my sample and important by another 34 percent. It can be helpful to think of forensic psychology as the social science equivalent of a contact sport. One of my forensic colleagues told me that clinical work is like playing golf, while forensic work is like running back kickoffs. The work is adversarial by its very nature in large part because it is closely associated with our adversarial justice system. Forensic psychologists operate in a very different cultural context than do other mental health professionals. While conflicts can and do arise in other areas of psychology, a case conference is not the same as a trial. Psychotherapists and other clinicians are used to approaching differences of opinion by reasoned discussion, dispassionate examination of the data, and consensus. In a case conference, differences of opinion are calmly discussed, usually without rancor, name calling, or purposeful misrepresentation of the views of other participants. In sharp contrast to this approach, the American justice system often encourages conflict, the idea being that through the vigorous debating of the issues and evidence of a case, the truth will be revealed. In a way, a trial can be likened to a football game. There is an offensive team and a defensive team (prosecution and defense, or plaintiff and defendant) that struggle to win the game by scoring points. The game has rules, and the players can do everything within the limits of the rules to win. There is a referee (the judge) who observes the action to make sure that the rules are obeyed. In the legal system, there are also professional ethics that lawyers and psychologists are supposed to follow without being reminded. Unfortunately, there are some attorneys and forensic professionals who subscribe to the philosophy of a football coach I knew who said it's not cheating if the ref doesn't call it.

This approach can be jarring and upsetting for those who are not accustomed to practicing psychology as a contact sport. Here are some vignettes drawn from actual practice that demonstrate just how nasty deposition and cross-examination can get.

The late Dr. Wilfrid Derby, Ph.D., ABPP, told me that he once took the oath that he would "tell the truth, so help me God" and was seated. During voir dire, opposing counsel asked him if he was a religious man. He replied that he was an agnostic and did not attend church. The lawyer then asked the court to dismiss him for having taken a religious oath when he did not believe in God. The judge disgustedly waved away the objection and the case proceeded.

I was once involved in a child abuse case on the side of the local branch of the state child abuse protective agency. It should be understood that in New Hampshire, and in most states, a psychologist's file at the licensing board is public. Someone working with the accused mother had managed to photocopy my application for licensure and brought it into court. I was then confronted with the fact that the file gave indications that I was not really licensed. I reviewed the materials and it became clear that certain documents in the file indicated that I was not yet licensed, because at the time I was applying for a license. They had removed the part of the file that showed that my application had been approved, and I pointed this out. The attorney for the mother then changed tactics and thrust a piece of paper into my hand, asking whether I had written it. I quickly ascertained that it was not my handwriting and that it had nothing to do with me, and I told the attorney this. He asked how I could be so sure, and I replied that for one thing, I never print when I write notes, and always use cursive. I stated, "And, counselor, I know how to spell 'psychologist'" (it had been misspelled in the document). He had obviously intended to embarrass me by pointing out that I could not be much of a psychologist if I couldn't even spell my title.

You might ask yourself why anyone would subject him/herself to this type of treatment. First, it is important to understand that these examples are provided because they are extreme. Most attorneys are reasonably pleasant and respectful, and when they are not, judges generally step in and prevent any unreasonable abuse of the expert. But if you decide to engage in this type of work, you have to understand that it is an adversarial environment. One of the reasons many psychologists gravitate to this area of practice is precisely because it is so adversarial. It can be interesting to see if your opinions and reasoning can withstand the kind of rigorous testing that going to court inevitably provides. Another reason is that some people just like to "mix it up" and view the court as a kind of arena. These are people who are competitive by nature and enjoy a brisk debate. It certainly adds an element of variety and excitement that can be missing in straight clinical practice. The downside is that being subjected to such tactics can be

---

STORIES FROM THE REAL WORLD

Many years ago I had a patient who fell on very bad times indeed. She had five children ranging from a few months old to nine years of age. She was hospitalized for more than six months for a refractory psychiatric condition. Her Air Force officer husband took her absence from their home as a personal affront. He initiated divorce proceedings. A year later I was subpoenaed to appear at the custody hearing. The husband's attorney was upset at my custody recommendations, which would have had the oldest child, a mature and decent young fellow who had become the caregiver to his brothers and sisters, visit his mother for two weeks each year until he reached his majority. This fellow was the one who asked for the visitation in the first place! I liked this young fellow a great deal.

The husband vigorously disagreed with this recommendation. His attorney confronted me with the accusation, "Doctor, I have it from reliable sources [sic, the husband] that you are having sexual intercourse with the wife! How can you possibly with a straight face make the recommendations you have just given in this court?"

My reply was straightforward. "You are a despicable degenerate of an attorney to accuse a man who has given yeoman service for free to a family that was in chaos. The wife is now employed, living independently, and is free of the mental health problems she experienced as a result of being married to a genuine bastard."

I was fortunate that the judge was favorably inclined toward me. He sat silently at his bench staring at the abusive attorney. The story was passed around the legal community with much humor and satisfaction. Apparently no psychologist had ever challenged this poor excuse for an attorney before.

John Wallace, Ph.D.

I am continually cross-examined about my late husband, Ralph Underwager (what he said in interviews, what he testified to in court, etc.). I do not think I should have to be cross-examined about what Ralph testified to in cases in which I was not involved. They criticize me for not doing laboratory research. I do archival research and write about research but I don't do laboratory studies with graduate students. They sneer at this. They make a big deal over the fact that, among my many speaking engagements, I have spoken at a few Victims of Child Abuse Laws (VOCAL) conferences. But it is more than this. Just last week a prosecutor in Arizona attempted to cross-examine me about the fact that when I met Ralph I was married to someone else. The judge wouldn't let him continue in this vein. But this question is frequently asked, even though I first met Ralph over 30 years ago and we were married over 25 years and I am a 66-year-old widow. It is in the packet of information that the National Center for the Prosecution of Child Abuse routinely sends out to prosecutors when I am retained by the defense. They always ask me what I am being paid for my testimony. I always answer, "Nothing, my testimony is not for sale. I am being paid for my time."

Hollida Wakefield, M.A.

One lawyer spent 90 minutes in voir dire on credentials I do not have. Much time was spent on my not being a "designated forensic psychologist," which is a Massachusetts credential unrelated to the parental fitness testimony I was giving. He also brought out that I was not a medical doctor, not a board-certified psychiatrist, and numerous other things. I finally added that I was not a licensed plumber, electrician, or cosmetologist, whereupon the judge told him to move on.

Michael Karson, Ph.D.

very stressful. It should also be borne in mind that sometimes these tactics work and you do come away feeling angry and humiliated. But this is part and parcel of this type of work, and you need to be able and willing to handle these pressures if you are going to be successful. Being intelligent, clinically skilled, and articulate is very important, but if you cannot put up with these tactics, you will have great difficulty succeeding in forensic practice. As the late Warren Zevon sang in his song "Boom Boom Mancini," "Some have the moves, and the right combinations, but if you can't take the punches, it don't mean a thing." The same thing (figuratively speaking) applies to forensic practice.

ADVANTAGES OF FORENSIC PRACTICE

It is important to point out that while forensic practice can be demanding and difficult, it also provides certain advantages over clinical practice. Depending on what is important to you, these advantages may greatly outweigh the disadvantages. One of the most obvious advantages is that forensic practice occurs outside of managed care. As all practicing psychologists are aware, this profession became substantially less attractive when managed care organizations took over the practice of mental health. The number of billable patient hours greatly decreased as fewer reimbursable sessions were approved by these organizations. Reimbursements have declined and there is very little money available for assessments of any kind. In addition, the amount of paperwork involved in seeing a patient in psychotherapy greatly increased. It is important to remember that a $70 hourly reimbursement is not really a $70 hour if it also involves 20 minutes filling out forms and half an hour on the phone trying to convince a case reviewer that the client really does need to be seen for more than five sessions. The only way to keep a clinical practice profitable is to increase the number of patients you see per week, and large caseloads are a recipe for stress and burnout. In addition, it must be remembered that there are a finite number of reimbursable hours in your market. Managed care has created a situation in which the same or a greater number of practitioners are chasing a shrinking pool of these hours. Many private practitioners have had to adjust their practices by trying to add consultation work, Social Security disability assessments, or other sources of supplementary income. A percentage have become disgusted and simply gotten jobs in clinics or in schools. The money is not as good, but there is less pressure and no insurance companies looking over your shoulder.

Forensic psychology is a managed-care-free zone. For one thing, insurance companies generally will not provide reimbursement for services that are not specifically therapeutic in nature. Much of the work of forensic psychologists is not, strictly speaking, therapeutic. Assessments of legal insanity, competence to stand trial, or child custody may have some bearing on the mental health of the participants but they are undertaken to advance the goals of the legal system. This can come as a shock to some forensic clients who are under the misapprehension that their child custody assessment or other forensic evaluation is likely to be covered by their insurance. But the fact of the matter is that forensic psychological cases are paid either by the individual seeking the services or by agreement with the courts. Many forensic psychologists require that a retainer be paid to them prior to their undertaking an assessment, while others take payment at the time of service. This greatly reduces the need for third-party billing and also makes it more likely that you will be paid your full fee. In one of my surveys of forensic psychologists, having a managed-care-free practice was considered by 63 percent of respondents to be one of the main positive features of this type of practice. While there are other ways of breaking free of managed care, such as coaching and consulting, forensic psychology is one excellent way of increasing reimbursement and lessening administrative paperwork.

A related advantage of forensic practice is that it is generally better paid than other forms of applied psychology. The American Psychological Association (APA) periodically does salary surveys for psychologists working in a variety of settings. Unfortunately, the APA does not have a separate category for forensic psychology and I was unable to find any studies of this issue. But in my conversations with my forensic colleagues across the country, there is general agreement that forensic work pays much better than clinical work. How much better will depend on your practice and your market, but 53 percent of my survey participants thought that this was a positive aspect of forensic psychology practice.

Another advantage of forensic practice is that it is intellectually stimulating. Of my survey respondents, 93 percent thought that this was a positive and enjoyable aspect of the practice of forensic psychology. Those reading this book who have done a considerable amount of psychotherapy know that while there are many satisfactions to that type of work, there can also be a certain monotony, particularly if you are the type of person who needs a lot of change and stimulation. Back when I was doing a great deal of work with conduct-disordered and oppositional-defiant teenagers, there came a certain point when they began to merge in my mind into one generic angry, sullen adolescent. It was at this point that I began to think about expanding my practice and making it more varied. Forensic psychology requires you to learn about a variety of new legal and psychological issues and also forces you to become knowledgeable and remain current with regard to the professional literature in your areas of practice. There is the challenge of testifying and dealing with hostile cross-examination as well as the demand to continually hone your skills.

In the same way, forensic psychology has less of certain types of stress than you might find in clinical practice. When you do a forensic assessment, there is a great deal less emotional connection with the client, and this can be an advantage. I find that doing a forensic assessment, which has a clear beginning, middle, and end, is much less emotionally draining than ongoing psychotherapy. There are far fewer of the interpersonal demands that can be so draining over a period of years and decades. Also, forensic psychology can get you out of the office. I have been lucky to be able to travel around the country in a way that I would never have been able to in straight clinical practice. And while business travel can have its own disadvantages, you do get to see other parts of the country. Even if your forensic practice is local or regional, you still leave your office to go to court and you come in contact with people such as lawyers, police officers, correctional officers, and bailiffs who can be very interesting and whom you would be unlikely to meet doing psychotherapy in your office.

DISADVANTAGES OF FORENSIC PRACTICE

Interestingly, my survey found that forensic psychologists see relatively few disadvantages to their chosen careers. Almost certainly, this is at least partially because these are people who have self-selected into this type of work. If they found it to be highly disadvantageous, they probably would do something else. The three factors that were seen as most disadvantageous were the adversarial nature of the work (41 percent), the unpleasant and disturbing aspects of some forensic cases (30 percent), and the greater exposure to malpractice suits and board complaints (23 percent).

The disadvantages of the adversarial nature of the work have been discussed in other parts of this book. It can be extremely stressful to have a highly trained attorney skillfully point out the weaknesses in your work and it is even more difficult when the criticisms are correct. However, even when you have done an excellent job there is going to be a certain percentage of cases in which the lawyer cross-examining you will be hostile, obnoxious, and devious. There is a saying among lawyers that when the facts of the case are to your advantage you should use the facts, when you do not have the facts but have the law on your side you should emphasize the law, and when you have neither the facts nor the law on your side you should pound on the expert. If you decide to pursue a career in forensic psychology, dealing with these types of hostile cross-examinations should be seen as part of the cost of doing business.

As far as the unpleasant and disturbing aspects of some cases are concerned, this is also an undeniable occupational hazard. Depending on what type of forensic work you do, you will see a side of life to which you would otherwise never have been exposed. Many aspects of criminal forensic practice involve the maltreatment of children, and this can be very difficult emotionally. Other cases can involve truly disturbing acts of interpersonal violence, complete with full-color pictures and vivid descriptions. I have had cases that have caused me significant emotional distress that took me awhile to stop thinking about. Over time I have been affected by these cases. For example, I no longer watch movies that are at all emotionally challenging, preferring to watch comedies and action films. People ask me if I have seen certain movies about emotionally tormented individuals, thinking that someone in my line of work would find such films interesting. Although there was a time when I would probably have been interested, I now get enough emotional Sturm und Drang all day long and do not need any more when I get home. Apparently, I am not the only one who feels this way. Of the participants in my survey, 38 percent answered yes to the question "Have you ever found aspects of a forensic case so emotionally upsetting that you were bothered by thoughts of the case for some time?"

It should be borne in mind that as a forensic psychologist you have a certain amount of control over what types of cases you take. If you would prefer not to be involved in cases with a high potential to be disturbing, you can specialize in areas such as child custody or testamentary capacity which, while challenging, are unlikely to involve anyone being chopped into pieces with a crosscut saw. In addition, just as physicians become used to blood and pain, forensic psychologists generally toughen up over time and learn to compartmentalize their feelings about their cases.

Finally, the increased exposure to malpractice suits and board complaints can be stressful, but the risk should not be blown out of proportion. Malpractice suits against psychologists of any type are reasonably rare. Board complaints, while more common, are also relatively infrequent and generally have positive outcomes for the psychologists involved. This issue is discussed more thoroughly in Chapter 5 dealing with risk management.

Overall, it has been my experience that most forensic psychologists are reasonably happy with their careers and feel positively about their day-to-day work. I asked my survey participants, "How positive do you find your work as a forensic psychologist?" Fifty-five percent had a very positive view of their work and an additional 36 percent found it to be generally positive. Only 9 percent characterize their experience as both positive and negative and no one found their work to be generally or very negative. If you have read this chapter and think that your qualities and attributes are a good match with a skill set required to be a successful forensic psychologist, if you put in the necessary preparation you are likely to find a career satisfying and stimulating.

In summary, the practice of forensic psychology requires a number of skills, attributes, and personal qualities that make it different from practice in other areas such as clinical, school, or counseling psychology. The skills and qualities include a high tolerance for certain types of stress and conflict, excellent assessment skills, a high level of objectivity, and a rigorous approach to data. The following quiz can be used as one way of gauging whether you have the qualities that will enable you to function well in this area of practice.

IS FORENSIC PRACTICE FOR YOU?

1. Does public speaking make you nervous? (If so, are you willing to work to overcome this?)
2. Can you think on your feet?
3. Do you have good report writing skills?
4. Can you tolerate conflict and adversity?
5. Are you committed to a scientific approach to your work?
6. Are you willing to work to constantly update your knowledge of the relevant literature?
7. Are you willing to constantly strive to be objective, questioning your own conclusions and methodology?
8. Do you have excellent testing and diagnostic skills?
9. Can you tolerate having your work scrutinized and criticized by attorneys, judges, and fellow professionals?
10. Will you be able to comfortably operate in an environment where the rules are different from those of the clinic?

CHAPTER 3

Preparing for Forensic Psychological Practice

W̶HAT YOU WILL LEARN:

As previously mentioned, this book is designed primarily for licensed psychologists who wish to shift some or all of their practices from clinical, counseling, or school psychology to forensic psychology, and to a lesser extent for graduate students in a doctoral program in psychology who are considering having a forensic component to their practice once they become licensed. This chapter discusses ways in which practitioners and graduate students can develop expertise in this area and establish their credentials as forensic psychologists.

WHO CAN CALL THEMSELVES FORENSIC PSYCHOLOGISTS?

It should be understood that while forensic psychology is designated as a specialty area of practice by the American Psychological Association (APA), it is not recognized in the same way as clinical, counseling, and school psychology. This is not to say that the existence of forensic psychology is ignored; there is an APA division (41, American Psychology–Law Society) for forensic practitioners. But there are no official guidelines for qualifying someone as a forensic psychologist. There are programs that offer a concentration in forensic psychology, but this is generally in the context of a clinical program. There are several programs that offer Ph.D.'s in forensic psychology, such as John Jay College in New York, but these programs are more geared for individuals who wish to teach or work in public policy. I am unaware of any state that would allow someone with a Ph.D. in forensic psychology to become licensed to practice. You need to have a Ph.D. in a specialty area in which you can be licensed (clinical, counseling, or school). So, what actually makes somebody a forensic psychologist?

Any licensed psychologist can call him/herself a forensic psychologist in nearly all jurisdictions. In many ways this is no different from practicing in any other subspecialty area. To give an example, a licensed clinician who has worked primarily with teenage delinquents in a community mental health clinic and then in a private practice setting may wish to begin doing marriage counseling. Under the code of ethics of the APA and the licensing laws of most states, this clinician would not have to go back to graduate school and obtain a degree in marriage counseling, because marriage counseling would be subsumed under the scope of practice allowed by his/her psychology license. At the same time, the ethics code makes it clear that individuals must be competent

60

in all areas in which they practice. The code does not explicitly state what a clinician has to do to be considered competent in a particular area. If one boils down the ethical requirements for moving into another subspecialty area, what the code really says is that clinicians should use their judgment in determining whether they are qualified to work with a particular client group. At the same time, if a problem occurs or there is a bad outcome, the onus will be on the clinician to show that he or she had acquired appropriate expertise before working with this new population.

This is different from what is supposed to happen when a clinician moves from one recognized specialty area to another. For example, my doctoral degree is in school psychology. Subsequent to receiving my doctorate, I decided that I wanted to expand my practice into clinical psychology. The APA ethics code makes it clear that to do so, I would have to pick up any courses in the clinical program that were not covered in my school psychology program. This was not an issue in my case, since my school psychology program almost completely overlapped the clinical program and actually required more credits than the clinical program, so few additional credits were required for the clinical psychology doctorate. The next step was to take a postdoctoral internship in clinical psychology, which I did in a state hospital for adult psychiatric patients. This having been done, I could, if I wished, call myself a clinical psychologist. As it happens, I have not done so and have generally referred to myself either as a licensed psychologist or as a forensic psychologist.

It should be noted that this may change in the future. There is a move afoot to make forensic psychology an official specialty area of the American Psychological Association and also to develop specific requirements for course work and training. At the same time, some forensic psychologists are opposed to codifying such requirements and prefer to leave the situation more open. After all, the best-known forensic psychologists practicing today did not complete programs in forensic psychology, so why is it necessary to make things more restrictive? This issue is still being actively debated. If such requirements are developed, almost anyone who has ever held him/herself up as a forensic practitioner will likely be grandfathered into the system and not required to go back to school. For this reason, if you are leaning toward moving into forensic practice, it would probably be a good idea to get cracking on the project.

GRADUATE AND POSTDOCTORAL TRAINING

CLINICAL PROGRAMS WITH FORENSIC SPECIALIZATION

Although this book is intended for psychologists who are already licensed or for graduate students and interns who are looking ahead, some mention should be made about graduate programs that have forensic concentrations. If you are contemplating a career in forensic psychology, the advantages of attending such a program are considerable. You would come out of graduate school with much more knowledge and experience in this area of psychology than graduates of straight clinical, counseling, or school programs. If your clinical forensic program offers the Ph.D. as opposed to Psy.D., you would probably have the added advantage of having written a dissertation on a forensic subject, which will be a plus when it is time to be qualified as an expert in court. Also, with a little imagination, the dissertation could be converted to a paper presentation, peer-reviewed article, or law review piece. You would also know, through your experiences in practicum, whether forensic practice is for you and, if so, what particular areas of the field appeal to you. Graduates of these programs will often have met and worked with experienced forensic psychologists who can help them make connections with other forensic practitioners who might hire them into their group practices, as well as lawyers, judges, child protection workers, and probation officers. Consequently, these graduate students will have done a great deal of networking even before they start their internships. Plus, they will also have a great deal of flexibility, being able to work in purely clinical, mixed clinical and forensic, and straight forensic settings. So, if you are pretty sure about what you want to do, a clinical program with a forensic focus is the power play and a really good idea.

BUILDING FORENSIC EXPERIENCE INTO YOUR GRADUATE PROGRAM

If you are already a graduate student, another route is to try to include as much forensic experience in your training as possible. If your program offers any forensic psychology courses, take them. Many programs require students to complete practica, and others have a distributed internship during graduate school that generally counts as one year of postdoctoral internship. How something done before you receive your doctorate can count as postdoctoral I don't know, but that is how it works in many programs. I think it has something to do with the difficulty of obtaining a paying postdoctoral internship these days. In any case, if you can possibly do some of this work in a forensic setting, you should do so. With practicum, the rules are flexible and you can often find or create a practicum in a forensic setting. Jails, juvenile detention centers, state hospitals with forensic units, group homes, and other such settings often have licensed mental health professionals on staff who would jump at the chance to have a graduate student help them with testing and/or counseling. It is often possible to seek out such a placement, talk to the staff about working in return for supervision, and then approach the professors who handle practicum placements and sell them on the idea. These experiences are an opportunity to learn about forensic psychology, build your forensic resume, and pick up letters of recommendation. You can then use these experiences as entry to a postdoctoral forensic internship.

It should be noted that this is generally easiest to do from a clinical psychology program rather than a counseling or school program. In my survey of forensic psychologists on the Psylaw-L Listserv of the American Psychology—Law Society and the American Board of Forensic Psychology (ABFP) listserv, 63 percent of those responding had degrees in clinical psychology. Only 17 percent came from counseling psychology programs, and a mere 4.3 percent came from school psychology programs (only two responders and one of them was me). This is probably because the skill set required for forensic work is closely related to that of clinical psychology. Clinical psychologists generally (but not always) work with patients with higher levels of psychopathology than do counseling or school psychologists and utilize techniques that are also required in forensic work. This is a generalization, but clinical graduates are generally perceived to have more experience working with hard core populations and are therefore more likely to be picked for forensic postdoctoral internships. Despite this, there are plenty of routes to forensic practice for those with counseling or school degrees.

COMPLETING A FORENSIC POSTDOCTORAL INTERNSHIP

Another way to establish your forensic credentials is to complete a postdoctoral forensic internship. In my survey of forensic psychologists, 19 percent had completed such an internship. There are advantages and disadvantages to taking this route. The first consideration is that forensic postdoctoral internships, like all postdoctoral internships in psychology, are increasingly difficult to come by. This is partly because psychologists are at a disadvantage regarding internships in comparison to master's-level clinicians. The problem is that master's-level mental health professionals generally complete their terminal degrees in two years, do one or two years of internship, and are then eligible for licensure. Once they are licensed, they can receive insurance reimbursement and work for a clinic or in a group practice or strike out on their own. Doctoral-level psychologists have to complete four years of study, and those in Ph.D. programs (as opposed to Psy.D.) often take a year to compete their dissertations. They subsequently have to complete another one to two years of internship to be able to sit for the licensing examination, and they cannot receive reimbursement until they are licensed.

One might think that a psychologist should be able to be licensed after two or three years of graduate school as a master's-level therapist, but this is usually not a possibility, at least partly because of competition and turf issues. Despite that fact that the skill set of master's-level clinicians is almost exactly the same as that of psychologists who have completed two or three years of graduate school (except that the master's-level therapists generally have no training in testing), most states have requirements for specific courses that effectively block psychologists from obtaining such a license. This is particularly problematic because the extra years required to complete a Ph.D. mean heavier tuition costs to complete the degree, as well as an increased length of time with no income.

The rise of managed care has also compounded this problem by decreasing the demand for diagnostic testing and increasing the use of less expensive master's-level clinicians. Adding to this is the fact that managed care companies have decreased the number of psychotherapy sessions that subscribers are allowed. From a purely economic standpoint, this means that there are the same numbers of mental health professionals chasing a diminishing number of reimbursable therapy hours. There is also a decrease in the number of paid postdoctoral internships available, and it is difficult for those psychologists who are not already independently wealthy to go yet another two years with little or no income.

That being said, there are some hopeful steps being taken. There are initiatives in a number of states to allow psychologists to sit for licensure when they complete their doctoral degrees, which would allow them to take paying jobs right out of graduate school. Some states are also mulling the idea of granting a provisional license to recently graduated Ph.D.'s to accomplish the same goal. Another important change is related to where psychologists can intern. At the present time, the APA only approves internships that take place in an organized setting (clinic, school, hospital, prison) with an internship program that meets certain standards. While it is not strictly necessary that an internship be APA-approved, some organizations (such as the Veterans Administration) will not hire a psychologist who has not completed an APA-approved internship. And if your internship was not APA-approved, before you can be licensed you have to demonstrate that your internship was equivalent to one approved by the APA. Some states are now allowing new Ph.D.'s to intern in private practice settings. This still leaves the problem of reimbursement to resolve, but this step increases the number of postdoctoral internships available and makes the process more user-friendly.

It should be noted that I am not suggesting that an internship has to be explicitly forensic in order to help you enter forensic practice. As you will see later, many successful and well-known forensic psychologists never completed any kind of forensic internship. The situation is similar in neuropsychology, which has been recognized as a specialty by the APA. Many of the top neuropsychologists practicing today never completed a neuropsychology internship. This is because in rapidly developing areas of practice, there are often no such internships available when the area of practice is just beginning to be recognized. For example, I frequently testify about how child sexual abuse assessments should be conducted. Lawyers who want to raise questions about my credentials in this area will ask what graduate-level courses I have taken in the area of child abuse. I have to say that I have never taken such a course, although I have taught about child abuse at a graduate level, written articles for peer-reviewed journals, and published a book on the subject. The reason for my lack of course work in this area is simple; there were no such courses back in 1978 when I started graduate school. There are now, but back then you could not take such courses because they did not exist.

There are some developments at the APA with regard to specialties that could have an impact on those who are not practicing now who may wish to in the future. Forensic psychology has been recognized as a specialty area by the APA, but unlike some other emerging specialties such as neuropsychology, there are as yet no recommended standards psychologists have to meet in order to officially call themselves forensic psychologists. Those who are practicing in this area do not as yet have to have taken any specific graduate courses, internships, or practica to hold themselves out as specialists in this area. Also, everyone who was working in this area before such standards are adopted will be considered grandfathered as forensic psychologists. But the issue is more complicated than this, unfortunately. No one organization owns psychology, not even the APA. Consequently, while the APA may have suggested standards for specialties, the standards do not have the force of law.

Unless your state or province specifically certifies or licenses in a specialty area (and while most do not, some do), once you are licensed as a psychologist, you can pretty much call yourself whatever you want. For example, whether your doctorate was in clinical, counseling, or school psychology, in most states you are simply licensed as a psychologist. In such states, if you want to say that you specialize in clinical psychology, no one will stop you. There are many psychologists who went to neuropsychological workshops, received supervision, and read books on the subject who hold themselves out as neuropsychologists even though they do not meet the specialty standards promulgated by the APA. In my experience, their assessments vary in quality, but many are pretty good.

Is it unethical to practice in this manner? The answer is open to debate. The APA ethics code makes it clear that you have to be competent to practice in a specific area of applied psychology. Are you, by definition, incompetent if you don't meet the letter of the standards? In my opinion, not really, since the specialty standards are considered aspirational rather than enforceable. But by the same token, you have to be sure that you know what you are doing before you undertake to practice in a new area. This is because the APA code makes it clear that the onus is on you to demonstrate that you had appropriate preparation in that area of practice. If a case goes south, it will be up to you to demonstrate that you were competent in that area; it won't be the board's responsibility to show that you were not. This is particularly important in forensic psychology, since forensic psychologists tend to draw board complaints at a higher rate than other psychologists.

At this point, forensic psychology has been around long enough that there are any number of forensic postdoctoral internships available. They vary widely in the extent to which their focus and content are completely, mostly, or partially forensic, and there are advantages and disadvantages to each. The main issue is the extent to which you want to be focused on forensic cases or whether you want to have a few more arrows in your quiver.

Having a postdoctoral internship in a setting such as the forensic unit of a state prison will mean that you will have tremendous experience performing competency, NGRI, and sexual predator evaluations and possibly a great deal of expertise in treating offender populations, but you will most likely learn nothing about marriage counseling, psychoeducational assessment, or a host of other subjects. This means that if you are sure you want to go into forensic practice or work in such a setting, you will have an advantage, but if you want to be able to find a job in a wider range of settings you may have problems.

A postdoctoral internship that allows you to work with both forensic and nonforensic populations provides you greater flexibility in the initial part of your career. You may find, particularly if you are in a small market, that there simply is not enough forensic work to fill your schedule, and it may be helpful to be able to present yourself as having experience and expertise in a number of areas. Personally, I think that the more subspecialties you can develop the better off you will be, but this is very much a matter of personal preference and marketing strategy. You do have a marketing strategy, right? No? Then you'd better check out Chapter 8 and *Getting Started in Private Practice* (Stout & Grand, 2005).

How Experienced Nonforensic Psychologists Can Prepare for Forensic Practice

Let's assume that you did not attend a clinical program with a forensic focus and did not complete a postdoctoral forensic internship. You manage to meet the requirements for licensure and pass, and now you are licensed as a psychologist in your state. Is it too late to begin working in forensic psychology? Not at all. There are any number of routes still open to you.

Starting Gradually in a Clinic or Group Practice

One of the most common approaches is to get a job in a clinic or group practice that will allow you to get started in forensic work a little at a time, and under supervision. This is a common route to any number of subspecialties, including forensic psychology. Just as many lawyers do a stint at the beginning of their careers in the public defender's office or the prosecutor's office as a first real job, community mental health clinics are often the first stop for newly minted licensed psychologists. The jobs do not pay very well at the outset, but usually provide sufficient income for survival and sometimes have opportunities for additional fee-for-service work depending on the clinic and your levels of energy and ambition. These clinics are often good places to gain experience and seasoning since they serve diverse populations with a wide variety of mental health problems. Some have programs for individuals with chronic psychosis and others have in-house treatment programs for batterers, sexual offenders, and other offender populations. In the same way, these clinics often serve victim populations, including sexual and domestic abuse survivors, who are treated in both group and individual modalities. If you demonstrate a willingness to work with tougher clients, you will almost certainly find yourself in demand.

It should be pointed out that it is common to feel that you are in over your head in these situations and worry that you are not experienced enough to do such work. These concerns should be taken seriously, but can be dealt with constructively. It should also be understood that in many cases, the clients with the most severe psychological problems are treated by the least experienced clinicians. This same tendency can be seen in state psychiatric hospitals. Generally, the last person hired gets the (from most people's perspective) least desirable client groups, and the more experienced clinicians get to work with the higher-functioning clients. This seems backwards and is, but it is the way things generally work, in my experience.

NEED FOR QUALITY SUPERVISION

It is important to insist on appropriate supervision by a senior clinician in this type of situation. This is important for several reasons. First, you will never get any better at working with a particular population if you don't receive feedback and constructive criticism. Experience by itself without feedback is of limited utility. One of my supervisors once likened receiving feedback to learning how to be an accurate archer. You shoot an arrow at the target and observe the arrow miss the target. You adjust your aim and the next few shots hit the target, but not consistently in the center. You continue taking shots and making adjustments until you can hit the bull's-eye most of the time. This process could not work if you were blindfolded, no matter how many shots you took, because you would never receive the feedback that would allow you to refine your aim. In the same way, simply talking to clients without getting feedback from your supervisor makes you the equivalent of a blind archer. I recall many years ago, a clinician who worked for the local child protection agency was in court and testified that she had assessed hundreds of children to see if they had been sexually abused. When the defense attorney asked her whether she had ever come to the correct conclusion in any of those cases she was rattled. There was no way she could know for sure, since there was almost never a source of outside verification of her conclusions.

A second reason for insisting on appropriate supervision is that the supervisor provides a degree of protection against board complaints and lawsuits if a case has a bad outcome or otherwise goes south. While this is more fully discussed in Chapter 5 on risk management, one of the best ways to demonstrate to a psychology board investigator that you showed due diligence on a case is documentation from yourself and the supervisor that you discussed the case with and followed the advice of a senior clinician.

Finally, a good supervisor can provide important emotional support, which will be necessary if you are working with more difficult populations. Make no mistake, this type of work is stressful, the more so if you are relatively inexperienced. You will need to be reassured that you are doing okay if you are, and helped to make changes if you are not. I vividly recall my anxiety when I started seeing my first official patients at an inner-city elementary school. I went to my supervisor about a particularly difficult adolescent I was seeing. I told him that I was very concerned that I was going to screw up the case and make a mistake. My supervisor laughed and said that no doubt I would make mistakes in this case and in many others if I was going to learn, and that I'd better get on with it.

Interestingly, this particular student did not appear to get better while I was seeing him. He called me vile names and laughed at my attempts to do anything therapeutic with him. He broke one of my Rorschach cards in half. Once he brought me a can of cola that he had vigorously shaken before offering it to me, and I was doused with soda. Sometimes he would be so abusive (verbally) that I would start laughing, not believing what I was hearing. I was so worried about what was happening that I asked my supervisor repeatedly to take me off the case, because I thought I was making him worse. My supervisor refused, telling me I was doing fine and that I needed to hang in there.

At the end of the school year I had to meet with the boy's parents, something I had been dreading. I had actually prepared myself to apologize to them. To my surprise, the father gave me a hearty handshake while his wife beamed at me. They told me that they did not know what I had done, but their son had had his best year ever in school and at home. His grades were way up, he had made friends, and he was even being nice to his little sister.

Stunned, I discussed this outcome with my supervisor, asking how it was possible. He had a number of theories, but the point is that without his support and confidence, I would have given up on the boy. Most cases are not this extreme, but there is always a need for clinicians starting out to have the technical and moral support of a thoughtful and experienced supervisor.

GAINING EXPERIENCE THROUGH HOSPITAL-BASED PRACTICE

A related way to acquire experience that can be useful in starting a forensic practice is to take a position in a state or private psychiatric hospital. Inpatient populations are made up of people who have either acute or chronic serious psychiatric problems and there are many opportunities for training. In private practice, managed care provides very little reimbursement for assessment, and as a result it can be difficult to develop good testing and diagnostic skills. These skills require practice, and hospitals are one of the few settings where a high volume of assessments are still performed. Since having excellent assessment skills is essential for forensic psychologists, the advantages of working in such a setting are obvious. It should be noted that many areas of forensic work involve assessments of individuals with long-standing severe mental illnesses such as schizophrenia, bipolar disorder, mental retardation, and various forms of brain damage. Contact with individuals with these conditions can be initially disturbing, and it takes practice to be able to be comfortable with these clients and to be able to communicate effectively. Working in a setting where these conditions are common allows you to relax with these clients. In addition, working in a psychiatric hospital provides exposure to and experience working with clients with a wide variety of conditions. Where but in a state hospital will you see patients with an encapsulated psychosis, Capgras' syndrome, multi-infarct dementia appearing as paranoid schizophrenia, Cotard's syndrome, Korsakoff's psychosis, erotomania, or Ganser's syndrome? Exposure to a wide variety of psychiatric conditions and diagnoses will help you develop the kind of differential diagnostic skills and hypothesis testing approach that will be extremely important in your forensic practice.

All of this being said, I am assuming that most of the people reading this book, other than graduate students, are psychologists who are already practicing clinical, counseling, or school psychology and who wish to move into forensic work either as an addition to their current practice or as the main focus of their practice. This is how most of the forensic psychologists practicing today got started. To use myself as an example, I had no real idea of what forensic psychologists did (I knew they existed) until I had gotten my Ph.D., completed my postdoctoral work, obtained my license, and been in private practice for several years. Let's assume you are an experienced, licensed psychologist working in a clinic, hospital, or private practice and you want to expand into forensic work. How can you acquire the expertise necessary to practice as a forensic psychologist? There are a number of methods, which are not mutually exclusive.

CONTINUING EDUCATION FOR FORENSIC PSYCHOLOGY

One of the most common ways of learning about forensic psychology is to attend continuing education workshops. These are offered all over the country, although many of the best forensic workshops are presented in large metropolitan areas. Workshops can be privately sponsored or put on by state psychological associations. You can also attend workshops at regional and national conferences. Since almost all psychologists have to complete a certain number of continuing education units (CEUs) in order to maintain their licenses, attending forensically themed offerings need not involve any expense above and beyond your usual cost of doing business. A number of organizations offer excellent programs that focus on forensic issues. Among the best are the programs offered by the American Academy of Forensic Psychology (the training arm of the American Board of Forensic Psychology). The AAFP typically offers a number of programs over several days in a particular location. In a recent training session, the following workshops were offered over a four-day period:

- Ethical Issues in Forensic Practice
- Threat Assessment: A Practical Approach to Prevent Targeted Violence

- Recent Developments in MMPI-2 Interpretation: Implications for Forensic Assessment
- Jury Selection: Research and Practice
- Advanced Topics in Expert Testimony: The Evidence
- Advanced Topics in Expert Testimony: The Presentation
- Forensic Assessment of Tort Liability and Damages
- Preparing for Board Certification in Forensic Psychology— ABPP
- Assessment for Parenting Planning in Child Custody Litigation

These workshops were all taught by recognized experts in these fields. While some of the workshops may be too advanced for those just starting out, they provide highly concentrated training and the most recent information on each subject. Further, they are reasonably affordable and the organization offers a discount that increases with each workshop you attend. If you were to attend all four days and take four workshops, without a doubt you would leave knowing a great deal about forensic psychology. The workshops sponsored by the American Board of Forensic Psychology have an added advantage for participants in that if you wish to apply for your diplomate in forensic psychology, each credit hour you receive in these workshops counts as two for purposes of your postlicensure experience.

In the same way, the American College of Forensic Psychology has a yearly three-day symposium that offers up to 30 paper presentations and offers CEUs for attendees. Various companies offer excellent workshops; those offered by Drew Levens and Associates often focus on forensic topics, and the presenters are knowledgeable and entertaining. The APA *Monitor on Psychology* has extensive listings of CEU workshops around the country, and you will almost certainly find more in your local psychology association news. My only caveat about workshops put on by local associations is that these organizations try to cater to a wide range of interests, and hard-core workshops on subjects of forensic interest may not be offered with any regularity.

Another recent development that can greatly add to your knowledge and expertise in forensic work is the burgeoning field of home study CEUs. Many companies and organizations, including the American Psychological Association, have begun to provide tests to accompany psychology books on a variety of subjects, including forensic psychology. The way this works is that you buy and read a book that is being offered as a home study program. Then, depending on the company offering the home study program, you take a test on the material. Some companies will send you a paper-and-pencil test, which you complete and send back. The tests are usually true-false or multiple choice and you have to answer a certain percentage of the questions correctly in order to receive credit. Generally, if you fail you get another chance and you are provided with feedback on which items you answered correctly or incorrectly. Other companies are more advanced from a technological standpoint. To give an example (and blatantly plug my own side business) my own continuing education company is called HPS-CE and can be viewed on the Web at www.hps-ce.com. We have many different types of offerings, but we specialize in forensic programs. We can send you a paper-and-pencil test if you wish, but you can also take the test online at your leisure and convenience. You can start the test in one session and finish another time. One of the better features of our site is that once you complete the test, you fire it off over the Internet, and if you pass you receive certificate of completion almost instantaneously. This can be particularly helpful if you have forgotten that you have to reapply for your license at the end of the week and you have neglected to get those three required ethics credits. There are other organizations offering online continuing education training, but you will have to research them to see what types of forensic programs they offer.

PRIVATE SUPERVISION: FINDING A FORENSIC SUPERVISOR/MENTOR

Another method of gaining experience and expertise in forensic psychology is to find an appropriately credentialed supervisor. If you are very lucky, you may find a true mentor who will guide your first steps in this new area of your practice. Many senior-level psychologists enjoy supervising other psychologists, and some will offer the supervision at a reduced fee for this reason. In my case, I was lucky enough to make the acquaintance of Dr. Wilfrid Derby back in 1986. I was looking for clinical case supervision, and I literally picked him out of the Manchester, New Hampshire, telephone book. I called him because he was a diplomate in both clinical and forensic psychology, and I knew that this meant he was probably a good bet. Dr. Derby was in his late 60s when I met him and had a solo practice that he and his wife ran out of an old converted carriage house. Psychology was his second career; prior to getting his doctorate, he had been Captain Derby of the United States Coast Guard. He had been a gunnery officer on battleships that defended the Atlantic convoys against the German U-boats in World War II. He had also commanded the United Nations survey ship on the Grand Banks off the coast of Newfoundland, and been an intelligence operative in Indonesia during the communist insurgency.

I began by seeing him every few weeks for case supervision. I had just gone into full-time private practice and wanted to hone my skills in a number of areas. After a few sessions he suggested that I begin focusing on forensic psychology. He explained that it was challenging, more lucrative than standard psychotherapy practice, and a nice break from seeing patients all day long. Dr. Derby had been doing a large number of psychological evaluations of juvenile delinquents at a local detention center, but it involved leaving the office and driving up there, and he was getting to the point that he had more private-pay forensic and neuropsychological cases than he could handle. I was already pretty experienced in doing evaluations of adolescents, so he started referring these cases to me and supervising my assessments.

Because of the contacts I made in this way, I was soon doing a high volume of these cases and becoming known to lawyers all over the state. From doing juvenile assessments, I gradually began receiving referrals for other types of assessments and I continued to receive supervision from Dr. Derby. Since New Hampshire was and is a small market without many forensic specialists, I was able to work on all kinds of forensic cases. From the beginning of our relationship, Dr. Derby encouraged me to obtain the diplomate in forensic psychology, which was very good advice. His assistance and guidance were immeasurably helpful to me in my career. I have read somewhere that if a person does not find a mentor by the age of 30, then that particular type of relationship is closed to them, and I was lucky to get in just under the wire.

It is not always possible to find a supervisor/mentor who will be as helpful as Dr. Derby was to me, but there are plenty of experienced forensic psychologists who will be willing to help you develop your skills and make contact with referral sources. Supervision can take a number of different forms. Some may wish to have weekly supervision; this is particularly helpful if you plan to become a diplomate in forensic psychology (see section on obtaining the ABPP) and you have been licensed at the independent practice level for a minimum of five years. Others may wish to obtain supervision on a case-by-case basis as you begin to receive referrals. For example, you may receive a referral for a risk assessment on a juvenile fire setter and feel that while you are willing to perform the assessment, you need guidance and oversight on the case. If your supervisor has relevant expertise, this may be an excellent chance to gain experience in this area. Supervisors can help you with test selection, data collection, overall methodology, interpretation of the results, and report writing. Still another style of supervision centers around specific issues. It may be that during an assessment, a specific issue related to a particular test may arise. For example, a subject may have equivocal scores on the validity scales of several tests and you may be in doubt as to how to interpret the results. Or you may wonder about what tests to use in a particular case. It is good to have a go-to person who can either field such questions or tell you where you can get them answered.

Ultimately, having personal supervision when entering a new area of psychological practice should be considered essential, and this is very much the case in forensic psychology. It is simply too easy to make serious mistakes in cases that could have very serious repercussions for the parties and for yourself if you do not have an experienced practitioner looking over your shoulder as you get started. This type of supervision may seem expensive, but in reality it is probably the best use of your training dollar. As mentioned, many psychologists lower their fees when doing supervision, partly out of solidarity with their fellow professionals and also because doing such supervision is a break from forensic and clinical work. Small-group supervision is another way to keep expenses down, and a supervisor may be willing to work in this manner. In any case, you should consider paying for supervision and investment in your career as part of the cost of doing business.

REQUIRED READING

Finally, the role of independent reading and study in developing a knowledge base in forensic psychology should not be underestimated. There are a number of books that many forensic psychologists would consider essential reading. I strongly recommend that the aspiring forensic psychologist read a selection of the following books to lay down a foundation of general knowledge about forensic psychology. These books are ones that I consider indispensable and are written for experienced psychologists wishing to make the transition to forensic work. They can be used in conjunction with any of the previously mentioned ways of developing expertise and a knowledge base. There are books that provide a thorough overview of this area of specialty and those which provide essential information about a specific area of forensic practice.

GENERAL OVERVIEWS

Psychological Evaluations for the Courts, Second Edition
By G. B. Melton, J. Petrila, N. G. Poythress, and C. Slobogin (1997)

This weighty tome is probably as close to being the bible of forensic practice as any book. It provides a history of the development of the U.S. legal system as well as an overview of the structure of the American system of justice. It also takes the reader systematically through the principles of law as it intersects with forensic psychology. The reader will be exposed to major legal cases that inform our practice, different theories relating to legal insanity, criminal and civil competencies, best interests of the child, and virtually every other major concept that will arise in forensic work. The authors also provide a general approach to the assessment of nearly all psycholegal issues that are likely to come up in forensic practice. Ethical issues are also carefully addressed. *Psychological Evaluations for the Courts* is not light reading, but if you take it a chapter at a time, you will finish knowing a great deal about how to practice forensic psychology. If I had to pick one book on the subject, this would be it. My only quibble is that the authors do not provide much information on the nuts and bolts of performing these assessments in the less than optimal conditions that often exist in the real world, but this is a minor criticism.

Evaluating Competencies: Forensic Assessments and Instruments,
  Second Edition
By Thomas Grisso (2002)

This is a very important book for a great many reasons. It lays out a rationale for assessment that is clear and logical and that can be effectively applied to a wide range of forensic issues. Dr. Grisso proposes a five-step model for assessing competencies, such as competency to stand trial, waive Miranda rights and/or confess, write a will, or parent a child. Briefly, the model consists of the following components:

1. *Functional.* In this part of the assessment, the psychologist tries to determine the extent to which the subject can do what is necessary to be considered competent to perform a particular task. For example, in a criminal case, does the defendant know enough

about standing trial (roles of the participants, adversarial nature of the proceedings, appreciation of the range of penalties, and chances of being found guilty) to be considered competent to stand trial?

2. *Causal.* If deficits in the subject's ability to understand what is being asked of him or her or to perform the tasks required are detected, what is causing these deficits? Is the subject psychotic, mentally retarded, or malingering? This step not only helps provide information to the court about the cause and severity of underlying problems, but in some cases it can help the court understand where the subject stands in relation to others on a particular measure.

3. *Person in situation.* In this step, the psychologist considers the subject's abilities and deficits in the particular context in which they will be required. This step attempts to allow for the fact that some types of cases make more demands on a defendant than others. For example, it is probably easier to stand trial for simple assault in a district court in a case in which there are few witnesses and the defendant will not have to testify than in a drug sales case in which there are multiple defendants, multiple charges, and a large number of witnesses.

4. *Conclusory.* This is the part of the assessment report in which the psychologist informs the court as to his/her opinion about the subject's competency. Grisso has always been justifiably ambivalent about this component, and there is disagreement in the field of forensic psychology about whether psychologists should offer such opinions about what is called the ultimate issue: the matter of law being decided by the court. Some, including Grisso, have argued that since the ultimate issue (competency to stand trial, legal insanity, child custody, etc.) is legal rather than psychological, practitioners should provide the court with information that will be helpful in coming to an opinion on these issues, but not state an opinion themselves. Those adhering to this position feel that to express such an opinion constitutes overreaching on the part of the psychologist and potentially usurps the role of the judge or jury. Those on the other side of this issue counter that their opinion on the ultimate issue is just one more piece of information that they are supplying to the court, which can give the opinion such weight as it feels appropriate. I personally try to play both sides of the issue. In the conclusion of my reports, I

state something like "While decisions about [ultimate issue before the court] rest with the court, it is my opinion that [defendant/plaintiff does/does not] meet the standards laid out in [legal statute/controlling case] for [appropriate competency]." In doing this, I let the judge know that I know who is in charge, while providing my opinion if he/she is interested. Those starting out in forensic practice would do well to understand this issue and develop their own approach.

5. *Remediation.* In some cases, it may be possible that if there are legitimate deficits in the subject's competency-related abilities, these could be improved to the point that the subject could possibly become competent. This is more likely to happen if the underlying condition is one that can be treated through education or medication. There is research that indicates that psychotic individuals can often be restored to competency through the use of psychotropic medications. However, if someone is incompetent because of a long-standing problem such as mental retardation or brain damage, treatment will probably not improve matters enough for the subject to be considered competent. In this part of the five-step methodology, the forensic psychologist provides an opinion about the prospects for improvement of the underlying condition.

In addition to providing an explanation of this model, Grisso gives the reader an overview of the legal standards that inform each area of competency addressed in the book, as well as explaining specifically how each of these competencies should be assessed. Finally, he reviews a wide range of psychological tests used in each of these areas and provides concise information about each test's reliability and validity. This book is indispensable for the forensic practitioner for many reasons, not the least of which is the way it provides a clear, logical, and usable evaluation methodology.

The Psychologist as Expert Witness, Second Edition
By Theodore H. Blau (2001)

This is another excellent general book on the subject with more emphasis than some of the others on helping the clinician make the transition to forensic work. There is less emphasis on theory and historical context and more stress placed on giving the reader a practical guide to the assessment of issues in the major areas of forensic practice. It is also illustrated with case examples, which are extremely helpful since they show the practical application of the assessment principles Dr. Blau addresses in the different sections of the book.

The Handbook of Forensic Psychology, Third Edition
Edited by Allen Hess and Irving Weiner (2005)

This is a newly revised edition of a classic text that many practitioners find indispensable. It is comprehensive but readable, and has more of a how-to practical focus than some of the other general references, while still providing a good deal of background and legal context for the forensic issues it covers. The book provides particularly helpful guidance on how to write effective forensic reports.

Essentials of Forensic Psychological Assessment
By Marc Ackerman (1999)

This book is different from the other general forensic texts mentioned earlier in that it is much shorter and less comprehensive. However, if you are considering entering forensic practice and would like a quick overview of some of the major areas of the field, this book is an excellent place to start. Dr. Ackerman is best known for his work in child custody evaluation and there is a good deal of material on that subject, but he also provides a practical overview of areas of practice such as competence to stand trial, insanity, and ethical issues in forensic psychology.

SPECIFIC TOPICS

Once you have obtained an overview of the field of forensic psychology by reading some or all of the general texts just mentioned, you will want to deepen your understanding of specific aspects of forensic psychology in which you wish to practice. The following are some of the best books in specialty areas of forensic practice.

Competence to Stand Trial. Competence to stand trial evaluations are some of the most commonly requested forensic evaluations. For a criminal defendant to proceed to trial, he must understand enough about the process to be able to assist his attorney in the trial and follow the proceedings. Most states use some version of the Dusky standard, which states that the defendant is competent if he has "sufficient present ability to consult with his lawyer with a reasonable degree of rational understanding—and . . . he has a rational as well as factual understanding of the proceedings against him." (*Dusky v. United States*, 362 U. S. 402, 80 S. Ct. 788 [1960]). The defense attorney, prosecutor, or judge all have an obligation to raise this issue if they come to suspect that a defendant lacks these abilities. Such evaluations generally involve using one of the commercially available competency tests to determine whether the defendant has any defects that might compromise his/her ability to meet the Dusky standard. If the defendant has a reasonable understanding of the process, the evaluation is finished. If problems are observed, the evaluator explores the reasons for these problems (mental retardation, psychosis, malingering) and the likelihood that the problem can be addressed through psychotherapy or medications.

Performing competency evaluations can be a good place for those wishing to specialize in criminal-related practice to get started. The legal standard is relatively straightforward, and well-researched tests are available to assess the issues involved.

Competency to Stand Trial Evaluation: A Manual for Practice
By Thomas Grisso (1988)

This slim volume is a minor classic of psychological writing. In fewer than 140 pages Dr. Grisso manages to provide a concise history of the concept of competency to stand trial, a review of the legal standards that govern this area of psychology and the law, a conceptual guide to approaching such assessments (utilizing the five steps mentioned in relation to his *Evaluating Competencies*), and a practical methodology for actually performing the evaluation. While many psychology books are longer than they have to be, this volume (more of a monograph than a book) provides readers with exactly what they need to know while avoiding redundancy and padding. I have often recommended this book to young lawyers in public defender's offices who are nervous about trying their first competency to stand trial case. I tell them to order a copy and read it, and I assure them that if they do so and pay attention to what they are reading, they will know as much or more about these assessments as the psychologists and psychiatrists they are cross-examining.

Waiver of Miranda Rights and Disputed Interrogations. These two areas are, in practice, closely related. The Miranda rights were designed as a protection for defendants who are in police custody who may not realize that they have constitutional rights to refrain from answering the questions of arresting officers, that statements they make to such officers may be used against them in trial, and that they may have a lawyer present to advise them, free of charge if they are indigent. Under the law it is not enough to simply tell defendants that they have these rights; the defendants must understand the function of these rights and make a voluntary and knowing waiver if they decide to answer their interrogators' questions or make a confession. To give an example, nearly everyone who ever watched a police show on TV knows that "You have the right to remain silent. Anything you say can and will be used against you in a court of law." I have frequently evaluated individuals who have, after being told this, made self-incriminating statements to police who were questioning them. I have asked them what the right to silence means and they are quick to tell me, "You don't have to say anything if you don't want to." I then ask how a particular defendant might decide to make statements or remain silent once they have been informed of the right. Sometimes they are unable to tell me how such a decision might be made and in other cases they will tell me that a defendant probably shouldn't say anything to the police without a lawyer present. In those cases, I follow up by asking why they gave an incriminating statement to the police without consulting with a lawyer after having been told that they have the right to a lawyer. Their answers vary. Sometimes they tell me that they had the impression that if they did not answer questions, the police would think that they were guilty. Sometimes they say that the police told them that they are just trying to help out and get to the bottom of the case. In other instances, they tell me that it was strongly suggested that things might not go so well for them if they did not cooperate. Whether these responses equal a knowing and voluntary waiver of their Miranda rights needs to be carefully assessed and is ultimately an issue for the court to decide. However, forensic psychologists are frequently brought in to assess defendants' competency to waive Miranda rights.

In the same way, once a defendant has waived Miranda rights, police interrogators may utilize a variety of techniques designed to elicit information from the defendant. Some of these techniques have been found to be psychologically coercive, and confessions have been thrown out as a result. There is also a body of research indicating that some clients have higher levels of interrogative suggestibility, and that individuals with certain characteristics (low IQ, learning disabilities, certain types of psychopathology, etc.) are more vulnerable to these techniques. As with the waiver of Miranda rights, mental health professionals are sometimes retained by council to assess the extent to which the techniques used by interrogators were unduly coercive and might have had the potential of producing a false confession. There are several books on the subject that should be considered essential reading for anyone wishing to become involved in this area of forensic practice.

The Psychology of Interrogations and Confessions: a Handbook
By Gisli H. Gudjonsson (2003)

Dr. Gudjonsson has written numerous articles and a number of books on the subject of interrogations and false confessions. This handbook is comprehensive and at the same time readable and entertaining. Dr. Gudjonsson has been involved in a number of high-profile false confession cases in the United Kingdom and has also developed an instrument designed to assess interrogative suggestibility. In this book he discusses a number of theories that attempt to explain false confessions and puts forward his own personal structure for understanding the thought processes of individuals who make such false confessions. The book is filled with illustrations from actual cases. Dr. Gudjonsson also provides concrete suggestions for assessment methodologies for psychologists performing assessments in this area of practice.

Interrogations and Disputed Confessions: a Manual for Forensic
Psychological Practice
By Greg DeClue (2005)

This recently published book complements the Gudjonsson handbook. Dr. DeClue, in addition to his general forensic work, is a police psychologist who works for several police departments in Florida. His book provides a great deal of specific information about American case law regarding confessions and firmly places his assessment methodology in the context of the law. As with Dr. Gudjonsson, he provides summation regarding the types of police tactics that may have the inadvertent effect of producing false confessions and makes recommendations for policies that would reduce this problem. Finally, Dr. DeClue demonstrates how Grisso's five-step model of competency assessment can be utilized to provide a rational framework for forensic assessments in these types of situations.

Insanity Evaluations. As previously mentioned, evaluations to determine whether a defendant meets the standards to be considered legally insane are sometimes referred to as not guilty by reason of insanity (NGRI) or mental state at time of offense (MSTO) assessments. While the use of the insanity defense is nowhere near as common as the general public supposes and is successful in a mere fraction of those cases that are actually brought to trial, it does come up in the course of forensic practice. Clearly, it would be inappropriate to undertake such an evaluation for the first time without supervision, but it is important to become knowledgeable about the legal and methodological issues involved in such cases.

Conducting Insanity Evaluations, Second Edition
By Richard Rogers and Daniel Shuman (2000)

The two authors of this volume are extremely well respected among forensic professionals for their work in a variety of areas. Here they provide the reader with a history of the development of the insanity defense from its origins in English common law to the legal standards used today. In one of the best and most comprehensive books on the subject, the authors provide clear instruction that will allow the reader to conduct such assessments in a manner that will withstand close legal and ethical scrutiny and also offer guidance regarding specific techniques, instruments, and methods.

Sexual Offender Evaluations. Forensic psychologists evaluate sexual offenders for a variety of reasons. In some cases, individuals convicted of sexual offenses utilize such evaluations at their sentencing hearings in order to suggest that outpatient treatment or a shorter sentence coupled with such treatment does not pose an undue risk to the community. As previously mentioned, many states have sexually violent predator laws and psychologists are utilized to help determine whether a particular offender meets the criteria for civil commitment as a sexually violent predator after having completed the designated prison sentence. Such cases also come up in the context of misdemeanor sexual assaults as well as in custody assessments in which inappropriate sexual contact between a parent and child becomes an issue.

This is an area of forensic psychology that is rapidly developing and controversial. This is not the place to go into a detailed discussion of the issues involved in the practice of doing such assessments and testifying in these cases, but there are some major issues that should be mentioned. One of these is that there are a number of schools of thought about the most accurate way to conduct sexual offender risk assessments. A number of models have been utilized over time. Some of these have fallen by the wayside, while others have become more accepted. At one time, many psychologists and psychiatrists utilized a purely clinical approach to such assessments. They would review records and interviews of the perpetrator and draw conclusions about recidivism risk based on their own idiosyncratic take on what they believed constitutes a risk factor. Since many of the risk factors these practitioners utilized were found to have little or no association with actual recidivism, these types of assessments tended to have low predictive validity and have been mostly, but not completely, abandoned in this field.

Another model that is now widely utilized is the empirically guided clinical assessment. Psychologists utilizing this model will choose an instrument such as the SVR-20, which lists 20 factors that have been shown empirically to correlate with sexually violent recidivism. They score each factor as present or absent, but do not use a numerical score to determine risk. Rather, they look at the data they have gathered in a clinical judgment regarding future risk.

Finally, some psychologists use what are called actuarial instruments in determining risk of sexual offense. These instruments are similar to those utilized in empirically guided clinical assessment, but are actually scored. The scores of the particular individual being assessed are then compared with others with similar scores and recidivism likelihood is calculated. It should be noted that some psychologists prefer to use a combination of techniques in doing such evaluations. This area of practice is controversial for a number of reasons. Some question whether sentencing offenders to a particular length of incarceration and then subsequently committing them to a correctional hospital for an indeterminate length of time is justified from a moral, legal, or clinical standpoint. Others question whether the instruments utilized in doing such assessments are accurate enough to inform the legal system. Despite this, there is a large demand for the services by both prosecutors and defense attorneys.

It is particularly important to develop a strong foundation in the research, theory, and practice of sexual offender assessment. The books recommended here are starting points, but reading them should not be considered sufficient preparation for practice in this area. Anyone considering doing these types of assessments should attend continuing education and training workshops with knowledgeable presenters and should also strongly consider individual supervision when getting started in this area.

Evaluating Sex Offenders: A Manual for Civil Commitments and Beyond
By Dennis M. Doren (2002)
This book focuses primarily, but not exclusively, on evaluating sexual offenders for civil commitment purposes. Dr. Doren addresses issues such as the specifics of different states' commitment procedures as well as who different states consider qualified to perform such evaluations. He critiques the different methodologies commonly used in performing such assessments and takes on the knotty issue of the diagnosis of paraphilia as defined by the *DSM-IV-TR*. Dr. Doren also provides a guide to writing evaluation reports and testifying on these issues in court.

Assessing Sex Offenders: Problems and Pitfalls
By Terence W. Campbell (2004)
   Dr. Campbell's book differs from that of Dr. Doren in that it is far more critical of the instruments and procedures used to assess sexual offenders. Dr. Campbell makes it clear that he feels that practice in this area is way beyond what is scientifically defensible and he is equally hard on empirically guided clinical assessment and actuarial techniques. The author recommends a much more conservative and circumscribed approach to the assessment of sexual offenders. Those wishing to work in this area should familiarize themselves with his opinions, since he is quite knowledgeable about this area of practice and also because it is likely that those attacking your testimony regarding sexual offender assessment will be familiar with similar issues.

Child Custody and Parenting Evaluations. Child custody is an important area for forensic psychologists. The large number of marriages that end in divorce creates an ongoing market for forensic psychologists. The services of psychologists who are knowledgeable in this area are in demand and there is no sign that the need for their services will be diminishing in the foreseeable future. Although some states have passed laws requiring mandatory child impact classes and mediation procedures for divorcing parents, this is unlikely to stem the tide of cases in which parents continue to disagree about custodial arrangements or to have difficulty co-parenting. At the same time, child custody is an area of practice that is fraught with difficulty and sometimes peril for forensic psychologists. Some research indicates that while complaints by mental health consumers to boards of psychology or mental health against psychologists are reasonably rare (an average of 2 or 3 percent per year, with a much smaller fraction of the complaints resulting in any adverse outcome for practitioners), the percentage is much higher when psychologists engage in child custody assessment.

There are several reasons for these difficulties. One of these is that an argument can be made that child custody assessment is a bit of a scientific backwater compared to practice in other areas such as criminal competency to stand trial or legal insanity assessments. This is not necessarily the fault of the practitioners. Custody evaluations are meant to be guided by the principle of the best interests of the child. Unfortunately, a myriad of factors goes into determining best interests: the fit between a child and his/her parents, parenting ability, the influence of siblings, specific psychological characteristics of the members of the family, and the desire for one or both parties to move out of the area, to name just a few. Additionally, there is very little empirical research to support the superiority of a particular custody arrangement, the advisability of overnight visitation for very young children, or other issues that frequently come up in divorce courts. Further complicating these types of assessments is the tendency of each parent to be defensive during such assessments; it can be very difficult to obtain an accurate picture of family member psychological functioning through the use of traditional tests and instruments. Finally, after a decision is made about custodial arrangements, it is not possible to determine whether a different arrangement might have been more or less beneficial; it is not possible to develop a control group for this type of research for practical reasons.

A number of psychologists have attempted to address these issues and help forensic psychologists practicing in the area of child custody to develop evaluation methodologies that are logical as well as scientifically and legally defensible.

Conducting Scientifically Crafted Child Custody Evaluations, Second Edition
By Jonathan W. Gould (2006)

In probably the single best resource in this area of practice Dr. Gould succinctly addresses the laws and ethical guidelines governing the area and provides a conservative, well-thought-out model of assessment based on those best-interest factors for which there is a general consensus of agreement. He then operationalizes these issues and recommends testing and interview procedures that provide essential information to the court that has jurisdiction over the family. A particular strength of this book is that Dr. Gould reviews the relevant research relating to general and specific issues and makes it clear when there is not sufficient research to draw firm conclusions.

Clinician's Guide to Child Custody Evaluations, 2006 Edition
By Marc Ackerman (2006)

Dr. Ackerman is a recognized expert in the field of child custody evaluations. This book provides a straightforward, well-written guide to ethics, methodology, specific instruments, and general information essential to conducting such assessments. It is a good basic text for those starting out in this area.

The Scientific Basis of Child Custody Decisions
Edited by Robert M. Galatzer-Levy and Louis Kraus (1999)

This edited volume looks at a variety of areas associated with custody assessment in terms of the scientific support (or lack thereof) that informs such practice. While it is a bit dismaying to see how little hard data supports this area of forensic practice, the book does provide critiques of what data does exist. This is a useful book for those testifying in this area of practice since it acquaints the practitioner with the underlying scientific support for custody assessment and the assessment of special issues related to custody.

Although child custody evaluations and parenting evaluations would seem to be the same thing, there are important differences. There is a good deal of overlap as far as methodology and assessment instrument are concerned but there are important differences in focus. Parenting evaluations generally come up in the context of legal proceedings in which a state's child protection agency has taken action against a parent as the result of allegations of child abuse or neglect, or they can come up in other contexts such as termination of parental rights. When parents' rights are terminated, they cease to have any legal rights in relation to their child, who is then free to be adopted by another party. Different states have different burdens of proof for child abuse and neglect proceedings and for termination cases. Unfortunately, many experienced child relations and forensic psychologists forget that there is an essential difference between custody assessment and parenting assessment. When the divorcing couple cannot decide on their own about important issues such as custodial time and visitation, a custody evaluation may be requested by the judge or the guardian *ad litem*. What follows is, in essence, a parenting contest in which the court utilizes the information provided by the psychologist-evaluator to determine which parent is likely to do a better job as the primary custodian of the family's children. In parenting assessments, the issue is whether the parents have or can acquire the basic ability to adequately care for their children, coupled with whether returning the children to the parents is in the children's best interest. In these situations, the issue is not whether foster parents or relatives with whom the children have been placed are better at parenting than the biological parents, even though this may in fact be the case. Despite this, it is clear that many clinicians approach parenting evaluations as though they were custody evaluations, which can create many problems for the court and for the expert. There are several excellent books on the subject.

Psychological Consultation in Parental Rights Cases
By Frank J. Dyer (1999)
This book provides an overview of the laws governing this area of forensic practice as well as a review of research related to the effects of foster care on children, rates of child reabuse after being returned to biological parents, and developmental issues associated with placement and adoption. Dr. Dyer also has a section dealing with common cross-examination tactics in this area of forensic practice that I found very helpful.

Parenting Evaluations for the Court
By Lois Oberlander Condie (2003)
This book covers much of the same ground as Dyer's *Psycholgical Consultation in Parental Rights Cases* but goes into much greater depth with regard to the psychology of parenting, laws and legislation regarding parental rights, and the effect of maltreatment on children. It also provides a very helpful guide to evaluation methodology and data interpretation.

Malingering and Defensiveness. It should be clear by this point that the sometimes adversarial nature of forensic assessment creates situations in which those being evaluated have strong motivations to attempt to influence the outcome of the assessment. This is very different from clinical work. While it is not uncommon for therapy patients to hold back information or put some type of spin on what they say to their therapists, it is uncommon for them to grossly misrepresent their actual state of affairs. Generally speaking, it makes little sense for a client to seek out a therapist and pretend to be depressed, anxious, or manic when they are not, since this would simply be a waste of time and money. The case is very different in forensic assessment. For example, criminal defendants may decide they are likely be treated with more leniency if they are seen as suffering from serious mental illness.

As a result, they may exaggerate cognitive or emotional difficulties or simply fabricate such problems.

At the other extreme, parents in custody disputes may be motivated to minimize or deny any problems and present themselves as perfectly adjusted. Individuals found guilty of driving under the influence may underrepresent their alcohol consumption, while personal injury litigants may exaggerate their emotional distress. When individuals present themselves as having impairments that are not objectively present for purposes of external gain, this is called malingering. Attempting to present an unrealistically positive view of oneself is referred to as defensiveness. Since forensic psychologists are no better than anyone else at determining who is telling the truth, it is important that they be familiar with techniques and methods for minimizing the impact of subjects' attempts at impression management on their conclusions. This is a complex undertaking, and there are many different approaches to detecting the presence of malingering or defensiveness in forensic evaluations.

STORIES FROM THE REAL WORLD

This is one of my favorite teaching stories. Picture in your mind:

I am in a room within Men's Central Jail in Los Angeles, California, where I do some of my evals. The defendant walks in. His hair is sticking out in all directions, with dust, pieces of paper, and other flotsam and jetsam both in it and on it. "Mr. Smith, I am Dr. Hirsch. Please come in and sit down." "Smith, Smith, Smith . . ." As the defendant repeats his name over and over again, he is picking at the air around him and seemingly bringing little things to his mouth to eat, as he chews after each deliverance to his lips. "Mr. Smith, please sit down." "Down, down, down . . ." Mr. Smith continues to pick at the air, engages in immediate echolalia, and sits down. "Mr. Smith, you have convinced me that your mental problems are so severe that you could not possibly go to trial without first going to a psychiatric hospital for treatment. You are free to leave." Mr. Smith gets up, walks out the door, and heads directly back to his unit.

(Just to be sure, I spoke to a sheriff's deputy who worked on the defendant's unit. He said that the defendant was fully functional, had never evidenced echolalia, and interacted with his peers without difficulty. Oh, I also asked about his hair. The deputies have never seen it with flotsam and jetsam.)

This happened in the 1960s and was my first introduction to forensic work.

Barry Hirsch, Ph.D.

Clinical Assessment of Malingering and Deception, Second Edition
Edited by Richard Rogers (1997)

This is the essential source for information on the subject of malingering and defensiveness. This edited volume has chapters on subjects such as malingerers psychosis, simulated amnesia, malingering of post-traumatic stress disorder, and children and deception. In addition, there is an in-depth treatment of psychometric assessment of malingering and defensiveness as well as up-to-date chapters on subjects such as the use of the polygraph, hypnosis, and drug-assisted interviews. The book should be considered required reading for anyone who is involved or wishes to become involved in forensic psychological assessment. Interestingly, this book achieved a certain notoriety outside of psychological circles when it became an issue in a multiple murder case in Wakefield, Massachusetts. On December 26, 2000, Michael McDermott killed seven of his co-workers at Edgewater Technologies. He had been informed that his company was going to garnish his wages at the behest of the IRS, to whom he owed $5,600. In an attempt to utilize an insanity defense, McDermott described many symptoms of psychosis prior to and during his attack. However, investigators found that he had researched the malingering of schizophrenia on the Internet and had actually obtained a copy of *Clinical Assessment of Malingering and Deception*. The discovery that he had been doing such research dealt a serious blow to the defense's argument that he had been operating under an insane delusion and was not responsible for his actions.

Documentation. The issue of documentation is covered in Chapter 5 dealing with risk management. The demands for good documentation are much higher in forensic psychology than in other areas of applied practice because of the high level of scrutiny to which your work will be subjected. Forensic psychologists generally develop a variety of specialized releases and forms to assist them in maintaining a high standard of documentation.

The Forensic Documentation Sourcebook: The Complete Resource for Forensic Mental Health Practice
By Theodore H. Blau, Ph.D., A. E. Jongsma, Fred L. Alberts Jr., Ph.D., and Fred L. Alberts (2004)

An excellent shortcut in the documentation process, particularly for those just starting out, this book contains a wide variety of documents and is accompanied by a compact disk that allows you to modify these documents any way you like. There are essential forms such as Forensic Intake, Authorization for Release of Psychological Information, Informed Consent, Family and Adult History, as well as forms designed to assist in custody, neuropsychological, and insanity evaluations. You can put your letterhead on the forms and make modifications so they match your particular practice, or you can use them just as they are provided. This is an extremely useful book that lets you avoid reinventing the wheel every time you need a new type of form.

MISCELLANEOUS READING

Coping with Psychiatric and Psychological Testimony
By J. Ziskin and D. Faust (1995)

It is not an exaggeration to say that the mere sight of this three-volume set on opposing counsel's table in court can strike fear in the heart of experienced forensic psychologists. Many guides to testifying in court actually have chapters that address how to deal with cross-examinations guided by these volumes. This work is a step-by-step guide for attorneys who wish to attack the testimony of psychologists and psychiatrists in court. It is not designed to be fair and balanced; rather, it is designed to help lawyers who are cross-examining forensic psychiatrists and psychologists to undermine the experts' testimony in a variety of ways. Ziskin and Faust provide information that allows lawyers to raise questions regarding the training of mental health professionals, the reliability of information they provide, the value (or lack thereof) of advanced degrees and board certifications, and the lack of scientific foundation for psychiatry and psychology generally. They go on to provide negative critiques of specific test instruments and diagnoses and also to supply specific cross-examination questions on topics such as confirmatory bias, anchoring effects, and false positives and negatives in diagnoses.

Although most lawyers are not familiar with this work, those who do familiarize themselves with it can be formidable opponents, which is why the sight of the three volumes in court can have such a demoralizing effect. There is even an expression to describe the experience of being worked over by a lawyer armed with *Coping with Psychiatric and Psychological Testimony*; it is called "getting Ziskinized." While quite expensive, I strongly recommend that all aspiring forensic psychologists try to get their hands on a copy and read it so as to be forewarned and forearmed against the kinds of attacks they will have to expect in this type of work. In addition, the book is thought-provoking and may inspire you to go to the literature on a particular topic in order to understand both sides of an issue addressed in a one-sided manner by the authors. It was my bedside reading for a number of years when I was starting out in my forensic practice, and it unquestionably improved my ability to testify and cope with cross-examination.

Whores of the Court: The Fraud of Psychiatric Testimony in the Rape of American Justice
By Margaret A. Hagen (1997)

In 1993, Dr. Hagen's older brother was sued for more than $3 million in a personal injury case in which recovered memory played a part. Dr. Hagen was so outraged by what she saw as a parade of allegedly expert witnesses for the prosecution and defense and the lack of scientific foundation for many of their claims that she began to research the basis of psycholegal testimony in the courts. The result is *Whores of the Court*, which is an unsettling yet entertaining polemic against the use of psychological experts in litigation. In this book Dr. Hagen takes on the insanity defense, recovered memories, therapies for sexual offenders and wife beaters, and a host of other topics near and dear to the hearts of mental health expert witnesses. While I disagree with much of what Dr. Hagen has to say, it is also clear that she is right on many subjects. She does an excellent job of showing that many studies that purport to support particular points of view congenial to forensic psychology are seriously flawed, and she also correctly decries the tendency of courts to give undue deference to the opinions of forensic practitioners. I think the book is important not only because of the points that Dr. Hagen makes but also because it forces those practicing in this area to demonstrate the scientific basis of their techniques and conclusions and it inspires critical thinking on the subjects.

CONCLUSION

In addition to attributes one must have to be successful in forensic psychology, there are also some disadvantages that those wishing to work in this field need to be able to tolerate. Again, this is a question of what you are willing to put up with in your professional life, and some may decide that it is not worth it. The adversarial (and some times abusive) nature of the psychologist's interaction with the legal system has been addressed in the previous vignettes. Forty percent of the forensic psychologists I surveyed thought that this aspect of their work made it less attractive and took away from their job satisfaction. But there are other sources of dissatisfaction. For example, 39 percent of those surveyed felt that practicing forensic psychology gave them greater exposure to malpractice claims and board complaints than other areas of practice. This turns out to be not just a perception, but a fact. Forensic psychologists do have greater exposure to these problems than do clinical, school, or counseling psychologists, particularly if they perform custody assessments. The good news is that malpractice claims against forensic psychologists, while more prevalent than in other areas of psychology, are nevertheless relatively rare. Also, while psychology board complaints are much more common, they still have a low base rate and a very high percentage of such complaints are found to be without merit. Of the small percentage in which a psychology board takes action, it is usually a confidential letter of concern or reprimand; more stringent sanctions are almost always reserved for gross incompetence, obvious misuse of influence or bias, financial misconduct, or sexual relations with a current or former client.

Despite the relatively low rate of board complaints against forensic psychologists, it is an issue for which you must prepare yourself when working in this area of practice. Some psychology boards are excellent and highly professional and some are infamous for their idiosyncratic and punitive approach to professionals who come to their attention. In addition, these boards are made up of volunteers who have limited terms in office, and a psychology board can go from quite reasonable to very unreasonable in a short period of time. Dealing with a board complaint can be extremely stressful, expensive, and time-consuming, even if the complaint is obviously without merit. For many psychologists, there's nothing quite so chilling as receiving a letter with a psychology board return address, particularly when it is not time for paying your yearly license fee. Dealing with board complaints will be addressed in Chapter 5 on risk management, but those wishing to move into forensic psychology practice must ask themselves about the extent to which they are willing to deal with these types of stresses as part of the cost of doing business.

The Business of Forensic Psychology

Up to this point, we have discussed forensic psychology practice from a number of different perspectives. In this section we discuss forensic practice specifically as a business. One of the problems with private practice for most psychologists is that generally they have gone into this line of work with no business training whatsoever. Although this has changed to some extent in recent years, most practitioners decided to go into this line of work with very little thought about the practical and financial aspects of their decision. Think back to your days in graduate school. When you were sitting in your first classes, did you, or did anyone else, ever raise your hand and ask, "Excuse me, professor, I was wondering—how much can you make as a clinical psychologist?" For many of us, there was no immediate need to ask these questions because our education and postdoctoral training pretty much led us along for six to eight years. We had four years of graduate school, maybe a year (or two) finishing a dissertation, and then pre- and postdoctoral internships that often led to a job in the same setting. Many psychologists find that they are comfortable with where they have ended up and continue to work at the community mental health center or the psychiatric hospital. A portion of psychologists decide to strike out on their own, either by doing a little fee-for-service work in a group practice in the evening or by picking up a consulting gig or two with a school or group home. A few dive right in and hang out a shingle, starting a full-time solo practice. And as discussed previously, some psychologists decide that forensic work is a good fit for them and get started in that area of practice, either as a sideline or as their main focus.

It is very important to note that the market for forensic psychology is likely to change in the foreseeable future. Until recently, forensic psychology was such a rapidly expanding area of practice that it was not really necessary to do much in the way of marketing in order to be successful. The demand for forensic services far outstripped the supply, and to some extent this is still the case. When I first began my practice, once it became known that I was willing to do forensic evaluations, the business simply came to my door. Probation officers, juvenile service officers, and lawyers were overjoyed to hear that there was someone in the area who could do these evaluations and was not afraid to go to court. The networking occurred all by itself; new lawyers would see me testify in court and ask for my card and I would get calls from all over the state asking for my services. My experience is not at all unique. I once went to a workshop featuring the noted forensic psychologist Charles Ewing, who said that when he got started in forensic psychology it was like being the best-looking guy on an all-girls softball team.

I strongly suspect that this is about to change for several reasons. It is important to bear in mind that there are a finite number of forensic evaluations available to be done in any market. The more forensic practitioners there are, the greater the level of competition will be. The pressures of managed care have made many clinical and counseling psychologists consider ways to get out of the rat race that psychotherapy practice has become. Forensic psychology is one route that many of them are considering, and their entrance into the market will inevitably increase competition. One limiting factor on this has been that many clinical practitioners simply do not want to go to court, and this means less competition for the relatively small number of psychologists who do not mind that type of thing. Another factor to consider is the increasing number of clinical psychology programs that provide forensic specializations. This is a recent development, but the graduates of these programs will soon be coming into the marketplace. These individuals will have jump-started their forensic careers by learning about forensic psychology and developing good assessment techniques even before they have completed their internships. Finally, as I mentioned the outset of this book, forensic psychology has become fashionable and is seen as an interesting, desirable career. I believe that these forces will make it necessary for those getting into the forensic psychology market in the near future to begin to think more seriously about how they are going to manage and market their practices.

In my experience, most of the psychologists who try private practice make a go of it. Some whom I know have been so squeezed or disgusted by managed care that they have gone back to the clinic or the school, but they are a minority. Problems arise, though, because of the lack of business savvy or even business mindedness that characterizes most psychologists. There are a number of fundamental issues that many psychologists entering such practice fail to understand or address in a conscious, explicit fashion, and this failure inevitably has a negative effect on their earnings. Here are some of these issues.

A FORENSIC PRACTICE IS A BUSINESS

This is often a concept that psychologists, forensic or otherwise, resist. As a group, we are so socialized to see ourselves as helpers with a mission that it seems somehow crass or undignified to think about ourselves as businesspeople. Many psychologists got into the field because they wanted to be of service to their fellow human beings. Psychologists as a group seem to agonize about nuances of ethics and boundaries that other professionals simply take in stride. Ethical discussions can often become as convoluted as Talmudic debates, and there are journals and workshops on subjects such as psychotherapy as a means of social justice and self-actualization. I have no objection to psychologists approaching their work in this manner, except when this attitude generally obscures the basic truth that private practice, forensic or otherwise, is a business. If you are uncomfortable with this approach, you should probably stay out of private practice in general and forensic psychology specifically and pursue your profession in an academic or institutional setting.

This is not a problem that is unique to psychologists. It occurs in any area of small business where people get involved without much business training. A restaurant consultant I know told me that he is often approached by people who want to start a small café or grill. His first question to them is "Why do you want to do this?" They often tell him that they love to cook, or that their wives make wonderful vegetable soup with only the finest ingredients. This consultant told me that these people have no conception of what they are getting into. They tell him they want to have a small restaurant, perhaps seating 40 people, and that they will attract business by providing low-priced quality meals. When he begins asking them questions about their plan, they are at a loss and often shocked by the reality of the business they want to get into. How much do they plan to charge for a meal? What do they imagine the cost of producing the meal will be? How many meals do they think they will be able to serve per day? Do they realize that even though they plan on having 10 tables that seat four, sometimes only two or three people will sit there, so that capacity is more likely 30 to 35 than 40? What about their location—how much automobile and foot traffic will pass by per day? If they are doing a coffeehouse in a strip mall, do they realize that they will need to have a noncompete clause in their lease because otherwise a Starbucks may pop up next to them and put them out of business? In this consultant's experience, less than 10 percent of these aspiring restaurateurs have given these matters any thought, or even know they exist as issues. In my experience, most psychologists striking out into private practice are even worse than these would-be café operators.

The idea of being a businessperson is repugnant to many psychologists for some of the aforementioned reasons. I even have mild attacks myself. For example, a large city near my practice holds a yearly bar association convention. The organization's publicist mentioned that for several years a number of psychologists had rented booths on the exhibitors' floor in order to meet lawyers and provide them with brochures and curricula vitae (CVs). I was curious about this idea and discussed it with some colleagues. Many of them expressed concern that such an obvious attempt to solicit business might be seen by the lawyers as crass and undignified, so I asked a number of lawyers I know about whether they would find such an approach undignified and off-putting. They laughed at this idea, and told me that their only interest was in finding a psychologist who could do what they needed him/her to do. One lawyer scoffed at the whole issue of trying to be dignified. "Sure, you will be very dignified, sitting in your office in a tweed jacket, puffing your pipe, with no clients." I should note that ultimately I did not rent a booth, but I made the decision based on a costs/benefits analysis rather than because of the dignity issue.

The private practice of forensic psychology is a business in most respects no different from any other. You are providing a service in return for money. As with all businesses, there are unique aspects and specialized techniques and knowledge, but the rules of the marketplace are immutable and inevitable. As a consequence, it is essential that you learn about business principles and marketing and approach entering a practice with these principles in mind. It is not the purpose of this book to lay out the specifics of developing a pro forma plan and a business plan, as there are many books that already do this. But to succeed and maximize the profitability of your practice, it is extremely important to approach private forensic practice as a business enterprise first and foremost.

This does not mean that you have to be obsessed with money to be successful, or mercenary or dishonest. As with other businesses, one of the most important components is to have a good product to sell. Using the comparison of running a restaurant, if the food is not good, it does not matter how slick your presentation is, how attractive your servers are, or what a great location you have; those factors may bring people in once but by themselves they won't bring them back. In the business of forensic psychology, you have only two products to sell and they are closely related. These are your expertise and the perception of your integrity. One without the other is of little use. With regard to your expertise, you have to have the ability to assist fact finders in their attempts to arrive at the truth of psycholegal issues. If you lack the appropriate expertise, you will fail to do what you have to do to supply the needed information, or worse, you will supply misinformation. You might neglect to consider all logical possibilities to explain what you observe, fail to elicit essential information in your interviews, misinterpret tests, or otherwise come to inaccurate conclusions. All of the integrity and honesty in the world will not help if you don't have the skills.

In the same way, you must be perceived as honest and ethical if you are going to survive in this line of work. If you engage in the practice of forensic psychology for any length of time, you will become well known to a network of judges, lawyers, as well as law enforcement and probation/parole officers. They don't always have to agree with you, but it is important that they believe that you are sincere in your opinions. Lawyers refer to expert witnesses who shape their opinions to meet their clients' needs as "hired guns" or, less politely, as "whores." Sometimes these labels are unfairly applied, but unfortunately, sometimes they are deserved. Some expert witnesses appear to run their practices in line with the motto "Whose bread I eat, his song I sing." There are strong pressures, some subtle and some less so, that can be brought to bear on forensic psychologists in their roles as expert witnesses, and these pressures can be hard to resist. There is the desire to please the lawyer who hired you, the desire to win the case, and the fear that if your conclusions don't match what the lawyer wants, you will lose a source of referrals. On top of this, it is a fact that you can actually make a great deal of money as a hired gun, but only for a while.

Once you get a reputation as a hired gun, you are pretty much out of business in that jurisdiction. Judges will give very little weight to your testimony, and lawyers will figure out that you don't do their cases much good. Opposing counsel will begin to start tracking your testimony, and you will be confronted with inconsistencies in your testimony and depositions that make it clear to everybody that you modify your conclusions to suit the lawyer by whom you were retained. This will lead to increasingly embarrassing cross-examinations and depositions in which you are systematically cut to pieces and hoist by your own petard. Eventually, if you want to stay in business you will have to leave town and start again where the professional community does not know you. Returning to our restaurant comparison, it is as though word has gotten around that your food tastes lousy and there will be a gradual but inevitable falloff of return customers. It simply won't matter how good your presentation is; you will be out of business. So, you have to have the skills and you have to have integrity as a foundation to forensic practice. The presentation and other elements can be improved over time.

The next point is closely related to the fact that you are running a business, but it is not exactly the same.

BUSINESSES REQUIRE INTELLIGENT MARKETING

Assuming you have come to terms with the fact that you are a businessperson, the next step to consider is how to market your business. Again, for many psychologists this is a difficult hurdle to overcome. As previously mentioned, marketing seems a bit undignified and crass to many psychologists, but it is absolutely necessary if you are going to get your forensic practice started and maximize profit. Consequently you need to answer a number of questions if you are going to effectively market your practice.

WHO IS YOUR MARKET?

All businesspeople, including forensic psychologists, need to decide who is likely to need their services. In the case of forensic private practice, the main source of referrals is generally lawyers, although certain types of agencies may also be good sources of business. If you are new to a jurisdiction, it can be difficult to get a sense of where the demand is, and you want there to be a good fit between the services you provide and the services that are in demand. For example, a fair number of psychologists across the United States are highly specialized in the assessment of sexual offenders to determine whether they meet the criteria for civil commitment under some of the relatively new sexually violent predators laws. However, if one of these experts came to, say, New Hampshire, with the intention of doing such work there, they would have a marketing problem. Why? Because, at the present time, New Hampshire is one of the states that does not have such a law. Consequently, these practitioners would have to pursue some other related type of referrals such as those involving presentencing assessments or sexual offender treatment. It pays to do a little research before committing yourself to a type of practice in a particular area.

In the same way, you may find yourself in a jurisdiction in which court-employed clinicians pretty much have the market cornered on competency assessments or juvenile delinquent evaluations. This doesn't mean that people with the money to get a second opinion can't hire you, but it limits the number of such assessments you can do, and also means that you will always be testifying for the defense, which is less desirable than dividing your work between prosecution and defense.

How Can You Get a Sense of the Market?

There are a number of ways to get a sense of what type of forensic psychological services are needed if you are new to the market. Two ways are to talk to other forensic psychologists and to potential referral sources.

Talk to the Competition. While some established forensic practitioners don't like to help out potential competitors, it has been my experience that many, if not most, forensic psychologists are generous and helpful to neophytes. I suspect that this is partly because that's the kind of people they are and partly because psychologists who are established in this area of practice are not worried about the competition that newcomers potentially pose. I am always happy to talk to psychologists thinking about getting started because it is a way to network and also because as a board-certified forensic psychologist with 20 years' experience, I am confident that it will be some time before they pose a threat to my practice.

One way to make such contacts is to pick up the phone book and cold-call a couple of forensic psychologists. You can also go to the American Board of Professional Psychology (ABPP) web site at www.abpp.org and see if there are any forensic diplomates in your area. I recommend that you simply tell them that you are trying to move into this area of practice and ask if they would be willing to talk to you, either by phone or at their office, about the market for forensic services in the area. Offering to take them to lunch is often a good way to make contact; everyone likes a free lunch. You can also meet forensic practitioners at state psychological association meetings, as well as regional meetings and conferences. There are also e-mail lists such as Psylaw-L that you can join and you can back-channel list members from your area and ask them about market conditions. You may run into people who don't care to help you out, but a straightforward approach often yields surprisingly positive results.

In the same way, you can often approach lawyers you have met and ask them about what type of services are in demand in your area. As with psychologists, I have generally found legal professionals to be generous with information about the market for forensic services, and it sometimes happens that talking to them in this way generates a referral down the road. You can cold-call lawyers from legal directories or the phone book who list areas of practice (criminal, civil, divorce/custody, etc.) that match your areas of developing expertise. Talking to the head lawyer at the local public defender's office is often very productive, since public defenders are always looking for new experts. Another way to network is to attend a legal continuing education program that deals with an area of interest for you. Local bar associations have web sites where they advertise upcoming workshops to their members. For example, the family law section may advertise a half-day workshop dealing with child custody. If you attend, you will learn a good deal about the laws and statutes governing child custody in your area, and you will also have the opportunity to rub shoulders with large numbers of lawyers who work in this area. Breaks in the program are a great opportunity to ask questions about what type of forensic services are in demand.

Talk to Potential Referral Sources. As previously mentioned, there are other groups of people who are or can provide information about potential referral sources. Adult and juvenile probation officers, educational advocates, school principals, and physicians may have information about the market for forensic services, and you should use any access you have (without being perceived as too aggressive) to talk to them. There is a great deal of information about the market for forensic services to be had for the asking, and asking can have the dual effect of generating business as well as information. It should be noted that what I am describing can be difficult for many psychologists who are unused to approaching people in this manner, and that talking in this way to strangers can be anxiety provoking, particularly when you are not in the kind of one-up position that being a therapist provides. My advice is to persevere and it will get easier. The ability to introduce yourself with ease to strangers and elicit information is a necessary skill closely related to the skills that you will need to be successful in forensic psychology. If you find that you cannot bring yourself to approach people in this manner, you might want to reconsider going into this area of practice.

What Do Lawyers Look For in Forensic Psychologists?

As part of my research for this book I developed an online survey using SurveyMonkey.com, which I posted on a number of lawyers' Listservs. The survey was designed to elicit information from lawyers about their utilization of mental health experts. Understanding what lawyers are looking for and how they utilize forensic psychologist services, it is possible to target your marketing more effectively. Services such as SurveyMonkey are easy to use and inexpensive and could be used to get a sense of the need for services in your area. I received 31 responses from attorneys who have used mental health professionals in their legal work. The results were interesting and help explain what lawyers are looking for in a mental health expert and where the expert services are likely to be needed.

Of the 31 respondents, 71 percent stated that they have used the services of mental health experts at least occasionally, 19 percent use experts regularly, and 3.2 percent make use of mental health experts frequently.

I asked what types of mental health experts the lawyers have engaged in their practices and how frequently. Doctoral-level psychologists were the most frequently utilized experts, with psychiatrists a close second. Expert services of licensed marriage and family counselors, master's-level counselors, and nurse practitioners were much more rarely used.

The expert testimony of mental health professionals was most frequently used in criminal cases by the defense. Other areas of high-demand utilization included child sexual abuse defense and testimony in personal injury cases for the plaintiff, as well as in child custody cases. There appeared to be less demand for work for prosecutors generally and for civil defense attorneys. However, this could be an artifact of the sample, which may disproportionately contain defense attorneys.

When asked which groups of mental health professionals had the most effective testimony, psychiatrists were considered to be most effective, with doctoral-level psychologists only slightly behind. Master's-level therapists and licensed marriage and family counselors were seen as least effective in their testimony.

Survey participants were provided with a list of qualities and attributes that mental health professionals might have or lack and asked to rate their relative importance. Interestingly, the ability to keep one's composure under cross-examination was the most highly rated quality, along with being familiar with the research in one's area of testimony, objectivity, and good presentation/speaking ability. Survey participants also felt that being confident and advocating vigorously for one's professional opinion were important qualities. Having media exposure, being physically attractive, and attending a prestigious graduate school were not considered to be important attributes or qualities.

When asked about qualities or behaviors that have a negative effect on a mental health expert's testimony, being underprepared for testimony or becoming emotional when challenged during cross-examination were seen as the biggest liabilities. The lawyers in this sample also do not like it when experts give equivocal, long-winded, or overly technical answers. Having a reputation as a hired gun and making poor eye contact with the judge or jury were both considered moderately negative. Testifying in many jurisdictions was not considered to be a liability. Interestingly, testifying frequently or infrequently was not considered to be an important issue.

The sidebars offer comments that were entered anonymously by lawyers in their responses to my SurveyMonkey survey.

LAWYERS' COMMENTS ON WHAT MAKES A FORENSIC PSYCHOLOGY EXPERT

- Preparation, focus, and credibility are more important than degrees and publications.
- Direct knowledge of parties/personalities in contest/at issue; preparation to include oral report and then written report to attorney; willingness to give forensic recommendations to attorney; willingness to meet with client/attorney at locations other than expert's office; knowledge and opinion of the reputation of opposing expert; previous experience with the specific judge in the case.
- A good mental health expert, in my opinion, comes into court prepared to take and defend a position. They need to be prepared to defend their position based on Daubert factors of reliability and relevance. They should be prepared to discuss the current status of the issue within the pertinent field and be prepared to cite some accepted peer-reviewed articles in support of their position. They should be prepared to defend their sources and explain why the research supports their conclusions. They should feel comfortable educating the court without being patronizing. The worst come in with a gut feeling, no science to back it up, and are not particularly helpful to anyone.
- Good communication skills always trump good credentials.
- Honest. Well prepared. Speaks in commonsense language a jury can understand. Independent thinker. High-quality professional reputation.

LAWYERS' COMMENTS REGARDING
WHAT MAKES FOR BAD EXPERT TESTIMONY

- Poor presentation, overuse of technical jargon, overprotective of own position, and unwilling to accept challenges and unable to turn them back.
- When testifying to finder of fact changing/modifying opinion as previously stated to examining/engaging attorney; in testimony being an advocate for a client rather than a reporter of objective-as-possible facts; willingness to modify previously testified-to opinion under cross-examination.
- Not prepared. Goes too far with opinions—selling them rather than presenting them fairly and honestly.
- Deviates from case with hypotheticals and unrelated materials—testifies about the mental health of individuals who are not patients, such as spouses of patients.

ESTABLISHING YOUR REFERRAL BASE

Now that you know something about potential sources of referrals, you need to begin letting them know that your services are available and that it would be a good idea for them to refer cases to you. As someone new to the market, you will have to get your foot in the door and start developing a referral base. A surprising amount of marketing will be required to produce a referral base large enough to support a private practice. Granted, it is likely that you already have some type of income from nonforensic cases, but if you would like to work primarily in the area of forensic psychology it will take a large number of lawyers, probation officers, and agencies to provide enough referrals to make your practice a going concern. To explain why this is the case, another analogy to the restaurant business is in order. Think about your favorite moderately priced restaurant, the one you go to with your spouse and your kids or to meet with some of your friends. Imagine that it seats about 40 people and is generally about three-quarters full when you go there. You probably have never thought about this (unless you're in the restaurant business), but the place probably needs a busy lunch and at least two turns (two sets of 30 diners) and maybe some bar business to be profitable. Now, how often do you go to that restaurant? Once or twice a week at most? And you are a good customer. The manager knows you by name and sometimes sends you over a complimentary glass of wine to show his appreciation. Now, think about it. That restaurant needs to serve around 100 people a day in order to make a profit. The best customers come in once or twice a week, but many others come in once or twice a month or less. Think about how many people have to visit that restaurant at least once a month for it to turn a profit. The restaurant owner will need literally thousands of people who like his restaurant and dine there at least occasionally for his business to be viable.

Now, think about a forensic practice. Let's assume that you specialize in child custody assessment. You may develop a referral network that includes a number of guardians *ad litem* who like your work and send you cases on a consistent basis. Even the busiest guardian *ad litem* in solo practice is going to have only five or six cases a year that require custody evaluations. And, for any number of reasons, he/she may not send every one of them to you, so maybe each guardian *ad litem* is good for four referrals per year. How many such evaluations will you need per year to make your practice profitable? Let's assume that you do these evaluations for an average cost of $2,500 per assessment and you run approximately 30 percent overhead. You will be netting $1,750 per assessment. If you want to make about $85,000 per year, that's about 40 custody assessments a year if that's all you do. You would need a referral base of at least 10 guardians *ad litem*, each sending you four assessments per year, but more likely you would need 20 or 30 lawyers who know you and like your work in this area to make your practice profitable. The same obviously goes for any specialty area of forensic psychology. Clearly, it is essential to network and establish connections with a large number of potential referral sources if you are going to be successful in the private practice of forensic psychology.

What methods of marketing are most successful? I posted an online survey to several forensic psychology Listservs that asked practitioners to rate a number of marketing strategies utilized by mental health professionals in their work. The highest-rated strategy was personal contact with lawyers/word of mouth, with 100 percent of the survey participants rating this as very effective. In my experience, they are correct. Lawyers like to meet potential experts, ask questions, and get a sense of how particular experts present themselves. They like to get an idea of how an expert would approach a case, and whether this approach is consistent with their own theory of the case. The problem with the personal contact/word of mouth approach is somewhat similar to the age-old dilemma of getting a job; employers want to hire somebody who has experience, but how to get the experience without being hired for the job? The clinician wishing to make a transition into forensic work generally starts out with few attorney contacts, so how is the word of mouth to be spread?

One excellent way of dealing with this problem is by utilizing the survey's second most highly rated strategy for obtaining referrals: giving talks to local bar association sections. Depending on where you live, bar associations can be structured in a number of ways. There is always a state bar association, but there may also be county- and city-level bar organizations. The bar associations of some large cities such as Boston and New York may be substantially larger than the state bar associations of places like Vermont and Nebraska. Larger bar associations are often divided into interest sections. For example, one section may cover domestic relations law and divorces, while others may cover criminal law, personal injury litigation, or probate law. These interest sections often meet monthly, and many of them like to feature a speaker or presentation on a topic of interest to the members of that section. There are few better ways to meet a large number of potential referral sources and begin developing a referral network than by volunteering to present on a topic of interest at one of the section meetings. These meetings are great venues for marketing because they have exactly the audience you are looking for all in one place. It is a great place to hand out your business cards, brochures, and CVs. I have done this type of presentation on many occasions and I am always approached by several attorneys after my talk who have specific questions and sometimes on-the-spot referrals.

To utilize this method of marketing, you need to check the web sites of your state, county, and city bar associations and get a sense of how each of these groups is organized. The head of each section is generally noted and their email addresses are often provided. A letter or email briefly describing your practice and your availability as a speaker on a number of section-related topics should be noted, and it is not a bad idea to attach your CV so that they can get a sense of your qualifications. Indicate that you will be calling within the week to follow up, and make sure that you do so. There are a number of different kinds of presentations you can suggest that are generally crowd pleasers. One type is a presentation in which you give an overview of a general topic of interest to that section. For example, the criminal law section may be interested in hearing an overview of the methodologies and tests currently utilized to determine competence to stand trial. Divorce lawyers may want to hear a general overview of the use of testing in custody evaluations, along with brief but thoughtful reviews of commonly utilized tests. The idea of these types of presentations is to inform the attorney audience about services that are available from forensic psychologists generally and by you specifically. The latter should be touched on very lightly; to turn the presentation into a long advertisement for your practice runs the risk of appearing crass and alienating potential referral sources.

Another type of presentation could be one in which you discuss a topic that is controversial for both lawyers and forensic psychologists. You can get an idea of what topics might fall into this category by watching the news and reviewing articles and local bar journals, which are often available online. I recommend that they be topical and controversial, but not too controversial; you want to provoke interest but not irritation and anger. Some examples of such topics would be the issue of parental relocation after divorce, the efficacy of sexual offender therapy, or the empirical basis of various therapies for post-traumatic stress disorder (PTSD). When giving such a talk, it is important to have a balanced presentation that honestly describes both sides of the issue at hand and to the extent possible simplifies the debate into terms that are understandable by nonpsychologists.

As previously mentioned, these types of presentations should not look or sound to the participants as nothing more than self-advertisements. The audience should definitely get the idea that you are knowledgeable about these topics and can provide services in that area if requested, but don't overdo it. Additionally, you should try to come across as professional, confident, well-spoken, and thoughtful, since what you are doing is really a job interview. Anything you can do to make the presentation interesting and clear will be important. At a minimum, you should provide an outline of your presentation on paper with your letterhead. You could use PowerPoint to add visual interest to your presentation. PowerPoint also allows you to print out the presentation in formats that allow participants to jot notes next to each presentation slide. You may wish to list important references on your presentation topic in your handouts. It can also be a good idea to provide copies of any articles you have written on the subject. As a presenter, you should dress professionally so as to make a good impression. Allow time for questions. A good rule of thumb is to use only 70 percent of the time allotted for the presentation in lecturing and 25 to 30 percent for a question-and-answer session. If your presentation is very tightly organized, you may wish to ask the audience to hold all but the most pressing questions for the end, but if you are comfortable with a little more freewheeling style, you can field questions as they arise.

Sometimes you may be offered an honorarium for speaking, but generally you will not. Don't worry about it and don't ask for a fee for this type of presentation, because you are getting exposure and publicity that you couldn't purchase if you wanted to. Advertisements, flyers, and newsletters can be very expensive (although they don't have to be). By contrast, when you give a presentation for a bar association interest section you get to strut your stuff for a whole roomful of exactly the kind of lawyers to whom you are marketing your services. Don't worry if it is a small room and a small audience. If you develop a relationship with even one of the lawyers present, the two hours you have spent giving a talk may translate into thousands of dollars' worth of referrals over time. And even if not one of the lawyers present actually sends you a case, they may very well go back to their law firms and leave your brochure on the lunch table or mention your name when one of their colleagues asks about local experts. I strongly recommend that anyone wishing to increase forensic referrals utilize speaking to bar associations and related organizations as one of their main marketing strategies and put time and energy into developing the skills to provide effective presentations. No other marketing method is as effective or provides this big a bang for the buck.

A related method of marketing targets groups other than lawyers. Presentations to child protective service (CPS) agencies were also highly rated by my online survey respondents as a method of generating referrals. Every state has an organization that handles allegations of child abuse and neglect, often generically referred to as child protective services. Additionally, all states have organizations that deal with issues related to juvenile delinquency. In some jurisdictions, these organizations are one and the same and in others they are separate. However, nearly all of them have requirements for ongoing training and are always looking for speakers. If you do forensic work in any of these areas, it is well worth talking to whoever organizes training for CPS workers. CPS caseworkers and supervisors are almost always looking for psychologists and other mental health professionals to perform assessments and court-ordered therapy. One of the best ways to become known to them is to give trainings and presentations on topics germane to their work. For example, you could give presentations on the treatment of juvenile sexual offenders, working with children with PTSD, and risk assessment with violent or suicidal adolescents.

Using Publications and Presentations

A number of the other highly rated methods of marketing your forensic practice involve different types of publishing. My survey participants rated publishing in legal journals and newsletters and publishing in peer-reviewed journals as effective methods of developing a forensic psychology referral base, with the former being more effective than the latter. In this part of the chapter we discuss how to use publication as a method of marketing your practice.

Many psychologists who enter private practice have never presented or published an academic paper. This is understandable for a number of reasons. First, clinical practice, by its very nature, is oriented toward a different market. Referrals for clinical practice come from many sources, such as physicians, guidance counselors, support groups, and other clinicians. These referrals are often based on the personal experience of these referral sources with the clinician, and not on the number of journal articles the clinician has written. Additionally, general clinicians are busy seeing clients and may have little time for writing or little interest in publishing, since it is unlikely to increase their referral bases or bring in more clients. Also, it can be difficult to do research as a clinician. Psychologists working in academic settings have graduate assistants to do some of the grunt labor of doing research. More importantly, they are actually paid to research and it is seen as part of their jobs. Clinicians have none of these advantages. Finally, clinicians often went into clinical work because their interests lay there as opposed to academic pursuits. All of these factors, and others, discourage clinicians from publishing or presenting academic articles.

As previously discussed, forensic psychologists obtain their referrals from lawyers, guardians *ad litem*, probation/parole officers, and in some cases clinicians. These sources are on the lookout for individuals who have the credentials and experience that can withstand vigorous voir dire and allow the practitioner to be qualified as an expert. There is a saying among lawyers that an expert is a guy from out of town who wrote a book. One way the aspiring forensic psychologist can establish his/her credentials is through a strong CV with an impressive list of publications and presentations. But how should someone who has never published begin? Many seasoned professionals who have never published harbor a suspicion that it is difficult to get published, and that those who do so are academic gods who live on Mount Olympus.

The reality is that it is much easier to present at conferences and publish academic papers than most psychologists think. There are many, many journals out there that need articles every month, particularly in emerging areas such as forensic psychology. In addition, there are many conferences that need paper presentations to fill up their annals volumes. Any clinician with a modicum of writing ability can get published. This is not to say that everyone can have their work published in a flagship journal such as the *American Psychologist*, but there are many second- and third-tier journals where entry is much easier. The same goes for presentations; it is considerably less difficult to have a paper accepted for presentation at a regional conference than at the annual meeting of the American Psychiatric Association. And, while presentations require the psychologists to actually show up and read their papers, if the psychologists have serious problems with public speaking, they have to either overcome this or reconsider their desire to work in this area of practice.

This is a good point to mention that one of the most important things that you have to do to market your forensic practice and maximize your profitability is to distinguish yourself from the mass of other practitioners. There are many practitioners who hold themselves up as forensic psychologists, and they are all competing for a finite number of referral hours and a limited amount of money. Effective marketing means not only getting the word out that you offer a service, but also convincing potential referral sources that you offer something special. Publishing takes some effort and there's always the chance that your first article or two may not be accepted. But having a list of presentations and publications on your CV demonstrates that you went to extra effort. Just as football coaches say that a good big player is better than a good small player, legal professionals will generally pick the individual with some publications as their expert over an equally skilled clinician or forensic psychologist who has none. Successful individuals in all kinds of fields increase their chances of success through seeking out and utilizing every possible advantage, and forensic psychology is no different. Presenting papers and publishing articles are two of the most effective methods of gaining advantages over competitors, and while doing so takes some effort and discipline, so does almost everything else worth doing.

General Considerations. In order for psychologists to use presentations and publications effectively, there are a number of basics they should know about different types of presentation venues and publications. This is because, generally speaking, lawyers and courts have different views of the relative weight that should be assigned to different types of articles and presentations than do mental health professionals, and if psychologists intend to use these methods as marketing tools, they should put their efforts where they will do the most good. Also, the use of these media should be seen as a progression from those venues that are easiest to break into initially to those that are more selective and provide the widest exposure to the desired market audience.

As previously stated, the legal profession has a different view of the relative weight that should be assigned to different types of publications than do mental health professionals. A useful analogy can be drawn from the world of magic and sleight of hand. There are hundreds of books and DVDs available to the aspiring magician that presents a myriad of methods for causing coins and scarves to vanish, transposing items, multiplying billiard balls, and linking rings. Some of these tricks are very complex and require many hours to perfect; some are not really practical no matter how long they are practiced. Professional magicians tend to use these complicated tricks as ways of impressing their peers; these types of tricks are sometimes referred to as magician pleasers. However, these are not the best tricks for presentation to lay audiences for purposes of pure entertainment. Some of the best-known professional magicians, when performing for nonmagicians, use tricks that are simple and can be performed by beginning and intermediate magicians. The pros do the tricks better, of course, but they realize that what impresses their peers does not necessarily impress the paying public. In the same way, publications that impress professional forensic psychologists do not necessarily have the same impact on the legal profession, which will supply the bulk of the forensic psychologist's paying customers.

To use the profession of psychology as an example, those who are more academically oriented see articles that appear in peer-reviewed journals as having the most merit. Non-peer-reviewed articles and even books are not even considered when advancement and tenure qualifications are assessed. Peer review is a process in which articles are sent to a number of experts in the field who are not told the author's identity. The article is accepted for publication only if it passes this scrutiny. Additionally, some journals are considered more prestigious than others. For example, the journals published by the divisions of the American Psychological Association are generally highly regarded. *Law and*

Human Behavior is published by Division 41 (American Psychology–Law Society) and is highly regarded in the field of forensic psychology. However, members of the legal profession are less attuned to which journals are well regarded in the field and tend to see one journal as very much like another. Additionally, many in the forensic psychologist's market audience are unfamiliar with the process and importance of peer review, although some are aware of the difference between peer-reviewed and non-peer-reviewed journals. As a consequence, a publication in a new or less-well-known journal may be given the same weight in court as one in *Law and Human Behavior*. The practical impact of this is that for purposes of marketing, articles published in lesser-known journals or journals that are just starting publication (and they pop up all the time) can have just as much impact as a marketing tool as one that runs in the most prestigious publication.

What to Write About? It is often said in writing fiction that authors should write about what they know. The same is true when using publication as a method of promoting forensic mental health practice. The psychologist considering writing an article should obviously know a good deal about the area in which he or she plans to write. This knowledge can be derived from graduate education, and one's dissertation is often a good place to start, since it generally requires the writer to perform a review of the literature in the subject area being researched. Often the review section of a dissertation, with some alteration, can form the basis of a review article on that subject. Other ways of gaining expertise include continuing education workshops, supervision, and review of the current literature. This process has been made much easier by the Internet. Psychologists over the age of 40 may recall a time when, if you wished to research a subject, you had to go to an actual mortar-and-brick library. This could be difficult if you lived in an area without a good academic library or if your college had a relatively small one. Not all libraries had extensive lists of journals, and specific books that were needed might already be checked out. Now it is easy to access many journals online through PubMed and PsychInfo databases, and subscriptions are available at reasonable prices. Many other journals allow consumers to purchase individual articles for a fee. As a consequence, it is now much easier to review the literature on a particular subject than it was in years past.

The psychologist can start the process by choosing an area of interest and then reading the current literature and journal articles. In doing so, certain trends and controversies in that area will become apparent. These issues provide fertile ground for articles that examine the controversy or issue from a new or synthetic perspective. Here are a few examples. A clinician who has experience treating adolescents with behavior problems may have an interest in the use of wilderness camps in the treatment of such clients. A review of the literature may indicate that there is disagreement about the efficacy of such programs, or that there appears to be little empirical research on the subject of any kind. This state of affairs provides the opportunity to write several different types of articles on the subject. A review article might present a brief history of the use of such programs, the results of research on outcomes of such interventions, or possibly the lack thereof. The author could then offer conclusions about the evidence of the efficacy of such programs overall and, depending on what the literature reveals, could urge caution in the use of wilderness programs for the treatment of delinquency or support the use of such programs (either wholeheartedly or cautiously), and also provide suggestions for further research.

Another example might involve a clinician who works with clients with attention deficit/hyperactivity disorder (ADHD). A review of the literature may reveal that the presence of ADHD has been an issue in the sentencing of criminals who appear to have problems with impulse control. Possible topics for articles related to this issue might include the extent to which ADHD meets the requirements for being considered a mental illness for the purposes of sentence mitigation, a review of the literature on ADHD and the ability to meaningfully utilize Miranda rights, the comorbidity of ADHD and conduct disorder or psychopathy, or a review of whether the treatment of teens with stimulant medication is related to less delinquency.

Certain trends and developments in the law can provide a rich source of ideas for articles. For example, in 1993 the United States Supreme Court handed down its ruling in the case of *Daubert v. Merrell Dow Pharmaceuticals*. This case had to do with what constituted scientific evidence and what was admissible in a court of law. Prior to this ruling, the federal government and most states had used the Frye standard when determining whether testimony was sufficiently scientific to be admitted in a particular case. The Frye standard indicated that an expert's testimony was scientific if its basis was generally accepted by the majority of the appropriate scientific community. However, in its Daubert ruling, the court developed a new, more rigorous test to determine the scientific validity of expert testimony. The elements of this test are:

- Has the scientific theory that underlies the proposed testimony been tested, or can it be tested?
- Has the scientific theory been subject to peer review?
- What is the error rate of the theory or technique, and are there controlling standards?
- Has the scientific community generally accepted the theory or technique?

Looking at this list of standards, it can easily be seen how a large number of subjects of forensic interest could be examined in the light of these requirements. An almost endless number of articles in the light of *Daubert v. Merrell Dow* can be imagined. For example, do the decisions of custody evaluators meet the Daubert standard? How about some of the more controversial syndromes, such as Munchausen syndrome by proxy, battered women's syndrome, black rage, or false memory syndrome? Do a particular state's guidelines for determining the dangerousness of juveniles being considered for transfer to adult court meet these standards? Obviously, writing such an article requires a thorough knowledge of the literature on the subject and at least a rudimentary grasp of research methodology, but obtaining such knowledge is well within the ability of a psychologist with an advanced degree, or should be.

It should be noted that the types of papers described here do not require the author to go out and conduct empirical research with human subjects, do statistical analysis, and gain human subject committee approval. These types of articles utilize literature reviews and the analysis of the author. Such articles have value because they summarize the literature on a particular subject of forensic interest and allow other practitioners to become knowledgeable on the subject quickly. It should also be understood that while ethical principles regarding plagiarism obviously must be observed, writing an article that is derivative of others' work is completely appropriate, as long as their work is properly acknowledged. Frankly, there is almost nothing in psychology (or any other subject, for that matter) that is completely original. Science is a process in which knowledge is built gradually on the work of others, much like a coral reef gradually grows layer by layer on the remains of earlier organisms. And even with review articles, the fact that someone has previously reviewed a subject does not mean that there will not be new research to review on that subject two years later.

Another type of article that may be practical for clinicians to undertake is survey research. Again, the use of the Internet has made such research much easier than in the past. There are even web sites that provide templates for the construction of online surveys such as surveymonkey.com. To give an example of how such research might be done by a clinician, consider the issue of parental alienation syndrome (PAS). This is a controversial issue, with supporters and detractors of the syndrome writing articles and reaction articles that in some cases are more polemic than scholarly. A review of the literature in this area will reveal that whereas many authors have strongly held opinions on the subject, there is very little hard data. One possibility might be to obtain a list of psychologists or guardians *ad litem* and send them (either by mail or by email) a survey that asks questions such as whether these professionals have ever worked with a case they thought might be PAS, how often this has occurred, what percentage of such cases seem to occur in contentious custody proceedings, and other information that might cast some light on this issue. Obviously, such a survey would not be the last word on the subject, but it would at least provide useful information and suggest directions for further research.

Two possible obstacles to academic writing are a lack of familiarity with American Psychological Association (APA) style requirements, as well as having writing skills that have fallen into disuse (or were never well developed in the first place). However, these need not be insurmountable problems. Obviously, if psychologists are serious about using academic writing to expand their forensic practices, at some point they will have to obtain the APA style manual and review it, which is not as difficult as it might initially appear. In addition, another valuable service provided on the Internet is the use of online academic editors. These services allow writers to pick an editor from a list of individuals with knowledge and experience in psychology, social work, or medical writing. These editors receive ratings from their customers (just like sellers on eBay) so it is possible to have some quality control in choosing one. Users set up an account and upload their article, which is returned to them having been copyedited, shaped up stylistically, and put in the appropriate format. These services are generally quite reasonably priced, ranging between $3 and $10 per page, depending in part on how fast you need the work done. At these rates, a 12-page article can receive professional editing for $36 to $120. While it is obviously better to develop the academic skills necessary for publication, the use of such editors is a good way to jump-start the process of getting into print.

Where to Publish? Deciding where to publish an article is an important decision. This part of the chapter offers suggestions for publishing articles in a manner that will provide the psychologist with the maximum exposure to the target audience.

It should be understood that using publications in this manner is best approached as a twofold process. Put simply, articles presented at conferences and published in peer-reviewed journals establish the psychologist's bona fides; articles published in law reviews and journals bring in the business. As previously mentioned, in order to be allowed to testify as an expert in a court of law, one needs to be qualified through a process known as voir dire. In a typical case, the lawyer who wishes to use the psychologist's testimony calls the psychologist to the stand and asks questions that reveal to the court the expert's qualifications. Typically, the expert is asked about educational background, training, and experience in the relevant area. Once this is done, opposing counsel can either agree that the psychologist is an expert for purposes of the case or challenge the psychologist's experience, credentials, and expert status. Whereas it is not necessary to have a long list of publications on your CV, it is tremendously helpful to be able to present concrete evidence that your peers (at least a few) thought your article good enough to be included in a conference or journal. In my experience, having published an article or two on the topic on which someone is being presented as an expert almost guarantees the acceptance of the testimony by the court.

This being the case, it is best to try to have your first efforts geared toward presentations at professional associations and peer-reviewed journals. This is because you have to establish yourself as an expert on a subject of forensic interest in order for the law publications to consider publishing your subsequent offerings. In addition, if you go about publishing thoughtfully, it is possible to create some synergy and make your efforts more efficient. The best way to explain this may be by a hypothetical example.

A psychologist who has begun doing psychological evaluations of juvenile delinquents for the courts begins doing competence to stand trial evaluations under supervision and finds this area of practice interesting. In the course of going to court, the psychologist learns that in her state, in order for a juvenile to plead guilty, the juvenile's lawyer must review an official waiver of rights with his client. This waiver contains information about all of the rights the juvenile will be giving up if he pleads guilty (his right to a speedy trial, his right to confront witnesses, his right to have each element of the charges against him proven, etc.), and the lawyer must tell the court whether the juvenile client understood the waiver and is pleading guilty willingly and knowingly. The psychologist, while waiting to testify, picks up a copy of the waiver and reviews it. In this case, our hypothetical psychologist used to work as a school psychologist and has experience with dyslexic students. Because of this knowledge, she notices that the reading level of the waiver form seems quite high, possibly too high for most juvenile delinquents (who she knows from her supervision and reading often have learning disabilities and/or low IQs), and she realizes that this might be a good subject for an article.

The psychologist goes back to her office and does a PsychInfo search on the readability of legal documents. She discovers that there are some articles in this area, but nothing specifically dealing with the readability of juvenile waivers. However, by reading these articles she has now developed the raw material for the review of the literature section of her article. She also discovers that there are a number of easy ways to analyze the readability (reading level) of documents. She uses one of these methods and discovers that her state's juvenile waiver is written at a 10th-grade level, which means that only 50 percent of average 10th graders will really understand the document. She realizes that the waiver is probably not understood by many of the younger delinquents and those with lower IQs and learning problems. She does her own analysis of the waiver and finds that it could be rendered easier to understand by using shorter sentences and words and explaining certain legal terms. She now has the outline of an interesting article; she has material for the review section, she has her methods section (the analysis of the readability), her conclusions (the waiver is too hard for much of the juvenile population with whom it is used), and recommendations for improving this state of affairs. She writes a 10-page article and either edits it herself if she is comfortable with APA style, has a colleague help her, or uses an online editing service. To her delight, she has now written her first academic article.

But how to get the article published? She could send it out to a peer-reviewed journal, but she has several concerns about this. One of her more academically oriented colleagues explains to her that the time from submission of an article to its publication may be one to two years. Additionally, the article may not be accepted by the first or even the second journal to which she applies. She would like to have some exposure faster than this. Luckily, her colleague explains to her that the fastest way to get an article out there is to present it at a conference. He explains that psychology, like other mental health disciplines, has a national organization, regional organizations, and subregional organizations. For example, there is the American Psychological Association, the Eastern Psychological Association, and the New England Psychological Association. All of these organizations have annual meetings with sessions at which papers can be read by authors. The psychologist goes online and finds that the New England Psychological Association is accepting proposals for papers at its annual meeting in nine months. There is an online application; the psychologist is surprised to find that she does not even have to send the whole paper—she only needs to complete short and long descriptions (abstracts) of her paper and she can submit these electronically, which she does. Several months later, she is thrilled to receive notification that her paper has been accepted for presentation at the conference. She goes to the conference and presents her paper to a small audience of 5 professors and 15 graduate students. She also brings 20 copies of her paper to hand out to the audience. That night she updates her CV's publication section with "The Readability of the Vermont Juvenile Waiver of Trial Notice." If she has a web site, (see section in this chapter on web sites) she may post the article for download and it may be picked up by one or more of the search engines, so that someone who searches for "juvenile waiver" or "waiver readability" may come up with her name.

A couple of months go by, and our psychologist decides to expand and update her paper for publication in a peer-reviewed print journal. She has found some additional references and studies that address some aspects of her subject, and she adds them to her review of the literature. She also finds an article that did not come to her attention when she was preparing her paper for presentation—an article that provides a methodology for determining what level of intellectual ability is required to comprehend materials written at different levels. She expands her article with material relating to the generally lower IQs of juveniles before the court as opposed to their nondelinquent peers, further bolstering her arguments regarding the potential obstacles that poorly designed waivers may create for youths before the court. Now the article is ready for submission to a journal; but which one? Several factors play a role in her choice. Some journals are highly selective and tend to publish only hard-research articles, so these would not be good choices. Other journals have a long lag time between submission and publication, and our psychologist is anxious to get into print. She talks to colleagues on her Listserv, and one of them suggests a newer forensic journal that is flexible as to the type of articles it prints and has a six-month to one-year publication time. She submits the article (following the format guidelines posted on the journal's web site) and is pleasantly surprised when the article is accepted for publication in the upcoming issue.

It is important to note that publishing in a journal an article that first saw the light of day as a presentation paper is not at all unethical or deceptive; many experienced authors use presentation at a conference as a way to do a shakedown on a paper that is designed for eventual journal publication. It would be a problem to send the exact same paper to a journal without alerting the editors that it had been previously presented, but if it is expanded and updated there is no problem. It should also be noted that peer-reviewed journals generally do not consider articles that have been simultaneously sent to other journals, so if you have an article to submit, decide carefully where to send it (one journal only), since if it is rejected you will have to start the process again.

Is the publication of the paper the end of the process? Luckily for our psychologist in this example, it is not. Good marketers make use of synergy, where one stone can kill multiple birds. Kano, the inventor of judo, had an important saying, which he meant to apply not just to unarmed combat, but to all human effort: "Minimum effort, maximum effect." This applies just as much to marketing expert forensic services as it does to unarmed combat. The key here is to use the published article (which having been written, does not require the effort of writing again) in as many ways as possible to advance the goal of publicity and promotion. Another way that the psychologist in this example can maximize the impact of her work is to look to legal publications.

It should be understood that there are many kinds of legal publications. They vary from highly prestigious university-based publications that are at least as difficult to get into as the most selective social science journals to trifold newsletters put out by county bar associations that are always looking for articles to fill out their content. It should also be remembered that there are many more lawyers than there are psychologists, so there are many more such legal publications than there are social science journals/papers/newsletters. In deciding where and how to repackage and republish her paper on the juvenile waiver for lawyers, our psychologist has several issues to keep in mind.

The first of these issues is her purpose in publishing for legal professionals. As previously mentioned, publication in peer-reviewed social science journals establishes your bona fides, while publication for lawyers brings in business. This principle is important to understand. Articles published in social science journals attest to the fact that the expert is, in fact, an expert. As previously mentioned, one of the best ways to ensure that a judge will accept you as an expert for purposes of court testimony is having actually published an article or articles on the subject at hand. Bear in mind that many successful forensic psychologists have never published an article of any kind and are qualified in court on the basis of their degrees, the workshops and trainings they have attended, their employment, and in smaller markets the fact that the judge knows of them either directly or by reputation. Having even a few publications (all other things being equal) can almost guarantee that the court will confer expert status on the psychologist. Additionally, having peer-reviewed publications to your credit may lead forensic peers to regard you as knowledgeable in a particular area. But it must be understood that enhancement of the forensic psychologist's standing among peers is unlikely to increase referrals. Why? It is partly because referrals come primarily from lawyers, and partly because the other forensic psychologists are your competition.

As a consequence, the type of article that you write for a law publication will differ from those of peer-reviewed journals in format and focus. For example, most law publications do not use APA style and will require you to conform to their format when it comes to citations; the smaller, local publications are often very flexible about format and style. Also, there is a much wider variety of types of articles which can be written because of the greater range of legal publications. For example, the state's main bar association journal is likely to be more scholarly and formal, and it is also likely to be to be highly selective. The trial lawyer's association, which has fewer members (but probably a higher proportion of lawyers who might require expert services) will often accept shorter, more informal articles on a wider variety of subjects. The weekly bar news (often in tabloid form) is even more relaxed and will frequently carry 1,500-word news pieces that require no references. All of these types of publications can be helpful in bringing the expert's practice to the attention of legal referral sources.

The second issue is what the forensic psychologist should write about for these publications. In the example of the psychologist who wrote the peer-reviewed article about her state's juvenile waiver, the fastest and easiest thing for her to do is to retool the article for the state bar journal or trial bar news. This can be done by making a number of simple changes in format and focus. For example, her review section could discuss the research on the waiver process with juveniles in more general terms, since her audience is now not made up of mental health professionals with backgrounds in methodology and statistics. In addition, it might make sense to do a brief review of important case law on a federal and state level that relates to this subject. The information regarding national trends can be obtained by reviewing some of the better current references on the subject in the mental health research literature and by consulting one or more of the authoritative forensic psychology reference texts. The local law can be trickier to obtain, and it is helpful to cultivate a few legal professionals who can give you the citations and explanations you need. Another change that the psychologist in this example can make would be to add material on the standard of practice for the practical assessment of waiver comprehension. This has the dual purpose of alerting the legal professionals reading the article that such evaluations are available, and even more importantly, that the author is ready to accept such referrals. Obviously, a light touch is needed here; it is important not to appear too obviously self-serving. It is not necessary to turn the article into an advertisement in order to make it clear that such services are available.

Assuming that the article is accepted, it can still be further utilized for publication elsewhere. Unlike peer-reviewed journals, many law publications do accept multiple submissions. As a consequence, the same article may be submitted to other legal publications in other locations. If the psychologist in our example lives in a large, populous state, she might consider submitting it in another large city in the state. If she works in the Northeast, she might consider legal publications in nearby states. Prospective publishers should be alerted to the fact that the article has been published elsewhere. Another approach would be to make small changes in the article to reflect the specific statutes and laws of each jurisdiction. Again, to use our example of the psychologist and the juvenile waiver article, different states could have different juvenile waiver forms with different readability levels, and each edition of the article could be tweaked to reflect these differences. The point is, the more the article or variations of the article are published in legal publications, the more the work of the psychologist will be exposed to potential referral sources. And since the bulk of the labor was expended on the original paper presentation, the use of different versions of the article and its publication in different types of legal journals and newsletters is a tremendously efficient way of promoting your practice to your target audience.

I have utilized this form of marketing on a number of occasions. Back in 1999 I wrote an article about a model for a limited child custody assessment and submitted it to the New Hampshire *Trial Bar News*, where it was accepted and published. This was an area of interest for me so I then submitted the article to the *Journal of Psychiatry and the Law* after making the focus more scholarly, expanding the content, and changing the format to meet the needs of that journal. The article was accepted and published in 2003. I have included both articles in Appendixes E and F so that those wishing to try this method of getting the most out of your writing will be able to see how it can be done.

OTHER FORMS OF MARKETING

A great deal has been written about the marketing of private psychology practices generally—for example, *Getting Started in Private Practice* (Stout & Grand, 2005)—and about utilizing such marketing techniques specifically for the promotion of forensic practice. There are a number of reasons for this, but one of the most important is that there has been a great demand for forensic psychological services and there has not been a real need for promotion. Many of the established forensic psychologists I've spoken to tell me that once word got around that they provided forensic assessments and testimony, that part of their practice simply took off and in many cases crowded out the other aspects of the practice. However, with the pressures of managed care, many psychologists have looked to forensic work as a way of breaking out of the managed care rat race, and competition is beginning to increase. That being the case, it is becoming more important for forensic psychologists generally and those just moving into this area of practice specifically to utilize efficient, intelligent marketing techniques that maximize exposure at minimal cost.

Advertising. One obvious method of attracting business would be to advertise in magazines and newspapers. Most of the participants in my survey felt that advertising in local newspapers was an ineffective way of gaining exposure, and I agree with this assessment. The problem with advertising in the local newspaper is that forensic psychology is a relatively specialized service, and advertising in a newspaper meant for general readership is simply not efficient. It makes more sense to advertise in bar association journals and newsletters, since the readership is almost entirely made up of the people who are likely to send you referrals. Despite this, many forensic psychologists have told me that such advertisements are ineffective as well, and that the only real way to develop a referral base is through word of mouth. I think this is an incorrect assumption that is based on a number of factors.

The first of these factors is, as previously mentioned, the fact that many forensic psychologists think that there is something undignified and crass about many types of practice promotion. There is a somewhat elitist perspective that as experts to the court we are somehow above the commercial fray. I guess this position is fine if you think that you have enough referrals and you are doing all the business you can handle. I strongly suspect that this will cease to be the case as more clinical psychologists with specializations in forensic psychology obtain their doctorates. I believe the second reason for the belief among many forensic psychologists that advertising does not bring in referrals is that since most of them lack real business training, they have not developed accurate methods for gauging the success of a particular series of ads and do not routinely do any type of cost/benefit analysis. Many practitioners who have tried advertising in law journals run the ad for a few months and see no obvious spike in business. This leads them to assume, sometimes falsely, that the ad is not effective. They do not know that if you are going to advertise effectively you have to have a mechanism for determining the financial return on your promotional activities.

Let's take an example. A forensic psychologist who is relatively new to the practice in his area decides to run an ad in his local bar association newsletter. He decides on a budget of $2,000. He takes out an eighth-of-a-page ad in the classified section of the journal that mentions his name, makes it clear that he is a forensic psychologist, and states that he has particular experience and expertise in the assessment of civil and criminal competencies. Given the price of the ad, he is able to run it for 10 months. How will he know if the ad is effective? Logically, the first thing he should do is to develop some method of determining whether any attorneys calling for the first time with referrals saw his ad and were influenced by it. The best way to do this is to routinely ask these lawyers how they heard about his practice and to keep track of their answers. If he does this, he will have a better idea of how effectively his ad is reaching potential referral sources. He may discover that the ad was highly effective and that it brought his practice to the attention of 10 attorneys, 8 of whom actually sent an evaluation his way. Assuming for the sake of simplicity that he charges roughly $1,000 for an assessment, this represents a $6,000 return on his $2,000 investment. The return will be even higher if he is asked to go to court and testify in any of these cases. Further, if he makes a good impression on these lawyers, they will undoubtedly sent him further referrals and mention him to other lawyers at their law firms, further increasing the return of the ad through word-of-mouth referrals.

In another scenario, the obvious return on the $2,000 advertisement may not be so large. For example, our psychologist may find that only two lawyers called him as a result of the ad, and that only one actually sent a referral. This would appear to be a $1,000 return on the $2,000 investment. But if the psychologist establishes a good relationship with that one attorney, it may generate multiple referrals over a period of years, again providing an excellent return on the initial advertising investment. It is important to note that if you do not keep some type of records about how referral sources found you, you will basically be shooting in the dark and have no idea of what type of impact your ads are having.

There's another factor that may have an influence on why many forensic psychologists feel that advertising is not an effective way to generate referrals. I told a friend of mine who has been involved in the advertising industry for 30 years that many of my forensic colleagues believe that advertising in print is ineffective and that they have never had any luck when they have attempted to use this medium. He thought about this for a moment and then said, "Have they ever considered the possibility that their ads stink?" I think that he had a point. As I have mentioned before, most psychologists go into private practice with little or no business training. There is no reason to believe that they would be any better at knowing a good print advertisement from a bad one than they are at any other aspect of business. It may be that their advertisements are amateurish or poorly designed and that is why they are ineffective.

So, how do you go about developing an effective print ad? One of the first things to remember is that you are not only trying to let potential referral sources know you exist, but you are also trying to distinguish yourself from your competition. If you don't have something

126

about your practice that differentiates you from the rest of the pack, you may wish to hold off on an expensive print advertisement campaign until you have developed a particular area of expertise that your ad can communicate. You should also be on the lookout for issues that are rapidly developing or that have been discussed in the local news or in legal publications. For example, in 2005 the New Hampshire legislature revised the laws governing child custody in divorce. In an effort to de-escalate conflict, the lawmakers changed the emphasis of divorce courts' decisions from designating the primary custodial parent to having both parents collaborate on a joint parenting plan. It is now incumbent on divorcing parents to sit down, together if they can or with a mediator if they cannot, and actually write out a joint parenting plan that explicitly lays out the manner in which they are going to divide child-related responsibilities such as medical care, academics, religious education, and a visitation schedule. The idea is that this will reduce conflict by placing less emphasis on winning or losing a custody war and more on coming together to make plans in the best interests of the family's children. How well this will work remains to be seen, but the legislature has mandated that marital matters, lawyers and parents need to approach their custody issues in this manner.

Since this approach is new to the New Hampshire market, most of the psychologists working in the child custody arena will still be geared toward doing traditional custody evaluations. If you are relatively new at this type of work, it will be difficult to break into the traditional child custody area when there are probably a number of forensic psychologists who have specialized in child custody for years and know all of the guardians *ad litem* (GALs) and divorce lawyers. But since the whole mediation/parenting plan approach is new, this creates a potential marketing area for the new practitioner who wants to work in the child custody field. There are several steps that could be taken that would prepare the way for an effective print advertisement.

First, you could do some self-study on the topic of developing joint parenting plans; there are articles on the Web, as well as on PsychInfo. There are also books on the subject, and workshops are cropping up as well. The point is to become adequately skilled in developing joint parenting plans and to develop a general protocol for approaching these matters. Having done so, you would now have the opportunity to begin marketing yourself in this area.

By picking up on this development in the field of child custody, you will have gained access to an emerging market, differentiated yourself from other custody-related practitioners, and minimized the advantage of their longer-term involvement in the community. That being done, you may decide to utilize print advertisements, along with other forms of promotion such as giving talks to bar sections and writing articles, in your marketing plan. You may even wish to consider partnering with a lawyer or other mental health professional who has training as a mediator to provide some type of package deal in which the two of you provide both services for a fixed fee.

It is important to give careful thought to where you want your print advertisement to appear. Continuing with the example of the psychologist who wishes to market assistance with joint parenting plans, some thought must be given to who makes up your market and where print ads are likely to be seen by potential clients. In this case, I would look for the legal publication in your area that is likely to have the greatest readership of those lawyers who specialize in domestic relations and child custody. It may be that your area has a trial lawyers association that has a newsletter or quarterly journal. This might very well be a better place to put your ad than the city or state bar association publications that are also read by attorneys who do not go to court or involve themselves in domestic relations. Another possibility is that the local bar association domestic relations interest section may have a small newsletter. The advantage of advertising in such publications is that the readership contains a more concentrated sampling of the lawyers with whom you wish to make contact. Also, because of the lower circulation, advertisements are likely to be less expensive and you can thus stretch your advertising dollar further.

The first thing to remember is that unless you happen to have been a graphic artist in a former career, or have a spouse or other close relative who happens to be one and will help you, don't try to do it yourself. There are many technical aspects of designing an effective ad requiring specialized knowledge that amateurs don't even know exist, let alone have the skills to pull off. There is a reason why the menus at expensive, well-known restaurants look so good compared to the ones that small diners create using their fourth grader's version of PrintShop; the expensive restaurants either utilize advertising firms or copy menus from other restaurants that have the style and feel that they're looking for. You could go to an advertising agency and have it develop your print advertisement for you, but advertising agencies tend to be expensive and I'm assuming that you don't have an unlimited advertising budget. What you need is a graphic designer to work with you in putting together the ad. Graphic designers can also be very expensive, particularly if they are working for an agency. Luckily, there are graphic designers working part-time or moonlighting who can be consulted at substantially reduced rates compared to what the advertising agencies charge. Finding these people involves a certain amount of investigation. You should look at the ads in the journals and newsletters where you are considering advertising and try to find out who designed some of the ones you like. If there are other psychologists with advertisements you could try calling them, but as the saying goes, Macy's doesn't tell Gimbel's. You'll probably have better luck contacting someone from another profession such as a lawyer, and this may also give you the opportunity to make contact with the possible referral source. Also, with the advent of the Internet, your graphic designer does not have to live in your hometown, and it is possible to find somebody on the other side of the country to set up your ad for you.

If we continue with our example of the psychologist who wants to distinguish him/herself in the area of assisting divorcing couples with joint parenting plans, it is apparent that the ad has to emphasize this service. This does mean that other areas of your work cannot be mentioned, but it will be important to highlight that feature of your practice. The same would be true if you are emphasizing any other part of your practice, whether it be criminal or civil competencies, sexual offender risk assessments, or personal injury work. I strongly recommend that you find some aspect of any of these areas that is new or rapidly developing, develop an area of expertise around that issue, and emphasize this expertise or service in any print advertisements you utilize. In the same way, think carefully about where the people whom you want to see your advertisement are likely to be looking. Finally, develop some method of tracking responses to your ad and the return on your advertising dollar; otherwise you will simply be like a blindfolded archer who shoots at a target but never receives feedback about the accuracy of each shot.

Web Sites. Forensic psychologists with whom I have spoken have mixed feelings about the usefulness of having a web site. Some feel that in this day and age, a web site is a necessary component of successful practice promotion. Others disagree, saying that most of their business is local rather than national; a forensic psychologist working in Pittsburgh, Pennsylvania, will derive little benefit from having his or her web site read in San Francisco. Although there are forensic psychologists with national reputations who actually do benefit from that aspect of having a web site, if you are reading *Getting Started in Forensic Psychology Practice* you probably don't fall into that category yet. It is worth looking at the web sites of some of the better-known forensic psychologists to get an idea of how such a site should look. Here are examples of a few web sites, some very elaborate and some more basic:

- www.forensis.org (Reid Meloy, Ph.D., ABPP [Forensic])
- www.psychconsulting.co.nz (Nick Lascelles)
- gregdeclue.myakkatech.com (Gregory DeClue, Ph.D., ABPP [Forensic])
- www.psychology-law.com (my own web site)

A web site is an excellent way to promote your practice for very little money. In addition, web sites have other uses besides simply being used as advertising, as will be discussed later in this section. I have a web site, and in general I've been happy with the results. It's a good place for attorneys (and clinical patients) to go when they are considering using my services.

STORIES FROM THE REAL WORLD

I have a web page explaining my approach in clinical (nonforensic) treatment. On that page, I state that I am "a strong believer in the role of culture in mental health," and that I "address the impact of societal oppression, racism, sexism, homophobia, poverty, and other forms of discrimination and hostility on clients' current circumstances and functioning." In a sexually violent predator (SVP) proceeding, a prosecutor cross-examined me regarding this statement, asking whether I wasn't just trying to excuse the defendant's behavior on cultural grounds (something that had not come up at all in my evaluation!). I had to explain the difference between my clinical treatment and forensic evaluation work.

I have a set of web pages that provide basic information on various forensic topics. One such topic is the forensic implications of alcoholic blackouts. In a confession suppression hearing, regarding the suggestibility of a 15-year-old defendant, the cross-examining attorney tried to introduce statements I'd made about alcoholic blackouts, which was not a topic I had testified about on direct examination. (The judge sustained an objection.)

Karen Franklin, Ph.D.

I moved from Illinois, where I was very well known, to Ohio, where I wasn't even in the phone book. I got two forensic cases immediately, from the web site. I also received much communication from people in Illinois who still needed to reach me but did not know my new office address. I am surprised at the number of hits I get each month, and how many web pages each person reviewed. I think it is very worthwhile to have a web site.

Marty Traver, Ph.D., clinical and forensic psychologist

My web site provides me an easy way to make reprints of my publications available to readers. It allows people who find my book at the publisher's web site to link to my web site and find me.

Gregory DeClue, Ph.D., ABPP (forensic)

One cautionary note for folks thinking about developing a web site is that the other side will scrutinize it for cross-examination fodder. So, as with anything else (such as publications, CVs, etc.), the more information you post, the more there is to go after you with. It's best not to post anything you are not prepared to defend in court.

If you do choose to have a web site, just as with print advertisements it is important that it not look amateurish. Consequently, if you are not a professional quality web site designer you should seek help from someone who does this professionally. As with print advertisements, one excellent way of finding a good web site designer is to look up the sites of other psychologists and find one that you like. Usually, the name of the designer will appear somewhere on the web site and you can contact the designer directly. Prices vary widely, so shop around; there are plenty of good part-timers out there who can set up your site and modify it as occasions demand.

A web site is not targeted to a particular audience in the same way that print ads are. But they do provide important benefits to your practice. Examples include:

- You can provide an in-depth description of your training and the areas of your expertise. When you have initial contacts with possible referral sources, you can direct them to your web site and all the information they need will be instantly and conveniently displayed for their inspection. You may wish to include your CV on the site.

- You can include downloadable copies of the papers you have written. You should bear in mind that when the commercial search engines such as Google send out their spiders to look for web sites to list, having useful content is one of the selection criteria they use. For this reason, having papers helps direct people to your site. Papers that you have presented at conferences can nearly always be posted without concerns about copyright (but check anyway). Bar journals and legal publications nearly always allow you to post papers that you have written and they have run, but you should call the editor to double-check. Peer-reviewed journals are trickier, since they often require that you sign over the copyright of your article to them. Despite this, many will allow you to post the text of your article on your site as long as it is not a scanned facsimile or PDF file of the article as it ran in the journal. Some journals may also want you to state where the article originally ran and link it to their web sites. Other journals are less relaxed about this, so be sure to check before posting. You could also do a shorter, modified version of an article with a link to the journal so that the article can be purchased by readers. However you do it, having some of your writings online in this way allows referral sources to get a sense of your opinions and expertise. In some cases, the web site may actually bring in a referral. As an example, let's suppose you practice in Pittsburgh and you presented your article entitled "The Practical Assessment of Testamentary Capacity: A Guide for Clinicians" at a regional conference. Since this is a specialized area even for forensic psychologists, an attorney in your area may need a psychologist with this expertise and not know where to look. If he does a search with the descriptors "forensic psychologist" and "Pittsburgh" and "testamentary" it is possible that your site may pop up.
- You can put printable directions to your office from the north, south, east, and west. Rather than spending time on the phone describing the various routes to your office for the umpteenth time, you can just direct tech-savvy folks to your site and let them download precise directions. You may also want to include a picture of your office to make things even easier.

- You should include a list of helpful links. You could add links to the APA ethical guidelines and code of conduct, as well as to the American Board of Forensic Psychology's ethical guidelines for forensic psychologists. Ken Pope's web site (www.kspope.com) has lots of great content with an emphasis on ethical issues, and Kim McKinzey's WebPsychEmpiricist (an innovative site at http://wpe.info that posts reprints and original articles and by-passes the whole peer review process) is a good bet. You could also provide links to your local board of psychology or mental health practice as well as your state psychological association.

Overall, while having a web site may not generate referrals in the way other types of marketing might do, it is an inexpensive way to provide information to potential referral sources. In addition, since most psychologists don't have one, having a slick-looking site makes you look a bit more professional and successful, which can't help but have positive effects in the long run.

Direct Mail. Direct mail is another marketing technique that is under-utilized by forensic psychologists. Interestingly, in my survey of experienced forensic psychologists this method of marketing received mixed ratings. Forty-six percent thought it was effective or very effective, while 31 percent thought it was neither effective nor ineffective. Fifteen percent thought that it was very ineffective. However, as with print advertisements, I suspect that part of the problem is that few forensic psychologists actually try it. Additionally, I think that many are affected by the conventional wisdom that only word of mouth is effective. Properly

---

PSYCHOLOGISTS' OPINIONS ABOUT DIRECT MAIL MARKETING

- I used it to get started—mailed to 250 law firms within my chosen traveling distance, and listed services that I was able to provide. Got maybe three jobs, but these led to others. Four years into my business, I never need to advertise now.
- Quarterly newsletter is sent to referral sources. The advantage seems to be favorable comments. The con is keeping up with consistent mailing each quarter.
- Mailings are probably of value when announcing the opening of one's practice, or a change of address or phone number, but not in general.

targeted direct mailing has worked well for psychologists in other specialties, and there's no reason why it should not work for a forensic psychologist. The sidebar highlights some opinions about direct mailing I received from one of my web surveys about how forensic psychologists obtain referrals.

Because of the specialized nature of forensic psychology, it is important to consider carefully where you want to put your energy and your money. As discussed previously, the major sources of referrals for forensic psychologists are lawyers. But depending on the situation in your area, there may be other important referral sources. For example, in your area, probation and parole officers may have a great deal of influence on where the individuals they supervise go for court-ordered assessment or therapy. In the same way, in some states programs for those found guilty of drunk driving are often referred for mandated aftercare which involves substance abuse counseling with a properly cre-

---

SAMPLE LETTER TO POTENTIAL REFERRAL SOURCE

Dear Superintendent Smith:

My name is Katherine Jones and I am a licensed psychologist in private practice in North Adams, Virginia. In addition to my general practice of child, adolescent, and adult psychotherapy, I have a specialty in the area of forensic psychology. I have a particular interest in the issue of violence in the schools, and I provide both consultation to schools regarding student violence and assessments of students and in-service training for staff members. I have written a paper entitled "Hit Lists and Online Threats: Assessing Violence Risk in the Schools," which I have enclosed with this letter. In the article I review current approaches to this type of risk assessment in educational settings and lay out what I believe is an effective and cost-efficient method for approaching this problem.

I would like to call you next week to discuss the services I provide in this area. You may be interested in checking my web site to get a sense of my background and interests (www.vaforensics.com). I look forward to speaking to you directly.

Sincerely,
Katherine Jones, Ph.D.
Virginia Licensed Psychologist #867
233 Main Street, Suite 201
North Adams, VA 33441
Phone: (233) 243-1212
Fax: (233) 243-2211
Email: ksmithpsych@rtsglobal.net

dentialed mental health professional. In still other cases, there may be a demand in schools for forensic psychologists to do assessments of students who have made threats or who have otherwise raised concerns about potential violence.

Direct mailing can take several forms. One type of mailing is simply a letter to a potential referral source that introduces you, briefly lays out your credentials in an area that might be of interest to them, and indicates that you will follow up with a call in the following week. A sample of this type of letter appears in the sidebar.

It can be seen that this letter is simply an introduction that makes a cold call a little less cold. The same type of letter could be sent to an attorney or chief parole officer as a way of making initial contact. If you have been given the contact's name by someone you both know, mention that person's name in the letter. In my experience, these types of targeted introductory letters are reasonably effective. You send them because you have some reason to suspect that the recipient may be in the market for the services you would like to provide, and the letters cost only the price of a stamp, an envelope, and a sheet of paper. Even if the person you contact has no immediate need for your services, you have at least made contact and added to your referral network. You should be sure to follow up in a timely manner. Also, you should keep track of the people you contact in this way and gradually build up a mailing list that you can use for other types of promotions.

It is worth putting some time and effort into the selection and design of your stationery and letterhead, since this is often going to be the first impression you make on your contacts. Style is to some extent a matter of taste, but it is important that your stationery be of good quality and that your letterhead be conservative. Remember, you are dealing with court-related matters and with lawyers, so you should attempt to present an impression of solidity and seriousness. It is different if you are specializing in play therapy with children or a related type of practice, because then a touch of whimsy may set the right tone. But as a forensic psychologist you will be dealing with lawyers who are defending clients who are accused of heinous crimes associated with long prison sentences, or victims of terrible abuse or accidents, or parents who may lose rights to their children. Because of the high stakes, you are going to want to project the impression that you are a serious individual who approaches your work in a professional manner. The stationery and letterhead need not be professionally printed if you have a decent ink-jet or laser printer, but it should not look like you simply used the first style that came along with your copy of Microsoft Word. Kinko's and other local print shops can be very helpful if you are not confident about designing your own letterhead. Your letterhead should include your name, your title (including license number if required in your state), full business address, phone and fax numbers, email address, and URL (uniform resource locator) of your web site, if you have one.

A second type of direct mailing involves developing a brochure and sending it to possible referral sources. This is different from an introductory letter in that it is designed to be sent as a mass mailing and does not necessarily involve specific personal follow-up. Colleagues of mine have simply gone through the lawyer listings in their local phone directories and selected those whose stated areas of practice match their own specialties. Once they had their mailing list, they developed a brochure giving an overview of their credentials and practice, areas of specialization, contact information, and a description of potential advantages of utilizing their services. Most also included directions to their offices or small maps.

SUMMARY

There is every reason to anticipate that forensic psychology is going to become increasingly competitive as time goes on. This creates a need to differentiate yourself from all of the other practitioners in your market who will be competing with you for a finite number of forensic referrals. The time is quickly passing when it has been enough to simply hang out your shingle and wait for lawyers and other referral sources to come to you. The judicious use of marketing techniques such as publications, web pages, print advertisements, and direct mailing can help get your forensic practice off to a robust start.

Risk Management in Forensic Practice

The term *risk management* means different things in different contexts. In forensic psychology, as with other types of clinical practice, there are two general types of risk: board complaints and malpractice actions. Thankfully, both are relatively rare in forensic psychology.

A 2004 article by Barbara Van Horne reviewing the frequency of board complaints against psychologists makes it clear that they are relatively rare and in the vast majority of cases do not result in any adverse action against the psychologist. Unfortunately, it is also the case that forensic psychologists are at higher risk of such complaints and lawsuits than those in clinical practice, especially if they do child–custody-related work (Kirkland & Kirkland, 2001). I would go so far as to say that if you are doing custody-related work, the occasional complaint needs to be seen as part of the cost of doing business.

The other piece of bad news as related to malpractice and board complaints is the emotional toll it can take and the large expenditure of time, money, and mental energy that dealing with these issues can require. Worse, these problems are almost never resolved quickly, and lawsuits and investigations can drag on for months and sometimes years. No matter how experienced you are, and how much equanimity you have cultivated, there is something extremely unsettling about getting a letter from your state board when you know it is not time to renew your license. You open the envelope and there is a list of the complaints from the disgruntled client, and you realize that you are going to have to respond to each and every charge, no matter how absurd they are or how much they deviate from the reality of the situation.

How forensic practitioners can cope with an actual board complaint will be discussed later in this chapter. But long before you receive a complaint, it is important to take steps to minimize your exposure to risk, and also to develop procedures and general approaches to your work that will make it less likely that your actions will lead to a substantiated complaint.

ANTICIPATE PROBLEMS

In a recent conversation I had with Michael Gottlieb, noted expert on psychological ethics, he told me that he thought one of the most important ways to minimize risk in any psychology practice is to anticipate problems. He explained that it is not enough to deal with issues as they come up, but that it is necessary to actively consider all of the potential problems that could arise in your practice generally, and specifically in particular cases. This is an excellent point and one that is even more important in forensic practice. When considering taking a referral, particularly if it has unusual aspects, you should sit down and think about all the ways it could go wrong and "snap back" on you. Often, potential problems with a case may not become clear until you have run through a variety of scenarios in your mind.

An example may be helpful. A number of companies maintain lists of psychologists to do independent medical examinations (IMEs) for organizations such as insurance companies. They are called IMEs even when psychologists do them. The issue may be fitness to return to work or workers' compensation–related issues. Some of these companies have elaborate informed consent forms that the evaluator must explain to the employee and have the individual sign. One of the companies that I have worked for has a clause in its forms that states that employees cannot receive the finished reports from me, but only from their attorneys if the cases go to court. In the same way, I am under contract with the company that referred the employee not to give him/her a copy of the report, which is technically the property of that company.

This all seems reasonably straightforward, and I had done a number of evaluations for a particular company without any kind of problem. Then the company referred a woman to me for an assessment of whether she was still psychiatrically disabled or could return to some type of work at her company. I carefully reviewed the informed consent papers with her and explained to her that she could not get the results from me after the evaluation was done. She understood and signed the papers, and we proceeded with the evaluation. I determined that she was exhibiting a moderate degree of symptom exaggeration and was likely to be able to work in some capacity. I sent out my report and heard nothing (which is good) for several months, when the client called and asked for a copy of my report. I reiterated that she had signed an agreement that she could not get the report from me and that I was not free to release it. She took this reasonably well and said she would call the company that sent her for the assessment.

After she hung up, I began to consider the matter and became a bit concerned. It occurred to me that New Hampshire, like many states, has laws on the books that make it clear that clients have a right to the contents of their files except under very specific circumstances. Signing a form that states that you will not ask the psychologist to cough up the report after the fact is not one of these circumstances. Neither is there any clause that states that clients can not withdraw their agreement regarding the release of the reports. If this client complained to the New Hampshire Board of Mental Health Practice and told them that I would not give her the report, might I not be in violation of the regulations? I called the company that referred this women and described my problem. They were pleasant, but told me that they thought the employee's agreement that she would not request the report from me was binding and that they expected me to abide by it, although they made it clear that if my local board put the squeeze on me, they would not sue me or cause problems if I had to release the report. I should mention that there was nothing about the report that made me unwilling to release it and that under normal circumstances I would have done just that.

I next called the Board of Mental Health Practice and asked the administrator what she thought. She told me that she would bring up the issue at the next board meeting and get back to me. About a month later she told me that it was the opinion of the board that the employee's signing the agreement that she would not receive the report from me trumped her general right to the report, and that if she complained about me, they would not find any misconduct on my part. So, my problem was solved—or was it?

The members of the board are not lawyers and they might be wrong about the legal issues in the case. Also, board members serve their terms and are replaced by new appointees; would a board with different personnel have a different view of the situation? I have asked a number of my lawyer friends about this and they have differing opinions. Some say the agreement trumps the regulations about file disclosure, while others say that you cannot sign away your rights in this manner. So, what initially appeared to be a very simple matter turned out to be anything but. In retrospect, my mistake was that when this new type of referral came my way, I did not stop to think what possible implications it might have.

It is this lack of thoughtful consideration that leads to many of the issues that end with psychologists coming before their local psychology boards, and in many cases, if they had given the matter a moment's thought, they could have avoided the problem. One obvious and unfortunately common example of this is when therapists and, on occasion, forensic evaluators may discuss people whom they have not met or evaluated in court-related matters. The most obvious example of this can occur when therapists work with children whose parents are divorced or divorcing. Unfortunately, some therapists have not yet come to understand that they should not be working with a child in this situation unless both parents are in agreement about the therapy or unless it has been ordered by a court. Worse, there are often situations in which these therapists become aligned with one parent or do not communicate with the other parent. Problems get serious when the therapist, with the best of intentions, writes a letter to the court stating that the child's difficulties are caused by the other parent's actions or that there should be no unsupervised visitation with that parent, based solely on the representations of the parent who brings the child to the sessions. The most cursory attempt to consider the possible ramifications of writing such a letter at the behest of, for example, a mother would raise the following considerations:

- The father is not likely to be happy about the therapist writing the letter. He may possibly say to himself something like "How could the therapist make such a recommendation? He/she doesn't even know me."
- It is possible that the father is as bad a person as the child's mother makes him out to be. If this is so, he will have few scruples about trying to get back at the therapist.
- It is also possible that he is not such a bad guy, and that some of the things the mother has said about him are either exaggerated or completely false. If this is so, the therapist is perpetrating an injustice.

All of this being the case, the father may decide to complain about the therapist to the board. This is very easy to do and requires only a pen, paper, an envelope, and a stamp. If the board finds that the therapist has been unethical and sanctions him/her, it will be public and the father may find out about it. This may lead to a malpractice action, since there are lawyers who specialize in suing mental health professionals, and they consider having a board find unethical conduct to be a very positive thing for a case.

This reasoning does not require advanced training in ethics or a law degree. It just involves a little consideration of the possible implications of taking a particular action. Why therapists make this mistake so often is complex, but a little foresight can save you a world of pain and anxiety.

Ethical questions can become even more complicated in situations in which a psychologist functions as a forensic evaluator. You would think that forensic psychologists, who we have established are more at risk than other clinicians with regard to board complaints and malpractice actions, would be very sensitive and proactive in these situations, and for the most part they are. But this does not prevent them from making very similar fundamental mistakes.

For a real-life situation, I was involved in a child custody case involving allegations of Munchausen syndrome by proxy, which is a rare and controversial diagnosis in which a parent, usually a mother, falsifies a child's medical condition by exaggerating, fabricating, or inducing physical illness. I was consulting on the case and had occasion to review the deposition of the other side's expert, an experienced child forensic psychologist working for a well-known university. The father in the case had retained the expert's services to review the mother's and the couple's three children's medical records and dropped off several boxes of paperwork related to the case. The expert's work on the case at the time she gave her deposition consisted entirely of a review of these records. She did not interview or test the children, mother, or father. On the basis of her review of these records the expert wrote a report in which she opined, among other things:

- The mother suffered from Munchausen syndrome, a situation in which a person exaggerates, fabricates, or induces illness in him/herself, as opposed to a proxy.
- This placed the mother at an undetermined but increased risk of perpetrating Munchausen syndrome by proxy on her children.
- The court should immediately transfer custody from the mother to the father.

How many possible problems can you spot in this scenario? Here are a few of the more obvious ones:

- The psychologist took the records from the father, rather than from the medical facilities themselves. She had no way of knowing if the records were complete or even if they had not been altered or fabricated. Remember, we live in a world in which computers and scanners are cheap and readily available. Think about it; what is to stop clients from taking a letter or report your wrote, scanning your signature and letterhead, and writing their own version of the report? We will discuss the issue of not taking anyone's word in greater depth, but it is always necessary to take reasonable precautions about the integrity of your data.

- The psychologist was making recommendations about persons she had not evaluated, and in the case of the mother and the children, persons she had never even met. It would have been only reasonable to have made an attempt to speak to the mother in this case. She might have provided data that would cause the psychologist to modify her opinion. For example, what if the mother had shown the psychologist records that the father had been married twice before and had raised the issue of Munchausen syndrome by proxy in both previous divorces?
- Related to the preceding point, the psychologist was recommending that custody be transferred to a person about whom she knew next to nothing. For all she knew, the father could be a wife batterer, a drug addict, or a pedophile. Even assuming she was right that there were important problems in the mother's parenting, she had no way of knowing whether the children would be better or worse off based on her recommendation of a custody change to the father, since she had not bothered to do even the most cursory check of the father's personal and/or parenting history.

I should point out that these are not mere abstract concerns; this expert was confronted by skilled attorneys with each and every issue listed above in agonizing detail. And the damage such sloppy work inflicts goes well beyond undermining the particular case. Once a judge sees this type of thing, the credibility of that expert in that court is damaged forever. As the saying goes, you get only one chance to make a first impression. So, how to avoid such ugly scenes? There are three essential rules to follow:

1. Be honest and fair.
2. Learn (really learn) the APA ethics code and the forensic guidelines.
3. Show your work—the data and techniques you utilized in reaching your conclusion.

HONESTY AND INTEGRITY: INDISPENSABLE FOR EXPERTS

This book has discussed many of the personal qualities that forensic psychologists require if they are to be successful in their chosen field. Although I have referenced the need for honesty and integrity in other sections, it is important that these qualities be discussed in the context of risk management. This is partly because they are highly effective as a general risk management policy and also because they will help you avoid many of the specific problems that have the potential to lead to a board complaint or malpractice action. While it is not invariably the case that an honest person has nothing to fear, honesty will keep you out of most sticky situations

You may be asking, what is there to be dishonest about in a forensic practice? You might be surprised at how much pressure there is to shade your evaluations in a particular direction and how strong the motivations, conscious and unconscious, can be to do just that. These temptations can be obvious or subtle, and the subtle ones are often the ones that cause the most trouble.

For example, if you do enough testifying you will eventually find yourself in a position where a cross-examining attorney is accurately pointing out some flaw or mistake in your report or data. Maybe you misscored something, misconstrued a study that you had read and referred to, or somehow missed an important piece of data. When this happens, the thing to do is to admit a mistake immediately. For one thing, you are under oath and that is what you promised to do. Also, your purpose in being in court is to assist in the process by providing accurate information, not to show how smart you are or that you are infallible. Unfortunately, I often see experts equivocate in these situations, using weasel words to avoid just coming out and saying that they were wrong. This kind of reaction is destructive to the fact-finding progress and bad for the expert as well. It is important to understand that the judge hearing your case is generally a reasonably intelligent human being. Although judges may not know much about the technical aspects of psychology, they certainly know the telltale signs of somebody who is trying to avoid acknowledging an honest mistake. This behavior will make them less likely to give your opinion much weight in that particular case specifically and in future testimony generally. Remember that on a very fundamental level, as a forensic psychologist the only things you have to sell are your expertise and the perception of your integrity. If you undermine the perception of your integrity by being less than straightforward in court, you have damaged one of your most important selling points and you will most likely never recoup this loss.

Aside from individuals who purposely slant their assessments because they actually are hired guns, there are often subtle pressures to shade your reports and testimony to please the attorney who is retain-

144

ing your services. All people, including psychologists, want to be liked. In the course of working with a particular attorney, you may develop a personal relationship. Attorneys can be very competitive and all of them hate to lose cases. Do not be surprised if an attorney presumes upon the relationship to try to get you to modify your conclusions. This has happened to me on many occasions. Recently, an attorney for whom I do a good deal of work referred a father who was involved in a child visitation dispute. He was alleged by his ex-wife to have made some kind of threat to her and his visitation rights had been temporarily suspended. The attorney wanted me to do a psychological evaluation that would reassure the court that he was unlikely to act on these alleged threats even if he had made them. Unfortunately, his Minnesota Multiphasic Personality Inventory–2 (MMPI-2) was similar to individuals who are angry, impulsive, and given to hostile verbal outbursts. When the attorney who had retained me received the report he tried to convince me that the section of the report that made reference to the problems should be taken out or at least softened. He kept me on the phone for some time trying to convince me that the threats had actually never been made. I had to be very firm in explaining the basis of my conclusions in my report and why they could not be changed. In addition to stating that I do not change reports unless there is an obvious factual error or misprint, I had to do some explaining about the nature of assessment. I pointed out that there are many MMPI-2 "cookbooks" out there and that any consulting psychologist who received the MMPI-2 protocol his client had produced could look up his code type and would know that I had left out important information about this individual's psychological profile. If this happened, it would almost certainly be pointed out in court, and in addition to making me look bad in that case, it would also undermine my effectiveness in that court for the rest of my career. After a good deal of explanation, the attorney was willing to accept my report as it was written.

There are lots of ways in which mental health professionals can affect the outcome of their assessments, and some of them are not easily detected by nonprofessionals. One of the ways I see most frequently is the practice of simply not assessing a particular issue or area of functioning if you do not think the result will be consistent with the outcome you are trying to produce. For example, if you are working for the prosecution in the area of competence to stand trial, you ask only basic factual questions of the defendant and stay away from tests such as the MacArthur Competence Assessment Tool—

Criminal Adjudication (MacCAT-CA), which looks at more subtle aspects of the defendant's grasp of the issues involved in standing trial. If you are doing a good deal of plaintiff's work and personal injury cases, you can emphasize clinical interviewing and avoid any tests with validity scales or any test specifically designed to measure symptom exaggeration. In the same way, if you are doing educational due process work and you are working for a school district that does not want to designate many students as educationally handicapped, you can choose an IQ test and an achievement battery that have a high level of correlation with each other in order to shrink the intelligence-achievement discrepancy. By contrast, if you are working for parents who want their child to be designated educationally handicapped, you can choose instruments that have a low level of correlation to expand the same discrepancy. The problem with this is that you are eventually going to run into an attorney who has some sophistication in this area, or the attorney may simply hire a psychologist consultant who will show him "where the bodies are buried" in your report. When this happens, you are going to have a very uncomfortable and unpleasant day on the stand as the attorney cross-examines you on these issues and confronts you with learned treatises that lay out in agonizing detail what you actually should have done in your assessment.

All of this unpleasantness can be avoided by making a decision at the outset of your career to be honest and to stick to your guns. Although this may occasionally have the effect of upsetting an attorney, in the long run it is the only real choice you have if you want to be successful in forensic psychology.

THE APA ETHICAL CODE AND SPECIALTY GUIDELINES FOR FORENSIC PSYCHOLOGISTS

The American Psychological Association Ethical Principles and Code of Conduct (hereafter referred to as the Code) was revised in 2002. The prior version of the Code (1993) had a section that specifically addressed forensic practice, but the 2002 revision subsumed this section under other, more general sections. The Code, along with additional regulations and laws in particular jurisdictions, governs the practice of psychology in general and forensic psychology specifically. There are also the Specialty Guidelines for Forensic Psychologists (hereafter the Guidelines) that were promulgated in 1991 by the American Psychology–Law Society, which address more specific aspects of forensic practice. The Guidelines are in the process of revision, but this is the version that is currently in use. It should be understood that the Code is described as "enforceable" and the Guidelines are aspirational in nature. This is an important and complex distinction that has sometimes caused confusion in board complaints. The issue has been to what extent psychologists can be reprimanded and/or sanctioned for conduct that falls below aspirational standards but does not violate the Code. Some boards have appeared to experience standards creep and have held psychologists to higher but nonenforceable standards. The moral here seems to be that you should try to have your assessments and testimony conform to the forensic aspirational standards (the Guidelines) to the greatest extent possible and practical.

This section is not intended as an exhaustive review of the APA Code and the Guidelines with all of their implications for psychologists, forensic or otherwise. The purpose of this section is to review those sections of the Code and the Guidelines that have particular relevance for risk management for those working in the forensic arena.

CONFLICTS BETWEEN ETHICS AND THE LAW

Section 1.02 of the Code, "Conflicts between Ethics and Law, Regulations and Other Governing Legal Authority," deals with situations in which the court asks you to do something that would not be illegal but might be professionally unethical. This happens more often than might be supposed. The Code indicates that when this happens, psychologists take reasonable steps to resolve the problem. If they do their best to sort out the conflict and still cannot get the court to see things their way, they are allowed to follow the requirements of the law. The Guidelines (section IV, G) basically echo this position and suggest that psychologists may attempt to resolve such conflicts by seeking professional consultation, retaining their own lawyers, or speaking directly to the lawyers in the case.

One common example of this is related to the previously discussed issues of the incompatibility of the roles of therapist and forensic evaluator. This distinction is a difficult one for legal professionals to understand because it is not an issue in the expert testimony of other types of professionals. For example, let's imagine that someone slips and falls on the ice in front of a store, is injured, and decides to sue the store owner. If the person breaks a leg, the physician who diagnosed and treated the broken leg may also serve as the expert in the case. Medical ethics do not draw the same type of distinction between the roles of expert witness/evaluator and treatment provider that the psychological profession does. This is not the place to engage in an in-depth discussion of why this is, but I think most experts in the area of psychological ethics would agree that the emotional nature of the therapist/client relationship is much deeper and more complicated than that which exists between an orthopedist and the patient whose leg he sets.

Unfortunately, lawyers and judges do not understand why psychologists make this distinction, and it can be difficult to explain. In addition, they are not bound by the APA Code or the Guidelines. Problems related to this distinction come up frequently in my practice and I think I am pretty typical in this respect. For example, I recently received a call from a lawyer who sometimes refers cases to me. He was representing the father of a 16-year-old boy in a custody dispute. The son, who had been placed in the primary physical custody of his mother when the divorce had been finalized, had basically refused to return to his mother's house after a visit with his father. In New Hampshire we have the Butterick standard, which states that the court can consider the wishes of a "mature minor" with regard to custody. The lawyer was going to court in a week and wanted me to evaluate the boy, and if I found that he was reasonably mature, I would testify to this at the hearing. The boy's mother was not going to be informed of the assessment and would not find out about my involvement until just before I came to court. I had a very hard time explaining that the Code and Guidelines strongly suggested that I not do this type of evaluation for several reasons:

- Section 9 of the standards makes it clear that my assessments and testimony need to be based on information and techniques sufficient to substantiate my findings. How could I go into court with a straight face and tell the judge that I was in a position to opine about this boy's emotional maturity when I had not even spoken to his mother, who was up until recently the boy's primary custodian? It might be the case that this lad holds his breath until he turns blue when denied his own way and that he and his father neglected to mention this. Or maybe the father wants to stop paying child support and promised his son a car if he would come and live with him.
- Section 3.04 makes it clear that I am supposed to take reasonable steps to avoid harming my clients. What if the father is a lousy

148

parent? What if he has been engaging in a campaign of denigration and lies against the mother and this is a case of what some call parental alienation? Might this boy not be harmed by living with his father under these circumstances? It seems to me that the least that could be expected of me in such a situation would be to involve the mother and hear her side of the story.

- I had no idea what was in this couple's divorce stipulation. What if there was a section, as in many such documents, stating that neither parent will take the child to a health care provider without the permission of the other parent? Now, it should be understood that I am not bound by the stipulations of someone else's divorce decree. I could not be found in contempt of court if I did the assessment. But doing so clearly goes against the intent of the court in such a case. Additionally, if I had done the evaluation without the permission or even knowledge of the mother, there would be an excellent chance that she would be upset and angry with me and complain to the board about me.

This last type of situation has been such a problem in my jurisdiction that the New Hampshire Board of Mental Health Practice has actually put the following on its web site:

January 21, 2004

JOINT CUSTODY

The Board held a discussion on the issue of joint custody because it is a current issue that presents difficulty to many clinicians. The Board presents this as information to the public.

"Joint custody" is a phrase that is commonly used to describe one of two things in a divorce context: either joint physical custody or joint legal custody. Joint physical custody means that both parents have a right to share physical custody of their child—for example, the parents live near each other and the child has a right to stay at either parent's home at any time during the week. Joint legal custody means both parents have the right to make major life decisions for their child. This is the type of custody that would involve the Board's licensees.

Joint legal custody is defined under RSA 458:17, III as including "all parental rights with the exception of physical custody which shall be awarded as the court deems most conducive to the benefit of the children." In general, New Hampshire has adopted a presumption that joint legal custody is in the best interest of children. RSA 458:17, II.

Joint legal custody means that "both parents hold legal responsibility and have equal rights regarding major decisions in the child's life including education, religion, and medical care. On the other hand, daily decisions of a more immediate nature are made by the parent-caretaker." New Hampshire Practice Series, Family Law, Sec. 14.07.

There are no New Hampshire cases, with published decisions, that state that a doctor or a mental health practitioner must obtain both parents' permission before treating a child if the parents have joint legal custody of the child. However, because both parents have "equal rights" to make decision regarding their child's education, religion, and medical care, they both have the right to consent to mental health treatment.

The one limitation to this general rule is that the individual divorce decree, or subsequent court orders, could authorize one parent over the other to make decisions regarding whom the child will treat with. For example, if the divorce decree says that both parents have joint legal custody, mom has physical custody, and mom can make the decision as to which medical care person will treat the child, then dad's consent is not needed. In this example, however, dad would have full right to access of his child's records and would have a right to talk or meet with the mental health practitioner for an update on his child's treatment. There could also be a subsequent order of the court that says that neither mom nor dad can change or add medical providers without further order of the court. In this type of case, a practitioner should not agree to treat a child until there is a specific court order allowing that practitioner to treat the child.

Because the individual divorce decrees or subsequent orders could provide further information that would be very important to mental health practitioners, the Board recommends that in each case of treatment of a child, the mental health practitioner might want to ask some variation of the following questions:

1) Are you married to the child's other parent?
2) If yes, does he/she consent to your child entering treatment with me? Will he/she sign a release? If no, explore the situation and determine if the practitioner feels comfortable treating a child without both parents' permission.
3) If no to #1, are you divorced?
4) If yes to #3, please provide me with a copy of your divorce decree and explain what your understanding of the legal custody arrangement is—for example do you [the parent bringing the child for treatment] get to decide which medical care providers your child treats with? Are there any subsequent orders from the court that deal with issues regarding medical treatment of the

child? I will need a copy of your divorce decree and any subsequent orders relating to medical treatment for my file before I can begin treatment unless the other parent is willing to sign the release to begin treatment.

5) If no to #3, what is your child's relationship with his/her other parent? [In this case, the mental health practitioner will need to determine if there is a legal relationship between the child and the other parent—such as a separation agreement or order for a married couple that is separated; or, in the case of a child born out of wedlock, an unmarried couple's custody agreement, a private custody contract/agreement, or a court order establishing a legal relationship with the child. The practitioner should obtain a copy of any such agreement or order. Again, it would be best if the practitioner could obtain both parents' permission before beginning treatment.]

One concern that licensees will raise is that by asking to see the divorce decree, any subsequent court order, or any custody agreement, they are being required to make a legal decision regarding whose consent is needed before they can begin treatment. However, technically under their Codes of Ethics, they are required to make sure that they have authority to treat a child. If a practitioner makes a diligent effort to obtain custody documents and makes a reasonable assessment of those records, that practitioner has met his/her responsibility under the Code of Ethics to have informed consent for treatment. Further, in some circumstances, a practitioner may want to contact his/her private legal counsel to assist in making the decision of who must consent to treatment.

This outline of how to provide informed consent and obtain a release/waiver of the mental health practitioner/client privilege is provided by the Board as guidance to practitioners. However, the Board does not guarantee that this outline encompasses every joint custody situation that may arise in practice. Practitioners must consider the individual circumstances of each joint custody situation and should seek advice specific to a situations when a practitioner is in doubt.

Even after I made these points the lawyer was still unsure about why I couldn't do the assessment. I explained that I don't turn down cases lightly, because that is how I make my living, but I could not jeopardize my license for one case, even if it created problems for him.

In the same way, I was recently contacted by an attorney who was defending a client accused of sexual harassment. He told me that he was concerned because the plaintiff's therapist, who works at a local feminist counseling center, was going to testify in the case. Not only was the therapist going to testify on her client's behalf, but she had done a forensic assessment of the client and was prepared to testify that the woman had post-traumatic stress disorder (PTSD) and that the proximate cause of her symptoms was the defendant's sexual harassment. She had not spoken to anyone about the client's situation, nor had she done anything to check the veracity of the client's representations. The icing on the cake was that she was willing to be paid on a contingency basis. The lawyer wanted me to send him materials (such as the relevant sections of the Code and Guidelines) so that he could demonstrate that the therapist's actions were unethical and that her methodology was unsound. I sent the materials, but luckily for me I was spared having to send a "Dear Unethical Colleague" letter because the case was settled and I never found out the therapist's name.

If you are starting out in forensic psychology, you obviously need to know the ethics of your profession, but you also need to be able to stick to your guns in the face of the demands of courts and lawyers who often neither know nor care about these issues. Aside from the type of problems already noted, if you do court-ordered therapy with sexual offenders, batterers, abusive or neglectful parents, or delinquents there will be other pressures. It is very common for lawyers for child protection agencies or prosecutor's offices to try to pressure psychologists to draw forensic conclusions on the basis of their therapeutic work with clients, and courts and lawyers have difficulty accepting psychologists' ethical qualms about this. After all, you speak to the client every week; who better than you to inform the court about their recidivism risk? You will have to learn to stick to your guns to the extent possible. At the same time, remember that if you have made reasonable efforts to explain the situation and the court is not buying it, you don't have to go to jail like a reporter protecting a confidential source. If you are the therapist and you have made clear the problems with giving such testimony and stated your various caveats, and the judge says that you have to state your opinion if you have one, do it.

The issue of conflicts between psychological ethics and the law comes up with regard to the release of records. In the previous version of the APA Code, there was a section that stated that psychologists were allowed to release records and test results only to an appropriately qualified mental health professional. Unfortunately, when a client puts his or her mental state at issue in a legal proceed-

ing such as a personal injury suit, opposing counsel is generally entitled to review the plaintiff's mental health records in a process known
as discovery. In the same way, you might perform a competency to
stand trial assessment and decide that the defendant is incompetent.
There may be another expert working for the prosecution who decides the defendant is competent. It is very likely that the prosecutor
is going to want to see your file, including the raw data, so that the
opposing expert can tell him/her how best to cross-examine you. Under the old Code, you could send your file to the opposing expert, but
not directly to the prosecutor. This was designed to prevent the im-
proper use of the data contained in the file by opposing counsel and
also to maintain test security.

Problems arose when lawyers felt they were entitled to the file
(which they almost always were) and obtained a valid subpoena from
the judge in the case to make the psychologist cough up the file without
using another mental health professional as an intermediary. When this
occurred, it created a situation in which it was necessary for the psychologist to retain his/her own lawyer and try to quash the subpoena.
This was inconvenient and expensive and usually meant a day out of
the office. There was a lively debate among forensic psychologists over
this particular provision of the Code. Many felt that the provision was
important, since lawyers don't understand the data and misuse it.
Those on the other side felt that the provision was misguided. After all,
if you were the expert designated to receive the data, what else would
you do but show it or give it to the lawyer who retained you? Also,
other experts (physicians, engineers, physical therapists) did not have
to go through this kind of song and dance every time their files were requested, so what made psychologists so different? I sided strongly with
the latter group against the provision.

When the 2003 revision of the Code came out, the obligation to send
file material only to qualified mental health professionals was dropped.
Under section 4.05, "Disclosures," the Code now states:

(a) Psychologists may disclose confidential information with the appropriate consent of the organizational client, the individual client/patient,
or another legally authorized person on behalf of the client/patient unless prohibited by law.
(b) Psychologists may disclose confidential information without the
consent of the individual only as mandated by law, or where permitted
by law for a valid purpose such as to (1) provide needed professional

services; (2) obtain appropriate professional consultations; (3) protect the client/patient, psychologist, or others from harm; or (4) obtain payment for services from a client/patient, in which instance disclosure is limited to the minimum that is necessary to achieve the purpose.

Additionally, the Health Insurance Portability and Accountability Act (HIPAA) regulations have also given clients much greater access to their health information and many states have regulations in place that entitle clients access to their files under almost all circumstances. There are some limitations on this and you should familiarize yourself with any important restrictions to file access in your jurisdiction. For example, some states allow a child therapist to withhold the child's therapy records from a parent if the therapist deems that such a release is very likely to have a serious negative impact on that child's well-being.

You will often run into the opposite problem, which is that many mental health professionals never became educated about the change in the regulations and the laws in this area. Because of this, they will sometimes refuse to release therapy or testing records unless it is to a mental health professional. In one recent case, a local police chief was concerned about the results of a pre-employment assessment by a local psychologist and he and the new hire requested the file in writing. Despite the fact that the psychologist was provided with a signed and witnessed release from the officer, he continued to refuse to disclose the results, citing the relevant section of the 1993 Code. It took a strongly worded letter from me advising him to check with the state psychological association's ethics board before he saw the error of his ways. The moral of the story is that you should take special care to educate yourself about the regulations and ethical standards that govern the release of records where you practice, because the issue is likely to come up frequently in forensic practice.

RESOLVING ETHICAL VIOLATIONS

If you begin undertaking forensic cases, you are going to come across ethical violations with some regularity. As mentioned earlier, you will see therapists giving opinions on the ultimate issue when their role was only that of therapist and they clearly have inadequate knowledge of the situation to be opining in that manner. Other situations will arise when you see other evaluators interpreting in an obviously unfair manner—for example, clearly favoring one parent over the other in a custody matter—for reasons known only to him/herself. Sometimes you will review a treatment file and find that the therapist appears not to believe in keeping notes or that there is clear evidence that when the file was subpoenaed, the therapist made a bunch of notes the next day and backdated them. You may see instances in which evaluators actually destroyed their notes prior to trial or deposition, or erased sections of them.

When this happens, what should you do? Section 1.04 of the Code, "Informal Resolution of Ethical Violations," suggests informal resolution of these issues unless the matter is so egregious that a board complaint becomes a necessity. The Code gives very little specific guidance as to where that particular line is drawn, but it is fairly clear that sexual improprieties and serious boundary violations require a report be filed. I think it is important to not set the bar too low in these types of situations. You don't want to potentially damage a fellow professional's career without a very good reason and you also don't need to make all of the other mental health professionals in your area loathe and fear you. Additionally, these types of situations can snap back on you when someone you report turns around and reports you right back. However, what if the case comes to the attention of the board of psychology through someone else, and it becomes clear that you knew about the problem and did nothing? That inaction could itself become an issue with the board. How can you handle such a situation in a way that is consistent with both the ethical standards of the profession and good risk management practices?

Stanley Brodsky and R. K. McKinzey have written an outstanding article on what to do in these situations, entitled "The Ethical Confrontation of the Unethical Forensic Colleague" (2002). They mention a number of scenarios that might warrant some type of response from the forensic psychologist who observes the possible ethical lapse. These include:

- A psychologist falsely testifies that he has a modestly important credential when in fact he does not.
- An opposing expert gives a test improperly or scores it incorrectly.
- The opposing psychologist gives a synopsis of the research on a topic such as children's memory or sexual offender recidivism rates but leaves out any mention of any literature that reaches other conclusions.

- The psychologist becomes aware that the opposing forensic evaluator had a therapeutic relationship with a client she then evaluated for the court.
- The opposing psychologist is clearly underprepared for the type of evaluation and/or testimony he provided.

Brodsky and McKinzey provide templates for letters that address this situation in an assertive but collegial manner. Having such a template at your disposal is very helpful, since you can then discharge your ethical obligation without creating more problems than you solve. The psychologist whom you suspect has fallen short of the Code is warned of your concern; what they do about it is their business, unless of course you come across further examples of such behavior in the future. If that were the case, it might represent a pattern of such behavior and could warrant stronger action on your part. The authors also provide similar templates for replies should you find yourself on the receiving end of a "Dear Unethical Colleague" letter as well as letters that both ask for and respond to requests for clarification regarding the original letter.

As an aside, the adversarial nature of forensic psychology practice leads to situations in which practitioners can become very upset and angry with each other. The self-confidence necessary to do well as a forensic psychologist has a flip side that can sometimes be arrogance. As a result, situations can arise in which a good deal of resentment and bad blood can develop between professionals. It is important to try to remain calm and not overreact to criticism of your work. If you receive a "Dear Unethical Colleague" letter or other types of professional criticism, try not to let anger overwhelm you. Take some time to consider the issues being raised, and perhaps chat with a colleague or supervisor. It is always possible that the author is partly or completely correct. If this is the case, after the underlying legal case is concluded you might want to consider acknowledging the usefulness of the criticism in your own letter.

PROFESSIONAL COMPETENCE

The section of the Code that deals with competence makes clear that you have to know what you are doing when you undertake to treat, consult, teach, or conduct research. The Code notes that if you are working with diverse populations and there is evidence that this is likely to have an impact on your approach to such clients, you need to take steps (classes, supervision, research, etc.) to acquire the requisite knowledge and skills, or refer the clients to somebody who does know this terrain. In the same way, section III of the Guidelines states that forensic psychologists must practice only in areas in which they have specialized knowledge, experience, education, and training. Subsections of III also urge forensic practitioners to let the court know what they are going to testify about, the boundaries of their knowledge and competence, and the factual basis of their qualifications as experts. Section 2.01 (f) of the Code states that forensic psychologists need to be familiar with the judicial or administrative rules governing their roles. The Guidelines go into more detail, noting that you should be familiar with the professional and legal standards that govern your roles as an expert as well as the civil rights of the participants.

This means, in practice, that if you are doing a competency to stand trial assessment, an NGRI, or a custody assessment, you should have a basic understanding of the law as it applies to what you are doing. This is a good suggestion, and I have seen cases in which neophyte forensic psychologists have thought that they understood what they were supposed to be doing when in fact they did not. One example of this that comes to mind involved a competence to stand trial evaluation referral. I had been doing them for some time and was supervised by a diplomate in forensic psychology, so I knew what was being asked and the laws governing my role. The lawyer asked me repeatedly if I understood the laws governing the determination of competence and was finally convinced when I cited the actual Dusky/Champagne standards that dictate the standards in New Hampshire. I was curious about why he was so concerned, and he told me that the judge in the case had been frustrated by the ignorance of several experts who had testified on this subject in his court recently. Later that day, the judge called me from his chambers and quizzed me about the law in this area of practice. After I convinced him that I knew what I was doing, I asked him about the other psychologists who had testified before him in these types of matters. It turns out that several newbies had come into court and testified about whether defendants were competent to drive a car, dress themselves, write checks, and perform other tasks, but had done nothing to provide the court with information about whether the defendants had a factual and rational understanding of the issues involved in standing trial, or whether they were able to consult with their attorneys with a reasonable degree of rational understanding. This would be like volunteering to train dogs if you didn't know what a dog was or what you were supposed to train them to do. Worse, they didn't even know that there was anything to know about this.

The implications of this beggar the imagination. It is obvious that these psychologists had never read a book or article on the subject of competency, or they would have known better. It is obvious they did not consult with any colleagues who were more knowledgeable or even Google "competence to stand trial." Further, they must not have thought about the fact that they would go to court where there would be lawyers who would minutely examine their methodology and results, that there would be a judge who was likely to become irate, and that they most likely would never be allowed to testify in that courtroom again. And it was so easy to avoid with a modicum of effort. As I have suggested in other sections, many aspects of the practice of forensic psychology are not exactly rocket science and are quite knowable by persons with doctoral-level psychology training. But there are things you do have to know. You have to read a book or two, attend some workshops, and get some supervision. You also need to know the psychological/legal situation in your jurisdiction for the assessment you are performing. You can do this by looking up the case law if you are familiar with legal research, or you can ask a lawyer you know. You don't need to have a lawyer's level of understanding of all the important cases that govern legal practice in that area, but you do have to have some idea what you are doing. Failure to meet this standard can have results that are embarrassing, painful, and really bad for your practice, not to mention potentially unethical.

Multiple Relationships and Conflicts of Interest

Section 3.05 of the Code and section IV of the Guidelines deal with the issue of multiple relationships. The Code defines multiple relationships as occurring when a psychologist is in one kind of relationship with a client and at the same time in another role with the client or with a person closely associated with the client, or promises to enter into either of these types of relationships in the future. There are many examples of problematic multiple relationships in the professional literature. Psychologists are enjoined from entering into multiple relationships if such a relationship could be reasonably anticipated to have a negative effect on the psychologist's objectivity, competence, or effectiveness in the performance of their professional function. If the dual role would not be reasonably expected to cause such problems, it is not unethical. It should be understood that this is an area of considerable debate among psychologists, and while there are roles that are clearly unethical (a custody evaluator, say, who is sleeping with the mother in the case), others, such as the evaluator's daughter being one of the client's softball teammates, are harder to figure. For an excellent discussion of these issues, go to Ken Pope's web site (www.kspope.com) and also read Jeffrey Younggren and Michael Gottlieb's 2004 article.

It should be understood that when you work in the forensic arena, you have to be even more conscious of potential role conflicts and anticipate problems before they occur. One of the most important ingredients for success in a forensic practice is a reputation for integrity and impartiality. If there is anything about a case that could raise doubts, it is important to take steps to resolve this. For example, you may belatedly discover that your sister-in-law has taken a job as a paralegal at a law firm that represents one of the parties in a custody case on which you are already working. How should this be resolved? The first step is to do a little soul-searching and decide whether this relative's presence at the law firm is likely to create a situation in which your objectivity is affected. Is your sister-in-law going to be angry if the results of your evaluation are adverse to her boss' client? Will it make things tense at Thanksgiving dinner? Will that lawyer try to use the connection to get you to modify your testimony? What about if the opposing lawyer finds out about the connection and uses the information to undermine your testimony by suggesting that you are in the pocket of the other law firm?

One way to avoid problems in this type of situation is to let all of the parties in the case know about the situation as soon as you find out about it. Calls and letters to both lawyers will prevent any perception that you had something to hide. If you believe that the issue will have no effect on your judgment and impartiality, you should say so; if not, you should withdraw from the case. It is far better to lose one case than to have your reputation as a straight shooter damaged.

Other types of multiple role problems can arise in a forensic practice. For example, if you work in a small to medium-sized market, you will almost certainly develop personal relationships with some of the attorneys with whom you work. You may find yourself becoming the favorite expert of a few attorneys who send you a good deal of work each year. This is not necessarily a problem, as long as it is clear that their clients are not going to get any special treatment as a result of this type of relationship. Be very wary of an attorney who tries to presume on this type of relationship to achieve a more favorable outcome for his/her client. If, though, they are willing to accept with equanimity a report that does not go their way, there will probably be no problems in the future. The lawyer who gets into a deep snit because a client had results that were unfavorable to his case is not someone you want to work with in any case.

In the same way, it is important not to become a rubber stamp for any group or organization. There is a tendency for psychologists who do a good deal of work for, say, the local child protection agency, a particular public defender's office, or an educational advocacy agency to begin, consciously or unconsciously, to adopt some of the views and perspectives of that group. You may have seen this yourself. There are some psychologists who do a large number of evaluations for the state child protective service agency and always seem to produce reports that match the case plan of the agency. If the agency is moving toward termination of parental rights in a case, the psychologist finds the parent unfit; if child abuse is suspected, it is confirmed by the consulting psychologist, who interviews the child however many times it takes to get a disclosure of abuse. Some other psychologists who work closely with a group that requests independent medical examinations (IMEs) in workers' compensation cases may always seem to feel that the subject is either malingering or exaggerating symptoms. Others who tend to work for prosecutors seem never to find anyone incompetent or legally insane.

Some of this may actually be legitimate and be a reflection of the forensic psychologist's views and practices. To give an example, when it comes to Munchausen syndrome by proxy cases, I am almost always called by the defense. This is not because I rubber-stamp all of these cases or simply don't believe that parents harm their children with medicine or the medical system. I actually have no doubt at all that this sometimes occurs because I have unfortunately seen covertly taken videos of mothers harming their children in this manner. But I do feel, based on my experience and research, that the Munchausen syndrome by proxy label is overly broad and wrongly lumps together a wide variety of parental behaviors and motivations with differing potential for harm to a child. I think that the so-called behavioral profile that has been developed to identify Munchausen mothers has no established reliability or validity, and I also feel that in mild to moderate cases of this type of child abuse, there is hope of family reunification. These views are much more congenial to the defense in these cases than are the views of other experts who believe that parental rights must always be terminated when such behavior is detected. Prosecutors are unlikely to call me in such a case. Since my views generally run contrary to their theories regarding these cases, they don't retain my services.

In the same way, forensic psychologists may develop a particular view of criminal or civil competency or other issues that places their views closer to either the prosecution or the defense in certain types of cases. Some experts believe that children are almost always accurate reporters of sexual abuse and that it is very difficult to implant a distorted memory of such events, whereas others genuinely believe that it happens all the time. Vigorously advocating for your opinion is not the same as shaping your testimony to a specific end, as long as you acknowledge that there are differing opinions and represent the basis of your opinions honestly. It is only when opinions are presented to achieve a particular outcome that ethical issues arise, both in terms of multiple relationship problems and in regard to other ethical principles.

From a risk management perspective, what should you do when such issues arise? A few simple steps will help head off problems down the road. First, as previously mentioned, try to anticipate problems. For example, you decide to have your offices repainted and you call a reputable painting outfit to do the job. To your surprise, one of the painters turns out to be someone who was a defendant in a trial in which you testified and in which he was acquitted four years previously. When you evaluated him, it was in another office, and you have not seen him since. Should you hire a different painter? In this situation you should think about what could go wrong. What if he does a lousy job and you have to complain about the shoddy work to his boss? There would be no real problem from a psychotherapy standpoint because you are not his therapist and never were. The case is over, and had a good outcome as far as the painter is concerned, and he is no longer a client of yours. So far, so good. You should approach the painter and ask him if there is anything about his working for you that concerns him. If he is fine with it, that is also good. Finally, you should also consult with a colleague or with the local psychology association's ethics board. Once all of this is done, even if some unforeseen problem arises and the painter files a complaint with the psychology board, you will be able to show that you didn't seek out the dual role for some advantage and that you took reasonable steps to deal with the issue, including seeking consultation and talking to the ex-client. This should go a long way toward protecting you in the unlikely event of some type of problem arising from the dual role.

The issues of conflicts of interest and exploitative relationships are dealt with in sections 3.06 and 3.08 of the Code, although the Guidelines go into more specifics regarding relationships. One issue that is specifically mentioned is that forensic psychologists must not take cases on a contingent basis. Taking a case on contingency means agreeing to provide services in a case, such as a civil lawsuit, with no up-front payment or retainer, and agreeing to be paid only if the plaintiff prevails in the lawsuit. This is a common practice among attorneys and they may suggest that you accept cases on this basis. This is not unethical for lawyers because their role is officially one of advocacy. It is emphatically not the role of forensic psychologists, who are supposed to do everything possible to avoid situations in which their impartiality is affected or there is even an appearance of a lack of evenhandedness. Obviously, if you are going to be paid your fee only if the plaintiff prevails, this is likely to exert a strong incentive to write a report that will be helpful to the lawyer who retained your services. Consequently, you should either be paid before the report is issued or agree to do the case pro bono (for no fee), but don't do the case for the possibility of payment in the future.

The Guidelines recognize that in small communities it may be necessary to take on treatment and forensic evaluation roles. The Guidelines recommend that when this cannot be completely avoided, the forensic psychologist take reasonable steps to avoid any negative impact on the client.

INFORMED CONSENT

Section 3.10 of the Code makes it clear that before you perform an evaluation or treat an individual, you have to provide the client with all of the important information about what is going to occur and the possible implications in understandable language. While this is important in all aspects of professional psychology, it can be argued that it is even more important in forensic psychology. This is because of the serious consequences and high stakes involved in forensic work. Depending on the type of case, the issue could be the possible loss of someone's children, personal freedom, or life. In addition, there are complexities involved in performing forensic assessments from an informed consent standpoint that do not arise in clinical work. As a consequence, you

162

should put a good deal of thought into your informed consent practices when practicing forensic psychology.

I recommend that you develop a consent form for your assessments and also for court-ordered therapy activities if you do such work. You may decide that you need different forms for different types of evaluations. Additionally, these forms should be seen as living documents that will change as your practice evolves and different types of situations arise. I also strongly recommend that you do not simply hand the forms to clients and have them read and sign them; I would go over each section of the form and explain what it means, answering any questions the client may have. The following are some of the material that should be covered in a consent form for forensic assessment.

Who You Are and Brief Overview of Your Credentials. Everybody has their own way of relating to clients, and my way will not be the same as yours. I generally tell clients the following:

> As you have probably figured out, I am Dr. Mart. I am licensed as a psychologist in New Hampshire and Massachusetts. Unlike medical doctors, psychologists are generally not certified by the state in specialty areas. You know how some medical doctors are pediatricians, some are surgeons, and others are neurologists? We don't have that type of thing as part of our licensing; you are either a psychologist or you are not. However, I am board certified as a forensic psychologist by the American Board of Forensic Psychology. Forensic psychologists specialize in dealing with cases that have some connection to courts or the legal system.

Often at this point clients tell me they thought forensic meant something that is involved with dead people or crime scene analysis, and I explain what "forensic" means.

Purpose of Evaluation. I then explain in a general way what I will be doing in the evaluation, saying that I have been asked by the client's attorney (or the court, or the guardian *ad litem*) to perform a psychological evaluation to help the court decide about the forensic issue.

At this point I describe the issues I will be examining in a general way. You have to be careful to give clients sufficient information about the general areas of inquiry while not giving them so much that they are tempted to try to engage in impression management or malingering. For example, in a competency to stand trial examination, you probably want to say something like "I am going to ask you questions and give you some tests to find out how much you know about court and standing trial" rather than "I am going to test you to see if you know enough about the legal system to be able to stand trial for these charges." The latter statement may tip clients off that if they do not know much, they won't have to stand trial, and encourage them to feign incompetence. Of course, they may already know this and malinger anyway, but that is a different issue.

Evaluation Process. In this section of the informed consent process, I explain, again in a general way, what I will be doing and about how long it will take. I discuss the fact that I am going to perform a mental status examination and explain that it is not a test, but just a way for me to be thorough and obtain basic information about them. Then, I will perform a clinical interview, which I explain is an opportunity for me to ask them about their background, personal history, and the specific issues related to the case at hand. I also say that I will be doing testing and explain, in a general way, what kind of tests I will be administering. I make it clear that they can ask questions at any time if they want clarification or don't understand what I am saying. Also, I assure them that I want them to be as comfortable as possible and that they can ask for breaks as needed. I emphasize that it is important to be as honest and straightforward as possible and explain the concepts of "faking good" and "faking bad," the fact that I have some ability to detect them (I don't say how), and the negative implications that invalid testing can have on the evaluation specifically and their case generally.

Nature of Our Relationship and Confidentiality. I now discuss the fact that while medical doctors sometimes both treat illnesses and injuries and also testify in cases regarding these injuries, psychologists either evaluate or treat, but don't do both with the same person. I make it clear that I am not treating them and I am not their therapist, but am serving in the role of evaluator. This means, I explain, that we do not have a doctor-patient relationship and that I may have things to say in my report that could have an adverse effect on their case. If they are referred by their lawyer and the evaluation is not court ordered, I explain that the assessment is confidential—not under doctor-patient privilege, but under attorney-client privilege, which basically amounts to the same thing. In these cases, I explain that if the client and the attorney decide that the report I generate is not helpful, they will be free to file it away and it will most likely never see the light of day. I also make it clear that I will not discuss the case with anyone unless the client provides me with a signed release giving me permission for such communication. In other types of cases, the evaluations are court ordered or are covered under some other type of agreement and I make it clear that the court will see the evaluation with or without the client's permission.

That being said, I explain that there are some issues that are not covered under confidentiality. These include any credible threats of violence against persons or property and that if such threats are made, I will notify the intended target and the local police. In the same way, I note that if I come to believe that a client is imminently suicidal, I will take steps such as calling the police and supporting involuntary hospitalization. I also explain that any new allegations of child abuse (not already before the court) require me to make a report to the appropriate agency, and the same goes for elder abuse.

I should mention that when performing custody assessments, I use a much more elaborate consent form that lays out in considerable detail what I am going to do with the parties.

The Code also makes clear that even when the individual being evaluated is not legally capable of giving informed consent (persons under guardianship, persons court ordered for evaluations of issues such as criminal or civil guardianship, or minors), psychologists should still explain as much of the aforementioned material as is appropriate. In addition, if others have legal responsibility for the subject of the evaluation, they need to be briefed in the same manner as is described earlier, and they are the ones who will sign any releases required.

All of this does not require a great deal of time and can usually be covered in about 15 minutes. Once I am done, I hand clients a form that summarizes all of this information and tell them to take their time and read it, and make sure that it actually says what I said it says before signing it. I find that clients appreciate the time taken to explain their situation and that it reduces their anxiety. I think that it is important to look at the situation from the clients' perspective. Whatever the reason they are in your office for a forensic assessment, it is a pretty good bet that it is not good news for them. They may be facing jail time, loss of child custody, termination from their job, or expulsion from school. It makes sense that they are apprehensive, and it is helpful if you make it clear that you understand their trepidation and want them to be as comfortable as possible under the circumstances. This also has the dual purpose of making the assessment go more smoothly.

INFORMATIONAL AGREEMENT FORM
PSYCHOLOGICAL EVALUATION

Eric G. Mart, Ph.D., ABPP
_____
EXAMINERS   EXAMINEE

1. Dr. Eric Mart has verbally reviewed with me the purpose and nature of this psychological evaluation.
2. Dr. Eric Mart has advised me that as a result of this evaluation, he will prepare a written report about my present psychological functioning, relevant medical/psychiatric/psychological history, and his professional opinion.
3. Dr. Eric Mart has advised me that as an examining psychologist he is not providing any psychological treatment to me, and that at no time am I his patient.
4. Dr. Eric Mart has further advised me that he does not have a doctor-patient relationship with me.
5. Dr. Eric Mart has told me that he might have a "duty to warn" if he becomes aware that I intend to inflict serious bodily harm to a specific individual or individuals, and he has a duty to protect the intended target(s), which may include alerting law enforcement officials, and could involve warning the potential victim directly.
6. Dr. Eric Mart will communicate the results of this evaluation verbally and/or in a written report to the following party or parties:

_____
PERSON/AGENCY TO RECEIVE INFORMATION

I have read the above statement, I understand it, and I agree to its conditions.

_____
SIGNATURE OF EXAMINEE OR LEGAL GUARDIAN   DATE

Being scrupulous about your informed consent procedures is particularly important in forensic matters, from both ethical and risk management perspectives. As regards risk management, it is inevitable that some of your clients are going to be unhappy with your conclusions. One of the things they may say in their dissatisfaction is that you never told them what your were doing or why, and had they known, they would not have agreed to have the evaluation or take the test. If you are careful in documenting the fact that you told them what you were planning and why, you can clearly demonstrate that this aspect of the disgruntled client's complaint is groundless. So by being careful about this issue, you are doing the right thing and protecting yourself. This is an example of what Benjamin Franklin referred to as "doing well by doing good."

RECORD KEEPING AND FEES

Section 6 of the Code and section VI, B of the Guidelines deal with the issue of record keeping and fees. This section of the Code has particular importance for forensic psychologists. Almost everything that is mentioned about record keeping for psychologists in general goes double for those practicing in the forensic arena. This is in part because of the far greater scrutiny that files generated in forensic cases draw. Clinical files are maintained for a number of important reasons. There is the need to document that the session occurred and to record what transpired during the therapy session. The Code makes it clear that the information included in the case file should be sufficient to allow for continuity of treatment if there is a long hiatus in treatment or if the patient transfers to another mental health treatment provider. While some of this also applies to forensic work, there are also other ethical and risk management–related reasons for carefully documenting the information related to a forensic assessment.

The documentation generated in a forensic assessment is very likely to be viewed by any number of persons with some type of involvement in the legal case that is the cause for the assessment referral. Your report and your raw data will be carefully reviewed by lawyers on both sides of the case. Guardians *ad litem*, probation officers, judges or hearing officers, and the client him/herself may ask for and receive your entire file including test protocols, billing records, and your handwritten notes. Because of this, the Guidelines state the following:

> Forensic psychologists have an obligation to document and be prepared to make available, subject to court order or the rules of evidence, all data that form the basis for their evidence or services. The standard to be applied to such documentation or recording anticipates that the detail and quality of such documentation will be subject to reasonable judicial scrutiny; this standard is higher than the normative standard for general clinical practice. When forensic psychologists conduct an examination or engage in the treatment of a party to a legal proceeding, with foreknowledge that their professional services will be used in an adjudicative forum, they incur a special responsibility to provide the best documentation possible under the circumstances.

Additionally, opposing counsel may hire their own consulting psychologist to review the file and see if your conclusions match your data. The involvement of this consultant may be known to you, or the consultant may be kept out of the picture and operate behind the scenes. When the latter happens, you will probably become aware of it because opposing counsel will be asking you questions on cross-examination that are far too technically sophisticated to be coming from an attorney, and you may be left wondering who is actually pulling the strings in your cross-examination.

You have probably heard that if it isn't written down, it doesn't exist. Again, this goes double for forensic cases. You will be asked in minute detail about what you did and did not ask the client during the evaluation. You do not want to be placed in the position of saying that you did not write it down, but you remember asking the question and the answer you received; your recollection will be treated with skepticism and in some cases outright derision. In the same way, you will want to be able to document how many times you spoke to the client(s), the lawyers, and your collateral sources and what you talked about. This sounds like a great deal of work and it can be, but there are steps you can take to minimize the amount of writing you have to do while at the same time improving your documentation.

The first of these is the use of forms, checklists, and structured and semistructured interviews. For those unfamiliar with structured and semistructured interviews, in structured interviews all of the questions are provided and they are always asked in exactly the same manner, just as the questions of the Wechsler IQ tests are meant to be read as written. In semistructured interviewing, there are topics and specific questions provided, but the interviewer is free to change the wording and approach the interview in a more flexible manner. There are a wide variety of these available commercially and it is not difficult to develop your own. The use of structured interviews can be particularly helpful for a number of reasons. Richard Rogers has written an excellent book (Rogers, 2001) in which he makes a strong case that psychologists do not use structured interviews enough. He makes the point that the use of these instruments increases the comprehensiveness of the assessment and ensures that all of the important data is collected in a standardized manner. In forensic testimony, opposing counsel will sometimes ask very specific and mildly obscure questions about what you discussed with the client in an attempt to make it appear that you did an incomplete, slapdash assessment. If you use a structured interview format, you will know exactly what you asked the client and how the client responded. After the opposition tries this a few times and it does not work, they will usually drop this ploy. Rogers also makes the point that if structured interviews are utilized in a standardized manner, psychologists can compare responses across clients and that different psychologists can compare responses and profiles in the same way that they can interpret an MMPI-2 administered by another psychologist. In this way, a clinical or forensic interview can actually have psychometric properties. Approaching interviews in this manner would allow for the development of a degree of precision that is missing from most assessments.

It should be pointed out that not everyone will want to approach forensic interviewing in this manner. Many well-known and respected forensic psychologists prefer to conduct wide-ranging interviews and would feel restricted by the use of a more structured format. This is fine, as long as you take detailed, legible notes. It should also be made clear that the approaches are not mutually exclusive; you could use a structured or semistructured interview and augment the information you elicit by including extensive discussions of answers and asking probing questions.

There are several ways to approach structured or semistructured data collection. One of these is to have the client fill out a biographical information form before you actually begin interviewing him/her. Again, there are forms that are commercially available for this purpose.

The Forensic Documentation Sourcebook by Theodore H. Blau and Fred

L. Alberts Jr. (2004) is a collection of all kinds of forms for use in a forensic practice including intake forms, releases of information, contact logs, mental status forms, and biographical/intake documents. Best of all, the book comes with a compact disk that allows you to upload the forms to your computer and modify them any way you wish to suit your personal tastes and the specific needs of your practice. Many of these forms and other types of resources are also available on the publisher's web site (www.wiley.com). You can access them by simply going to the site, clicking on the psychology section, and then accessing the TheraForms section of the web page. The forms are available at a very reasonable cost, and once you have downloaded them, there is no per-use cost.

Stuart Greenberg, Ph.D. ABPP (Forensic), sells excellent, comprehensive forms for child custody and other forensic purposes. They can be obtained by writing him: Stuart Greenberg, Ph.D., 1217–24th Ave. E., Seattle, WA 98112.

Psychological Assessment Resources (PAR) (www.parinc.com) sells a well-designed Personal History Checklist in both adolescent and adult forms. This can be sent to the client as part of an intake package or you can have the client fill it out at your office prior to initiating the interview. For an additional charge, you can buy unlimited-use software that will allow you or a clerical assistant to input the client's responses and the software turns the responses into a narrative report that can be cut and pasted into your psychological report. PAR also has Mental Status Checklists for children, adolescents, and adults, which also have computer scoring programs. These forms can be used as interview drivers; you ask the client all of the relevant questions and check off the responses.

Multi-Health Systems (www.mhs.com) sells a similar program (Psychological/Social History Report), but it can be taken at the computer. The company also has a Psychiatric Mental Status program that can also be taken at the computer or on a form you can print out. Finally, the Chemical Dependency Assessment Profile focuses on substance abuse–related issues, and is very comprehensive.

It should be pointed out that while the computerized personal history and mental status programs are convenient and save time, the narratives they output will need considerable modification before they are included in a report. Some cutting and pasting is possible, but because of the nature of the report writing software, the narratives tend to be a bit stilted and awkward and will need to be changed to fit your narrative style if the information is to be included in your final reports. But, whether you use a form-driven personal history or a more freewheeling approach, obtaining a thorough personal history will provide you a context and foundation for the conclusions you reach in your assessment while also satisfying the requirements of the APA Code. Further, you will never have a problem with being found not to have asked important questions such as "Have you ever been in trouble with the law prior to the present matter?" or "Have you been thinking about harming yourself lately?" or "Is anyone being physically abusive to you?" The use of structured and semistructured interviews, checklists, and self-report forms will ensure that while you may miss more subtle or obscure information, you will at least hit your marks on the really important, basic information that is the bedrock of a good forensic assessment.

With regard to your handwritten notes, try to make them as legible as possible and minimize the use of personal shorthand that would be difficult for a third party to decipher. It will not be possible to completely avoid problems with legibility, since you will be taking notes on the fly, but do the best you can. If your handwriting is really hard to read, you may find yourself having to have the notes transcribed. While you will probably not have to pay for this, you will have to take time out of your busy day to read your notes into a tape recorder, and it can be particularly embarrassing if you find that in places you cannot read your own handwriting. Also, since you will not be able to take verbatim notes, you will have to be thoughtful about how to decide what to write down and what to leave out as incidental. Again, this is where structured and semistructured interviews can be helpful, since the questions you are asking (or a close approximation) will already be written down. I have on occasion been asked in court what exactly I asked the client and it was very helpful to be able to read the actual question I used. In a recent case, I was involved in a competence to stand trial case and was testifying in a New Hampshire district court. I thought the defendant was incompetent based in large part on her response to a standardized competency instrument called the MacArthur Competence Assessment Tool — Criminal Adjudication (MacCAT-CA). When I got to court, I discovered that the opposing psychiatrist had also given the same test subsequent to my assessment. Interestingly, the defendant was described by the opposing expert as much more articulate and knowledgeable than I had found her to be. After hearing both my testimony and the psychiatrist's, the judge commented on this and asked that he be provided with copies of the raw data from both assessment files so that he could see what the defendant had actually said in response to questions about standing trial as opposed to any paraphrasing. When the decision came down, he had found that the client was not competent to stand trial, in large part on the basis of her actual responses to my questions about the adjudication process. The moral here is that your file should be clear enough to allow the court to be able to scrutinize your data and draw conclusions.

There is an underlying practical/ethical/risk management issue related to documentation here that is of great importance. Joel Dvoskin, Ph.D., ABPP, has often spoken about this as the need to "show your work." In his discussions with me, Dr. Dvoskin has compared the process of doing a forensic assessment and providing testimony to being in junior high school, when the teacher graded you not just on whether you got the right answer on your algebra problem, but also on showing your work. This was so that the teacher could see how you arrived at your answer. In the same way, it is not enough to be right in your assessments, and often it is not possible to "be right" in the sense this term is generally used. Instead, Dr. Dvoskin suggests that we should remember that our role in court is to assist the judge and/or jury in coming to their own conclusions. Dr. Dvoskin points out that the best way to fulfill this role is to provide documentation and testimony that show the relationship between the conclusions you reached and the data and techniques you utilized. This allows the judge and jury to come to their own decisions about the adequacy of your methods and the weight that should be afforded your conclusions. They may not agree with you all the time, but at least you won't look like you are trying to hide the ball.

Other information that should be documented includes subsequent phone conversations with clients, lawyers, guardians, and other parties in the case. This is particularly important when talking to opposing counsel. This is because there is, for all practical purposes, no such thing as an off-the-record conversation with a lawyer. Always assume that what you say will be noted and in some cases used to undermine your testimony, so you had best have your own contemporaneous notes of the conversation in case an attempt is made to distort what you said. For this reason, try very hard not to be angry or sarcastic, and don't attempt to be humorous in these conversations, since that may also be used against you.

Remember to keep all correspondence related to the case in the file.

Also, find out how long you have to retain records in forensic cases in your jurisdiction. My state requires that records be kept for seven years past the conclusion of the case with an adult, and seven years past the age of majority in the case of a minor. One problem that can arise for this is finding enough storage space for all of the data you will accumulate in the course of your forensic practice. Forensic psychologists generate a lot more paper than those in clinical practice. This is because of the large amount of data that a forensic assessment can generate. I have had cases in which three or four file boxes of records have been shipped to me for a single case. Much more common are files that are several inches thick, and in some cases further legal documentation is routinely sent for months until the case is finally settled. You can quickly find yourself needing an astonishing amount of file space and may wind up using your basement and crawl space for dead storage. Unfortunately, you will receive requests for reports and files for years after you have completed your work on the case, for Social Security disability determinations or from new therapists who have heard that there is a diagnostic evaluation out there somewhere.

There are several approaches to handling the problem of storage of dead files. One approach that some psychologists endorse is waiting until the case has been settled and then removing all of the material you did not actually produce. You can either shred this material or send it back to the lawyer who retained you. You retain only the material that you actually generated in the process of completing your assessment. This is acceptable because the case is concluded and the extraneous material is not original, so if there is a need for it by the parties in the future, it can be obtained again from the lawyers on the case or from the original sources. Some psychologists have actually taken to scanning their files and saving the material on CDs. Those who do it swear by this way of storing files, but it can be labor intensive if you don't have much office support. As far as endless requests for records and reports are concerned, once again you should check with your local board and see what your state's regulations allow. New Hampshire is fairly typical in allowing psychologists to charge 50 cents per page for copying. You can develop a form letter that quotes the regulation and provide an estimate of the copying charges, and inform the person requesting the file that you will not start copying until the check clears. I find that in most cases I don't hear from the person again. Lawyers are usually not a problem, since they expect to be billed for such services. Clearly, if the file is not large and the client needs it for a legitimate reason, such as receiving SSI payments, you should consider simply absorbing the expense as part of the price of doing business.

One further documentation issue needs to be addressed, and this is the recording or videotaping of interviews. There is a good deal of debate regarding the advisability of this practice and there are good arguments on both sides. These arguments are similar to the debate about whether interviews of children suspected of being sexually abused should be recorded. In the latter debate, proponents feel that the use of audiotape or videotape allows the evaluator to avoid having to put so much energy into verbatim notes and to pay more attention to the interview process. Also, having the interview recorded means that the exact words of the interviewer and the child are preserved and available to the judge and/or jury. Those who are against recording are concerned that the child might be made to feel self-conscious. There is also concern that in trial the defense attorney could seize on minor inconsistencies in the child's statements or small problems in the investigator's interviewing technique and use them to undermine the case. At the present time, the balance has shifted firmly to the pro-recording side in the area of child abuse investigation.

It must be understood that we are not discussing covert taping. Taping without permission is certainly unethical (no informed consent, for one thing) and may be illegal in your jurisdiction. Some states allow you to record your conversation with another person without permission; in others, if you do this without the other person's permission you can be guilty of a misdemeanor or even a felony, so don't even consider it. But should you record some or all of your assessments? Again, there are advantages and disadvantages.

On the one hand, taping may cramp your style and make you and the client uncomfortable. Also, any verbal gaffs and awkward or confusing questions may be used by opposing counsel to suggest that you are unskilled or lack expertise. On the other hand, having a verbatim recording of what was actually said may be extremely helpful, particularly if you have a feeling that the client is likely to be disgruntled about your conclusions and is the type of individual who might try to make your life difficult. My personal feeling about this is that making a verbatim recording can be very useful because it allows you to really show your work and makes it so that nobody has to take your word about what you and the client said or did.

Personally, I record in some cases and not in others. It should not be surprising to the reader by this point to learn that I most frequently record custody assessments. It has been my experience that it is custody litigants who are most likely to take umbrage when the report is issued and who also are most likely to make a board complaint against you. Some members of this client group will either twist your statements, take them out of context, or make things up out of whole cloth. Having a record of what was actually said can save you a great deal of stress if they do "jump ugly." Also, the fact that they know that there is such a record may keep them from heading down that road in the first place. There are lots of clues that a case may mean trouble before you get down to the actual assessment. One or both of the clients may have already made complaints about the children's therapists, the guardian *ad litem*, the attorneys, and the judge. If you take the case, there is a pretty good chance that you are going to be next on the list. In the same way, some litigants will call before their appointments and attempt to almost depose you about your methods, experience, reports in other cases, and so on. This is also a bad sign.

If you get a bad feeling about a case because of these or other danger signs, this would be a good time to consider recording. Clearly, if one party is taped, so is the other. You should decide whether the tapes will be provided to counsel along with the report, and you should get a signed agreement either way. Using a video camera is one possibility, but it can be expensive and cumbersome to use and to make copies for the parties. An audio recording is a better way, and there are a number of ways to go from a technology standpoint. You could simply get a decent-quality tape recorder, preferably with stereo microphones for better sound quality. This has the advantage of being inexpensive and simple, but you will be interrupted every 45 minutes to change the tape, and the tapes can add up in a long interview. You will also need a dubbing deck if you want to make copies. Another possibility is to purchase one of the new flash–memory based digital recorders now available. They have a number of advantages. They are small and un-obtrusive and they can record for a long time. I bought one made by Sony. It is about the size of two packs of gum and can record for four hours at its lowest-quality setting, which is still better than a tape recording. These digital recorders also come with software and a USB cable that allows you to send the recording to your computer, where you can then burn it to as many CDs as you wish. Finally, some forensic psychologists I know use a minidisk setup. In practice it works like a digital recorder, except that the data is saved to a minidisk instead of a flash card. One of these recorders can hold even more data than a digital recorder.

One last caveat about recording: I strongly suggest that even though you are using a video camera or recorder, you should still take enough notes that you can reconstruct the session if there is some problem with your technology. You do not want to be put in a situation where a four-hour interview is completely lost and needs to be either completely reconstructed from memory or repeated in its entirety. A pen and a legal pad may be low-tech, but they make up for that in dependability and ease of use.

ASSESSMENT METHODS AND PROCEDURES

Section 9 of the Code and Section VI, A and C of the Guidelines deal with this issue of assessment methods and procedures. The Code makes it clear that when you perform an assessment, you should use sufficient techniques to support your diagnoses, evaluative statements, and conclusions. In the same way, the Guidelines state that forensic psychologists, having gained the requisite knowledge to perform assessments that meet the accepted standards of practice, are also obligated to use that knowledge to select tests, procedures, and methods of data collection appropriate to the task at hand.

These standards have a number of practical implications from an ethics/risk management standpoint. They mean that you should have a rationale for how you go about your assessments and treatment and that you should be able to articulate this rationale in a way that makes logical sense. The best way to do this is to become knowledgeable about how authorities in the particular forensic area in which you are working approach their work and then, to the extent practical, follow their lead. Several examples come to mind. As previously discussed, Thomas Grisso's five-step methodology for determination of competencies provides a logical and practical structure for any number of different types of assessments, but is particularly useful for evaluations of competence to stand trial and/or waive Miranda rights. When I go to court on competence to stand trial cases, I always suggest that the attorney who called me ask me in court to explain my assessment rationale. When asked this on direct examination, I explain the five steps and this provides a context for the judge to understand what I did and why. I find this is very helpful, since it allows the judge to make his or her own decisions about the adequacy of my assessment and also because it never hurts to show your respect for the court and the legal process by explicitly showing your work.

In the same way, if you are doing a custody assessment, using the general evaluative methodologies laid out by Jonathan Gould in *Conducting Scientifically Crafted Child Custody Evaluations* (2006) or the approach discussed by Marc Ackerman in a number of books provides a structure and rationale for your assessments that can be clearly articulated to the court. I am not suggesting that you have to adopt each and every aspect of these authors' suggestions, but the alternative is to develop some idiosyncratic method of your own, which is highly unlikely to be an improvement over the practices of the top experts in the field. It may be that you will eventually develop an innovative and forensically defensible methodology of your own, but if you are that expert at this point, you probably don't need to be reading this book. And it is not as if you don't see forensic practitioners who seem to be making it up as they go along.

As an example, I recently evaluated a woman in a case involving termination of parental rights. As mentioned in the "Required Reading" section of Chapter 3, there are a number of references that tell you almost everything you need to know about these types of assessments (Dyer, Condie). These authors and other authorities in this area of forensic practice provide general methodologies for assessment, suggestions about what data to collect and how to interpret it, and reviews of specific instruments for this type of assessment. This is what I try to do, and it has a number of advantages: I don't have to reinvent the wheel every time I do an assessment and it makes me less vulnerable to cross-examination aimed at undermining my testimony; also, it provides a framework that allows me to present a logical nexus between the data I utilized and the conclusions I drew. In this particular case, the opposing expert did not utilize any methodology she could articulate for the court and this created difficulties when she was cross-examined. In addition, she utilized the Thematic Apperception Test (TAT), the non-Exner Rorschach (which she did not score quantitatively), human figure drawings, and the Three Wishes Technique. Now, this is not the place to debate the place of projective instruments in psychological assessment; the debate on this issue is large, ongoing, and acrimonious, with respected practitioners on both sides. But there is a more important issue in this particular case, and that is whether the tests and techniques being utilized have any demonstrated validity for the particular forensic issues being assessed. I have searched the literature and I have been unable to find a single empirical study that indicates that the TAT, Rorschach, or Three Wishes tests have been shown to provide any information about an individual's parental fitness. This is important, since the Code (9.02, "Use of Assessments") makes it clear that psychologists should use tests and other techniques "in a manner and for purposes that are appropriate in the light of the research on or evidence of the usefulness and proper application of the techniques." Similarly, the same section states, "Psychologists use assessment instruments whose validity and reliability have been established for use with members of the population tested."

Using techniques that have such an attenuated relationship to the issue being assessed makes an expert very vulnerable on cross-examination. Think of the possibilities:

- "Doctor, what is the reliability of the Three Wishes Technique?" (There is no established reliability.)
- "And generally speaking, the validity of a psychological test cannot be higher than the reliability, correct?"
- "Doctor, can you explain what empirical research is, as opposed to, say, case studies or clinical anecdotes?"
- "And can you cite a single empirical study that links someone's responses on the Three Wishes Technique to any aspect of parenting ability?" (None exist.)
- "And despite the lack of any reliable science to suggest that this technique has any utility in assessing any of the issues before the court, you decided to use it?"
- "And you did this despite the fact that there are any number of psychological instruments that have been shown to be reliable and valid for assessing these issues?"

I don't think that you want to be on the receiving end of that kind of cross-examination, particularly when you could have avoided that unpleasantness through the simple expedient of making yourself knowledgeable about the standards of practice in this area of forensic assessment.

There is a good deal of debate on what constitutes the tests that are acceptable for forensic evaluations. In an article entitled "What Tests Are Acceptable for Use in Forensic Evaluations? A Survey of Experts" (2003), Stephen J. Lally surveyed 64 psychologists who had received the diplomate from the American Board of Forensic Psychology. The results were very interesting and demonstrated a range of opinions about a variety of popular psychological tests. Dr. Lally rated the tests as recommended, acceptable, equivocal-unacceptable, and no opinion, and further divided the tests as acceptable for specific forensic purposes such as evaluations of mental state at time of offense, risk for violence, and competency to waive Miranda rights. Although this article has a relatively small sample, it is a very knowledgeable sample and does provide insight into what types of tests are generally accepted in this field.

Some interesting patterns emerged in the survey. For example, Dr. Lally notes that in conducting mental state at time of offense evaluations, the Wechsler Adult Intelligence Scales–III (WAIS-III) and the Minnesota Multiphasic Personality Inventory–2 (MMPI-2) were recommended or found acceptable. The Rogers Criminal Responsibility Scales (R-CRAS), Halstead-Reitan, Personality Assessment Scales (PAI), Luria-Nebraska, Millon Clinical Multiaxial Inventory–III (MCMI-III), and Stanford-Binet were also found acceptable. However, the Rorschach and 16 PF were found equivocal-unacceptable, and projective drawings, TAT, and sentence completion tests were found unacceptable for this purpose.

In risk for violence evaluations, the Psychopathy Checklist–Revised (PCL-R) was recommended and the MMPI-2, Psychopathy Checklist–Screening Version (PCL-SV), Violence Risk Appraisal Guide (VRAG), WAIS-III, and PAI were considered acceptable. Projective techniques such as projective drawings, TAT, sentence completion, and Rorschach were all found unacceptable. Whereas this article doesn't assert the last word on the subject, it seems evident that forensic psychologists would do well to use those instruments that are rated recommended or acceptable because doing so will make their methodology much easier to defend during cross-examination; you could even cite Dr. Lally's article as support for your work. Think of how much grief the psychologist who utilized the Three Wishes Technique could have avoided if she had read Dr. Lally's article.

Another related issue that is implicit in the Code and explicit in the Guidelines is that of corroboration. Section IV, F of the Guidelines notes that the hearsay exception and other rules governing expert testimony place a special ethical burden on forensic psychologists. To understand why this is, it is important to know what the hearsay exception is. In a court of law, there are two types of witnesses—lay or fact witnesses and expert witnesses. Lay witnesses must generally (but not always) limit their testimony to what they saw with their own eyes and heard with their own ears. They cannot testify about what other people said to them because the person who made the original statement is not available to be cross-examined and the judge and/or jury cannot independently make judgments about the veracity of that person and his or her statements. An example of this would be that a lay witness cannot testify that a child's day care provider said that the child's father was surly and unpleasant in his interactions with the day care center's director. Questions about the father's behavior at the day care center should be asked directly of the day care center's director and not brought into court thirdhand. There are a number exceptions to the hearsay rule. For example, excited utterances, which are statements related to startling events made by individuals under the stress of the excitement caused by these events may be admissible in court even though they are hearsay. In the same way, declarations of present state of mind, while hearsay, are often admitted into trial. Reports of statements such as "I am really upset" or "This situation depresses me" may be admitted to show that the person making the statement actually was upset or depressed. Because of another hearsay exception, expert witnesses can testify about what persons involved in their assessments said to them and also make judgments about their mental state and demeanor. A forensic expert can testify about what a client said in a session, review and discuss the contents of education and therapy records created by persons the psychologist has never met, or report on interviews conducted with collateral data sources. This is part of the reason that being qualified as an expert is so important, since it designates the psychologist as an expert who is not bound by the hearsay rule.

This being the case, the Guidelines note that experts should not use information acquired through hearsay in an irresponsible manner. The Guidelines urge forensic psychologists to minimize their reliance on hearsay and to attempt to corroborate such information when possible. When this is not possible, it is strongly suggested that if psychologists decide to use uncorroborated hearsay in drawing their conclusions, they have an affirmative obligation to make the status of this information clear.

It is important to understand the concept of affirmative obligation, because it is important in the practice of forensic psychology. From a practical standpoint, what it means is that psychologists have to bring certain information forward in their report and in their direct examination. They cannot attempt to hide the ball and not mention the limitations of their data until it is brought out by opposing counsel's clever cross-examination. So, if there are important limitations on your data, you need to make them clear in your reports and in your testimony. For example, I often use the Adult-Adolescent Parenting Inventory–2 (AAPI-2) in custody and parenting examinations. This is a brief test that presents the client with 40 statements related to parenting young children, to which the parent can respond on a five-point scale that goes from strongly agree to strongly disagree. It has scales that include the parent's attitude toward corporal punishment, children's autonomy and independence, and the parent's tendency to reverse roles. However, the test has important limitations. It has no validity scales to help detect a parent's attempts to "fake good." Additionally, the statements are face valid. For example, when it comes to corporal punishment, there are statements similar to "I think that when children misbehave, they need a good hard spanking" (not a real AAPI-2 question). It is entirely possible that parents may agree with this statement and actually spank their children frequently, but realize that this is not likely to be well received by the evaluator. For this reason, they may "strongly disagree" with the statement on the test. My purpose in giving the test is that while some parents may "talk the talk" on paper but not "walk the walk," those who cannot even articulate appropriate parenting attitudes in a parenting evaluation are very likely to have real problems in their parenting styles. As a consequence, I make sure to note in my report that while Parent A may articulate appropriate parenting attitudes on the test, this is not a guarantee that he or she actually behaves in this manner with the children. It would be problematic and possibly unethical to present AAPI-2 results as though they were really predictive of parenting behavior.

In the same way, when it comes to forensic assessments, there is also an obligation to utilize a hypothesis testing model. Section IV, C of the Guidelines notes, "As an expert conducting an evaluation, treatment, consultation or scholarly/empirical investigation, the forensic psychologist maintains professional integrity by examining the issue at hand from all reasonable perspectives, actively seeking information that will differentially test plausible rival hypotheses." This is a very important point and it underlines one of the factors that make good forensic assessment so valuable to the courts. This approach is discussed in the section on investigatory ability in Chapter 2, but is worth touching on again. Let's imagine that you are referred a case in which a family was in a motor vehicle accident and their 17-year-old daughter experienced whiplash injuries that have caused persistent discomfort. Subsequent to the accident, the young woman develops symptoms of an eating disorder. The plaintiffs in the case allege that the pain from the accident is the cause of the daughter's symptoms. The initial discovery indicates that the daughter had previously had some symptoms of bulimia, which had been successfully treated by a local therapist. There is also information that the family has experienced moderate levels of conflict over the years, and that many of the issues are unrelated to the eating disorder (financial stress, substance abuse, etc.).

Even before you start the formal assessment, there are a number of competing hypotheses that suggest themselves in this case:

1. The new symptoms of eating disorder were directly caused by the accident; none of the previously existing problems are involved.
2. The symptoms of the eating disorder are an exacerbation of the preexisting condition, but would not have appeared absent the accident.
3. The symptoms of the eating disorder are caused by the combination of the accident, new family stressors, and the daughter's difficulties adjusting to going off to college; the accident was mildly to moderately contributive.
4. The accident had nothing to do with the new symptoms; they had already begun to manifest themselves several weeks before the crash occurred.

As a forensic psychologist, you have an obligation to explore the evidence that supports or undermines each of these hypotheses, and also to explore any new hypotheses that are suggested by the data you collect in the course of your assessment. In practice this means that in any case in which you are involved you should be able to articulate all the alternative theories of the case that you considered in arriving at your conclusions. Considering alternative hypotheses in a systematic manner is important from the perspectives of both ethics and risk management. For one thing, approaching assessments with a hypothesis testing model serves as a debiasing technique, because it makes it harder to ignore possibilities in a case. This is because once you have formulated the hypothesis, it is difficult to neglect it. For example, suppose I make a list of five alternative hypotheses that may apply to a competency to stand trial assessment:

1. The client falls short of the legal standard due to mental illness or cognitive deficiency.
2. The client appears to fall short of the standard and has mental illness or cognitive deficiency, but is exaggerating the level of his/her impairment, making it difficult to be sure of his/her standing relative to the legal standard.
3. The client is malingering, claiming deficits that have no objective basis in an effort to manipulate the outcome of the assessment.
4. The client has minor deficits that could create problems during trial but should not undermine competence if the court is aware of potential difficulties.
5. The client has no difficulties that would interfere with his/her ability to stand trial.

If one generates these hypotheses and then take steps to develop each one, a number of steps would logically follow. For example, the psychologist who performs the evaluation in this scenario would need to do testing and gather information to determine whether the client actually suffers from a mental condition that could have an effect on his/her understanding of the trial process and ability to assist his/her attorney. Additionally, since the issue of underperformance or frank malingering has been raised, it would be logical for the psychologist to gather data and use clinical and psychometric techniques to test these possibilities. It can be seen that if one employs a hypothesis testing model in assessment, the structure almost forces one to be objective and to avoid obvious bias, and it is allegations of bias that will sometimes lead to complaints by disgruntled parties to boards of psychology and more rarely to malpractice actions.

Another important issue related to assessments is raised by 9.08 of the Code ("Obsolete Tests and Outdated Test Results"). You should not use older versions of tests when newer, restandardized versions of the tests become available. For example, I have noticed that a new version of the Wide Range Achievement Test (WRAT-4) has recently been released. I sometimes use the WRAT-3 for academic screening in certain situations, but if I wish to continue using it I will have to upgrade to the new version in the near future. I know that it is expensive to replace tests, but if you wish to do evaluations of the highest quality, you do not really have a choice. It is also good practice for other reasons. For one thing, some attorneys are knowledgeable enough (or are working with a psychologist they hired who tipped them off) to know that you are using an obsolete test and they will not hesitate to bring it up in your cross-examination. This can be an awkward situation when you are put in the position of explaining that you are either too cheap to keep your tests up-to-date or oblivious to developments in your field. Also, since it is unethical to use these outdated tests, there is nothing to prevent a disgruntled litigant from complaining about this to the board of psychology in your neighborhood.

OTHER IMPORTANT ETHICS/RISK MANAGEMENT ISSUES

Section IV, B of the Guidelines (Relationships) states that "forensic psychologists do not provide professional services to parties to legal proceeding on the basis of 'contingent fees,' when those services involve the offering of expert testimony to a court or administrative body, or when they call upon the psychologist to make affirmations or representations intended to be relied upon by third parties." This is another area in which there is a disconnect between lawyers and forensic psychologists. You are probably familiar with contingency payment arrangements even if you have not heard them called this. You often see lawyers in television commercials or in print ads who state something like "We don't get paid until you do." This usually comes up in the context of personal injury cases, and what they mean is that the plaintiff puts up no money in advance and will pay the lawyer a percentage of the award if and when the case is won. Obviously, lawyers who work on this basis have to be selective about what cases they take and become involved only in those cases in which the plaintiff has a reasonable chance of prevailing. This is not considered unethical because it allows plaintiffs with very little money to have their day in court and have representation. In addition, attorneys are expected to be ethical but they are not expected to be impartial; their role is vigorous advocacy within the rules laid out by professional ethics and the rules of evidence. Lawyers are not expected to be objective when advocating for their clients.

As mentioned previously, this is a very different role from that of the forensic evaluator. Forensic psychologists are expected to be fair and impartial in their approach to cases and they cannot be afraid to give the attorney who engaged their services some bad news about the case. It has been suggested that psychologists can determine an impartiality quotient for their work by calculating the percentage of the time that they come to conclusions that are uncongenial to the parties who retained their services. If you find that, by a remarkable coincidence, your conclusions always support the position of the party who retained you, you need to take a hard look at your objectivity; after all, what are the chances of such remarkable good luck? As a consequence of this demand for objectivity and integrity, the Code and the Guidelines communicate, over and over again, the need for psychologists to avoid relationships that have the potential for creating bias. Being paid on a contingency basis is an obvious example of this type of problem. How objective am I likely to be if I put in 10 hours on an assessment of an accident victim and find that he/she is likely malingering or feigning symptoms of post-traumatic stress disorder? What if my finding that the client is exaggerating symptoms or malingering deflates the case before it even starts? There is even an excellent chance the jury may not find in favor of someone who actually has PTSD, in which case nobody gets paid. It is important that we be honest with ourselves about these pressures and influences. None of us are completely resistant to temptation, financial or otherwise. Taking a case on contingency can have subtle and not-so-subtle effects on your objectivity and the outcome of your assessment, so the best thing to do is to avoid ever being placed in that position.

I should note that this can be harder than one might expect. First, lawyers are very good at persuading people, and most psychologists are not used to being approached in that manner. Lawyers also tend to be much more assertive and are not afraid of putting pressure of one kind or another on a prospective expert. Also, there can be a strong incentive to work on this basis if the plaintiff is a sympathetic individual who has no money to hire an expert. It is easy to rationalize that while others might be tempted to modify their testimony as the result of a contingency fee to be paid sometime in the future, you are far too honest and conscientious to be so influenced. I can promise you, it isn't true and the best way to avoid finding yourself in a compromising situation is to refuse to take cases on a contingency basis under any circumstances. If the plaintiff really needs your services and can't pay you, section IV, C of the Guidelines has the answer for you: "Forensic psychologists who derive a substantial portion of their income from fee-for-service arrangements should offer some portion of the professional services on a pro bono or reduced fee basis where the public interest or the welfare of clients may be inhibited by insufficient financial resources." You have an obligation to do some work on a low-fee or no-fee basis. If you're so inclined, you can negotiate a lower rate for your services or waive your fee altogether in selected cases. Doing so will provide you with good karma and perhaps a reward in the next life. In this life, you may find that helping out occasionally improves your reputation and makes some attorneys more inclined to seek out your services with paying clients in the future.

According to Guidelines IV, D, "Forensic psychologists do not provide professional forensic services to a defendant or to any party in, or in contemplation of, a legal proceeding prior to that individual's representation by counsel, except for persons judicially determined, where appropriate, to be handling their representation pro se." What this means is that you should probably not become involved in a case in which a defendant is not represented by a lawyer. There are a number of good reasons for this, and this is a situation that has come up in my practice perhaps more frequently than is the case with most forensic psychologists. Because of my work in the area of Munchausen syndrome by proxy, I often receive calls from mothers who have had their children removed from their custody by their local child protective service agency and want my help. They are often desperate and sometimes tearful, and their stories are very compelling. Unfortunately, many of them are not represented by counsel for a variety of reasons. Sometimes they have fired their lawyers, sometimes they have run out of money, and sometimes they cannot find an attorney who feels qualified to defend them in this specialized and obscure area. By doing a Google search or checking certain bulletin boards, they come across my name and call me or write me. I am happy to talk to them to find out what's going on in their cases, but I always explain to them that the person I really need to speak to at this point is their lawyer. When they hear this, they often try to convince me that I should help them despite the fact that they have no lawyer. When this happens I carefully explain my role as an expert witness. To help them understand, I try to explain that an expert is like an arrow while the lawyers are like the bow; the arrow cannot be delivered without the bow and I cannot do a direct examination of myself on the witness stand. Individuals who are involved in the legal system without the guidance of an attorney often don't know where in the process their case stands, whether the court is even willing to hear expert testimony, or even if they have any legal recourse at this stage of the case. Under the circumstances, if you agree to do an evaluation with pro se clients, there is a certain likelihood that the evaluation will do them no good even if it comes out as supporting their position, and you will have taken their money without helping them. I believe it is an important principle of forensic practice to make sure that even before you come to the point where you make a diagnosis or address a psycholegal issue, you should make sure that there is some purpose for the work you're doing.

Section 9.01 (b) of the Code states that psychologists should provide opinions about the psychological characteristics of individuals only after they've conducted examinations of those individuals adequate to support their conclusions. This section also suggests that there are some statements you can make about individuals you have not evaluated based on other types of information you have gathered, but you have to make a reasonable effort to conduct a face-to-face assessment. If for some reason such an assessment is not practical, you are under an obligation to note the effort you made to try to interview that individual and the reasons why it was not possible. Further, if you are going to make statements about an individual you have not assessed, you have an obligation to discuss the impact of your limited information and conclusions and also limit the nature and scope of the type of comments you would be making.

Section IV, H of the Guidelines says almost exactly the same thing. It should be made clear that there are certain types of evaluations in which it is simply not possible to interview or test the subject. The most obvious example of this would be psychological autopsies and evaluations of testamentary capacity and undue influence when the testator (person making the will) is deceased. There is nothing unethical about these types of evaluations, but it is still probably advisable to note that you would have had a better idea of whether a deceased testator was demented if you had been able to administer neuropsychological testing yourself, rather than having to rely on medical records.

As previously mentioned, making statements about someone you have not assessed can be very risky if you do not heed the warnings of the Code and Guidelines. It is easy to become carried away by the narrative of a person who is describing past sexual abuse by a parent, a clergyman, or an abusive husband and simply take the alleged victim at his/her word. The obvious problem is that when you do this, you have basically decided that a person whom you have never interviewed is in fact guilty of sexual abuse or domestic violence. It is important to remember that even the most experienced psychologists are not human lie detectors, and that we can be misled or fooled outright as easily as anyone else. This type of thing comes up often in child abuse cases. Some years back, I consulted on a case in which the biological father was alleged to have been physically abusive to his son. The mother took the son to a psychologist who interviewed the mother and son together in the same room and also separately. Based on the statements of the mother and son, the psychologist diagnosed the son with post-traumatic stress disorder, the cause of which was the father's physical abuse. It is interesting to note the circularity of this reasoning.

How do you know this child has post-traumatic stress?

Because he was physically abused by his father.

How do you know that he was physically abused by his father?

Because he has post-traumatic stress.

The psychologist did not attempt to corroborate the accounts of the mother and son, nor did she do any testing or attempt to determine the veracity of the statements in any way. Interestingly, this case eventually went to court. On cross-examination, the psychologist was asked whether she made any effort to speak to the father and ask him for his side of the story. She actually stated, under oath, that she never interviewed the fathers in these situations because they would simply deny that they had committed the acts of abuse. As luck would have it, I had been retained by the father's attorney, and I assisted in the writing of her cross-examination. The attorney who retained me had the psychologist read the pertinent sections of the Code out loud to the court, and then asked her detailed questions about why those sections were included in the Code. She was then asked to describe the ways in which she had attempted to conduct the type of interview required by the Code. She was also asked to point out where in her report she had discussed the impact of the lack of the type of information that a face-to-face interview would afford on the reliability and accuracy of her report, and the ways in which she had limited the scope of her report to reflect this lack of information. She had, of course, done none of these things, and I will admit to feeling a certain satisfaction when I saw her exit the courtroom red-faced and furious. Interestingly, the boy was court-ordered into counseling with a very good psychotherapist who was knowledgeable about these matters and did not prejudge the situation. In a matter of months, this child admitted that his mother had pressured him into making false statements about his father, and the court gradually allowed the resumption of full visitation.

This is another example of where ethical behavior and risk management come together. The father in this case could easily have complained to the psychology board about the conduct of the diagnosing psychologist, and I think that it would have been an open-and-shut case since the Code is quite unambiguous about the ethical requirements in these types of situations. If the psychology board had made a finding of professional misconduct in the case, it is quite possible that the father could have retained an attorney and sued the psychologist for damages. This could have meant a year or two of weekly supervision for the psychologist with the attendant expenses, requirements for extra continuing education and ethics training, the publication of the finding of misconduct, and the possible loss of the psychologist's contracts with various managed care organizations. Not only is following the Code and Guidelines in these types of situations the right thing to do, but it also can save you thousands of dollars and untold angst. All you have to do is follow the rules and be a little humble about the limitations of your knowledge. The decisions we make as forensic psychologists can have very serious effects on people's lives, and we should keep this in mind before we run off at the mouth and express opinions based on a sense of outrage rather than on the type of data we are supposed to elicit.

BOARD COMPLAINTS

Before we leave the issue of risk management in forensic practice it is important to touch on the issue of complaints made about psychologists to boards of psychology or mental health practice. In recent years, this issue has begun to be studied in some detail. The information that has been elicited presents a sort of "good news, bad news" scenario. The good news is that the actual rate of board complaints against psychologists in general is quite low. Most states report that between 2 and 4 percent of psychologists are the focus of a complaint in any given year, and that the vast majority of these complaints are screened out, with no action being taken against the psychologist. Consequently, the overall risk of a psychologist having a substantiated complaint against them is quite low. To look at the statistics another way, unless it is the same 2 to 4 percent who have complaints against them every year, if you stay in practice for 20 years the likelihood of your eventually having some type of complaint made against you is bound to go up. The bad news is that if you engage in certain areas of forensic psychology, you are much more likely than average to have a complaint made against you. The area that is most risky from that standpoint is custody assessment. In one of my surveys I asked 45 practicing forensic psychologists about their perception of the risk of psychology board complaints in their field versus other areas of clinical practice. Of the respondents, 25 percent thought that the risk in forensic psychology was much higher, and another 36 percent thought that the risk was somewhat higher than in clinical practice. I also asked them to rate their perception of the risk of board complaints and/or malpractice claims for specific forensic activities. Child custody assessment was considered the most risky activity in this respect, with 62 percent of participants rating this area of practice as very risky. Other areas that were considered to have above-average risk were child abuse assessment and testimony and police fitness for duty assessments. Interestingly, 40 percent of my sample have had a complaint to their board made against them, and 20 percent have been sued for malpractice. Clearly, another cost of doing business for forensic psychologists is a much higher rate of having to deal with complaints made against them by unhappy litigants.

If it has not happened to you, it may be difficult to understand how unpleasant the experience of having a complaint made against you can be. Although it is easy to tell yourself that there is little likelihood that the complaint will have a significant impact on your practice or your life, the reality of the situation is that this is not the case. It is a very disturbing and unsettling experience to receive an envelope from the local board of psychology when you know that it is not time to pay your dues. These types of complaints threaten your livelihood and your sense of yourself as a competent professional. They normally take a very long time to resolve even if everything goes well, and you may find yourself spending months obsessing about the minutiae of the assessment or testimony associated with the complaint. And you may have good reason. In my experience, most boards of psychology or mental health practice are fair and do a professional job in dealing with these types of complaints. However, this is not always the case and there are boards that act irresponsibly or overreact for reasons known only to their membership. Consequently, for this reason and for a number of others, every complaint made against you should be taken extremely seriously. There are, however, steps that you can take to increase the likelihood that if a complaint is made it will be screened out, or failing that, ways in which you can minimize your chances of having the complaint stick.

One of the first things to do is to buy the maximum amount of board complaint insurance that you can get from your malpractice insurance company. This kind of insurance rider is inexpensive and is a real bargain. If your current insurance company does not offer it, I strongly recommend you find another company. Remember, you are much more likely to experience a board complaint than you are to be sued for malpractice, so board complaint insurance is a necessity, particularly in forensic psychology.

The second thing is to be a bit selective when you take cases, particularly in the custody area. While there is no guarantee that seemingly reasonable custody litigants will not turn on you in the end, there are certain behaviors that greatly increase the likelihood that they will complain about you. For example, if one of the parties has already complained to the bar association and judicial conduct committee about his/her previous lawyer, the guardian *ad litem*, and the judge in the case, it is a pretty safe bet that you will be next and you may wish to consider not taking the case. If you do get a sense that the case is taking a turn in the direction of a possible complaint, seek supervision for your work and be particularly diligent about documentation. In this way, should a complaint be made you can report to the board that you appropriately sought consultation and you already have someone in your corner if the complaint goes beyond the screening phase.

Generally, once a complaint is actually made, your board will request a copy of your file and a written response to the letter of complaint they received. At this point, you should take several important steps. The first of these is to contact your board complaint insurance company and let them know what has occurred. This will free up the money you will need to deal properly with the complaint. Also, if you have managed care contracts you should look them over because some managed care panels require that you report any complaints made against you even in the investigatory stage. The next thing to do is to get a good lawyer. You should talk to some of your colleagues about which lawyers in your area are knowledgeable about these types of issues. Generally, there are several lawyers in a given metropolitan area who have experience helping psychologists deal with board complaints. You should find someone who understands the process and who is responsive to your requests. It is a good idea to find such a lawyer before you need one so you do not have to scramble around at the last minute.

Very often, the issues in the complaint are fairly straightforward and are either true or not true. For example, a psychologist may be accused by an angry husband of having a romantic relationship with the guardian *ad litem*, who recommended custody to the wife. This is either true or untrue and if it is true you are in big trouble. If it is not, then there is not a pressing need for a complicated ethical analysis of something you simply did not do. However, ambiguous situations do arise. If you have any question about whether you may have inadvertently engaged in some ethical lapse, you should seek consultation to determine whether this is the case. I recommend that you consult someone with a reputation as an expert in the forensic area that is the issue in the complaint such as custody and who also has a background in psychological ethics. The consultant can review your file and report and tell you whether they think that there is a problem. If there is, talk to your attorney about how you should approach the board about whatever the problem is. If the expert thinks that you have not engaged in any such lapses, you can use his/her expert services if the case goes beyond the investigation stage. These services will generally be paid for out of your board complaint insurance, but be sure to discuss this with your lawyer and your insurance carrier.

You should work with your lawyer to craft a written response to the letter of complaint. It is important to address all the issues in the letter in a serious matter, even if the issues raised are absurd or ridiculous. It is very important not to be sarcastic, angry, or high-handed in your response, as this will almost certainly produce a negative reaction. Your lawyer will help you write your response in language that will lay out your perspective on the case in the most advantageous way possible. This is often a laborious process, but it is essential since it may have the effect of stopping the process from going any further and save you a great deal of stress and strain.

Rarely, the board will decide that the case requires further investigation. They may have you interviewed by a professional investigator or they may use the services of psychologists who volunteer to assist the board. This may occur at your office, at your lawyer's office, or at the investigator's office. In some cases, the lawyer for the board may be present. My advice is to have your lawyer present and to treat the interview as though it were court testimony. I would recommend that the interview be taped if that is allowed, so that any questions about what has actually been said can be easily resolved. Everything that you have read about how to testify in court applies in this situation. Keep your answers succinct, do not lose your temper, and do not try to be funny. If the investigation reaches this stage, you should probably have your expert write a report and you should have it ready to give to the investigator. Assuming that you, your attorney, and your expert have all concluded that you have not had any ethical lapses, giving the investigator the report sends an important message. That message is that if you have to go to a hearing, there will be testimony from a respected expert in the field that you engaged in no unethical behavior.

It should be pointed out that one thing that will work to your advantage is that psychology boards generally hate to actually have hearings. Just as in criminal prosecutions, nearly all board complaints are settled through plea bargaining. This makes sense, since if a psychologist actually acted in an unethical manner the individual will want to cut the best deal they can for themselves. On the off chance that you may be dealing with a board that is inclined to be unreasonable, letting them know that you are quite willing to go to a hearing can often have a positive effect on their approach to the case. I am personally aware of a number of cases in which psychologists who, at least in my opinion, had committed no unethical acts were offered plea bargains by psychology boards. These agreements sometimes had requirements that would have been very detrimental to the practice of the psychologists, including years of supervision, informing all of the managed care panels, and having the substantiated complaint be a matter of public record. The negotiations on these agreements went back and forth for months until the psychologists reach the point where they flatly turned down any agreements and said that they were willing to go to a hearing. When they did this, the boards of psychology involved simply dropped the cases and sent them private letters of reprimand. This behavior on the part of the boards in these cases makes it clear that when push came to shove, they preferred to drop the case rather than go to the trouble and potential embarrassment of having a public hearing.

Ultimately, the best way to minimize your exposure to problems related to board complaints is to engage in good risk management practices. When in doubt, seek consultation and if the case looks like it might be trouble, do not take it. In my own work, if a case begins to look like one or both parties are going to be unreasonably disgruntled, I try to be proactive in my approach. I often tell people that if they think I am the problem, the problem can be easily solved because I will give them their money back and get out of the case. I always make sure to discuss any case in which I think a complaint might be a possibility with colleagues, both for guidance and for the protection it affords me. This is seldom required, but you should be willing to take similar steps if it becomes necessary. If you should become involved in this process, it is important to talk to colleagues for moral support and to practice good self-care. Finally, I have been involved in supervising a number of individuals who committed relatively minor ethical violations and who were required to obtain supervision by their board of psychology. The good news is that despite having the substantiated complaint become public knowledge and having to tell all of their managed care panels about what had occurred, none of them experienced any real damage to their careers. It is only those who engage in more egregious types of behavior such as sexual boundary violations or fraud who have lost their licenses or been forced to leave the profession. Consequently, while these complaints should be taken very seriously, the actual risk of serious damage is slight.

Performing Evaluations

The purpose of this chapter is to provide an overview of how different types of forensic evaluations are actually performed. It is very important to note that none of these descriptions are meant to be utilized as step-by-step guides that will allow you to begin performing such evaluations if you have never done them before. As mentioned in Chapter 3, "Preparing for Forensic Psychological Practice," it is strongly recommended that before you attempt to do any kind of forensic evaluation, you should have at a minimum prepared yourself by reading current books and articles on the subject, attending continuing education workshops, and obtaining supervision from someone knowledgeable about this area of practice. It should also be understood that your clinical assessment skills should be well developed; forensic assessments are no place to develop basic testing technique. Attempting to perform such assessments with insufficient training and knowledge is a recipe for problems, both for you and for the client. It should always be borne in mind that these types of assessments are going to receive a great deal of scrutiny from the lawyers in the case, the court, and the jury and that you may be called to account for what you have written or what you have concluded in considerable detail. As has been previously stated, the courtroom is an adversarial arena and is very different from the collegial atmosphere of the case conference, and aside from any of the other negative consequences of performing a substandard evaluation, you will find it extremely uncomfortable to have obvious deficiencies in your work and preparation explicated in front of a live audience. Finally, as was discussed in the preceding chapter on risk management and ethics, it is unethical to perform evaluations when you have not become competent by virtue of formal education, study, and training.

That being said, it is important to have some sense of how these assessments can be approached. This chapter outlines procedures for performing some of the more common types of forensic assessments but it is far from being an exhaustive guide. It also discusses general issues in forensic assessment, the nuts and bolts of what you should actually do, from setting up your work space to writing your report. It should be noted that there is no one way to do a good evaluation, although it could be argued that some steps are indispensable. Some forensic psychologists are very test oriented, whereas others rely much more heavily on extensive interviewing and review of collateral information. Most fall somewhere in between on this spectrum. As long as the evaluation answers the referral questions, uses established techniques that can withstand evidentiary challenges, and clearly demonstrates the relationship between the conclusions drawn and the data relied upon, honorable psychologists can disagree about specific methods. As you become experienced in this area of practice you will undoubtedly develop your own style, favorite techniques, and general methodology for approaching different types of court-related evaluations.

THE SETTING

Where you physically do your forensic work is more complicated than in general clinical practice for several reasons. First, you will be doing a much higher volume of psychological testing than is usual for those in clinical practice, and this will have an effect on how you set up your physical space. Additionally, you may have the kind of forensic practice in which you are required to perform assessments in many different settings such as jails, prisons, schools, and group homes. This section offers some concrete suggestions about how to prepare for performing forensic assessments in and outside of your office.

YOUR OFFICE

If you are going to perform forensic evaluations, you obviously need office space in which to do them. Ideally, it is best to have some type of dedicated testing space in addition to your consulting room if you are going to be doing a high volume of assessments. One reason is that you are going to need space for a testing table and probably a computer, and your consulting room will probably not be big enough to contain this equipment in addition to the chairs or couches you use to see individual clients or families, and the personal work space where you answer phone calls and write your reports. Another issue is that some of the testing your client may be doing for you can take several hours. With some tests you have to sit across from the client and administer them, but others, such as the MMPI-2, do not require much direct involvement from the psychologist after the task has been explained. If the client is taking such a test in your consulting room, you will be unable to take phone calls, write reports, or do anything else that involves possible violations of confidentiality. You do not want your patients taking tests in the waiting room, particularly if you are in a group practice and there will be other people sitting there in addition to your client. Waiting rooms are generally not good places for this type of testing, since test security issues can arise and there are likely to be distractions. In addition, taking the MMPI-2 on a clipboard while sitting in a straight-backed waiting room chair is likely to be an uncomfortable and fatiguing experience for the client. If you are in a group practice that has extra office space or a conference room, this could be used as your testing room, although it will be necessary to put together a sign-up sheet to make sure that there are not conflicts about the use of the room and of specific tests owned by the group.

A point about home offices: A number of my colleagues who specialize in general psychotherapy have made the decision to work out of their homes. For most of them this is a good arrangement and it saves them money. I do not think that this is a good idea for anyone who is going to practice forensic psychology. It is important to remember that many of the people you will be evaluating either are accused of or have been found guilty of criminal behavior. It is simply not a good idea for them to know too much about you, particularly about where you live. The best arrangement for a forensic psychologist, in my opinion, is to work in a different town than the one in which you live. There is going to be a proportion of individuals whom you assess who are not going to be happy with the outcome of your evaluation. You do not need to be seeing them every day in the supermarket. Other problems can crop up as well. For example, several years ago I had severe neck and shoulder pain that I thought was a muscle spasm caused by some athletic injuries I had sustained in my misspent youth. I booked a session with a masseur who had been recommended by one of my neighbors. I was lying on my stomach and the masseur was working on my neck and shoulders. He had mentioned a number of times that I seemed familiar to him, but I did not recall ever having met him. Finally, he paused with his hands on my neck and said, "Wait, now I remember you. You did a child custody assessment five years ago about whether my son should move away with his mother." I tried to keep my voice calm and asked casually, "So, how did I do?" While I was saying this, I was trying to figure out whether I could roll away from him off the table if he had been unhappy with the outcome of the assessment. Luckily for me, he had been pleased with the results.

OUTSIDE THE OFFICE

One issue for those starting out in forensic psychology to consider is that a certain percentage of your assessments will take place outside of your office. This can present significant logistical problems and can be more of an obstacle that might seem apparent. Evaluations can take place at prisons, jails, juvenile facilities, group homes, nursing homes, and lawyers' offices. All the settings have the potential to present a number of obstacles to your completing your evaluation in a professional manner. For this reason, there are number of steps that should be taken to prepare for out-of-office assessments.

When you are contacted by a lawyer about performing such an assessment, you need to make it clear that you require their assistance in getting into the facility where the client is located. In my experience, prisons and jails are the most difficult places to do assessments unless you go to these places frequently and develop a relationship with the staff. Every correctional facility seems to have its own unique system with regard to allowing psychologists access to assessment clients. Some of them require some type of court order for you to be admitted. Others will accept a phone call from you explaining that you need to see the client and do not require any corroboration that you are a professional doing your job. Complications can arise no matter how careful you are in setting up the time and place for your assessment. You may call up the facility and ask to speak to whoever is in charge of arranging such visits. After being shuttled around from phone extension to phone extension, you may find yourself speaking to a shift commander, nurse, administrator, or assistant warden, who may or may not want you to fax over a court order for the assessment or a letter from the lawyer. It is very important to discuss what you plan to do in some detail. For example, I once drove several hours to an out-of-state prison where I had made it clear with the administrator that I would be doing a psychological evaluation with one of the inmates. When I arrived, the correctional officers in charge of screening visitors initially refused to allow me to bring in any of my psychological tests and told me that I was limited to one pen and a pad of paper. I asked to speak to the administrator with whom I had made arrangements and was told that she was not present in the building. I tried to explain that a psychological evaluation necessitated the use of psychological tests but was received unsympathetically. I asked if I could talk to somebody in the mental health department and was told that there was no one in today. This was actually quite unlikely since this was a very large prison and undoubtedly had a proportionally large staff of mental health personnel. I eventually called the lawyer who had engaged my services. He made a series of phone calls to the prison and eventually was able to effect my entry with my psychological tests, but only after I had wasted an hour and a half. There have been other occasions on which I have confirmed my appointment by phone and by mail only to be turned away at the jail because they had given the only contact visit room to an attorney and there was no place for me to test. For this reason, even after you speak to the appropriate administrator and set up the appointment, you should call to reconfirm on the day of the assessment just to make sure that the people on duty know you are coming. It is frequently the case that the person you have spoken to has not posted or communicated your appointment to the person who will actually be in charge on the day you come to the facility.

It is also important to talk to the administrator who is setting up the assessment about your minimal needs for testing. You are going to need a reasonable degree of privacy, a table or desk, and adequate lighting. Some smaller jails simply do not have this kind of space. Nearly all jails have rooms for attorneys and their clients to meet privately, and this is generally where you will end up. These vary in size and adequacy. Several summers ago I did an evaluation in a prison and was given a small cubicle in which to test. It was an extremely hot day and there were no fans, air-conditioning, or ventilation of any kind as far as I could tell. It was so hot in the room that sweat was dripping off my nose onto my writing pad, and by the time I left my shirt was saturated. I had to go back to see the client again and spoke to the lawyer about the situation. He was angry and told me that he had specifically arranged for me to be given space in the medical wing, which was air-conditioned. He called and spoke to the people with whom he had initially arranged the assessment and was assured that when I went back I would be taken to that wing. When I came the second time no one had the slightest idea of what I was talking about and I was placed back into the cubicle from hell to complete my assessment. Do the best you can about explaining your needs, but do not be too surprised if they are not met.

Scheduling and timing can also be a problem. Some jails and prisons are flexible in this regard, while others offer limited windows of opportunity for these assessments. Most of the jails and prisons I have visited have lockdown periods for the inmates in which everyone goes back to their cells so that they can be counted and accounted for. Some of these facilities will allow the inmate to continue working with you during these periods, while others will curtail your session during lockdown. Some jails let you continue working, but will basically lock you down in your testing room and you will not be able to leave until the head count is over. You may find yourself sitting around for 45 minutes to an hour after you have completed your assessment, so be prepared.

It is important to be flexible with your schedule on days when you go to these types of facilities. They are run around their own scheduling needs and are not particularly accommodating. You may find that despite the fact that you booked a session for nine o'clock, you may cool your heels in the waiting room for an hour or more before someone finally comes to escort you to where you need to go. Also, some of these facilities can be surprisingly disorganized. At one prison I was ushered into a huge room used for family visits where I was to test. I sat and waited for the inmate to be brought to me, but time went on and he did not appear. I was locked in the room and there was no one to ask about the situation. I had no idea whether anyone knew that I was even in the building, but I assumed that someone would eventually come in and notice me. An hour and 45 minutes later there was a shift change and a correctional officer walked into the room and saw me. She was startled and wanted to know how I had gotten there. Apparently, the correctional officer who had escorted me there had forgotten to call for the inmate and also forgot that I have been left there. On another occasion, I was left locked in a room with the defendant in the secure psychiatric ward of a prison and despite my repeatedly pressing the button that in theory alerted the staff to the fact that I was finished, no one came for several hours. Luckily, the defendant was a pleasant enough fellow, which was good because if he had decided to strangle me no one would have noticed for some time. Because these situations arise with some frequency, if you go to a prison to test you should probably clear off more time on your schedule than you think you will need.

Since you do not want to drive two hours to the state prison and find that you have forgotten materials that you need to complete the assessment, you should carefully check and make sure that you have everything that you need before you leave your office. Depending on what type of assessment you are doing, you may have a lot of equipment to bring with you. You should probably have what is referred to as a sample case, which is a large briefcase that can hold all of your files, tests, and other materials you will need. You may want to consider typing up a checklist of what you will need and going over it before you depart. I like to have visual confirmation that everything I need is in the sample case, including directions to the facility, copies of the letters or court orders that allow me to perform the assessment, and plenty of pencils, pens, and writing pads.

Another thing to consider is that in contrast to your office, where you can put someone at a table in your testing room to take the MMPI-2, leave the office manager to monitor the testing, and go return phone calls in your consulting room, you are stuck in the attorney/client room with the defendant throughout the entire assessment. I recommend that you bring some reading material to pass the time when you are waiting for the client to finish this type of testing. I do not recommend working on other case files, since they may be examined when you are screened to enter the prison, and because the person being evaluated may observe information that allows them to identify the client in the file.

Another issue to resolve is whether you can bring your laptop computer with you. Some prisons and jails will allow it and others will not, and there appears to be no rhyme or reason as to why this is the case. I prefer to be able to bring my laptop because of tests I have loaded onto it, but I make sure that I have paper-and-pencil versions of all the tests I want to give. Also, bring the power supply to the computer, as you do not want your battery to run out in the middle of the MMPI-2. Of course, there may or may not be an outlet in the attorney/client room you have been given.

Unless you are wearing a business suit or the female equivalent thereof, you should try to remember to inquire about the dress code at the jail or prison. In the past, I would dress quite casually when I went to jails or prisons since it did not seem that important to make any kind of impression on the staff or the inmate. I made the mistake of wearing blue jeans and a sweater to one prison, only to find that since the prisoners were dressed in denim, visitors were not allowed to wear this fabric. I told them I would go find the closest Wal-Mart and buy myself a pair of casual slacks, but the correctional officer relented and allowed me in with my jeans "just this once." I am told by colleagues that other facilities have dress codes that do not allow khaki slacks, so it pays to check about what you can and cannot wear.

Remember that jails and prisons get to decide what they will and will not allow and they are not used to debating their policies. There is no point in arguing with them because you cannot win; a patient, pleasant, but assertive attitude will serve you best in these settings.

General Procedures

Before the client arrives, you should have already provided the individual with some basic information. You should make clients aware of how long the evaluation is likely to take, how much it is likely to cost, and generally what you plan to do. I am generally paid at the time of service, but sometimes take a retainer. It is also useful to inquire discreetly about clients' reading ability and familiarity with/ability to use a computer for testing. This will allow you to choose appropriate instruments; if they have difficulty reading you may, for example, want to use the taped version of the MMPI-2 and make other similar modifications to your approach to assessment. Tell them to bring their reading glasses if they require them for close paperwork. You may wish to send them a packet with materials that they can fill out before they come in. The package can contain detailed directions to your office as well as any forms you want them to fill out before they arrive. These can include personal history questionnaires, custody/visitation worksheets, and other documents that will reduce the amount of time it takes to elicit this information. My supervisor, Wilfrid Derby, Ph.D., used to explain to patients that this kept him from having to be a high-priced secretary.

When clients arrive, either you or the office manager can give them whatever paperwork needs to be filled out. In my practice we have clients fill out a fact sheet that provides their contact information and also outlines information regarding the limits of confidentiality, my duty to warn and take other steps if threats against others are made, or if I become concerned that the client may be suicidal. The sheet also outlines the steps that I have to take if the client brings up information suggesting that he/she is engaging in child abuse or elder abuse that is not already known to the court. I usually include a release of information to the client's lawyer. I may obtain more releases after speaking to the client so I can interview important sources of collateral information.

Occasionally, I have encountered individuals who do not want their reports sent to their attorneys, nor do they want to give me permission to talk to their attorneys until they (the clients) see how the assessment goes or determine whether they like the report. If this occurs I make it very clear that it is my policy to send reports in the first instance to the attorney. I explain that the reason for this is that these days people have computers and scanners and that someone could easily take a copy of my report, scan the letterhead and my signature, and make changes to the report. For this reason, I want the report sent to clients' lawyers first, since they are unlikely to jeopardize their careers on behalf of one client. Additionally, I need to have the ability to communicate with clients' lawyers to do what I consider to be a professional job. I politely but firmly make it clear that I will not do the assessment if I cannot follow this policy. Rarely have clients refused to give me a release to speak to their attorneys and send them the report, but when it happens, I stick to my guns. This kind of suspiciousness on the part of clients is almost always a bad sign and an indication that they are going to be trouble down the road. In my opinion, it is important to be alert to these types of signs as one method of risk management. If you have a bad feeling about the assessment and the client at the start, you should take these feelings seriously. As Robert De Niro's character said in the movie *Ronin*, "If there is any doubt, there's no doubt." If the evaluation is immediately starting out on the wrong foot, you should either postpone the assessment until the client speaks to his/her attorney or simply refer the client to somebody else. Generally, I have little or no trouble getting the releases that I need to perform the assessment.

When I introduce myself to clients, I tell them who I am and shake hands if they initiate it. In my office we offer water and decaffeinated coffee, which we keep in a carafe on a bookshelf out of reach of children who sometimes share the waiting room. We provide decaffeinated coffee because I feel that my clients are generally tense enough when they come for the assessment. We also have caffeinated tea that we can offer to people who feel they are starting to fade or otherwise need a lift. One possible solution to providing coffee is to buy one of the cup-at-a-time coffeemakers that use individual packets of different types. I also make it a point to have some kind of food such as packaged peanut butter crackers or cookies in my break room, since evaluations can take the better part of the day and clients can get hungry.

After the introductions, I lead clients to my consulting room and indicate where I want them to sit. I am aware of the practice of some psychotherapists of providing a number of seats and letting clients choose where they wish to sit. Possibly, they think there is something diagnostic about which chair clients take or whether they ask for guidance. Harry Stack Sullivan and H. S. Perry, in *The Psychiatric Interview* (1972) discuss this and come to the conclusion that this is simply bad manners on the part of the therapist, and I share their opinion. Also, since I am taking notes and am right-handed, I like to sit to the right of the client so that I can lean my clipboard on my left knee or thigh. I think it is important that the chairs be reasonably comfortable and provide good back support, since you are going to be spending a great deal of time sitting there. Some type of small table between the chairs is helpful, since you can put your coffee there and also keep extra pens, papers, and whatever other forms you may be using on top.

Once we are seated, I make a little small talk ("Any trouble finding the place?") and then I ask clients if they understand, in a general way, why they have been sent for an assessment. I want to know whether we are on the same page with regard to what we are going to be doing and why. If we are in agreement, we move on and if not, I attempt to explain it. If there is some kind of serious confusion I will allow clients to speak privately to their attorneys by phone or we can sometimes reschedule, but this rarely happens. At this point I go through my Evaluation Agreement form as described in Chapter 5 on risk management so that clients can give informed consent for the assessment. That being done, I explain that I want them to be comfortable and that they should tell me if they need a break, want water, or need to go outside to smoke a cigarette. I also emphasize that I am in no hurry and have scheduled plenty of time for the assessment.

Once this has been done, my next step is almost always to perform a mental status examination. As I mentioned previously, I use the Mental Status Checklist (either for adults or for adolescents) published by Psychological Assessment Resources (PAR) as an interview driver. I almost never skip this step, because I believe, along with most other experienced forensic psychologists, that the mental status examination is an indispensable part of nearly all forensic assessments. Doing such an examination provides you with information about clients' appearance, distinguishing features, style of speech and expression, and many other characteristics that may be important in coming to your conclusions. A good mental status examination provides information about clients' objective presentation, medical history, current medications, stated and observed psychiatric symptoms, substance use, recent changes in appetite, weight, sleep pattern, and many other factors that are essential for ruling in or ruling out a wide variety of conditions. I strongly recommend that anyone starting out in forensic psychology acquire the skills to do a good mental status examination.

As previously mentioned, there are any number of structured and semistructured mental status forms on the market, and which you use is a matter of personal choice and taste. I like the Mental Status Check-list by PAR because it is comprehensive and also because of the soft-ware that allows you to input clients' answers and your observations and print out a narrative report. This report, with modifications, can be cut and pasted into your report and can be a real time saver. I also find that providing a good deal of structure in the early stage of the assess-ment is helpful as an information-gathering tool. Clients get into a rhythm of answering questions as they are put to them, and when more sensitive questions are asked, they often answer automatically. Part of this is that questions like "What is your sexual orientation?" is asked in the same manner and tone as "Are you currently employed?" The use of this type of questioning approach often prompts people to give more straightforward answers. This can be helpful when you are ask-ing questions about substance abuse, depression, suicidality, violent ideation, or whether the client has been a victim of sexual abuse or do-mestic violence.

The next stage of the evaluation is the clinical interview. Again, this can be structured, semistructured, or unstructured depending on your tastes and preferences. I generally ask questions about where clients were born and about their family life and upbringing. In addition, I question them about their adjustment to school, whether they had disciplinary problems in school or delinquency in the community, and any other problems that affected their develop-ment. I generally ask about relationships and friendships. If the eval-uation is not related to sexual offending or related issues I generally tread lightly on issues related to sexuality. In general, it is best not to ask many highly personal questions about issues that are not directly related to the issue for which clients are being assessed, since it is an invasion of privacy and tends to make people uncomfortable and de-fensive. With adult clients I ask about what they did post–high school and what they have done for work since they graduated from high school or college. With adolescent or child clients I often ask them about what they would like to do in the future. I also ask about hobbies, avocations, and other interests, since this a often provides important information and also gives me a sense of who clients are as people. Having covered general background material, I begin to ask questions about the matter that has led to the evaluation. I raise the subject by asking a few general questions. I also let clients know that I have read materials that provided information about the case prior to their coming in. I do this for several reasons. One is that I want to be free to bring up these matters and I do not want clients to feel that I have held back this information in order to trick or trap them. I also am putting them on notice that I have this information and may, for example, know that they have prior convictions or gave a statement to the police or that I have read the alleged victim statements about what occurred. In some cases this motivates clients to be more forthcoming about the case, since there is no point in trying to deny that certain things occurred.

In this phase of the clinical interview, in many cases, clients do most of the work. Once I open up the topic of the allegations against them or the charges facing them, they may simply give me their version of what occurred in considerable detail. At other times, certain clarifying questions must be asked or clients may need help to stay on topic. There are clients who have very problematic styles of communication and these need to be addressed in different ways. Some clients give extremely detailed and sometimes circumstantial or tangential accounts of their situations. They can go on and on for hours talking about issues that have only a very tenuous relationship to the present circumstances and the matter at hand. This can be extremely frustrating and fatiguing and it is often difficult to know what you should be taking notes on during the seemingly endless narrative of irrelevancies. It helps to try to be sympathetic, since these are often people with many worries on their minds and they may not have had a chance to talk to anyone about them. I will often try to use a number of maneuvers to steer them back to more relevant topics.

Sometimes it is necessary to be firm and start structuring the interview, cutting off the client with specific questions. One particularly difficult interview occurred when I was asked to do a competency assessment of a Spanish-speaking individual in a jail. I do not speak Spanish, but no Spanish-speaking forensic evaluator was available so I utilized the services of a professional interpreter. Using interpreters lengthens the interview in any case, since everything has to be translated back and forth. This particular defendant was being assessed for competence because he simply would not stop talking in court. During some preliminary hearings he had talked over the judge and over his attorneys, keeping up a running stream of comments about his distress, the unfairness of the proceedings, his prayers for the health of his attorney and his attorney's family members, and prayers to the Virgin Mary. Despite the attempts of his lawyer to quiet him, he kept talking, and this also occurred during consultations with his attorney outside of court as well. When I met with him at the jail, the defendant continued to do the same thing, talking over my questions and endlessly elaborating his answers. I had allowed plenty of time for the evaluation, but it was taking far too long and the interpreter was going to have to leave before we completed everything that I needed to do. Finally, in desperation, I used what little Spanish I knew to try to get the defendant to be quiet and respond to my questions. I told him "*¿Señor, solamente sí, no, o no sé. Comprende?*" This stemmed the flow for a short time but in a few minutes he was back to talking incessantly. Ultimately, I stopped the interview and with the permission of the defendant and his attorney I spoke to the psychiatrist who worked at the jail. The psychiatrist examined the defendant and prescribed a tranquilizer, which calmed the defendant down and greatly reduced his verbal flow. I was able to reexamine him and found that he appeared to be competent to stand trial now that he was less anxious.

Infrequently, it is necessary to be very firm with clients who are not being straightforward. For example, in one of my cases, the defendant was being very evasive. Questions such as "Were you convicted on those charges?" would seem to be straightforward enough, but I could not get a straight answer. When asked whether he had been convicted of domestic violence against his girlfriend, this client continued to answer, "I pled nolo" (nolo contendere, meaning I do not wish to contend) which was unresponsive to the question. We went back and forth on this several times and I finally confronted him, telling him that his refusal to answer my question in a straightforward manner made me question his veracity in his other answers. He took some umbrage at this, but I pointed out that he knew what a conviction was and he was simply trying to avoid telling me what I knew to be the truth. As this type of behavior continued I ultimately told him that he needed to answer my questions and I would give him some opportunity to clarify or state his opinion. I also told him that if he could not see his way clear to be more cooperative, I would simply conclude the interview and he could find someone else to assess him. In this particular case, setting firm limits brought the interview process back under control and we were able to finish the assessment.

In other cases, clients volunteer little or no information and getting them to answer questions is like pulling teeth. Sometimes this is due to their underlying psychological condition and other times it is simply a matter of their trying in a rather unsophisticated manner to avoid unpleasant topics. When this happens it is helpful to start asking more specific questions and politely but firmly insisting on an answer. Whereas it is generally preferable to elicit a free narrative, when clients are answering questions minimally in an attempt to hold back information it is necessary to get much more specific. This is a common interviewing technique in settings where people are generally motivated to withhold potentially embarrassing and damaging information, such as substance abuse assessments. As a consequence, clinicians who work with these populations want to keep asking questions with greater and greater specificity. For example, individuals with alcohol use problems frequently minimize their consumption. If you ask them how much they drink, they will say that they drink moderately or occasionally. For that reason, it is important to ask repeated questions such as "How much beer do you drink?" "How much wine do you drink?" "How much hard liquor do you drink?" Often this type of repeated question will elicit more accurate information than one that is simpler and more general.

In performing the clinical interview, it is important to remember that people need to tell their story. For this reason, it is important to be reasonably patient when clients give you more detail than you need, while at the same time not letting the interview get out of hand. It is also important to strike a balance between friendliness and formality. Since you are not functioning as a psychotherapist, being too friendly and sympathetic can mislead clients and make them feel that you are on their side when in fact you are on no one's side. Too much friendliness and self-disclosure is inappropriate when the results of your assessment may very well be unflattering to clients, who may then feel betrayed and angry. This can be a difficult transition for those who have worked as therapists to make, since joining skills are so important in that type of practice and they may be difficult to turn off.

PERFORMING SPECIFIC TYPES OF ASSESSMENTS

After the mental status examination and clinical interview are completed, it is time to move on to perform whatever testing is appropriate. What to do at this stage will depend very much on what type of forensic assessment you are performing. This section provides an overview of methods and instruments used in a variety of forensic evaluations. It is not intended to be exhaustive and is not a substitute for proper preparation and supervision.

COMPETENCE TO STAND TRIAL

Competence to stand trial assessments are often the foundation of a healthy criminal forensic practice. Depending on your location, there may be a demand for these types of evaluations. How often the issue is raised varies from jurisdiction to jurisdiction. While it is important to know what you doing when performing such evaluations, they are relatively easy to undertake. This is true for a number of reasons. For one thing, the law which governs competency to stand trial is fairly straightforward. Most states use some variation of the standard laid out in *Dusky v. United States* (1960), which states that a defendant has to have sufficient present ability to consult with his attorney with a reasonable degree of rational understanding, and have a rational as well as factual grasp of the proceedings against him. The factual component is generally taken to mean that the defendant understands, in a general way, the roles of the participants, the charges against him, the possible range of penalties, and other facts that are important in standing trial. The term *rational* means that defendants not only know these facts but understand their implications in a way that will allow them to meaningfully participate in their own trials. It should be noted that defendants' understanding does not have to be perfect or up to the standard of a lawyer, but they do need to have sufficient ability to be able to generally follow what is going on in the courtroom and understand the choices they have to make.

Another reason competency evaluations are relatively simple to perform is that there has been a great deal of research into this area of practice over the years. In 1973, the legal criteria outlined in the Dusky standard were made operational by A. Louis McGarry and colleagues at Harvard University. They had outlined 13 components that they believed formed the underpinnings of the factual and rational understanding detailed in the Dusky standard (Lipsitt, Lelos, & McGarry, 1971).

1. Appraisal of available legal defenses.
2. Unmanageable behavior.
3. Quality of relating to attorney.
4. Planning of legal strategy, including guilty plea to lesser charges where pertinent.
5. Appraisal of the role of:
   - Defense counsel
   - Prosecuting attorney

- Judge
- Jury
- Defendant
- Witnesses

6. Understanding of court procedure.
7. Appreciation of charges.
8. Appreciation of range and nature of possible penalties.
9. Appraisal of likely outcome.
10. Capacity to disclose to attorney available pertinent facts relating to offense, including defendant's movements, timing, mental state, and actions at time of offense.
11. Capacity to realistically challenge prosecution witnesses.
12. Capacity to testify relevantly.
13. Self-defeating versus self-serving motivation.

While different authorities in the field have looked at the underlying capacities involved in standing trial in different ways, these 13 criteria have been and continue to be highly influential.

Finally, because these evaluations are so commonly performed, good assessment tools for competence to stand trial have been developed and are readily available.

The Competence Assessment Instrument is a semistructured interview developed by the McGarry group that closely follows these 13 criteria. Some forensic psychologists utilize a rating system that allows the defendant's performance on each of the 13 components to be scored on a 1 to 5 scale where 1 represents total incapacity and 5 indicates no incapacity, but many who use the instrument do not use the rating system.

The Fitness Interview Test—Revised is a structured instrument that was originally developed to assess the competence of criminal defendants in Canada. It is divided into three general areas: ability to understand the nature of the proceedings and factual knowledge of criminal prosecutions, the ability to understand the consequences of the proceedings, and the ability to communicate effectively with counsel and assist in defense.

The MacArthur Competence Assessment Tool—Criminal Adjudication (MacCAT-CA) was published in 1999. It is probably the most sophisticated of the competence assessment tools now available. The test is divided into three sections. The first section, Understanding, is primarily related to the factual component of the Dusky standard. The

211

second section, Reasoning, examines the defendant's ability to identify the salient pieces of information that would need to be communicated to an attorney. These sections use a vignette of a fight between two individuals, one of whom assaults the other. The last section, Appreciation, is designed to measure the extent to which defendants understand the implications of the situation and also to what extent their grasp of their case is influence by disordered thinking. Unlike the other instruments mentioned, the MacCAT-CA has norms that allow the forensic psychologist to inform the court of where the defendant stands in relation to other individuals who were found competent or incompetent by courts. In addition, the MacCAT-CA is structured so that on many of the questions, if defendants give an incorrect answer or do not know the correct answer, they are given the correct information and then asked to repeat it in their own words. This allows the evaluator to develop both a sense of what defendants know and do not know about the adjudication process as well as the extent to which they can be educated about going to court. This helps rule out the possibility that the defendant has simply never been told about some of these issues.

In order to give the reader a sense of how competence assessments can be approached, I have included in Appendix A an analysis of a case involving juvenile competence to stand trial. This analysis was provided as one of my work samples when I was applying to become a diplomate in forensic psychology through the American Board of Forensic Psychology. This lays out my thought process, methodology, and findings in that case. The actual report that was submitted to the court (modified so that the subject is not identifiable) is presented in Appendix B.

Insanity/Mental State at Time of Offense/ Not Guilty by Reason of Insanity

The determination of legal insanity is another issue that can arise in criminal court related forensic practice. These evaluations generally come up with less frequency than assessments of competence to stand trial. Part of this has to do with how cases are structured. If defendants are so grossly impaired in their thinking and understanding that they are found incompetent, then they are not tried and there can be no insanity defense unless they are restored to competence. Consequently, many individuals who might be found legally insane never reach the point of being assessed as to their mental state at the time of their offense because they were screened out as incompetent at the outset of the adjudication process. The other issue is that contrary to what is commonly believed, the insanity defense is rarely used. It is estimated that the insanity defense is raised in less than 1 percent of criminal cases. Success rates for the insanity defense when it is raised vary widely from jurisdiction to jurisdiction. It should also be understood that legal insanity is not the same thing as mental illness. An individual can have a very serious mental illness such as schizophrenia and still be legally sane.

To understand the issue of legal insanity, it is important to know something about the law and specifically about the issue of criminal responsibility. Under the law, there are two components in a criminal act. The first of these is the behavior that is illegal, such as murder, assault, or robbery. This component of a criminal offense is known as the *actus reus*. The second component is the intention to commit a crime, which is known as the *mens rea*, literally a guilty mind. In order for individuals to be considered legally culpable for their acts, both *actus reus* and *mens rea* must be present. To use an example from my own experience, back in the mid-1980s I completed a postdoctoral retraining internship at a state hospital in Ohio. Much of my work there involved the treatment of individuals who suffered from both mental retardation and psychosis. Many individuals who have these problems have other medical problems such as seizure disorders. There was one young man at the hospital who periodically had severe grand mal seizures. Unfortunately, after he partially regained consciousness subsequent to seizure, he would become combative and attack anyone who approached him. I recall one incident in which I was in the day room of the hospital ward. I heard this patient give the characteristic cry that he made when the seizures came on him, and then I heard a sickening thud as his head struck the floor. A nurse and I ran into the room and found the young man lying on the floor bleeding profusely from a cut on his head. As we tried to stanch the bleeding, the patient partially regained consciousness and began punching and kicking me. I was forced to try to restrain him and spent several very frightening minutes wrestling with him, covered with his blood. Eventually additional staff came and were able to restrain him until he completely regained consciousness. In this case, the police were not called and the patient was not charged with assault, despite having punched and kicked me several times. As is sometimes the case with people who have seizure disorders, he had no recollection of his attack on me, nor did he have any control over his behavior.

His postseizure combativeness was what is called an automatism in that he was acting automatically, without conscious control. Consequently, even though he had performed the *actus reus* (attacking me) he lacked *mens rea*.

There is a long history in Western civilization of certain individuals being thought to be too gravely impaired to be considered culpable for illegal acts. Hebrew, Roman, and English common law all recognized that some individuals lacked the ability to understand the difference between right and wrong. In American law, a number of legal standards have been developed that define legal insanity. Some states utilize the M'Naughton standard. This standard is named after Daniel M'Naughton, who in 1843 shot and killed the personal secretary of Sir Robert Peel, the Prime Minister of Britain and the head of the Tory party. Mr. M'Naughton was apparently paranoid and believed that he was being persecuted by the prime minister and his party. He shot the secretary thinking that he was Prime Minister Peel. He was acquitted by reason of insanity at his trial, and this caused an uproar throughout the nation. The M'Naughton standard as it has been applied in American law in recent times states that persons are legally insane if, at the time of their offense, they did not understand the wrongfulness of their actions or they were unable to control their impulses if they knew they were wrong. Further, this lack of understanding or incapacity to control their actions has to result from a mental disease or defect. The other standard that is widely used is the American Law Institute (ALI) standard. The ALI standard states that individuals are not criminally responsible if at the time of their offense they were unable to appreciate the nature and quality or wrongfulness of their acts and that this inability is caused by a severe mental illness or defect.

It should be noted that the modern ALI standard was modified after the public outcry that resulted from the insanity acquittal of John Hinckley after his attempted assassination of President Ronald Reagan. The American Bar Association and the American Psychiatric Association both backed a move to remove from the insanity standard the criteria related to the defendant's ability to control his or her actions. It was argued that modern psychiatry was simply not advanced enough to differentiate whether individuals could not control their impulses or simply chose not to do so. The federal courts and many states have adopted this approach in their status with regard to insanity. In the past, other standards for legal insanity have been developed and utilized. In the case of *Durham v. United States* (1954) Judge David

214

Bazelon of the District of Columbia Circuit Court of Appeals ruled that a jury could find a defendant not guilty by reason of insanity if the defendant's criminal actions were the product of a mental disease or defect. For this reason, this legal standard is sometimes referred to as the "product test." This is clearly a much broader standard than M'-Naughton or ALI and allows for the introduction of all manner of expert testimony. This vagueness of the standard created a great deal of chaos in the judicial system and it was dropped in nearly all jurisdictions. The only state in which a form of this standard is currently utilized is my own state of New Hampshire. The New Hampshire state motto is "Live Free or Die," and there is a tradition of judicial independence and deference to the judgments of juries. Because of the use of the product test, New Hampshire juries who sit on cases in which the insanity defense is introduced are instructed that "legal insanity is what you think it is." It is interesting to note that despite the vagueness of the standard, there are very few successful acquittals by reason of insanity in New Hampshire.

It should be noted that a number of states also provide for a verdict of guilty but mentally ill. In theory, this verdict allows juries to find defendants guilty of crimes of which they are accused, but also acknowledges the need for defendants to be treated until they are restored to sanity. There has been a good deal of criticism of this approach to mentally disordered offenders, in part because many jurisdictions that implemented it did not create an infrastructure for the care and treatment of defendants so designated.

ASSESSMENT OF LEGAL INSANITY

The assessment of legal insanity is different from most types of forensic evaluations because it is essentially retrospective. The question before the court and before the evaluating psychologist is not defendants' current state of mind or psychological functioning, but their state of mind as it relates to the standard for legal insanity being utilized at the time of the offense. Other types of evaluations such as competence to stand trial are designed to assess the individual's ability in the here and now. For example, a hypothetical defendant could be a woman diagnosed with paranoid schizophrenia whose symptoms may be well controlled by medication. When she is medicated, she may have no difficulty understanding right from wrong or conforming her actions to the dictates of the law. However, it is possible that her crime was committed during

215

a period of time when, through no fault of her own, she was unable to take her medication. Because of this, the calm, reasonably lucid individual who sits before the evaluator may reflect a very different mental state than that which was present at the time of the offense. For this reason, although all good forensic evaluations involve careful review of records, it is even more central to insanity evaluations. Generally speaking, there are a number of components that characterize high-quality evaluations of this type.

Even though insanity evaluations are oriented toward the individual's mental state at the time of the offense, it is still important to conduct a careful mental status examination and thorough clinical interview. Although the defendant's current mental state is not the focus of the assessment, it may provide important information regarding the defendant's past mental condition. For example, if the defendant presents as paranoid with well-developed and organized delusions of persecution, this increases the likelihood that he/she was in a similar mental state at the time of the offense. Many of the diagnoses that are associated with legal insanity are not likely to suddenly appear and then disappear, although this can happen. The reasons for the mental status examination have been discussed previously. The clinical interview should cover a variety of topics, including the defendant's life history, the history of his/her mental illness, previous involvement in criminal activity, as well as involvement in various forms of treatment, such as medication, psychotherapy, and hospitalization. Clearly, clients should also be carefully questioned about the events that led up to the commission of the crime in question, including their thoughts, feelings, and any indication of disordered or confused thinking. The clinical interview should not be rushed and in some cases may have to be done over a series of days.

Generally, unless recent psychological testing has been performed, it will be necessary to do a battery of tests. At a minimum, the defendant should receive some type of intelligence test. Since the defendant's level of intellect may be an issue in the case, it is not recommended that an IQ screening test be utilized. Performing a comprehensive test such as the Wechsler Adult Intelligence Scales–III, Reynolds Intellectual Assessment Scales, or the Woodcock-Johnson–III will provide reliable information in cases where processing difficulties or subnormal intelligence are likely to be an issue. I would also recommend that you not use short forms of these tests. This is because in addition to the fact that the abbreviated tests give less reliable information, there is a high likelihood that opposing counsel will seize on your nonstandard administration and make an issue of it on cross-examination. If brain damage or other organic conditions emerged as an issue in the case, you need to determine whether your expertise in that area of evaluation is sufficient. If it is, you may choose to give either a fixed battery (Halstead Reitan, Luria-Nebraska) or flexible battery. While there is a good deal of debate in a neuropsychological community about which approach is better, both approaches have been successfully utilized in forensic cases. If you do not feel confident about administering these types of tests, one possibility is to have a fellow professional with more experience in this area perform a neuropsychological assessment. Of course, if it appears at the outset that neuropsychological assessment is going to be an important part of the case and you do not have sufficient experience or expertise in this area, you should refer the case to someone who does.

As far as personality testing is concerned, the administration of the MMPI-2 should probably be considered indispensable. While other personality tests such as the Personality Assessment Inventory or the Millon Clinical Multiaxial Inventory–III may be used as well, the Minnesota Multiphasic Personality Inventory–2 (MMPI-2) is the instrument that has been used for many years in clinical and forensic settings and is the most reliable and best-researched instrument for this purpose. You should clearly have a solid background in the interpretation of the MMPI-2 before performing insanity evaluations or most other forms of forensic assessment. Again, while some forensic psychologists disagree, it is my opinion that projective instruments should be avoided in these cases due to their lack of established reliability and validity. One possible exception is the Rorschach. While the Rorschach Comprehensive System remains controversial, even the critics of the test feel that one of the things that it does do well is detect psychotic thinking. For this reason, if you have been trained in the Comprehensive System, you might wish to employ the Rorschach if psychosis is an issue in the case.

Because insanity in this context is a legal rather than a psychological construct, there are few psychological tests specifically designed to assess legal insanity. One exception is the Rogers Criminal Responsibility Assessment Scales (RCRAS). This instrument is designed to assist forensic evaluators in assessing the individual elements of the ALI and M'Naughton standards. The RCRAS helps evaluators to structure their observations and information regarding different elements of the defendant's behavior and mental state at the time of the offense and fit them into the legal criteria. Although legal insanity cannot be reduced to a numeric score, I have found the instrument useful in organizing my thoughts and perceptions about these types of cases.

In addition to using standard psychological tests in assessing legal insanity, it is extremely important to take steps to assess the possibility of malingering. In many cases, defendants become aware that it will be to their advantage to be found not guilty by reason of insanity. This gives them a strong motivation to exaggerate their psychopathology, and it is important to take steps to rule out such exaggeration as an explanation for observed symptoms. There are both clinical and psychometric approaches to the assessment of malingering. One extremely useful source of information with regard to malingering is the validity scales of the MMPI-2. The scales are useful in detecting symptom exaggeration and random responding. The validity scales of other instruments such as the Personality Assessment Inventory (PAI) and the Millon Clinical Multiaxial Inventory–III (MCMI-III) are also useful sources of data, although they are not as sensitive or as well researched as the MMPI-2 scales. A number of tests specifically designed to assess malingering are also commercially available. Richard Rogers has developed the Structured Interview of Reported Symptoms (SIRS) for the detection of malingering of psychiatric symptoms. The SIRS is a structured interview that approaches possible malingering from a number of directions. It asks questions about very specific and unlikely symptom combinations, repeats questions to assess consistency, and also utilizes the psychologist's observations of discrepancies between the defendant's description of his/her behavior and actual behavior during the assessment. The SIRS is scored on a number of scales that measure the extent to which the defendant endorses symptoms that are infrequently noted in genuine psychiatric patients, symptoms that are overly blatant, or a large number of symptoms that are reported to be of extreme or unbearable severity. Depending on how many items are endorsed on the scale, the client may be rated as honest in responding, indeterminate, likely malingering, and probably malingering. This test is very useful for assessing individuals who are trying to feign severe mental illness.

There are also clinical indicia of the malingering of serious mental illness. In a chapter in *Clinical Assessment of Malingering and Deception* (2nd ed.), edited by Richard Rogers (1997), Philip Resnick, M.D., provides a clinical decision model for the assessment of malingered psychosis:

Meets the Following Criteria:

A. Understandable motive to malinger
B. Variability of presentation as observed in at least one of the following:
   1. Marked discrepancies in interview and noninterview behavior
   2. Inconsistencies in reported psychotic symptoms
   3. Contradictions between reported prior episodes and documented psychiatric history
C. Improbable psychiatric symptoms as evidenced by at least one of the following:
   1. Reporting elaborate psychiatric symptoms which lack common paranoid, grandiose, or religious themes
   2. Sudden emergence of purported psychotic symptoms to explain antisocial behavior
   3. Atypical hallucinations or delusions
D. Confirmation of malingered psychosis by either:
   1. Admission of malingering following confrontation
   2. Presence of strong corroborative information such as psychometric data or past history of dissimulation

In addition to the malingering of psychiatric symptoms, some individuals will attempt to malinger cognitive deficits, such as problems with memory or some normal intellectual ability. As with the malingering of psychiatric symptoms, there are both psychometric and clinical methods of assessing such malingering. There are a number of commercially available tests that assess both malingering and underperformance. Many of these utilize what has come to be called "forced choice testing." The Test of Memory Malingering (TOMM) is typical of these types of tests. In administering the TOMM, the evaluator shows the subject a series of 50 simple line drawings, one at a time. He/she is then shown cards or computer screens that have two line drawings on them. One of the drawings is from the series of 50 previously viewed and the other is new. The subject is forced to choose which of the drawings he/she has previously viewed. The series of 50 pictures is presented twice and there is an optional delayed trial in which the initial list is not shown. Malingering is detected in several ways on this test. First, the task itself, remembering 50 line drawings, sounds as though it would be difficult to laypersons but in fact is very easy. Nearly all individuals who are not brain-damaged or moderately to severely retarded can usually remember 48 out of the 50 pictures on the first trial without difficulty, since cued memory is utilized. Consequently, any score much below 46 on any of the trials is highly suspicious for malingering. Also, it should be remembered that since there are only two choices, even a blindfolded individual would get approximately 50 percent of the pictures correct. Anyone scoring below chance must logically have known the correct answer and purposely chosen the wrong one. There are a number of other tests utilizing this model that are available for both manual and computer-based administration and they should be employed whenever such malingering is suspected.

After the psychological evaluation of the defendant is completed, it is important to seek out and utilize third-party data. The evaluating psychologist should attempt to obtain a complete set of the defendant's mental health records, as well as information about past criminal history. Clearly, since defendants in these types of situations have a high potential for dissimulation, it is not sufficient to simply take their word regarding their history and circumstances. It is important to determine whether the symptoms that are observed during the face-to-face evaluation are consistent with past clinical history or suddenly emerged after the defendant was apprehended and charged. The evaluator may discover that although the defendant has been psychiatrically hospitalized, the records indicate that those working with the defendant over the years have frequently raised the issue of symptom exaggeration or malingering. It will also be very important to review arrest reports, which provide information about the defendant's behavior, demeanor, and the presence or absence of obvious impairment or intoxication at the time of his/her arrest. Any records of the defendant's movements and activities leading up to the arrest may also be important, since they provide information about the extent to which the defendant was planful with regard to the crime as well as the extent to which he/she gives evidence of understanding to some extent the wrongfulness of the contemplated actions.

When all this information is collected, the forensic psychologist summarizes it in his/her report. As has been previously mentioned, the issue of providing an ultimate issue opinion with regard to the defendant's legal sanity or lack thereof has been the subject of some discussion among forensic psychologists. My personal opinion, and I believe the opinion of most in the field, is that the court will give whatever weight to your conclusion it deems appropriate, and that judges and juries will want to hear your opinion for what it is worth. The difficulty comes in when one has to try to move from psychological conclusions (the defendant's *DSM-IV-TR* diagnosis, ability to reason, extent to which thought processes are affected by delusions and hallucinations) to the legal issue of whether the defendant understood the wrongfulness of his/her actions or could control his/her behavior. In my opinion, the best way to approach this is to clearly state your reasons for coming to your conclusions and describe the data on which you relied in relation to these conclusions. If you show your work in this manner, the judge and/or jury will be able to evaluate your rationale and the adequacy of your data and give it the weight they believe it deserves. In this way, even if they do not agree with your view of the case, they will likely respect your opinions and the integrity of your work.

Munchausen Syndrome by Proxy

Munchausen syndrome by proxy, which is also known as factitious disorder by proxy, is a relatively rare and controversial diagnosis. It is called factitious disorder by proxy in the *DSM-IV-TR* and is included in an appendix in the volume for those diagnoses that require further study before they will be made official. There are four basic diagnostic criteria for the condition. The first is that the perpetrator must exaggerate, fabricate, or induce symptoms of illness in someone under his/her control. This pattern of behavior is mostly seen between mothers and their children, but the entry criteria for the disorder could be met by a caretaker doing the same thing to an elderly person, and there are even case studies of individuals using their pets in this way. A second criterion is that the exaggeration, fabrication, or induction of illness is done for the purpose of obtaining the secondary gain associated with taking on the sick role by proxy. (In factitious disorder or Munchausen syndrome without the "by proxy" modifier, afflicted individuals fake illness in themselves to take on the sick role, while in the "by proxy" condition another is used.) Secondary gain is any covert advantage that is not directly related to one's stated goal (the health of one's child) and is unconscious. External gain is a conscious advantage, like time off from work or money. The third criterion is that the perpetrator's behavior is not better explained by another condition, so if a schizophrenic mother became convinced that her child was ill based on some type of delusion, this would not be factitious disorder by proxy. Finally, the behavior of the perpetrator must not be for obvious external advantage, so apparently exaggerating a child's illness in an attempt to obtain disability payments would also not qualify for the diagnosis.

This disorder has gained a certain amount of notoriety because of its unusual nature. In addition, it has been discussed in the popular media. The Bruce Willis movie *The Sixth Sense* includes a subplot about a case of factitious disorder by proxy, and the rapper Eminem has a song in which he states his belief that he was a victim of this behavior. There have been a number of high-profile cases that have been reported in the national media as well. I am including material on performing evaluations of factitious disorder by proxy for two reasons. One of these is that such evaluations are, in essence, no different than any other type of child abuse assessment. The other reason is that it is something that I became involved in starting in 1997 and gained a modest degree of notoriety for my work in this area. Performing assessments of possible factitious disorder by proxy cases and testifying in both civil and criminal trials involving this issue became an important subspecialty in my forensic practice. Describing how this occurred will give the reader a sense of how a niche practice can be developed and at the same time an idea of how such assessments can be done.

Between 1987 and 1998 I did a great deal of work for New Hampshire's Division of Children, Youth, and Families (DCYF). I performed evaluations on juvenile delinquents, children suspected of being abused, and also abusive parents who had to undergo court-ordered assessments as part of their agreements with DCYF. I also did psychotherapy with all of these groups. I would testify in these cases when requested, and I also began doing some work for the defense. In 1997 I was called by a local attorney who was defending the woman accused of perpetrating factitious disorder by proxy on her infant daughter. The attorney told me that he had called a number of psychologists and no one had even heard of factitious disorder by proxy, let alone knew anything about it. Just by chance, I did know something about the diagnosis. The previous year I had attended the convention of the American Psychological Association and wandered into a symposium on this diagnosis. This did not constitute a great deal of training, but it made me the most expert person to whom the attorney had access. In preparing to take the case, I read the available literature on the subject, including probably the best-known book at that time, *Hurting for Love* by Herb Schreier and Judith Libow (1993). I was appalled by what I found.

The literature on the subject was highly speculative and was based on a few case studies. There were only a few quasi-empirical studies that can only be considered preliminary work. Despite this, those who were writing about the subject of factitious disorder by proxy had developed a behavioral profile of mothers that they considered to be probative of this disorder. The profile covered such a wide range of behaviors that nearly any parent who had a seriously ill child was likely to have a few, and one of the criteria that was put forward in all seriousness was that denying that one has perpetrated factitious disorder by proxy is a sign of factitious disorder by proxy.

Since I had done a great deal of work in the area of child sexual abuse, I was sensitized to the issue of the base rate problem and the applications of Bayes' theorem to diagnosis and prediction. The base rate problem arises when psychologists or anyone else attempts to make diagnoses about phenomena that are very rare. An example of this would be assessing the dangerousness of high school students who make threats of violence in their school. In a post-Columbine world, parents and school administrators are extremely sensitive to these types of threats, and attempts have been made to develop systems of assessment that differentiate truly dangerous from nondangerous students. The problem is that the phenomenon of school shootings is thankfully so rare that any attempt at assessment will almost certainly produce an unacceptable rate of false positives. In this example, a false positive would be classifying a student as a potential killer when he is not, and a false negative would be classifying a truly dangerous student as harmless.

To explain why the base rate problem creates such difficulties in classification, let us assume that 1 out of 100,000 students suspected of being dangerous actually is likely to go on a killing spree. Let us also assume that we develop a procedure that is 90 percent accurate at detecting these dangerous students, and that the false negative rate is 5 percent, as is the false positive rate. If we use this procedure with all 100,000 students we will probably identify the one potential school shooter. However, we will also misidentify 5 percent of the 100,000 students as dangerous when they actually are not. This means that we will misidentify approximately 5000 students as dangerous.

The base rate problem comes up in sexual abuse cases, particularly when professionals attempt to use a behavioral profile to decide which children have actually been abused. Many of the behaviors that have been noted as possibly indicative of sexual abuse have a very high base rate in the nonabused population, which is much larger than those who have been abused. For this reason, these types of behavioral profiles are also likely to produce an unacceptable false positive rate.

223

This was obviously (at least to me) a problem with factitious disorder by proxy. Published estimates of the incidence of factitious disorder by proxy ranged between one and six pediatric cases out of one million. The base rate of this disorder is therefore extremely low. Some authors have suggested that the rate is actually much higher because of the undetected cases, but this is like stating that there are many undiscovered islands in the Pacific Ocean; we will not actually know how many there are until they are discovered. It is also a principle of medical and psychological diagnoses that if a disease or condition is rare and the diagnostic procedures not extremely accurate, the condition will be overdiagnosed. Despite this, my reading on the subject indicated that nearly all the authors had forgotten or neglected this principle and the implications of the base rate problem. I thought that this was an important point because factitious disorder by proxy was starting to be an issue in more and more child protection cases. Attorney Tom Ryan, who handled a number of high-profile factitious disorder by proxy cases, was quoted as saying that the condition was becoming the "disease du jour."

I was at this time approximately 41 years old and I had never written an academic paper. I had gone from working in the schools to private practice, and aside from teaching a few graduate classes as an adjunct assistant professor, I had not gone the route of academia. I had always assumed on some level that psychology papers in journals were written by academic gods who lived on Mount Olympus. I spoke to a colleague about how one did a paper and where to submit it. He was very helpful and told me that one of the fastest ways to disseminate information to the psychological community is to present a paper at a regional conference. He also suggested that presenting a paper in this way would help me organize my thoughts and that I could then expand what I had written into a journal article. Most importantly, he encouraged me and told me that there were plenty of journals looking for articles.

I took his advice and submitted a paper entitled "Problems with the Diagnosis of Factitious Disorder by Proxy in Forensic Settings" to the Eastern Psychological Association, which was having its convention in Boston that year. To my surprise, it was accepted. I presented the paper and handed out copies to those who were interested. What I had not anticipated was the speed with which information such as my paper could make it onto the Internet. Soon after I presented the paper I began receiving calls from desperate mothers who had been accused of

224

factitious disorder by proxy and from their lawyers. For the first time in my career lawyers were offering to fly me around the country to testify in these types of cases. What I did not know at the time was that I had stumbled on a niche; there were plenty of experts who were ready and willing to apply the factitious disorder by proxy pseudoscience and testify for the prosecution, but I was one of the first mental health professionals to raise questions about the accuracy of this diagnosis. While this was going on, I did further research and expanded the paper. I submitted it to a forensic journal and it was accepted and published within eight months of submission.

Over the next few years, I testified regarding factitious disorder by proxy in courts throughout the country. I testified in one of the high-profile cases and began receiving attention from the media. I appeared on *20/20*, ABC News, and BBC radio. One of my cases was covered by Court TV and my testimony was filmed and broadcast, along with comments by the analysts on the quality of my testimony and presentation (thankfully very positive). I was also interviewed by investigative reporters from the *New York Times* and the *New Yorker*. While all this was going on I published several more papers dealing with different issues of factitious disorder by proxy. I also wrote a book entitled *Munchausen Syndrome by Proxy Reconsidered* in 2002. Since this issue was topical, I wanted to get the book into print as quickly as possible. As luck would have it, my wife is a copy editor and layout artist and we decided to self-publish. After receiving the books from the printer, we sold them off of our web site and also through Amazon.com. Although I am not sure I would recommend self-publishing to others, we did reasonably well with the book, and it still sells steadily. This is because it is really the only book that would be helpful to the defense in a factitious disorder by proxy case. Because of this, almost every lawyer who is defending such a case buys a copy, and many parents who are accused also purchase one. The book was reviewed favorably in a number of journals and was also mentioned in *Psychology Today* and several other magazines.

Since that time I have continued to receive referrals for assessments and testimony in these cases. Sometimes my work involves actually assessing the accused individual and other times I testify about my concerns about the reliability and validity of the factitious disorder by proxy diagnosis. I should point out that even at the point when I was receiving the most referrals of this kind, they were far from the bulk of my forensic work. But the notoriety I received regarding this issue brought me to the attention of a larger group of referral sources. It has been particularly helpful in the New England area, since it has expanded my referral network to include Maine, Vermont, Massachusetts, and Rhode Island. I should also point out that none of the methodological and scientific concerns I raised about factitious disorder by proxy were original with me. What I did that no one else had done up to that point was to apply issues such as the base rate problem to an emerging issue. If you wish to develop a specialty that will differentiate you from others working in your general area of forensics, you should be alert to emerging problems and trends and be prepared to seize your opportunity when it presents itself.

As with the juvenile competence assessment described earlier, I am including both the analysis of a case that I did for my American Board of Forensic Psychology work sample in Appendix C and the actual report that I provided to the court in Appendix D so that my approach to these cases can be understood.

Testifying in Court and Depositions

Testifying in court can be extremely anxiety provoking, but can also be intellectually challenging and stimulating. After all the preparation involved in deciding to branch out into forensic work, becoming skilled, and performing assessments, it could be argued that stepping into the witness box constitutes the real moment of truth. Testifying well is a skill to which entire books have been devoted. This chapter is designed to give you a general understanding of what is involved and how to prepare.

MEET WITH THE RETAINING ATTORNEY

Preparing to testify actually begins well before you step into a courtroom. Good preparation is one way to deal with anxiety because the better prepared you are the less you have to worry about. One of the first steps to take is to meet with the attorney who has retained your services to go over your testimony. It is important to insist on this type of preparation because otherwise you may find that the attorney is asking you questions that can boomerang and actually harm his case or he may not ask the right questions to allow you to make the points that you need to present. It can be extremely difficult to work with underprepared attorneys, and it is difficult enough to testify without having to try to do their work as well as your own. Direct testimony works best when it is choreographed in advance. I actually find it helpful to outline my testimony and provide the outline to the attorney who retained my services (however, do not bring the outline onto the stand with you, since opposing counsel is entitled to take your file out of your hands and look through it). When you know what to expect by way of questions and the attorney knows what to expect with regard to your answers, the attorney can give you the openings you need to fully explain your conclusions and how you arrived at them. Discussing the testimony in advance also allows you to alert the attorney to any potential problems in your testimony. Very often, it is best that these issues be raised on direct testimony. For example, it is important to raise any limitations on your data and their impact on the reliability of your conclusions in your direct testimony rather than having it come out on cross-examination. Bringing these limitations to the attention of the judge and/or jury serves several purposes. First, it allows you to live up to your obligations under the APA Code to make such information known. Additionally, it helps to reinforce the fact that you are in court to provide information and not as an advocate. Finally, if it is brought

228

out on cross-examination rather than on direct testimony it can have the effect of making you look shifty or dishonest.

Another important part of your preparation with the retaining attorney is to discuss how he thinks your cross-examination is likely to go. I always ask attorneys how they think opposing counsel is likely to "come at me." Since lawyers are better at legal strategy than psychologists are, discussion of potential cross-examination issues can be very helpful. The lawyer who retained your services will probably have a pretty good idea of how the cross-examination will go. Depending on what issues he thinks may be important, you may want to double-check your sources or download articles for review.

If there are outstanding issues regarding your fee for testifying, they should be cleared up with the attorney before you go to court. This is important for several reasons. Just as you should not do an evaluation on a contingency basis, neither should you testify before you are paid for your time. Either the attorney should have your retainer for testimony when you meet or you should make it clear that you will have to receive the payment at least 48 hours before you testify or you will not be appearing. Attorneys understand this and are not put out by this request; be very wary if they give you a hard time about this. Generally, unless the attorney is someone you really trust, you should not agree to be paid in court either before or after testimony. If you agree to this, you will often find that the client or attorney does not have the check, and in any case, being seen accepting payment at the court does not make a good impression. Also, in criminal cases, if the defendant is found guilty, he or she may be sentenced to a lengthy incarceration and will be unavailable to make payments and probably unconcerned about the bill. In other types of cases, you can become very unimportant to the client after you have testified and it can be very difficult to collect fees after the fact, particularly if the client does not prevail. For all these reasons, get your check before you testify.

As mentioned previously, there are evidentiary standards that are used to determine the admissibility of scientific evidence. You should know whether you are in a Frye or Daubert state and be ready to deal with challenges to your methods on either basis. For example, you may use an instrument such as the Gudjonsson Suggestibility Scales in a disputed confession case. You should be prepared to describe the scientific basis for the utility of the test, and it may also be helpful to check into whether it has been admitted in cases in your own and in other jurisdictions. It may be helpful to list scholarly articles that address the use of the instruments you used. You should be prepared to explain to the court the extent to which your methods are testable and have been accepted by the forensic psychological community and the error rate of the instruments.

You also want to go over the contents of your file and remove any attorney/expert work product. Work product is a name for those materials that were generated not as part of your assessment but through your communication about the case with the attorney. For example, the attorney who retained your services may have sent you a letter that provides you with a summary of his view of the case. This would be work product, and opposing counsel is not entitled to view it. These types of materials can be removed from your file and placed somewhere else. Obviously, you never remove or alter anything from your file that you produced as part of your assessment. In addition to being unethical, it is an easy way to look dishonest. Even if there is something in the file that may potentially reflect badly on you, do not change it. As Americans have learned through many political scandals, the cover-up always causes more trouble than the underlying offense. If you made some kind of mistake, be prepared to say so in a straightforward manner. Remember that you will probably have to appear before the judge again, and it is more important to impress him/her with your integrity that to score points in a particular case.

CUE BOOKS

Depending on your personal style, you may want to utilize a cue book in your testimony. A cue book is simply a three-ring binder with tabs that contains material you may want to refer to during the testimony. What you put in the cue book will depend on the types of cases in which you testify and what type of material you find useful. This is a perfectly legitimate method of preparing for testimony, since you are not expected to have memorized the entire psychology database. Should you be asked a technical question about test construction or some other relatively obscure issue, you can simply open your cue book and look up the relevant material. Materials that can be included in a cue book include:

- Articles on the specific topic on which you are testifying.
- Copied pages from test manuals.
- The APA Ethical Standards and Code of Conduct.

- Relevant legal standards.
- Relevant court decisions.
- Lists of references.

Some attorneys may ask highly technical questions as a way of trying to undercut the court's perception of your expertise. They may ask questions such as "What is the interrater reliability of the MacCAT-CA?"—something I would not expect the average forensic psychologist to know off the top of his/her head. Now, there is nothing wrong with saying that you have not memorized the manual and do not know the specific number, but that you recall that it has excellent interrater reliability. It can be more effective to simply consult your cue book and give the attorney the actual number. This has the dual effect of buttressing the impression of your expertise and also discouraging further questions in this type. There is a cue book written by Theodore Blau, Ph.D., and Fred Alberts Jr., Ph.D., which is commercially available, or you can develop your own. You may end up with several cue books if you work in a number of areas of forensic psychology.

PRETRIAL PREPARATION

There are several steps that should be taken before you leave for court. One of these is to sit down and carefully review the case file and your report. Very often a good deal of time has passed between when you did the assessment and when you actually testify, so it is understandable that you may not recall everything that was said to you or the results of every test that you gave. You should refamiliarize yourself with the case so that it will be easier to answer questions in direct testimony and on cross-examination. If you were deposed in the case, you should review the transcript of your deposition since your statements will almost certainly form the basis of some of your cross-examination. You will also want to organize your file so that when on the stand you do not spend a lot of time shuffling through papers. Depending on the size of the file, you may want to use tabs; this may not be necessary with smaller files. You should make sure that you have included three or four copies of your curriculum vitae (CV) and your report, since the attorneys may not have made extra copies to distribute to the judge or to opposing counsel. I personally organize my file for court in what I have found to be the order in which I will need the materials. I put the CV on top, since I will be using a copy during the qualification process. My report comes next, followed

231

by test protocols and my notes. Finally, I include the supporting materials for the case in roughly chronological order if applicable. Sometimes everything will fit into a plain manila file and sometimes one or more expandable files are necessary. I have had cases in which I had to bring several file boxes to court. When this much material must be transported, it is very helpful to have a collapsible luggage carrier. If you testify frequently, you will probably want to have several types of briefcases. When the file is small I generally carry a small padfolio. I have a larger briefcase that can hold my computer and an expandable file, and for a case with really large amounts of data I use my sample case.

There are many small details involved in going to court that can cause considerable problems if they are neglected. This is particularly true if you are traveling far from your office to testify. One of the first things you will need to do is get directions to the court and estimate travel time. You should print out directions using Yahoo! maps or MapQuest, and this will also give you an estimate of travel time. You can also check to see if the court has a web site. If it does, it will often have driving directions from the various points of the compass. Remember, though, that these maps are not always accurate and it can be helpful to have a good road atlas as well as the downloaded map. Also, bear in mind that there will be occasions when you take a wrong turn or get stuck in traffic, so you should allow plenty of extra time above and beyond what is recommended, particularly if this is your first time at this particular court. Also remember that if you are driving more than a few hours you will probably want to stop somewhere to get something to eat before you go into the court; many courts do not have vending machines or places to eat. I try to avoid eating too much fast food on the road and I often pack a cooler with drinks and reasonably healthy food for longer trips. You can stick a couple of power bars in your briefcase as well for emergencies, and it is probably a good idea to bring a bottle of water as well. If possible, talk to the attorney who has retained you about where to park, and do not forget to bring plenty of quarters for parking meters.

Before you leave the office, check and double-check that you have all the materials you will need to testify. You do not want to drive three hours only to discover that you have left the file in your office or have grabbed the wrong file. I have developed a procedure of checking the file before leaving the office and double-checking before I get into the car. This may seem a bit obsessive, but the stakes in these cases are high and I do not want to undermine the case through carelessness.

HOW TO DRESS

While casual attire is often acceptable in clinical settings, it is important to dress appropriately for court appearances. How formally you dress is partly a function of the type of case in which you are testifying. In local district courts or juvenile courts, lawyers, juvenile probation officers, and court personnel tend to be a little less formal as far as dress is concerned. Male forensic psychologists testifying in these settings can usually get away with a sport jacket, an oxford shirt, a tie, and a pair of khaki pants. My female colleagues have suggested that how to dress for court is more complicated for women, but there is some consensus. They generally suggest a simple hairstyle, light makeup, and either understated jewelry or no jewelry at all. Professional-looking skirted suits are preferred and wearing tailored pantsuits is controversial.

Criminal cases and cases being heard in superior or federal courts require more formal attire. Forensic psychologists should basically dress like lawyers in conservative business suits. Also, the court is not the place for whimsical or flashy clothing. While a child psychologist may find it helpful in clinical settings to wear a tie covered with reproductions of children's drawings or cartoon figures, this would not be appropriate for court. Remember that you are trying to present yourself as a serious, thoughtful individual and you should dress the part. I know that this runs counter to how many psychologists feel about outward appearances. As a field, we are supposed to look beyond people's superficial presentations and value what lies underneath, and it can rub us the wrong way to have to put on what feels like a uniform. But it must be borne in mind that part of what we are doing is performing and playing a part. You can express your individuality someplace else; in court you are trying to impress the judge and jury with your knowledge, honesty, and gravitas, and dressing properly will help with the last aspect.

It is also a good idea to have a complete set of clothing suitable for testifying stashed in a closet at your office for emergencies. If you do much forensic work, it is inevitable that eventually a lawyer will call you from court saying your testimony is needed in one hour. Signals may have been crossed or the lawyer may have simply forgotten to inform you of when your testimony was required. This has unfortunately happened to me on days when I did not expect to see clients at the office and was working on reports in jeans, a sweatshirt, and worn-out track shoes. I did not have time to go home to change and made the decision to simply show up as I was. Luckily, I was testifying before a district court judge who knew me well and my apology for my casual dress was accepted. Now I try to have a sport jacket, tie, and slacks ready to go at my office so that I can be presentable on very short notice.

ARRIVING AT COURT

Once you get to the courthouse, you should be ready to go through screening and the metal detector. Get your keys, spare change, cell phone, beeper, and anything else metallic out of your pockets and ready to go into the small plastic basket that will be provided. Lately, I have noticed that federal courts are not allowing nonlawyers to bring in cell phones, and they make you check them at the front desk. If I can remember that this is the case, I leave my cell phone in my car locked in the glove compartment. If I forget and do not feel like going back to my car I have learned a trick to keep me from forgetting my cell phone at the desk. I have the bailiff lock up my keys along with my cell phone. If I forget to pick up my cell phone, I will not get far without my keys and will be reminded to come back. If you are allowed to take your cell phone into court, check and double-check that it is turned off. In my experience, nothing annoys the judge as much as a cell phone going off in his/her courtroom. In some of the courts where I testify this will result in an immediate hundred-dollar fine, and in others the phone is simply confiscated.

Most courts have case lists that will tell you which courtroom to go to. Once you get to the courtroom you can let the bailiff know that you have arrived and he/she will inform the attorney who retained your services. Depending on the case, you may be allowed to sit in the courtroom and observe. In some cases, the retaining attorney may specifically request this, since he/she may want you to hear opposing experts' opinions and possibly rebut them. In other cases, witnesses are sequestered outside the courtroom. If this is the case, avoid talking to other witnesses or anyone else about the case. This is where having brought some reading material comes in very handy.

Remember the courts run on their own time frame, and are not particularly concerned about your schedule. It is quite possible that your testimony will not be reached on the day that you have been scheduled and you may have to reschedule for a later date. I was once called to testify in a juvenile competence to stand trial case in a local district court. In these types of cases, I am generally paid by the court. I was told to arrive at one o'clock on Friday afternoon. The judge spent the entire session taking pleas in other cases and did not reach us that day. I was told to come back the following Friday, when the same thing happened despite the fact that I told the juvenile clerk that the court was paying for my time and the bill was mounting. The third Friday I came back to court I finally was called to testify at 3:30 and finished up at 6:00. When the judge received my bill, he was apparently quite upset and had his clerk notify me that he wanted a private meeting with me in his chambers to discuss the bill. I told the clerk I was happy to come speak to the judge, but I asked that he explain to him that it was the long wait that had run up the bill and not my assessment or testimony. After this was explained, the clerk called back and told me that there was no need for the meeting. From that time onward I was hustled into court to testify the moment I arrived in the building.

If possible, see if you can arrange to meet with the attorney who retained you before you testify. For example, it may be possible to meet for lunch or even in one of the conference rooms at the court. The attorney can bring you up to date on what has happened before you arrived. It may be that an opposing expert has brought up a particular issue that bears on your testimony or has answered a question in a way that the attorney you are working with wants you to address specifically. It is also possible that they have criticized some aspect of your report or your conclusions and that this needs to be considered before you take the stand. Having a little time to confer before you testify will allow you and the attorney to work out how you will address these issues during your direct testimony. The attorney may also have got the sense of how opposing counsel is going to approach the cross-examination, and this type of heads-up can be very helpful in avoiding unpleasant surprises.

You may be called to testify immediately, or you may spend a length of time cooling your heels in the courtroom, in the waiting area, or in a conference room if one is available. Remember not to talk to any of the other witnesses or to opposing counsel, unless you have the permission of the lawyer who is working with you. Remember that no conversation with a lawyer is ever off the record. Waiting to testify can be almost as anxiety provoking as the actual testimony. It is important to be aware of your anxiety level without dwelling on it in a counterproductive manner. It actually took me a good deal of time to realize just how tense I was getting before testimony. One day I had occasion to consider my behavior while waiting. I noticed that I often paced like a caged animal. If there was someone to talk to I often chattered incessantly, and I noticed that I would go to the men's room frequently. I generally was not aware of any anxiety on the stand since I was concentrating so hard on my testimony, but I noticed that after I finished testifying and was excused, I often flushed and broke out into a sweat. Looking at my behavior and reactions from an outside perspective, it suddenly occurred to me that not only was I anxious, I was wound as tightly as a banjo string, although I had little awareness of this. This was particularly ironic when one considers that I am a psychologist and I am supposed to be attuned to emotions, whether others' or my own. Once I realized this I began taking steps to reduce my anxiety. The steps included stress inoculation and meditation techniques. As most psychologists are aware, there is a curvilinear relationship between anxiety and performance. A certain amount of anxiety is helpful even in complex activities such as forensic testimony because it keeps us alert and aware of what is going on around us. Too much anxiety can negatively affect our performance and presentation. Clearly, it is normal and reasonable to be a bit anxious when testifying in court. The trick is to find personal techniques that keep the anxiety to an optimal and manageable level. What works for me may not work for you. I find that reading helps, although it is generally a mistake to bring anything too technical such as psychology articles or books. Lighter reading such as newspapers, magazines, and novels are probably a better bet. Books on tape are good and you can listen to them on the ride to court as well. You can subscribe to Audible.com and download books on tape to your iPod or MP3 player. You can also load up your MP3 player with music and that helps to pass the time and distract you from the matter at hand. A Game Boy or other handheld gaming system is also a possibility. Do not forget to bring extra batteries.

There are a few last-minute issues before you testify. Try not to be hungry or thirsty when you take the stand; it is distracting to have your stomach rumble while you are trying to make an important point about psychometrics. Stop in the restroom shortly before you are scheduled to go on. The Duke of Wellington had this advice for his soldiers about what to do before going into battle: "Make water whenever you can." This advice applies equally to forensic psychologists preparing to testify. Also make sure that your fastenings are secure before you leave the restroom.

In addition to methods of passing the time and distracting yourself

Keeping Your Cool in Court

Joel Dvoskin, Ph.D., ABPP, offers the following top 10 suggestions for keeping your cool in court:

10. Two words: *ka-ching.* Or, as Steve Martin once sang, "And the most amazing thing of all . . . is that I get paid . . . for doing . . . this!"
9. Never apologize for getting paid for your time. If you feel apologetic, call a plumber and ask him or her to do something easy in your house. It will cure your guilt more or less permanently.
8. Try not to think of yourself as winning or losing the case.
7. Remember that you are just evidence—you know, like a footprint or maggots eating at a wound. It's not a pretty job, but somebody has to do it. (And see #10.)
6. There are at least two sides to every story. If every word out of your mouth supports the side that called you, you are probably not telling the whole truth, and you deserve to get embarrassed.
5. When the other side scores a point, which they will, concede it gladly.
4. Listen carefully to the question before you begin to formulate an answer. The best way to avoid being thrown off by rapid-fire questions is to maintain a professional and thoughtful pace. If you'll forgive a sports analogy, it's like stepping out of the batter's box. This is not the SAT, and you can take all the time you need to answer.
3. Tell the truth.
2. There is no such thing as "the truth." (Gotcha!) All you can do is state your objective opinion and the evidence upon which it is based. If you think it's "the truth," you're overshooting badly, and you will make the mistake of thinking the other side's expert is a liar, just for disagreeing with you. This happens frequently, and makes one look like a pompous ass.

And the number one way to avoid losing your cool is (drumroll):

1. Remember, it's not about you.

while waiting to testify, self-talk techniques can also be helpful. First, it is important to remind yourself that you are not the person on trial. My wife often wishes me good luck when I leave to testify and I tell her half jokingly that I am not the one who needs the luck. In criminal cases, I am coming home at the end of the day however my testimony goes, because I am not charged with any crime. In civil cases, I have already received my fee and will be able to cover my expenses whether the jury finds for the plaintiff or for the defendant. This does not mean that I do not want to do well. It is important to me to try to do well in any activity, and being a successful forensic psychologist is a big part of my personal identity. In addition, doing well in direct testimony and cross-examination in the case will often help my practice since it may lead to new referrals. But ultimately, the case is not about me and that takes off a great deal of pressure. Whether you are dealing with a criminal or civil case, it can be very helpful to remind yourself that you are there to assist the court, not to advocate for anyone or anything other than your professional opinion. When you realize this, much of the psychological pressure tends to dissipate. There is a tendency to think of yourself as trying to win the case. This is a mistake, because it encourages you to worry about making or losing points. If you focus instead on explaining what you did and why you did it to the best of your ability, there is much less at stake from a psychological standpoint.

Another thing to remember is that most of the time, the lawyers who cross-examine you are more afraid of you that you are of them. As I have mentioned earlier in the book, it can be quite intimidating to step into a courtroom because you are now operating on the turf of the legal profession and not in the clinic or consulting room as you are accustomed. You are in a legal environment and there is a tendency to feel that you are at a great disadvantage because you are not a legal professional. But by the same token, the lawyers who cross-examine you are not psychologists. While they may have taken seminars or read about the subject on which you are going to testify, you know a lot more about what you are doing than they ever will. While they may in some cases use clever cross-examination techniques designed to confuse you or trip you up, you are the expert on interviewing, testing, and other subjects related to your work as a forensic psychologist. You should also remember that if the lawyer cross-examining you manages to mischaracterize your testimony or box you in so that you cannot explain something fully, the lawyer who retained you will have the opportunity to undertake a redirect examination that will allow you to fully clarify what you are trying to say. In the same way, if opposing counsel starts to badger you, mischaracterize testimony, or otherwise act in an abusive manner, the attorney who retained you will likely object. Clearly, there are techniques you will need to develop in order to deal effectively with cross-examination, but it is important to remember that you are not at as much of a disadvantage as you might think you are.

Before you actually testify, try to get a look at the courtroom to determine the location of the witness box. If you do not have a chance to find out, ask the lawyer who calls you where it is when you enter the courtroom. You do not want to wander around the courtroom looking lost. Walk directly to the witness box and put down your folder or briefcase, but remain standing and wait to be sworn in. Either the lawyer who called you or other court personnel will ask you to raise your right hand and swear to tell the truth. If you are not religious and object to taking an oath that includes "so help me God," some states allow use of an alternative oath in which you affirm to tell the truth rather than swearing to God. You should let the bailiff know ahead of time that you wish to do this. Do not take your seat until told to do so. When you sit down, put your file on the desk and then acknowledge the judge by saying "Good morning" or "Good afternoon" and address him or her as "your honor" or "judge." If there is a jury, you may wish to acknowledge them by looking at them and smiling. Some experts will actually greet the jury by saying something like "Good morning, ladies and gentlemen," but this is not essential.

Your general demeanor when testifying is important. You should not be too full of yourself or pompous. For the most part you should be yourself. Harry Stack Sullivan made the point that a therapist should not try to take on a persona that one cannot sustain. As I mentioned earlier in the book, my mentor was Dr. Wilfrid Derby. Dr. Derby was a graduate of the United States Coast Guard Academy and had a distinguished career as a gunnery officer during World War II and a ship commander later in his career. When I met him he was already 68 years old. Like many officers, he had a very dignified demeanor and that upright posture that seems to be characteristic of those who come out of the armed forces academies. His short white beard was always neatly trimmed and in a tweed suit he looked like the quintessential college professor. He also had a stentorian voice and excellent diction. All of this, combined with his knowledge of clinical and forensic psychology, made him an ideal expert witness; nobody could have looked the part more. It is natural to try to emulate your teacher or supervisor. Certainly, the way I approach assessments and write reports is greatly influenced by what Dr. Derby taught me. It became clear early on, though, that I could not effectively emulate his style of testimony. For one thing, I was much younger and simply did not radiate the same gravitas that he did. I lack the military bearing and sense of command that Dr. Derby brought to the courtroom. And even if I did try to imitate his style, it was not something that I could keep up for any length of time. Over time, I had to develop a style that was appropriate to the courtroom but not too much of a stretch for me to sustain. My style is more informal than Dr. Derby's was, and I am a bit more animated and emotional in my presentation. In developing your own courtroom persona, you should try to be yourself to the extent that your personal characteristics meet the requirements of providing such testimony. Err on the side of seriousness and formality at first and you can loosen up little by little. A certain amount of trial and error will be required before you become at ease with your presentation. Once this occurs, you can spend less time thinking about your way of presentation and more time concentrating on making your points.

There are also certain behaviors and reactions that should be avoided in the courtroom. One of the most important things is to not allow yourself to become angry. Some attorneys can be very provocative, and it can be very difficult not to respond in kind. Many of these types of attacks are almost clichés: "How much are you being paid for your testimony today?" "You are not a medical doctor, are you?" It is important to have the self-discipline not to snap back when questioned in this manner. Other lawyers can be quite aggressive. One prosecutor who cross-examined me would start at the back of the courtroom and stride forward shaking his finger and barking out his questions aggressively, and he would finish up about six inches from my face. I believe this is designed to intimidate, but it only angered me, although I was able to keep it inside. Some attorneys can be nasty and sarcastic, and they do this even when it is a bench trial and there is no jury to impress. On one occasion I testified in an educational due process case and opposing counsel was someone who had cross-examined me before in a different case. While the hearing officer was changing the tape in the tape recorder that was used in lieu of having a court reporter, the lawyer glared at me and with a voice dripping with sarcasm told me, "It is a pleasure to see you again, doctor." I answered that it was equally a pleasure for me, and there may have been a certain amount of sarcasm in my reply as well. He then said, glaring all the while, "It would be an even greater pleasure to meet you outside of the courtroom sometime," clearly implying that he would like to settle his differences with me through fisticuffs. I experienced a small adrenaline rush and somewhat ill-advisedly told him that I, too, would like to meet him outside the courtroom and any time or place was good for me. Looking back at this exchange I feel silly; was it really advisable to meet in a parking lot somewhere and duke it out with an educational attorney? Luckily, the hearing officer missed the entire exchange; I do not feel that my response would have increased my credibility in his eyes had he heard it.

The only time I have actually really lost my temper in court was in a civil child abuse case. I was testifying for the mother who was accused of abusing her daughter. The lawyer for the local child protection agency was someone whom I already did not like because of her tendency to be nasty and abusive to parents who were involved in the child protective system. Throughout my testimony, she repeatedly tried to cut me off or force me into yes/no answers and also made repeated nasty comments about my evaluation and general level of expertise. After several hours of this she tried to cut me off one too many times, telling me to simply answer the question. With a raised voice and spittle flying from my lips I told her I would answer the questions if she would stop trying to cut me off. Luckily, the judge was someone I had testified before on a number of other occasions and he was getting annoyed by this lawyer as well. He instructed her to let me finish my answers and that was that. However, if I had been in a different courtroom my loss of control could have had a negative effect on the case.

One excellent book to read that may help in dealing with anger in the courtroom and elsewhere is Thomas Cleary's 1991 translation of *The Art of War* by Sun Tzu. This book is about warfare but has many applications to everyday life. Sun Tzu, who was a general during the warring states period of China over 2,000 years ago, stressed the advantage of careful consideration before taking action, stating, "Those who are skilled in combat did not become angered, those who are skilled in winning did not become afraid. Thus the wise win before the fight, while the ignorant fight to win." Applied to providing forensic psychological testimony, this can be taken to mean that if you are well prepared and know your material, you can set aside anger and fear and simply do your job effectively. In his foreword, Cleary notes that we often consider the angry man to be ruthless when in fact such a person is an emotionalist, giving vent to his feelings in a way that does not advance his agenda. Cleary notes that the truly ruthless man remains objective and uses his opponent's lack of emotional control to his own advantage. This is easy to say but harder to do. Perhaps the most important way of avoiding becoming angry and giving vent to your emotions in a counterproductive manner is to not take others' provocative behaviors personally.

I first learned the importance of this approach not in a court of law but in my family's restaurant. If you have ever worked in a restaurant you know that while most people are reasonably pleasant, there are always a few who cannot be pleased and who appear to be looking for an opportunity to be dissatisfied. They complain about the service, the food, how long their orders take, and anything else they can think of. At times I would be called over to a table by a waiter or waitress to try to mollify such customers. Sometimes they were so provocative that it was extremely difficult for me not to simply give them their money back and tell them to get the hell out of the restaurant. I would watch my father when he had a similar situation and I noticed that he never became upset or irritated no matter how obnoxious the customer became. I asked him to tell me his secret, and he explained that when people came into the restaurant they ceased to be people as far as he was concerned and became customers. The purpose of having customers was to sell them food and drink and realize a profit. He jokingly told me that he felt that they did not actually have faces but were bodies with dollar signs where their heads should be. Looking at the situation from this perspective, he took nothing they said personally and so never became angry. He did not lose sight of his goal and if this involved speaking to a provocative and obnoxious customer in a way that would ultimately settle them down, that was just part of the job. In the same way, as a forensic expert in the courtroom, if you stay focused on your role, which is to provide testimony to assist the trier of fact with technical information beyond the understanding of the average layperson, the shenanigans of obnoxious attorneys should not affect you because you do not take them personally. Your challenge is to make your points skillfully in the face of such cross-examination. If you remember that the process is not about you, then you are less likely to rise to the bait and respond inappropriately.

Another important point to keep in mind about testifying is that you should not be reluctant to say that you do not know an answer or cannot answer a question. You are not omniscient and nobody expects you to know everything. You may be asked questions beyond your areas of expertise, or asked to make predictions that you cannot make with any degree of accuracy. When this happens, tell the truth and say you do not know or cannot answer. Answering this way has several advantages. Most importantly, it is the truth and you swore to tell the truth when you took the stand. Also, evasions and equivocations make you look shifty to the judge and jury, and that is the last thing you want. Stating honestly and straightforwardly that you do not know the answer to a question helps the judge and jury to see you as someone who is trying to assist the fact-finding process rather than someone with an ax to grind.

While this advice and other guides to testify will help you, if you are serious about becoming an expert at expert testimony, there are other steps you should take. Try to review transcripts of your testimony or depositions to get a sense of how you sounded to others. When I first had the opportunity to do this I was surprised by how many sentences I was starting with "Well," and how often I was inserting "you know" into my testimony. Becoming conscious of this and getting it under control was beneficial to my presentation. If at all possible, you should listen to recordings of your testimony or view videotapes. It is possible to ask permission of the clerk of the court to have a colleague or a member of your office staff videotape your testimony, and permission is often given. In some types of cases, such as child abuse or neglect, such taping by non–court personnel is not allowed. Being able to view videos of my testimony in a number of cases had a tremendous effect on how I testified in subsequent cases. I made changes to my posture, the pace of my speaking, and the amount of eye contact I made with the jury based on what I saw in the videotapes. It can be difficult to watch yourself and you will need to have a strong ego, but seeing yourself in action is tremendously helpful.

You should look at the attorney questioning you when he or she asks a question, but to the extent possible, you should direct your answers to the judge or jury. This can be hard to do and takes some practice, but you should try to do it at least some of the time. You should certainly do it when you want to emphasize a particular point. Looking at the judge or jury when answering is a way of acknowledging that you know who the important people in the courtroom are and also increases the impact of your testimony. This can be difficult, too, during a heated cross-examination and is not always possible. However, turning to address the jury or judge is one good way of slowing down the pace of testimony and allowing you to think of your answers more effectively.

When answering questions, it is important to speak at a reasonably slow pace that can be easily understood by the judge and the jury. In addition, you do not want to speak so quickly that the court reporter has difficulty transcribing your testimony. I have a tendency to speak rapidly and I have often been interrupted in my replies by irritated court reporters who asked me to repeat what I said and to please slow down. Since I noticed a problem I have made a conscious effort to enunciate and speak more slowly, and I believe this has made my testimony more effective. I also try to pause briefly before answering in order to make sure I am answering the question correctly. When you testify, remember that there is no rush. You are entitled to take your time in formulating your response. Some attorneys cross-examine in a rapid-fire manner designed to make it difficult for you to give any deliberation to your answers. It is easy to become caught up in this and start replying rapidly, but this is a mistake. Years ago, when I was practicing judo I had a very deliberate style that emphasized counters to my opponent's attacks. I remember in one match my opponent was much quicker than I was and scampered around the mat like a waterbug. I started moving faster, trying to keep up. During a break, my teacher pulled me aside and told me not to try to keep up with my opponent in that way and to slow the match down. "Do not do what he does, do what you do, and remember—never let your opponent dictate the pace of the match" was the advice he gave me. The same is true in relation to court testimony. To the extent possible, answer at the pace and in the manner with which you are comfortable and do not let yourself be hurried.

In the same way, some attorneys will try to force you to answer yes or no to a question that does not lend itself to such an answer. For example, one common cross-examination question that has almost become a cliché is some variation of "Now, doctor, psychology is more of an art than a science, isn't that correct?" Obviously, a yes or no answer is not an adequate reply to this question. Some aspects of psychology are just as scientific as physics, whereas others really are more of an art. To lump all areas of applied psychology into either the "art" or the "science" category would not be accurate, and as a consequence this question requires a more involved response. In many cases, as you begin to reply the lawyer will attempt to cut you off, stating something like "A simple yes or no will suffice, doctor." If you do not feel that you can answer accurately with a yes or no, you may say so. In some courts you can ask the judge if you can clarify and you may be allowed to. Generally, if you do not feel you can answer with a yes or no the court will have the attorney ask another question or generally move on. Sometimes the judge will instruct you to answer with a yes or no and allow you to expand on your response, and sometimes your answer can be clarified on redirect examination.

Cross-examining attorneys will also attempt to cut off your answers if they do not like the way they are going, even if they do not try to box you into a yes/no answer. For example, an attorney may ask you a question such as "Doctor, IQ tests are not very reliable, are they?" My lawyer friends have made it clear that this is a very bad question to ask, since it is a principle of cross-examination never to ask a question to which you do not already know the answer. By asking such a question, the lawyer has opened the door for you to do several things. You should answer this question in considerable detail. You can show the judge and or jury that you are very knowledgeable about the technical aspects of these types of tests and about scientific methodology in general. In addition, you can lay a foundation to show that your estimate of the plaintiff's or defendant's intellectual abilities is quite well considered and accurate. So, once this type of question is asked, you may want to give a mini lecture about different types of reliability, what types of reliability have been calculated for the IQ test you utilized, the standard error of measure of the test you selected, and the sources of external validity that were used in developing the test. It is at this point that the attorney may try to cut off your answer, but you should feel free to press on until you have made your point or the judge tells you to stop.

At other times you will be asked questions that are so complicated and have so many dependent clauses that you will not be able to follow them. Questions may contain three or four hypothetical suppositions, all of which you are to bear in mind and take account of in answering the lawyer's question. Questions may be so complicated by the time you get to the end of them you will not remember how they began. When in doubt, simply state that you cannot follow the question and ask if it can be restated. Do this as many times as necessary until the question is asked in a form that you can understand. Do not worry if the attorney questioning you becomes irritated or even irate; you have a right to understand the question before you answer it.

Another common cross-examination tactic is to incorrectly restate something you said earlier in your testimony. This incorrect restatement may be subtly embedded in the question or may be presented as a preamble. These types of questions often take the form of "Do you still beat your wife?" For example, "Doctor, you stated earlier that psychologists were incapable of telling whether someone was malingering. Now you state that you believe the plaintiff was not malingering during your examination. How do you reconcile these two statements?" It turns out that what you said was that psychologists were actually quite accurate in detecting certain types of malingering although it was not possible in all cases to be 100 percent sure. When this happens, do not let the attorney push you around. Feel free to state, "Counselor, that is an inaccurate representation of my testimony." You do not have to allow anyone to misrepresent your testimony. Often the attorney you are working with will object when this happens, but be prepared to stick up for yourself.

Some mention should be made of how depositions differ from courtroom testimony. Depositions are taken by opposing counsel as a time-saving device as well as a way of getting a sense of what you are going to testify about. They can take place in the lawyer's office or in your own office and there is generally a court reporter present. The format is more relaxed than court and generally the deposition will include yourself, the lawyer who retained your services, and opposing counsel as well as the reporter. Sometimes a defendant or plaintiff will be present. There is no judge at a deposition, but your testimony is given under oath. You should prepare for deposition in the same way you prepare for court testimony, organizing your file and reviewing your assessment materials and reports. Bring extra copies of your CV and your report in case they are needed. One difference between court testimony and depositions is that the attorney you are working with may object to questions asked by opposing counsel, but then tell you that you may answer. Occasionally you will be instructed not to answer a question. All of this is part of the record, and rulings may be made by the judge after he/she has reviewed the deposition. You can dress a bit more casually but you should still look professional.

Part of the purpose of the deposition is to gather information about your proposed testimony at trial. For this reason, questions may be more freewheeling and may not be asked in any particular order. In depositions it is best to answer as minimally as possible and not give a dissertation when a simple yes or no will suffice. If you talk too much, you are bound to say something that can be used to undermine your testimony at trial, so answer questions accurately but minimally. You should also be aware that it is sometimes permissible to refuse to answer questions. For example, let us imagine that past substance abuse by a parent becomes an issue in a custody case. The attorney may ask you about your assessment of this problem in the parent and other appropriate questions. However, he may also start asking you about your own history of substance abuse or lack thereof. You can refuse to answer this question on the grounds that it is not relevant to the issue at hand. You may get an argument about this from the attorney, but do not be afraid to stand your ground. The attorney asking the question will threaten to bring the matter to the judge, who may refuse to let you testify on these grounds, but this is very unlikely to happen if the question is outrageous or really is irrelevant.

Clearly, no book can completely prepare you for testifying in court, and experience is the best teacher. You will have to learn for yourself what works for you and how best to prepare. As time goes by it will become more comfortable in the courtroom and testifying will become almost second nature. Keep these basic principles and practices in mind and you will do fine:

- Be well prepared for your testimony.
- Organize your file.
- Get good directions to the court and allow extra time for travel.
- Dress conservatively.
- Address the judge and/or jury, not the lawyer questioning you.
- Do not lose your temper.
- Do not try to be humorous.
- Take your time in answering.
- Be sure you understand the question.
- Do not be afraid to ask for clarification.
- Do not let anyone mischaracterize your words or opinions.
- Remember that you are on the stand to assist the court and not to advocate.

ABPP Work Sample: Competency to Stand Trial Evaluation

RATIONALE, METHODS, AND DISCUSSION

BACKGROUND INFORMATION

The subject of this assessment, John Doe, was 10 years old at the time of the evaluation. He was before the court on juvenile charges of arson. A review of the police investigation indicated that the alleged incident took place in a foster home where he was spending a weekend as part of a respite. John apparently took a cigarette lighter and set fire to the drapes in the room in which he was supposed to be sleeping. Mrs. X., who lives in the home and was supervising John, heard the smoke alarm, and her husband put out the fire with a fire extinguisher. Both the wall and the ceiling of the room were damaged as a result of the fire. Mrs. X. alleged that John told her he had set the fire and showed no apparent remorse. John was uninjured in the incident.

As a rule, competency evaluations are first sent to a forensic psychiatrist who works for the State of New Hampshire at the prison's secure psychiatric unit. If the defense attorney is dissatisfied with the results of the evaluation, he or she can request an independent evaluation; it is usually in this capacity that I enter these cases. However, in this case both prosecution and defense agreed to bypass the state psychiatrist and have me perform the competency evaluation instead. It was my understanding that this course of action was agreed to in this case because of the state psychiatrist's lack of experience in working with children and young adolescents.

LEGAL AND FORENSIC PSYCHOLOGY ISSUES

In New Hampshire, competency evaluations are governed by the Dusky standard and by a closely related New Hampshire case called *State v. Champagne* (1985). According to these standards, it is the evaluator's job to assist the court in determining whether the defendant has a factual and rational grasp of the issues related to standing trial, as well as sufficient present ability to assist the counsel in his or her defense. Since New Hampshire has no specific standards that address competency issues for very young defendants, the adult standards apply.

Relevant Theories, Research, and Statutory/Case Law. In performing competency evaluations, I follow the five-point rationale for assessment laid out by Grisso in his 1998 book, *Competency to Stand Trial Evaluation*. This system includes five objectives for competency evaluations: functional, causal, interactive, conclusory, and prescriptive. Since I performed this evaluation, I have found Grisso's *Forensic Evaluation of Juveniles* (1998) very helpful; however, the book was not available at that time.

The first objective requires a functional assessment of the client's ability to deal with the issues related to standing trial. I use one or more of a variety of instruments to satisfy this criterion, including the Competency Assessment Instrument (CAI) and the Fitness Interview Test–Revised. (The MacCAT-CA was not yet available at the time this assessment was performed.) Using the results of this testing, I assess the defendant's general understanding of court-related issues and gather information about his or her abilities relating to the 13 criteria laid out in "Competency for Trial: A Screening Instrument" (Lipsitt, Lelos, & McGarry, 1971).

If the defendant is shown to have a reasonable grasp of the issues involved in standing trial, there is no need to go on to the other objectives in Grisso's system. However, If the subject demonstrates significant difficulties with the functional aspects of the assessment, the next step is to try to uncover the psychological causes, if any, of the defendant's difficulties. These could include subnormal cognitive abilities, mental illness, neuropsychological problems, or malingering. If a recent psychological evaluation that touches on these issues is available, it might explain any observed deficits in the factual, rational understanding of the trial process. If not, I generally use a variety of tests to assess these abilities. These usually consist of a short IQ test, such as the Kaufman

Brief Intelligence Test (KBIT), screening tests such as the Kaufman Functional Academic Skills Test and the Kaufman Short Neuropsychological Assessment Procedure, and a personality inventory, such as the Minnesota Multiphasic Personality Inventory–2 or the Personality Assessment Inventory, to assess psychopathology.

In juvenile cases, I use the same competency assessment instruments, but substitute age-appropriate psychological tests such as the Millon Adolescent Clinical Inventory (MACI) and/or the Jesness Inventory, as well as rating scales filled out by parents or teachers such as the Behavior Assessment System for Children—Parent Rating Scales (BASC-PRS), the Personality Inventory for Children, or the Conners Parent Rating Scale.

In every case I conduct a clinical interview, and in most cases I administer a structured mental status examination. For this purpose I generally use the Mental Status Checklist series put out by Psychological Assessment Resources. In cases where I am dealing with a younger child, I may instead have the parent or guardian fill out a Developmental History Checklist, since this supplies the background information I need and is more likely to be accurate than the child's self-report. In using this method, I have been influenced by Richard Rogers's excellent *Handbook of Diagnostic and Structured Interviewing: A Guide for Psychologists* (2001). Using a structured mental status interview allows me to acquire a great deal of information about the client in a relatively short period of time. In addition, having used these interviews on many occasions, I am able to compare answers across clients.

For the detection of malingering I use instruments specifically designed for this purpose, such as the Structured Interview of Reported Symptoms, above and beyond those provided by the validity scales of the Personality Assessment Inventory and Minnesota Multiphasic Personality Inventory–2. In juvenile cases, I utilize the validity scales on the self-report inventories that have them, such as the MACI. One reason that I prefer the Behavior Assessment System for Children tests to the Conners scales is the fact that they have validity indexes. Having gathered information about the causal component of competence, I compare the individual's observed or assessed deficits with any difficulties he or she might have had with the functional portion of the evaluation, in order to determine whether there is a logical connection between them.

In order to apply the third objective of Grisso's system, the interactive component, it is necessary to take into account the complexity of

251

the issues involved in the case, together with the findings from the causal portion of the evaluation. For example, it is easier for a somewhat limited defendant to understand the issues involved in standing trial for simple assault than the issues involved in standing trial for a fraud case. In the same way, children and adolescents are tried in juvenile court, where the atmosphere is more informal and the lawyers and defense attorneys have more experience working with young defendants. This generally makes it easier for juvenile defendants to follow the proceedings compared to the faster pace of an adult criminal trial.

Grisso identifies a conclusory objective for competency evaluations, but recommends that it not be included in most reports. I have personally struggled with this issue in my work in the New Hampshire courts. I agree with Dr. Grisso that such ultimate issue testimony can have the unintended effect of focusing the fact finder's decision on the conclusions of the assessing psychologist, rather than leaving the fact finder to draw his or her own conclusions. In fact, I have known some judges to hand down decisions stating that "Dr. Mart found the defendant competent to stand trial."

Although I am not comfortable with this phrasing, it is clear to me through long experience that the judges I have worked with throughout New Hampshire prefer that I express my conclusions about competency in my report and in my testimony. Ultimate issue testimony is not precluded under New Hampshire law; in addition, the opposing expert invariably expresses a conclusory opinion, even if I do not, and the opposing side will likely prevail under these circumstances in which their expert states their conclusion and I do not. As a result, I generally give my opinion along with a tactful acknowledgment that the ultimate determination of competency rests with the finder of fact.

In addressing the prescriptive objective in Grisso's system, I attempt to determine through my evaluation whether there is any chance that the defendant can be rendered competent through treatment, and if so the nature and likely duration of such treatment.

ETHICAL ISSUES

There are a number of ethical issues that have relevance for the type of evaluation I am describing. Forensic evaluations require careful documentation. In addition, the section of the American Psychological Association Ethical Standards that relates to forensic work makes it clear that methods and procedures that are adequate to assess the issue at hand completely must be employed. This implies that every reasonable logical hypothesis related to the case should be examined closely. In addition, the defendant and his or her attorney need to be informed of the purpose and scope of the evaluation and the limits of confidentiality in the case. In this particular case, given the seriousness of the offenses alleged and the young age of the alleged perpetrator, I made it a point to go over all of these issues with the defendant, his attorney, and his parent.

CLINICAL DESCRIPTION AND BACKGROUND INFORMATION

John was seen for evaluation of his competence to stand trial on October 28, 1998. He was brought in for the evaluation by his adoptive mother, Mrs. Doe. Previous to evaluating John, I interviewed Mrs. Doe about John's developmental history and general background information. In cases such as this I prefer to use a semistructured or structured interview. In this case I used the Developmental History Checklist for Children produced by Psychological Assessment Resources, Inc. as an interview driver. I was able to obtain the following information from Mrs. Doe:

John was primarily referred due to the arson charges. However, he has a variety of other concurrent problems. These include being argumentative with his mother, behavior problems both at home and in school, and nocturnal enuresis. John is in a full-time special education placement at the local public school. He is in fourth grade. He is a middle child with two natural siblings. His family is supported by his adoptive mother's employment, and the family is middle-class. Mrs. Doe has little knowledge of the details of his early history. She does know that his natural mother was in her 20s at the time of John's birth and that he had a normal delivery. He weighed approximately seven pounds at birth. She told me that he was primarily cared for by foster parents and his maternal aunt. Developmental milestones were reached within normal limits. John was difficult to toilet train.

Between the ages of two and five years John was cared for by foster parents. His gross motor development was normal but he had difficulties in language development and he was slow to learn his ABCs. John attended infant day care, preschool, and kindergarten. He had behavior problems in kindergarten and frequently needed to be disciplined. His academic performance was described as slow and he received special education services while in kindergarten. He started the first grade at age six. It is reported that he got along poorly with his teacher and continued to have disciplinary problems. His grades deteriorated despite continued special education placement. Problems in many academic skill areas were noted, including concentration, organization, paying attention, vocabulary and expression, and subnormal intelligence. Mrs. Doe told me that his problems with behavior, academic performance, and distractibility continue up to the present time. At the time of my evaluation John was being seen for psychotherapy and also being treated for attention deficit/hyperactivity disorder (ADHD). He has sleep problems including refusing to go to bed and refusing to get up as well as unresolved enuresis.

Previous to my interviewing John, I was able to observe him interact with his adoptive mother in my waiting room. He was extremely active and needed frequent redirection. He was very fidgety and was pulling toys and magazines off the shelves and racks despite his adoptive mother's attempts to control him. He came to my office willingly but was very distractible. It was difficult for me to keep him focused on my questions and testing, despite frequent breaks and positive reinforcement for good effort. John had some articulation problems and was difficult to understand at times. After talking to John briefly about his home situation, hobbies, and other neutral subjects, I asked questions from the Competence to Stand Trial Assessment Instrument. It was very difficult to get coherent answers from John and I believe this was due to both his distractibility and his problems with language processing. I explored his understanding of the roles of those who would be participating in his trial. John was unable to name his attorney. I asked him to describe the job of his attorney and he told me that his attorney "tells me what your mom is going to say, she is the boss." I asked him to clarify this and he told me that his attorney would ask questions. I asked what kind of questions his attorney would ask him, and John told me he would ask "about the fire, did you light this fire?" John was very confused about the role of the prosecuting attorney. I tried to clarify this for him by telling him that I was talking about the attorney who sat at the other table at court. John did not understand this and appeared to believe that he would sit at one table with his lawyer and his mother would sit at the other table. John was unable to tell me the role of the judge. I asked him what the judge looked like and he told me that the judge and his case had no glasses and wore a black suit but John could not tell me what the judge would do in the trial. John was unaware that he was the defendant and when I explained that he was he told me that his job was to "say yes and no your honor, blah, blah." John was unable to tell me anything about the role of witnesses in the trial.

Nor could John tell me anything about how he might be defended against the arson charges or how he might explain his way out of these charges. I asked him what would happen if he moved around or talked without permission in court and John appeared to believe that he could do whatever he wanted to in the court while the adults were speaking. I asked him what he was charged with and he told me that he had lit a fire, but he did not know the formal name for the charge. I asked him if this was a big or little charge and he told me that it was a big charge and that people might be afraid of him as a result of this charge. I asked John about what could happen to him if he was found guilty. He told me that the worst thing that could happen would be that he could "be put in a prison with grown-ups until I'm 18 or 19, 18 or 20." I asked him if the judge could decide to go easier on him and he told me that he could possibly go home; however, it was clear to me that John was very confused about these concepts and did not really understand my questions. He did not understand what probation is and his answers were difficult to follow. I asked what he thought his chances were of being found not guilty and it became clear that he did not understand the words "guilty" and "innocent." I asked him what he would do if a witness told a lie about him the courtroom and he told me that he would run away.

I asked John about the events of the night of the fire to assess his ability to disclose accurate information to his attorney. He initially told me that he didn't remember what happened, but when I encouraged him he told me that he had set a curtain on fire. I asked him who had put it out and he told me that two fire trucks and the fire chief had done so. This was inaccurate since according to the police reports it was Mr. X. who had put the fire out with a fire extinguisher. John was able to tell me the name of the family where he was having his weekend respite. He told me that the police took him in a police car to the station and then took him home to his family.

My assessment of John's performance on the CAI indicated that he had severe deficits in both his factual and rational understanding of the issues involved in standing trial. Following Grisso's methodology, I used a number of psychological tests to assess possible causes of these observed functional deficits above and beyond the obvious factor of his young age. I assessed John's level of intellectual functioning using the Kaufman Brief Intelligence Test. It was my feeling that KBIT would provide sufficient information about his verbal and nonverbal reasoning abilities to meet the needs of the competency evaluation. In most competency to stand trial evaluations, whether with adults or juveniles, it is my opinion that a screening instrument such as the KBIT is sufficient to determine a general range of intellectual functioning and that the administration of a more comprehensive test such as one of the Wechsler IQ scales is unnecessary. On this administration of the KBIT, John achieved a vocabulary standard score of 78, which falls in the borderline range; a matrices standard score of 70, which falls in the mildly retarded to borderline range, and a full-scale IQ of 71, which also falls in the mildly retarded to borderline range. It was clear to me from the scores that in addition to his obvious problems with concentration and attention, as well as his youth, John's subnormal intelligence clearly had a significant impact on his ability to understand the issues involved in standing trial.

I administered the reading and spelling subtests from the Wide Range Achievement Test–3 to assess his ability to deal with written material that might play a role in a trial. John achieved a reading standard score of 72 (second-grade level) and a spelling standard score of 78 (first-grade level). These results indicate that he is two to three years below grade level in reading and spelling. These results are also consistent with his scores on the KBIT.

In order to try to assess John's emotional functioning I gave his adoptive mother the Behavior Assessment System for Children — Parent Rating Scales. I did not administer the self-report version to John because of his extremely poor reading level and because I thought that his adoptive mother would be a more reliable informant than he would be. The caution indexes of the BASC-PRS were all within acceptable limits. Critical items included "threatens to hurt others," "plays with fire," and "wets bed." John's T score (a measure of deviation from the mean score when the mean in 50 and the standard deviation is 10) on the Clinical Scales Overview of the BASC-PRS was 75, which is in the clinically significant range. He showed a preponderance of externalizing over internalizing behavior problems. John had a score of 87 on the conduct problems scale, indicating significant behavioral deficits characterized by disruptive and socially deviant behaviors. He also had a clinical elevation on the aggression scale, indicating high levels of hostility and verbal or physical threatening behaviors toward others. John's score of 73 on the hyperactivity scale was in the clinical range and indicates strong tendencies toward impulsivity. These scores were all consistent with his mother's report.

John's T score of 69 on the depression scale was only one point below the clinical level. Elevations on this scale of the BASC-PRS indicate that he struggles with feelings of sadness, unhappiness, and stress. His scores of 68 on the attention problems and atypicality scales indicate that he is in transitional range in these areas with high levels of distractibility as well as behaviors that are considered unusual or odd by others. John's scores on the adaptive behavior section of the BASC-PRS indicate significant problems in adaptability, social skills, and leadership. Taken as a whole, the results of the BASC-PRS indicate that John has psychopathology of the type and severity to partially explain his difficulties understanding issues related to standing trial.

In considering the causal component of the deficits in John's grasp of the issues involved in standing trial, my review of the police reports, my interview with his adoptive mother, my clinical interview and observations with John himself, and results of psychometric testing provide important information. The results of the KBIT made clear that his intellectual abilities were well below average, and results of the WRAT-3 were commensurate with his measured intellectual abilities. The results of the BASC-PRS indicated very significant emotional problems in a number of areas including conduct, aggression, hyperactivity, and attention. His scores on measures of adaptive functioning were similarly low. While I did not conduct specific tests to assess malingering (I am unaware of any for children in this age range), the BASC-PRS was valid and the results of testing were consistent with information elicited from the developmental history and the police reports. It was my opinion that these factors, along with John's chronological age, satisfied the causal component of this competency evaluation by answering the question posed by Grisso: "What is the most plausible explanation for deficits in the defendant's specific competency abilities described in the functional evaluation?"

The next component that needed to be addressed in this competency methodology is the interactive component. In considering the interactive component, I considered John's abilities and deficits in the context of the type of case in which he was involved. Some types of cases, such as embezzlement or bank fraud, are highly complex and require that the defendant be able to follow complicated arguments and remember large amounts of factual information. Other cases, such as some simple assaults or shoplifting, are relatively simple and place fewer demands on the defendant's cognitive abilities. In this case, the allegations were quite simple. John was accused of setting the drapes on fire in the room where he was the only occupant. Issues such as specific sequences of events or large numbers of different people being involved were not a part of this case. In addition, this case, had it gone forward, would have been tried before a juvenile court justice with a great deal of experience working with adolescents and children. In my experience in the New Hampshire district courts, the justices are very sensitive to issues such as the attention spans of juvenile defendants as well as their limitations in the areas of vocabulary and understanding of court procedure. Even so, however, in this case John was one of the youngest defendants with whom I have been involved and had, in addition, significant deficits in cognitive abilities, attention, and information processing. I had concerns about his ability to meet the legal standard for competence to stand trial in this jurisdiction even taking interactive variables into account.

RESULTS AND CONCLUSIONS

In the conclusion to my report I reiterated my findings that John was a child who had serious cognitive deficits as well as significant emotional problems. I detailed his long involvement with special education and the fact that he was diagnosed and was being treated for ADHD. I also stated that his diagnostic picture was a complicated one with elements of depression, ADHD, conduct disorder, and borderline intellectual functioning. It was my conclusion that John had very serious difficulties comprehending and responding to issues involved in standing trial. His problems in standing trial included his low level of cognitive ability, his chronological age, his emotional problems, and his difficulty with behavioral control. I gave my conclusory statement in the following form: "As a result, while the decision of competency rests with the finder of fact, it is my opinion that John falls far short of the standards laid out in Dusky and Champagne. In addition, it is my opinion that his abilities in this area are unlikely to change in the foreseeable future."

ACCOUNT OF CONTACTS, COURT TESTIMONY, AND OUTCOME

In this case, it was decided by agreement between John's attorney, the district court prosecutor, and the presiding justice that the parties would accept my judgment about John's ability to stand trial. I spoke only to John's attorney in preparing for the evaluation and he supplied me with the police reports related to the case. Because of the prior agreement between the parties, the court decided that there was no need for my testimony in this case. John was found to be incompetent by the court, and his attorney told me that steps have been taken by John's school and the local developmental disability agency to develop better plans for supervision and respite.

Sample Psychological Report: Competency to Stand Trial Evaluation

Psychological Report

Name: John Doe

Age: 10

D.O.B.: August 2, 1988

Sex: Male

Date Interviewed: October 28, 1998

Date of Report: November 16, 1998

Referral and Background Information

John was referred for court-ordered evaluation of his competency to stand trial. John is before the court on charges related to his having set a curtain on fire while in a respite home. John's difficulty controlling his behavior and focusing during his interview with his attorney, as well as his intellectual and emotional problems, led his attorney to raise the issue of competency.

John's adoptive mother, Jane Doe, was interviewed and also filled out a developmental history checklist. In addition to John's delinquent charges, she indicated that he also has behavioral problems in school and at home. John attends full-time special education classes. He is in the fourth grade in a public school. His grades are reported to be poor. Mrs. Doe reports that John has particular difficulty in the areas of reading and math. John is currently being treated for ADHD.

EVALUATION TECHNIQUES

Clinical interview
Developmental history
Competence to Stand Trial Assessment Form
Behavior Assessment System for Children — Parent Rating Scales
Kaufman Brief Intelligence Test
Wide Range Achievement Test–3

RESULTS AND CONCLUSIONS

COMPETENCE TO STAND TRIAL ASSESSMENT FORM

The Competency Assessment Instrument (CAI) is a semi-structured interview designed to assess issues that relate to standing trial. In this case I modified the vocabulary of the questions due to John's age and cognitive deficits.

It was extremely difficult to keep John focused on the CAI, as he was very restless and distractible. He often gave only minimal answers or simply stated "I don't know" so that it was difficult to tell whether he actually understood. I asked him about the roles of court personnel. He was unable to tell me the name of his lawyer. John told me that his lawyer's job was to "tell me what your mom is going to say, she is the boss." He also told me that his lawyer would ask questions about whether he set the fire. John seemed very confused about the role of the prosecutor, even when I explained that he was the other lawyer at the other table in court. John appeared to believe that he sat with his lawyer at one table and his mother sat at the other. John was unable to tell me the job of the judge, but did tell me that the judge has "a black suit." I asked John what his job was in the trial and he told me that he would "say yes and no your honor, blah blah." He was unable to tell me the role of witnesses. He told me that if a witness told a lie about him in court, he would run away. He seems to believe that he can move around the courtroom freely during the trial.

John does not know the formal name of his charge, but knows he was charged with setting a fire, and he is aware that this is a serious charge. I asked what could happen to him if he was found guilty, and he told me that he could "be put in a prison with grown-ups until I'm 18 or 19, 18 or 20." He thought that he might also be allowed to go home, but it was hard to follow him when he discussed this. I also could not understand his answer when I asked him about probation due to the confused and jumbled nature of his thoughts. John did not understand the concepts of guilt or innocence. He was able to tell me some of the details from the night the fire occurred, suggesting he is capable of relating these facts to his attorney. He believes the incident in question occurred "a few months ago."

BEHAVIOR ASSESSMENT SYSTEM FOR CHILDREN— PARENT RATING SCALES

The Behavior Assessment System for Children (BASC) is an integrated system designed to facilitate the differential diagnosis and classification of a variety of emotional and behavioral disorders of children. It was administered in this case to determine if John has any emotional/behavioral problems that might have an effect on his ability to stand trial.

This inventory was completed by John's mother, Jane Doe, and the results are based on her rating of John's behavior. Any scores in the clinically significant range suggest a high level of maladjustment. Scores in the at-risk range identify either a significant problem that may not be severe enough to require formal treatment or a potential or developing problem that needs careful monitoring.

Clinical Scales Overview. John's T score on the Behavioral Symptoms Index, which is a measure of overall problem behaviors, is 75 and in the clinically significant range. His problem behaviors are most often seen in disruptive externalizing behaviors and internal overcontrol. It should also be noted that John's score on the Externalizing Problems Composite is significantly higher than his score on the Internalizing Problems Composite.

John's T score of 87 on the Externalizing Problems Composite is in the clinically significant range. His individual scale scores indicate disruptive problems in three areas—conduct, aggression, and hyperactivity. John's T scores on the conduct problems, aggression, and hyperactivity scales are in the clinically significant range. He very often engages in highly disruptive and socially deviant behaviors, acts in a hostile manner that is verbally or physically threatening to others, rushes through work and activities, and acts without thinking.

John's T score of 54 on the Internalizing Problems Composite is in the average range. However, his T score of 69 on the depression scale is in the at-risk range and reflects some problems in that area. He tends to have feelings of unhappiness, sadness, and stress that may result in an inability to carry out daily activities.

Additional Clinical Scales. John's T scores on the attention problems and atypicality scales are in the at-risk range. He tends to daydream or be easily distracted and unable to concentrate more than momentarily, and tends to behave in ways that are considered immature or odd.

Adaptive Skills Composite. On the Adaptive Skills Composite, John's T score of 29 is in the clinically significant range. His scores on individual scales reflect some problems with adaptability, social skills, and leadership. John's T score of 27 on the adaptability scale is in the clinically significant range. He often has difficulty adjusting to new social situations and demands, such as changes in routine, new teachers, or shifts from one task to another. John's T scores on the social skills and leadership scales are in the at-risk range. He tends not to interact successfully with peers and adults. He sometimes does not work well with others, participate in extracurricular activities, or contribute to solving group problems.

Diagnostic Considerations. John's ratings are relatively high compared to the general population on the items related to attention deficit/hyperactivity disorder, combined type, conduct disorder, major depression, and oppositional defiant disorder.

Kaufman Brief Intelligence Test

The Kaufman Brief Intelligence Test (KBIT) is a short IQ screening test. The test provides vocabulary and matrices subtest scores that are equivalent to the verbal and performance scores of the Wechsler tests. The two subtests are combined to derive a full-scale IQ.

On the KBIT, John had a vocabulary score of 78, a matrices score of 70, and a full-scale KBIT IQ of 71. These scores place his current level of intellectual functioning in the borderline to mildly retarded range.

Wide Range Achievement Test–3

John was administered the reading and spelling subtests of the WRAT-3, which is a brief screening test for academic achievement. John achieved a reading standard score of 72 and a spelling standard score of 78. These scores both fall in the well below average range compared to his peers, and are commensurate with his KBIT IQ scores.

SUMMARY AND RECOMMENDATIONS

The results of this evaluation indicate that John is a child with significant cognitive deficits as well as serious behavioral/emotional problems. He has a long history of involvement in special education and is currently being treated for ADHD. His diagnostic picture is complex, with elements of depression, ADHD, conduct disorder, and borderline intellectual functioning.

From the standpoint of competency to stand trial, John had serious difficulties with the questions I asked him related to this issue. These difficulties stem from a combination of his low level of intellectual abilities, problems with attention and self-control, his chronological age, and emotional issues. These create problems both in managing his behavior during the interview (let alone in court) and in understanding the concepts involved in standing trial. As a result, while the decision of competency rests with the finder of fact, it is my opinion that John falls far short of the standards laid out in Dusky and Champagne. In addition, it is my opinion that his abilities in this area are unlikely to change in the foreseeable future.

Eric Mart, Ph. D.

Eric Mart, Ph.D.
Certified Psychologist

ABPP Work Sample: Munchausen Syndrome by Proxy Evaluation

INTRODUCTION

This case involved allegations of factitious disorder by proxy (FDBP), also known as Munchausen syndrome by proxy. I became involved in this case as a result of my familiarity with FDBP through a previous case in which I had been involved, and through my research and writing on the subject.

My first involvement in this type of case occurred in the fall of 1997, when I was retained by a local defense attorney to evaluate a woman whom the New Hampshire Division of Youth and Family Services (DCYF) had accused of perpetrating FDBP on her child. At that time I was doing a considerable amount of work as an independent provider for the Division of Children, Youth, and Families (DCYF), in addition to providing evaluations and testimony for defense counsel in child abuse cases when I felt it was appropriate. I had done a great deal of work in the area of child abuse and had also read about FDBP and attended workshops on the subject, but had not been directly involved in an FDBP case. Therefore, in order to prepare for my work in this case, I searched the PsychLit database for articles on the subject of FDBP and visited local academic libraries in order to read the full text of as many articles as possible.

The flaws that I found in the literature on FDBP led me to write "Munchausen's Syndrome by Proxy: Psycho-Legal Issues," a paper I presented at the February 1998 annual meeting of the Eastern Psychological Association. Further research led me to publish my article

"Problems with the Diagnosis of Factitious Disorder by Proxy in Forensic Settings" in the January 1999 issue of the *American Journal of Forensic Psychology,* and in October 1999 I presented "Factitious Disorder by Proxy and the Federal Rules of Evidence," in a poster session at the ABA/APA conference in Washington, D.C.

As a result of my publications and the experience I have accumulated on FDBP over the past two years, I have been contacted by attorneys representing mothers accused of FDBP in various states, as well as the United Kingdom and Canada. I have been qualified as an expert on FDBP in courts in New Hampshire, Vermont, New Jersey, North Carolina, Florida, and Louisiana. In some cases I have been asked to evaluate the accused, but the majority of cases have involved dissertational testimony related to motions *ad limine* (motions to exclude) and/or direct testimony in child dependency and criminal cases.

The work sample presented here concerns a case that took place in New Jersey. I was contacted in the summer of 1998 by an attorney representing a woman accused of perpetrating FDBP on her two foster children. The attorney, who had obtained my name through an organization he found on the Internet known as Mothers Against Munchausen's Allegations (MAMA), retained me to evaluate his client, to review the complete medical records, and to testify in court if necessary.

FORENSIC PSYCHOLOGICAL ISSUES

As I conceptualize this case, the first forensic psychological issue that needs to be addressed in my evaluation and review of the case materials concerns the specific nature of and factual basis for the allegations. In FDBP cases it is essential to review the entire medical record in order to examine this issue, as there is often a problem in these cases that is not seen as frequently in other types of child abuse cases. Specifically, the accusers often base their allegations of FDBP on what they consider to be a number of suspicious circumstances, but do not make it clear what they believe the parent did that was abusive or neglectful. Often, what I have called "the bill of particulars" is absent in these cases, and the allegations are based on subjective data that has been utilized without reference to probability or base rate.

The second forensic issue in this case concerns the purpose of the evaluation. As I see it, this purpose is not to determine whether a particular client matches the "FDBP profile," since I do not believe that

268

such a profile has been adequately researched and may not exist. Rather, the purpose is to gather information that may lead to the development of various hypotheses that could explain the circumstances in the case and the behaviors exhibited by the alleged perpetrator that have been ascribed to FDBP.

ETHICAL ISSUES

From an ethical standpoint, the issues involved in this type of evaluation are similar to those that are applicable to other types of forensic evaluations. The American Psychological Association's "Ethical Principles of Psychologists and Code of Conduct," section 7 ("Forensic Activities"), indicates that forensic psychologists must comply with all provisions of the general ethical code to the extent that they apply to forensic activities. In addition, forensic psychologists are required to base their work on appropriate knowledge and competence in the areas related to the cases in which they are involved. In this case, the basis of my expertise and knowledge was my thorough review of the literature in the area of FDBP and my background, training, and experience in the area of child abuse in general.

Section 7.02 of the "Ethical Principles of Psychologists and Code of Conduct" has particular relevance in this type of case. The code states: "Psychologists' forensic assessments, recommendations, and reports are based on information and techniques (including personal interviews of the individual, when appropriate) sufficient to provide appropriate substantiation for their findings" (American Psychological Association, 1994). This is important in FDBP cases, since it is necessary to review the entire medical and psychological files on the children and the parent in question. It is also necessary for the evaluator to avoid confirmatory bias and generate and evaluate all reasonable alternative hypotheses in FDBP cases. It should be noted that there are a number of well-known experts in this area who frequently diagnose individuals with FDBP without having met with them.

RELEVANT CASE AND STATUTORY LAW AND ADMINISTRATIVE REGULATIONS

It should be understood that FDBP cases are covered by the same local statutes that cover child abuse in general. There are not, to my knowledge, any statutes that specifically address FDBP, and this is important to remember in these types of cases. In many cases, the focus appears to shift from the issue of whether the alleged abuser did or did not cause a child harm or the risk of harm to a quasi-diagnostic issue.

CLINICAL DESCRIPTION AND
BACKGROUND INFORMATION

This case involved the assessment of a woman who was accused of perpetrating factitious disorder by proxy (FDBP), also known as Munchausen syndrome by proxy, against her two infant foster children. The client, Joan Smith, had been charged with child abuse and neglect under New Jersey law.

Mrs. Smith's alleged victims were African-American fraternal twins, a boy and a girl. The infants had been removed from their natural mother, who was incarcerated at the time of their delivery, due to her inability to care for them. The infants were born with congenital syphilis, and were also distressed due to their having been exposed to cocaine, alcohol, and marijuana in utero. They were found to be cocaine positive at birth, and they were born with extra digits, which were removed early in their hospitalization. Mrs. Smith took the infants into care some weeks after their birth, when they were released from the intensive neonatal unit at the local hospital. During the year that the infants were in her care, they were diagnosed with a variety of medical and developmental problems, including gastroesophageal reflux, asthma, seizures, and developmental delay. Toward the end of their year in Mrs. Smith's care, one of the social workers involved in the case became concerned that no one outside of the Smith family had ever seen any of the symptoms of the disorders for which the children were being treated, and it was at this time that Mrs. Smith came under suspicion as a perpetrator of FDBP.

An investigation was undertaken without the knowledge of the Smith family, and in December 1998, social workers from the New Jersey Division of Youth and Family Services came to the Smith residence without warning and removed the children. In my interview with Mrs. Smith, she told me that she and her husband were given no explanation for the removal other than the infants' illness, and were puzzled by this explanation since the babies had begun to improve physically at that time. She also said that when she called the child protective service (CPS) office following the removal she was told that as foster parents they had no right to an explanation. The couple retained

270

legal counsel and attended a meeting at the CPS regional office. At this meeting they were told that the children had been removed as a result of FDBP allegations against Mrs. Smith. Mr. and Mrs. Smith were subsequently charged with child abuse, and it was at this time that their attorney contacted me to request my services in this case.

CONTACTS

Although I made attempts to contact the guardian *ad litem* in this case, she did not return my telephone calls and as a result I was not able to speak with her. I also attempted to contact CPS. However, it was made clear to me by the state's attorney that the agency would not allow its workers to speak with me. As a result, my collateral sources of information were limited to Dr. G., who was the consulting neurologist in the case before the children were taken into the care of CPS, and several of Mrs. Smith's neighbors, whom I contacted at her request. In addition, I reviewed the complete medical and CPS records of the twins and consulted with Mrs. Smith's attorney in preparing my report and testimony.

METHODOLOGY AND RATIONALE

This evaluation involved a thorough review of the voluminous medical records in this case. In addition to a review of records and collateral interviews, the evaluation consisted of a clinical interview, a mental status examination, and several psychological tests including the Child Abuse Potential Inventory, the Adult-Adolescent Parenting Inventory, the Minnesota Multiphasic Personality Inventory–2 (MMPI-2), and the Shipley Institute of Living Scale.

CLINICAL FINDINGS

My interview with Mrs. Smith took place in my office on July 8, 1998, when she flew to Manchester from New Jersey. I began the interview with the mental status evaluation, utilizing the Mental Status Checklist for Adults as an interview driver. At the time of the evaluation, Mrs. Smith was 33 years old. She is half Caucasian and half Cherokee Indian. Her occupation of the past few years has been homemaker and foster mother. Mrs. Smith did not complete high school but did obtain her GED. She also said that she had taken some courses in business school. She reported that her major presenting problem was the allegation of child abuse through FDBP, which had led her to obtain the evaluation. She also told me that she was experiencing depression secondary to the abuse case.

Mrs. Smith appeared to be her chronological age. She is below average in height; her weight is proportional to her height. Mrs. Smith's eyes are blue and her hair is blond. She was appropriately dressed and her hygiene was good. Mrs. Smith required the use of glasses for reading. Her gait and posture were normal and her level of motor behavior was unremarkable. She was alert and had no trouble attending to the evaluation. During the evaluation Mrs. Smith's facial expression was appropriate to the matters being discussed and her eye contact was appropriate. Speech quantity and quality were normal and there was no sign of any type of speech impairment or articulation problem. Her mood was generally calm and cheerful except when she discussed the loss of her foster children. On several occasions when discussing this loss she became sad and tearful. Her affect was appropriate.

Mrs. Smith reported that she had experienced episodes of moderate depression frequently during the past six months prior to the evaluation. Her symptoms of depression included poor appetite, loss of interests, guilt, sleep disturbance, fatigue, and an initial weight loss following the removal of the twins. Mrs. Smith was not observed to be notably anxious during the evaluation; however, she did report that she had experienced mild situational anxiety frequently during the six months prior to the evaluation. Mrs. Smith's thought processes were logical and coherent. She did not report delusions or hallucinations, and gave no signs of these problems. She denied common compulsions or obsessive thoughts. She reported a phobia related to heights but did not find it to interfere with her daily activities. Mrs. Smith reported no recent disturbances of consciousness. Her attention and concentration were normal and she was oriented in all spheres. She gave no evidence of serious problems in language, either expressive or receptive. I estimated her intelligence level to be average.

Mrs. Smith told me that she was not receiving medical treatment for any condition at the time of the interview, nor did she have any concerns about physical problems that had not been treated. She is a nonsmoker, having quit some years ago. She reported that she does not drink, has never used drugs, and has no history of alcohol abuse. After her initial weight loss, her weight has stabilized and her appetite is normal. Mrs. Smith told me that she had developed sleep problems recently, including insomnia, frequent wakening, and restlessness.

With the exception of the allegations of child abuse and neglect, Mrs. Smith reported no previous legal history and no history of violent acts or violent ideation. Mrs. Smith is married and is in her first marriage. Her spouse is employed in sales. She and her husband live in their own house with three adopted children, aged 6, 5, and 4. The couple also has two natural children aged 15 and 11.

After performing the mental status examination, I interviewed Mrs. Smith about the case. She told me that on January 8, 1997, she picked up Babies A and B (as they were referred to in this case) at the neonatal unit of the hospital in which they were being treated. Mrs. Smith told me that she was under the impression that the babies had been on paregoric in the hospital and that Baby A had been intubated.

Mrs. Smith told me that the children were very quiet during the two-hour ride home from the hospital, but began screaming the next morning at 3 A.M. She said that the only way to soothe them was by swaddling and rocking them. According to Mrs. Smith, not long after this they began spitting up frequently. She said that the doctors who were monitoring the children told her to thicken their formula with cereal to help them keep it down, but this did not appear to help much. The babies were eventually diagnosed with gastroesophageal reflux disorder and were prescribed a number of medications to treat the condition. Mr. and Mrs. Smith also observed the babies having tremors, which they characterized as involving shaking of the limbs, staring, and lip quivering. Although the babies had normal electroencephalograms (EEGs), they were diagnosed with seizure disorders. The twins received numerous medical specialty consultations, including pulmonary, gastroenterology, endocrinology, developmental, and genetic consultations. It was noted that the infants had a variety of problems, including malformed ears, skeletal abnormalities, and asthma. In addition, it was noted that the children were developmentally delayed.

After interviewing Mrs. Smith, I administered several psychological tests. One of these was the Adult-Adolescent Parenting Inventory (AAPI). This test is normed on both abusive and nonabusive adults and adolescents. I find the test useful in determining whether a parent can at least articulate parenting attitudes and beliefs that are generally considered to be appropriate in dealing with young children. The test has four scales; the Inappropriate Expectations scale, which measures the parents' understanding of children's growth and development; the Corporal Punishment scale, which measures a parent's knowledge of and beliefs in methods of child discipline which do not involve physical punishment; The Role Reversal Scale, which measures the extent to which parents relate to their children as objects for their own gratification; and the Empathy scale, which measures the extent to which parents understand children's emotional needs. Mrs. Smith's scores on the Corporal Punishment, Role Reversal, and Empathy scales were all average to above average. Her score on the Inappropriate Expectations scale was slightly below average, suggesting some mild deficits in her understanding of children's growth and development.

Mrs. Smith was also administered the Child Abuse Potential Inventory (CAPI). I chose this test in order to obtain data about Mrs. Smith's propensity toward physical child abuse. Unfortunately, Mrs. Smith produced an elevation on the Lie scale of the test, which resulted in an elevated Fake-Good index and rendered the test invalid. It is not clear why she had such a defensive response set on this particular test, as she was forthcoming in my interview and her MMPI-2 was valid. One possible explanation for certain difficulties she had on the tests will be discussed later in this part of the work sample.

On the MMPI-2 Mrs. Smith produced a valid protocol with a single elevation on scale 7. This elevation, suggesting problems with anxiety, shyness, and guilt, was consistent with my general impression of Mrs. Smith. It was clear in the course of my conversation with her that one of the reasons why she became involved in foster care was that it allowed her to do what she saw as important work in a private setting (her home) with children, who are less likely to be critical of her or put her on the spot than adults might be. Considering the results of her MMPI-2 in the context of my interview with her, it was my impression that she had mild characterological problems of the dependent or avoidant type but gave no indication of more serious psychopathology.

I also administered the Shipley Institute for Living Scale in order to screen for general intellectual ability. On the Shipley Mrs. Smith achieved a Vocabulary T score of 46 and an Abstraction T score of 49. Her total T score of 49 produced a Wechsler Adult Intelligence Sale–R (WAIS-R) IQ equivalent of 93. This result was roughly commensurate with a partial WAIS-R, administered on January 17, 1998, on which she achieved a verbal IQ of 82; given the standard errors of measurement of the Shipley and partial WAIS-R, it is likely that her intellectual abilities fall in the low average to average range. While the Shipley is a relatively coarse screening instrument, there were indications from the Conceptual Quotient score that Mrs. Smith has some difficulties with certain types of information processing. This is consistent with her self-report of dyslexia and difficulties with school achievement. I would have liked to develop more information about this issue by giving her a Woodcock-Johnson or similar achievement test, but I was operating under very tight time constraints and had to prioritize my use of time.

CONCLUSIONS

Based on the results of the testing, Mrs. Smith appears to possess low average to average intellectual abilities. She has difficulty processing certain types of information, and this is consistent with her history of dyslexia and poor school achievement. In addition, she appears to have difficulties with word finding and a certain dysfluency in her use of language.

Mrs. Smith's results on the MMPI-2 indicate that she is a generally well-adjusted individual who has a tendency to be shy and reserved. There are indications that she has some fears of social interactions with others, and feels that she might not be liked or might meet with criticism and disapproval. Mrs. Smith has some symptoms of an avoidant personality disorder; however, there is no sign of any Axis I psychopathology.

Her performance on the Child Abuse Potential Inventory was invalid and consequently not interpretable. Her scores on the Adult-Adolescent Personality Inventory indicate that she is able to articulate child rearing attitudes in the areas of Empathy, Role Reversal, and Corporal Punishment. Her slightly below-average score on the Inappropriate Expectations scale was difficult to explain, given the amount of time she has spent rearing her own children, as well as adopting and fostering others. I hypothesized that this mild deficit might be related to her difficulties with information processing.

It is important to note that the main purpose of the psychological testing and interview portion of this evaluation was not designed to decide whether Mrs. Smith had or did not have the profile of an FDBP perpetrator. At the time I met with Mrs. Smith I did not believe that the presence of characteristics supposedly associated with FDBP was probative of Mrs. Smith's having abused her children, nor did I believe that the absence of such characteristics indicated that she had not abused them. This was because of the lack of scientific data about the reliability and validity of the putative FDBP profile. My purpose in conducting the evaluation was to gather information that might support or undermine any of the alternative hypotheses that I had generated in my exploration of this case. Some of these alternative hypotheses were:

1. Mrs. Smith was guilty of consciously inducing or fabricating all of the reported medical symptoms in the twins.
2. Mrs. Smith was guilty of consciously inducing or fabricating some but not all of the reported medical symptoms in the twins.
3. Mrs. Smith was guilty of exaggerating bona fide medical symptoms in the twins.
4. Mrs. Smith saw symptoms where there were none, due to factors such as misinterpretation of normal infant behavior or anxiety.
5. Mrs. Smith accurately observed medical symptoms in the children, which the doctors employed by CPS to review the records inappropriately discounted.

Although the purpose of the examination was not to decide whether Mrs. Smith had or did not have the profile of an FDBP perpetrator, it was necessary to address the issue in my report, since prosecution experts in these cases frequently use the FDBP behavioral profile to diagnose the accused with the disorder in order to establish a motive in the case. Consequently, I included the following statement in my report.

Although some well-known experts who specialize in the diagnosis of Munchausen syndrome by proxy contend that there is a characteristic psychological profile, this has not been established by scientific research. However, assuming that the FDBP behavioral profile has some validity, Mrs. Smith's profile does not fit this "characteristic" pattern. The scientific literature that exists on the subject theorizes that the personality characteristics of Munchausen mothers place them in the "Cluster B" group of personality disorders, that is, individuals with antisocial, narcissistic, or histrionic personality styles. Mrs. Smith's personality disorder falls in the "Cluster C" group, which includes avoidant, dependent, and obsessive-compulsive disorders. Her valid MMPI-2 results indicate that she is a shy person who has difficulty in interactions with authority figures. I observed some of this apprehension in my own interview with her, although she became more relaxed as the evaluation went on. Logic suggests that a shy person who finds interactions with unfamiliar persons aversive would not actively seek attention by fabricating illnesses in children under her care.

The results of the parenting instruments I administered also do not support a factitious disorder by proxy diagnosis. A parent who would consciously and knowingly subject her child to painful, invasive, and possibly dangerous medical procedures for her own gratification could be expected to have deficits in empathy for their child. Mrs. Smith's scores on the AAPI, however, indicate that she has above-average levels of empathy. Nor is her role reversal score unusual.

Much of my time in this case was taken up with reviewing the complete and voluminous medical files on both babies, which amounted to thousands of pages. These included medical records, CPS notes, and evaluations undertaken by physicians hired by CPS to determine whether this was a case of FDBP. I did not receive all of these records at the same time. Mrs. Smith's attorney had great difficulty with issues of discovery and it was only some weeks before my actual testimony that I received the last of the records. Interestingly, these last records were highly significant for reasons I will detail later in the work sample.

The case against Mrs. Smith rested primarily on reports by physicians that were provided at the request of CPS. One was written by Dr. C. on December 17, 1997, and the other was written by Dr. M. on May 13, 1998.

Dr. C. stated in her report that she had reviewed the records on Babies A and B; my subsequent investigation indicated that she had reviewed only portions of the records, and that important documents that might have influenced her conclusion were either neglected by her or not supplied to her. Dr. C. briefly reviewed the medical history of the infants in her report, mentioning that they were delivered at 40 weeks gestation by cesarean section and that pregnancy was complicated by maternal use of cocaine and a history of maternal syphilis. Dr. C. also stated that no problems were recorded in records of the twins' seven-week hospital stay after their birth. This particular statement, that no problems were noted when the twins were neonates, was important in the prosecution of the case. This is because it was the prosecution's theory that no medical problems were observed with the children until they began to reside with Mrs. Smith, and that the problems disappeared immediately upon their removal from the Smith home. There were comments in the record by CPS personnel that Mrs. Smith had falsely stated that the babies had been intubated at the nursery when in fact they had not been intubated. However, a careful review of the records revealed that one of the babies had been seen to be "blue and tachypneic" and had been suctioned with a tube on one occasion. This entry is important because it contradicts the contention that there were no problems observed in the children during their stay at the nursery. In a situation such as this case, one instance of falsification is extremely important. For example, if it is alleged (as it was in this case) that a mother is fabricating reports of seizures in a child, and this allegation is supported by statements that no CPS worker or physician has ever observed a seizure, one instance of a reliable witness observing a seizure is much more important than the statements of those who did not witness a seizure.

A related issue that came up several times in the course of the case against Mrs. Smith concerned her statements that both of the babies had been treated with paregoric while at the border nursery. A careful review of the medical records indicated that they had, in fact, not been treated with paregoric. When I questioned Mrs. Smith about her statements, she gave the following explanation. She told me that when she went to the nursery to pick up the twins the nursery seemed unusually quiet. Mrs. Smith told me that when she asked a nurse why the infants were quiet, the nurse said, "They are all on paregoric." Mrs. Smith told me that she took this statement literally, and since the twins were in the nursery she assumed the statement applied to them as well. It should be noted that there is no evidence in the record that any of the physicians working with the twins ever made any medical decisions or ordered any treatment on the basis of this representation. While it is possible that Mrs. Smith made this misrepresentation to the doctors consciously, consistent with a diagnosis of FDBP, it seems far more likely that this was simply an example of her somewhat concrete communication style.

In her report Dr. C. also noted a contradiction between Mrs. Smith's reports that the twins were spitting up and vomiting frequently and the fact that individuals working on the case did not observe these behaviors, nor did medical tests, such as an upper gastrointestinal study or pH probe, give results consistent with gastroesophageal reflux disease.

In addition, Dr. C. reported that Mrs. Smith had mentioned that the children had seizures, and "has described both grand mal seizures, and episodes of 'tremors' with staring and 'lip twitching' which occur frequently. . . . As far as I can tell from the records, no one but the foster mother has observed these seizures."

If Mrs. Smith had indeed been the only one to observe the symptoms, this would be evidence that would support a diagnosis of FDBP or some form of medical child abuse, and as a result Dr. C.'s comments in the report were of great concern. However, in my interview with Mrs. Smith I had asked her for the names of individuals who had independently observed tremors and vomiting in the twins. She gave me several names and telephone numbers, and as part of my evaluation I contacted these individuals. One of these individuals, a neighbor of the Smiths, told me that she had seen the babies vomiting on many occasions. In addition, she said that she had been interviewed by CPS investigators and had told them this, but felt that she had not been taken seriously. Another woman whom I contacted had done some babysitting for the twins, and she told me that she had observed tremors, staring spells, and frequent vomiting in both infants. This individual also told me that she worked as a supervisor in a women's shelter and was used to seeing these types of symptoms in children who had been exposed to drugs and alcohol during pregnancy. She told me that she had gone out of her way to inform Mrs. Smith about the tremors and had urged her to seek a neurological consultation. Finally, I spoke with Mr. Smith, who supported his wife's version of the children's health and told me he had seen frequent episodes of tremors and vomiting when his wife was not present. While Mr. Smith's objectivity might be questioned, it appeared to me to be a stretch to assume that he would allow the medical abuse of these infants simply to please his wife.

In addition to these contacts, even the documents that had been provided by CPS up to this point offered evidence to falsify the accusation. The caseworker who saw the twins just before they were removed from Mrs. Smith's custody had commented in her notes on the visit that one of the babies had "a few small amounts of emesis." While this observation does not suggest the kind of frequent high-volume vomiting that Mrs. Smith and her husband observed, it does once again falsify the premise that no professional had ever seen the babies vomiting.

Shortly before I completed my report, the court ordered that CPS produce the last of the records in the case. I was surprised to find that there were many more records of individuals who knew the Smith family and had observed the infants having episodes of vomiting and tremors. Of particular importance was a letter from a physical therapist who had worked with the children from the age of seven months. In her letter to CPS she stated:

> Please accept this letter to confirm that I was in fact witness to the profuse, excessive vomiting performed by [Babies A and B]. I began working with [Babies A and B] when they were about seven months old. I had discussed this vomiting with their foster-mother, [Joan Smith], and I even encouraged her to discuss this symptom with the twins' M.D. in hopes that with proper diagnosis and treatment it could be brought under control.
>
> I had been very pleased as the months passed and with extensive speech therapy and appropriate medication that the vomiting had been drastically reduced. [Baby B] had even gone through several physical therapy sessions without vomiting in the past month or two.

It was of great concern to me that this information did not appear in any reports produced by CPS or by Drs. C. and M. It should also be noted that the twins were removed shortly after the period of time referenced in the above quotation, indicating that they had already improved greatly. This piece of information is important when one considers that in this and other FDBP cases, the sudden and dramatic improvement of a child's medical condition after removal is put forth as a robust indicator of FDBP.

In reviewing the report written by Dr. M., I also found serious problems and misrepresentations. I believe this was due in part to the fact that he had not done a complete review of the records, but had reviewed only selected portions that were supplied to him by CPS. The documentation of the babies' symptoms by neighbors and by the physical therapist were apparently not supplied to Dr. M. He stated in his report that the babies' medical problems resolved rapidly once they were placed out of the Smith household, and that this was indicative of FDBP. In the last paragraph of his brief report he also stated:

> In addition, the entire constellation of features with multisystem disease, switching of primary hospital affiliations, the children who reported to have reflux but did not have objective evidence of reflux (actually at a

weight above their expected weight for height) all supports the diagnosis of fictitious [*sic*] signs and symptoms. Consequently, prudent care of these children would be to not return them to the [Smiths] and find alternative foster or adoptive care. In their book, *Hurting for Love*, Schreier and Lebo [*sic*] express their opinion that perpetrators of Munchausen syndrome by proxy continue to perpetrate the charade by compulsion. I believe these children would not be safe in the Smith foster home.

It should be noted that while frequent switching of doctors and/or hospitals has been remarked on in the clinical literature as being a sign of FDBP, Mrs. Smith had switched hospitals only once due to her dissatisfaction with a hospital's slow response to an emergency call. The switch to another reputable hospital was made with the approval of CPS, and one of the caseworkers from that agency actually accompanied Mrs. Smith to the new hospital to assist her with the transition of care. There is nothing in the record to suggest that anyone was concerned or had suspicions about her at the time of the transition, and in any case, one change of providers does not appear to meet the criterion of frequent transitions.

It should also be noted that the allegations against Mrs. Smith occurred in a context of conflict between Mrs. Smith and the CPS nurse/caseworker who supervised her foster care of the twins. Several months before the allegations of FDBP were brought against Mrs. Smith, there had been conflict between this caseworker and Mrs. Smith about rates of payment and the level of service to be provided for the twins. This resulted in considerable animosity between the two women. This particular caseworker was later praised in records by her supervisor for her tireless efforts to bring this situation (the alleged FDBP) to the attention of the doctors and other authorities in this case. This information was never alluded to by either Dr. C. or Dr. M., and it is not clear whether they did not know about it or they chose to ignore it. While it may seem improbable to suggest that personal animosity and malice on the part of a CPS worker may have been a factor in this case, given the extremely low base rate of FDBP, this alternative explanation may be no more farfetched than the possibility of FDBP. Although it is not possible to determine the base rate of situations such as CPS workers or physicians using the diagnosis of FDBP to undermine or injure a parent, there are documented cases of such situations. Because there is an ethical requirement for forensic psychologists to generate and investigate alternative hypotheses, this issue should have been considered, but was not, by the evaluating physicians.

As part of my data gathering for my report and testimony, I called Dr. G., who was the consulting neurologist on this case before the children were taken into the care of CPS. He told me that Mrs. Smith was always appropriate in her consultations with him and that he saw nothing suspicious about her behavior or the symptoms she was reporting. Dr. G. told me that Mrs. Smith had not brought the children in more than was necessary, and that the symptoms she described were consistent with their history of exposure to intrauterine cocaine. He also said that it was not uncommon for the symptoms of tremor, reflux, and the breathing problems associated with reflux in cocaine-exposed children to resolve rapidly at about one year of age, which is when the children were taken into care by CPS. Dr. G. did not think it was unusual that physicians had not observed tremors or seizures in the children, since he seldom was present during the seizures of his other epileptic patients.

COURT TESTIMONY AND OUTCOME

On December 22, 1998, I traveled to a coastal town in New Jersey in order to testify in this case the following day. I met with the Smiths' attorney the night before the testimony in order to discuss the attorney's direct examination and possible cross-examination tactics. My direct testimony the following morning began with general issues and moved to specific ones directly related to this case. I was qualified as an expert in forensic psychology, child abuse, and Munchausen syndrome by proxy with only minor questioning from the prosecution. In my direct testimony the following morning, the attorney for the defendant had me review my involvement in cases of FDBP, discussing my initial involvement in such cases through the New Hampshire DCYF, my subsequent research into the subject, my Eastern Psychological Association presentation, and my article, which at the time was scheduled to be published in the *American Journal of Forensic Psychology* the following month.

After being qualified as an expert, I began by addressing general issues and then moving to specific issues directly related to this case. The first general issue I addressed concerned problems I had observed with the diagnosis of FDBP. These fell into two groups: data collection and data analysis.

The problems with data collection that I discussed included the difficulties in obtaining discovery materials from CPS, the reliance of investigators in these cases on secondary sources, and selective review of materials. I expressed my opinion that a careful review of all medical records was necessary in order to understand the history of the child's medical problems and their temporal relation to parental involvement. Because many children diagnosed as victims of FDBP have complicated medical histories and often have bona fide complaints in addition to those alleged by the parents, the records are often voluminous, and CPS agencies are reluctant to produce the entire file. Whether this is due to the difficulty and expense of copying such a large volume of records, disorganization, or reluctance to share this material is difficult to gauge. In addition, investigators often rely on secondary sources, such as reports, letters, and opinions derived from someone else's review of the medical records. This reliance on secondary sources can have the effect of creating systematic error, since any errors or misinterpretations made by the initial evaluator are perpetuated and become accepted as facts when they may in reality be distortions of the actual material.

In addressing the problems that I had observed concerning data analysis, I discussed the problem of confirmatory bias, that relates to the failure by evaluators to develop all reasonable alternative hypotheses and to rigorously attempt to develop information which either supports or undercuts these hypotheses. In my testimony I stated that it had been apparent to me in my involvement in these cases that once the diagnosis of FDBP has been raised, all efforts by those evaluating the case became directed toward confirming the diagnosis. A related problem is the selective review of materials. Frequently the evaluator, rather than going through the painstaking work of reading each page of the record, instead selects and reviews only documents that support his or her initial theory. This is another way in which important relevant information that might disconfirm the hypothesis of FDBP is neglected or ignored. In these cases, medical records are routinely scanned for pieces of information that would support the FDBP diagnosis, whereas data that points in another direction are either given insufficient weight or ignored altogether.

In my testimony I stated that confirmatory bias is a normal human tendency that requires effort and a rigorous evaluation methodology to combat. Confirmatory bias in the case of FDBP is a particular problem since there are no clear exclusionary criteria, and those criteria that exist are subjective. For example, misreporting aspects of the child's medical history is considered to be a sign of FDBP, but there are no quantitative guidelines for how much misrepresentation equals substantial misrepresentation for the purposes of making the diagnosis.

Another issue related to data analysis to which I testified concerned the use of vague and unproven profile data in making the FDBP diagnosis. In my testimony I gave examples, drawn from my articles, about how the use of such data was likely to lead to a high level of false positive diagnosis. I also discussed the issue of the base rate problem and the application of Bayes' theorem to the issue of the misdiagnosis of FDBP. However, I found it difficult to get these ideas across in a way that was understandable to the court, which is not surprising considering the difficulty that many psychologists have in understanding these issues. Through the use of analogy, I attempted to illustrate how these factors were likely to lead to a high rate of false positive diagnosis. The example I gave involved the use of the tuberculin tine test. I explained that if an upper-middle-class American took a tine test and had a reaction, the physician would then employ the more accurate blood test to make the diagnosis of tuberculosis, but would recognize that the likelihood that the tine test result represented a true positive diagnosis was slim. In contrast, if a poor African villager received the tine test and had a similar reaction, and this result would be quite likely to represent a true positive diagnosis of tuberculosis. I then explained that the reason for the different probabilities associated with the same reaction in two different individuals had to do with the different base rates of the disease in the two populations. Because of the extremely low incidence of TB in the upper-middle-class American population, the likelihood of a false positive result was actually higher than the incidence of tuberculosis in this group, which lent itself to false positive diagnosis. However, in the African village the rate of tuberculosis was probably high enough that the likelihood of a true positive diagnosis using this test was far greater than the false positive rate of the test. I related this example to the empirical literature on the subject of FDBP, which indicates that the disease is extremely rare and therefore likely to be overdiagnosed, particularly because the diagnostic criteria and methods used for the diagnosis are so imprecise.

In moving to specific issues directly related to this case, the bulk of my direct testimony concerned the relationship of the general issues regarding data collection and analysis to the actual facts of the allegations against Mrs. Smith. I have detailed most of these issues in my discussion of the report I submitted to the court, such as the fact that numerous individuals had in fact seen many of the symptoms that were alleged to be factitious in nature, as well as other alternative explanations for data supposedly pointing to FDBP as the most likely reason for the twins' difficulties. I also included other examples in which important data had been neglected in the case against Mrs. Smith. For example, one of the ways in which Mrs. Smith's account of the male twin's medical history was alleged to have been at variance with the actual medical record concerned her statement that there had been some suspicion that the child may have had a pituitary tumor. The report of the CPS worker stated that there was no record of this suspicion, and that the MRI that was performed showed no sign of such a tumor. However, a careful review of the records revealed that when the MRI had been performed, the radiologist who first read the films had seen what he thought was a mass in the region of the pituitary and recommended further tests to determine whether it was malignant or benign. It was only after a second radiologist reviewed the films that the possibility of a tumor was ruled out. It is not clear when or if this information was given to the mother, but her statement at the time it was made appears to have been accurate. Consequently, any conclusions about the mother's veracity in her reporting of the medical history of the child that were based on this particular issue were incorrect. I pointed out to the court that while as a psychologist I am not qualified to evaluate an MRI, the sequence, timing, and conclusions about the presence or absence of a particular symptom or condition can be assessed, and this example demonstrates the importance of such an assessment.

My cross-examination by the CPS attorney was surprisingly limited, in that he focused most of his energy on pointing out that I was not a medical doctor and had not examined the twins independently. I acknowledged that medical diagnosis was outside of my scope of practice and that I had made this clear on direct examination. I should point out that the CPS attorney had made no attempt to contact me in advance of the trial to ask questions about my report or to obtain the contents of my file on Mrs. Smith, and as a result I believe he was unprepared for my testimony. One of the problems for the prosecution in this case was that I was the only expert in the case who had actually been qualified as an expert on FDBP in any jurisdiction, and I was also the only expert in the case who had presented a peer-reviewed paper at a major conference.

The guardian *ad litem* in the case asked only one or two questions, which were designed to clarify some aspect of my testimony. To my surprise, it was the judge who asked the most difficult questions of me and offered the most resistance to my conclusions. In my experience, it is not unusual for judges in these types of cases to ask a few questions to clarify points of the expert's testimony. In this case, however, the judge spent 45 minutes in what I can only describe as a vigorous cross-examination of my statements in direct testimony, which for me was unprecedented. Among other things, she asked me how it was that the medical doctors who had testified in the case had stated that FDBP is underdiagnosed while I appeared to be stating that it was most likely overdiagnosed. I told her that, unlike the physicians in this case, I am a forensic scientist. I explained that the majority of physicians are trained in an apprentice model and generally do not have extensive experience or course work in statistics or scientific methodology. I explained to the judge that I had based my estimate of the base rate of FDBP on the handful of empirical articles available on the subject, and that in every case the indications were that FDBP was extremely rare. I also explained that I took my responsibility as an expert witness to supply the court with scientific and technical information very seriously and felt it was best to rely on scientific data rather than clinical judgment or hunches. In response to further questions on the subject I told the judge that if she asked any physician what would happen in the abstract if a medical condition was extremely rare and tests used to diagnose it were imprecise, they would almost certainly tell her that the condition would be overdiagnosed. It was my opinion that it was unfortunate that CPS and the physicians in this case appeared to be neglecting this principle of diagnosis.

It was six months before I heard about the verdict in the case from the attorney for the Smiths. The judge had stated in her opinion that she had heard conflicting testimony about the issue of FDBP in the case and that she had serious doubts that Mrs. Smith had intentionally done anything to harm the twins. However, she pointed out that under the controlling statute in the state of New Jersey, if the parent exposed the child to potentially harmful medications and medical procedures, this constituted abuse even if it was unintentional and done for what the parent believed were the best reasons. Consequently, the abuse case against Mrs. Smith was founded (i.e., the judge found abuse or neglect to be present). It should also be noted that the twins had been living in a new foster home for over a year at this point and were adjusting well.

In the state of New Jersey, if one child in a family is deemed to be abused or at risk, all of the children in the family are considered to be at risk. Under the circumstances, Mrs. Smith could have lost not only the twins but her other children, both natural and adopted, and it is clear from the record that CPS had considered removing the other children. However, the judge closed the case after her verdict, preventing this from occurring. While I am no longer privy to the ongoing developments in this case, Mrs. Smith's attorney told me that Mrs. Smith had found another lawyer and was pursuing an appeal.

Sample Psychological Report: Munchausen Syndrome by Proxy Evaluation

PSYCHOLOGICAL REPORT

Name: Joan Smith
Age: 33
D.O.B.: June 8, 1965
Sex: Female

Date Interviewed: July 8, 1998
Date of Report: October 12, 1998

REFERRAL AND BACKGROUND INFORMATION

Joan Smith was referred for evaluation by her attorney. She is at present involved in a child abuse/neglect case with the New Jersey child protective service (CPS) agency. The case involves two African-American twin infants who were cared for by Mrs. Smith and her husband. The infants were approximately seven weeks old when the Smiths took them into their home as foster children, and they lived with the Smiths for about 11 months. They were removed by CPS when the caseworkers involved in monitoring the children began to suspect that Mrs. Smith was suffering from Munchausen syndrome by proxy or factitious disorder by proxy (FDBP). This allegation was based on what CPS workers believed was evidence that Mrs. Smith had provided the children's physicians with inaccurate information about their medical history, and had possibly fabricated symptoms of developmental delay, asthma or respiratory problems, seizures or tremors, and esophageal reflux. CPS documents also indicate that caseworkers believed that the children's health status improved dramatically when they were removed from the Smiths' house, and that this supports the diagnosis of Munchausen syndrome by proxy.

This evaluation consists of a psychological assessment of Mrs. Smith's cognitive and emotional status and of her parenting ability as measured by standardized instruments, as well as an examination of the methodology used by CPS caseworkers and providers in arriving at this diagnosis. In addition, I have included a copy of my paper "Problems with the Diagnosis of Factitious Disorder by Proxy in Forensic Settings." A shorter version of this paper was presented at the Eastern Psychological Association's annual meeting in Boston in February 1998, and the attached version will be published in a forthcoming issue of the *American Journal of Forensic Psychology*.

EVALUATION TECHNIQUES

Clinical interview
Mental status examination
Adult-Adolescent Parenting Inventory
Child Abuse Potential Inventory
Minnesota Multiphasic Personality Inventory–2
Shipley Institute of Living Scale

In addition to the results of structured interviews and psychometric testing, my conclusions in this report are based on telephone interviews with collateral data sources and on my review of the voluminous medical and social documentation of the children (hereafter referred to individually as Babies A and B, A being the male and B being the female), which was provided under seal by CPS.

RESULTS OF THE INTERVIEW

Mrs. Smith told me in our interview that the children were seven weeks old when she took them into her care. They had been removed from their natural mother, who had abused substances including alcohol and cocaine during her pregnancy. According to Mrs. Smith, the birth mother had had only two prenatal visits during the children's gestation, and had also spent time in jail during the pregnancy. Mrs. Smith reported to me that she has two natural children aged 15 and 11, and three adopted children aged 6, 5, and 4. In addition, she reported that she has provided foster care for approximately 11 children in five years.

Mrs. Smith told me that the children were found to be positive for cocaine at birth and suffered from congenital syphilis. In addition, both infants had extra digits, which were removed before the Smiths took them into care. No other problems were related to her by CPS. Mrs. Smith told me that on the day she first took them home the children were very quiet during the two-hour drive from Newark to her home. However, she said that at 3:00 A.M. the following morning the twins began crying and screaming, but said that it seemed to help when she swaddled and rocked them. She reported that soon after this the twins began to spit up frequently, and were seen by doctors one week later.

According to Mrs. Smith, after she discussed the twins' continued vomiting with doctors, she was told to adjust the feeding position and thicken the formula with cereal. She reported that in February the twins were diagnosed with esophageal reflux and were put on medication for this. She also noted that the children were suffering from tremors, which caused their lips to quiver. Their doctor attributed this to cocaine withdrawal. An electroencephalogram was done at this time, and the results were normal. An MRI showed the possibility of some type of tumor or shadow on Baby A's pituitary, but a subsequent reading of the images by another doctor ruled out a problem in this area.

Around the beginning of August 1997, Mrs. Smith became dissatisfied with the response of the Cooper Hospital to what she believed was some type of seizure that one of the children was having. She told her social worker, who arranged for the children to go to the Dupont Pen Mart Clinic, and accompanied her to the hospital with the records of the twins. The children received various evaluations there, including pulmonary, gastrointestinal, neurological, developmental, and genetic consults. Between August and December, the children's asthma was treated with various medications and the use of a nebulizer. At the end of August they were given electroencephalograms. They were seen by Dr. G., a neurologist, and were placed on phenobarbital. According to Mrs. Smith, for the next seven or eight months the twins exhibited tremors and shakes, and Mr. Smith thought he observed one of the children foaming at the mouth. Mrs. Smith reported that on November 14 or 15, 1997, Baby A began wheezing. He was given a nebulizer treatment, but it did not help and he would not eat. At this point the home health care aide arrived and saw the child wheezing. The baby was taken to the hospital emergency room, where he was given oxygen and further breathing treatments. On December 3, Baby B underwent a sleep study and a bowel biopsy. Mild apnea was noted, but the doctors did not feel that there was a need for an apnea monitor.

Mrs. Smith reported that on December 29, 1997, CPS workers took the children back into care without explanation, other than to say that they were sick. Mrs. Smith stated that the children's various conditions were at this point beginning to improve.

RESULTS OF TESTING

MENTAL STATUS EXAMINATION

Presenting Problem. Ms. Smith is a 33-year old white female who was referred for evaluation by her attorney. She was evaluated in my office. Mrs. Smith's major presenting problem was reported as being allegations of factitious disorder by proxy. Other concurrent problems include depression.

Physical and Behavioral Description. Mrs. Smith's appearance is consistent with her stated age. She is of below-average height and of average weight for her build. Her eyes are blue; color of hair is blond. Mrs. Smith's manner of dress was appropriate to the office setting and her hygiene appeared to be good. In completing the interview, she required the use of glasses. Mrs. Smith's gait, posture, and motor behavior during the interview were normal.

During the interview Mrs. Smith was alert, and her level of responsiveness did not show obvious effects of pain, medications, or drugs. There were no overt signs of distress during the interview. Mrs. Smith's facial expression was appropriate to the content of the interview topic.

Eye contact during the interview was appropriately focused. Speech quantity, both spontaneously and in response to questions, was normal. Speech quality was normal.

Emotional Status. Mrs. Smith's mood was calm and cheerful. Her affect, or emotional responsiveness, was appropriate to the content of the discussion. She reported current feelings of moderate depression, and indicated that she had experienced frequent episodes of depression in the past six months. Of the common specific symptoms of depression, Mrs. Smith reported experiencing poor appetite, the loss of usual interests, guilt, sleep disturbance, fatigue, and weight loss. No signs of

292

anxiety were observed during the interview. Mrs. Smith admitted to mild feelings of anxiety and reported experiencing episodes of anxiety frequently in the previous six months. Review of common symptoms of anxiety revealed that Mrs. Smith experiences excessive sweating.

Mrs. Smith's thought processes were logical and coherent. Content of thought focused on concerns regarding the presenting problem. There were no indications of the presence of delusions, common compulsions, or obsessive thoughts. She reported that she suffers from a persistent, irrational fear of heights. Auditory, visual, and olfactory hallucinations were denied. Mrs. Smith has no recent history of loss of consciousness, seizures, or blackouts.

Evaluation of cognitive processes indicated that Mrs. Smith's attention and concentration skills were normal. She was oriented for person, place, and time. Immediate, recent, and remote memories were intact. No amnesia was reported. There was no evidence of unconscious fabrication of responses, as sometimes occurs with memory disorders. Mrs. Smith's intellectual ability was estimated as being in the average range. There was no indication of notable decline of intellectual ability. Computational skills were judged to be within normal limits. Evaluation of language skills revealed no evidence of aphasia. There was no obvious evidence of other cognitive deficits typically associated with brain dysfunction.

Health and Habits. Review of Mrs. Smith's medical status revealed that she is not currently being treated for any medical disorder. She reported no concerns about medical problems. She is a former smoker. She denied any use of alcohol or illicit drugs. There has been a recent change in Mrs. Smith's sleep pattern, which is now marked by insomnia, frequent awakening, and restlessness.

Legal Issues/Aggressive Behavior. Mrs. Smith reported no previous history of significant legal problems. She denied any history of suicide attempts or violent acts toward others, including family members. Current thoughts of self-injury or violence to others were denied. Her demeanor during the interview gave no indication of aggressive or violent behavior.

Current Living Situation. Review of Mrs. Smith's current living situation reveals that she is presently working at home. According to Mrs. Smith, she obtained her high school equivalency degree and attended business school. She is in her first marriage. Her husband is employed in sales. The Smiths live in a house with their two natural children and three adopted children. Mrs. Smith described the quality of the marital and family relationships as being good.

Adult-Adolescent Parenting Inventory

The AAPI is designed to evaluate a parent's stated attitudes about parenting and compare them to attitudes of both normal and abusive parents. Parents who demonstrate deficits on the AAPI are very likely to exhibit those deficits in their interactions with their offspring.

The test is scored on four clinical scales. The Inappropriate Expectations scale measures the parent's knowledge of child growth and development; the Empathy scale assesses the parent's ability to nurture a child and to understand his or her needs; the Corporal Punishment scale indicates the parent's attitudes toward physical force in dealing with children; the Role Reversal scale measures the parent's tendency to use children to satisfy his or her own needs.

Mrs. Smith's score on the Inappropriate Expectations scale of the AAPI was slightly below average compared to nonabusive parents. Individuals with low scores on the Inappropriate Expectations scale may show a lack of understanding of children's developmental capabilities, and may expect their children to achieve at a higher level than they are capable of. These individuals may feel personally inadequate or may feel inadequate as parents, and may judge their own competence as parents by their children's achievements.

Mrs. Smith's score on the Empathy scale was above average, suggesting that she has better than average ability to understand children's needs and meet their needs in this area. Her score on the Corporal Punishment scale was above average and indicates that she does not endorse physical coercion as a means of dealing with children's problem behaviors. Mrs. Smith's score on the Role Reversal scale of the AAPI was average, indicating that she does not use her children as objects for her own gratification.

Child Abuse Potential Inventory

The Child Abuse Potential Inventory (CAPI) is a 160-question test designed for use as a screening tool in detecting actual or potential physical child abuse by individuals who are reported and investigated for suspected child abuse. Research indicates that, at the time of testing, individuals with elevated abuse scale scores have characteristics, traits, and parenting styles similar to those of confirmed physical child abusers.

Mrs. Smith's responses produced an elevation on the Lie scale and the Fake-Good index of the CAPI validity scales. This pattern generally represents an attempt by the respondent to present herself in a positive light. As a result, Mrs. Smith's abuse and factor scale scores may be unduly lowered and cannot be interpreted.

Mrs. Smith also obtained an elevation on the Problems with Child/Self scale of the CAPI. Those who obtain high scores on this scale perceive their children as limited in ability and competency, and perceive themselves as limited in physical ability. These individuals tend to have physical problems, such as poor health or physical handicaps. They describe their children as being burdened with special problems. Information from the twins' medical records suggests that this is an accurate reflection of their condition.

MINNESOTA MULTIPHASIC PERSONALITY INVENTORY–2

The Minnesota Multiphasic Personality Inventory–2 (MMPI-2) is an objective personality inventory with three validity scales, 10 clinical scales, and a number of content and research scales.

Mrs. Smith's scores on the validity scales of the MMPI-2 indicate that she was open and honest in completing the test, and that the clinical scale configuration is an accurate reflection of her actual emotional functioning.

Mrs. Smith has only one elevated clinical scale (7). Individuals with this profile are happy most of the time, and they generally feel cheerful. They are easily frightened, though, and often phobic. They are in good physical health and as able to work as they ever were. These individuals are very shy and reserved, and are easily embarrassed. They tend not to have behavioral problems because of their social isolation and fear of social interaction. They describe their home life as being pleasant.

SHIPLEY INSTITUTE FOR LIVING SCALE

The Shipley Institute of Living Scale is a brief IQ screening instrument. Mrs. Smith's performance on the Shipley places her overall level of intellectual ability in the low average to average range. There are indications that she has some difficulties with certain types of information processing. Mrs. Smith told me that she is dyslexic and that she had trouble with academics in school. A partial Wechsler Adult Intelligence Scales–R (WAIS-R) performed by Sharon Peterson, Ph.D., on January 17, 1998, indicated that Mrs. Smith's verbal IQ is 82, which places her in the low average range. Three performance subtests were administered, and Mrs. Smith's average on these was 8, which falls in the low average to average range.

SUMMARY AND RECOMMENDATIONS

The results of this psychological evaluation indicate that Mrs. Smith is an individual of low average intellectual abilities. In addition, she appears to have difficulty processing certain types of information, and this is consistent with the history she gives of dyslexia. Results of the MMPI-2 indicate that she is a generally well-adjusted individual who at the same time is somewhat shy and reserved. She has some fears of social interaction with other individuals if she feels that she might not be liked or approved of. Most individuals with this profile are diagnosed as having avoidant personality disorders. Mrs. Smith's performance on the Child Abuse Potential Inventory was invalid and consequently not interpretable. However, her scores on the AAPI indicate that she is able to understand and meet the emotional needs of young children and that she avoids corporal punishment, preferring to use other methods of discipline. She does not use her children as objects for her own gratification. She does have a slightly below average ability to understand children's developmental needs, and this may be related to her difficulties with information processing.

The diagnosis of Munchausen syndrome by proxy, or factitious disorder by proxy, is listed in the *Diagnostic and Statistical Manual (DSM-IV)* of the American Psychiatric Association in a section reserved for diagnoses that require further study. The criteria for a diagnosis of factitious disorder by proxy are:

> Intentional production or feigning of physical or psychological signs or symptoms in another person who is under the individual's care.
> The motivation for the perpetrator's behavior is to assume the sick role by proxy.
> External incentives for the behavior (such as economic gain) are absent.
> The behavior is not better accounted for by another mental disorder.

In diagnosing this condition, it is essential to verify that all four of the criteria are satisfied. This means that, even if there is undeniable proof that the suspected perpetrator feigned or induced symptoms in the patient, unless her behavior was intentional and motivated by a desire to assume the sick role by proxy, and unless there is no external incentive or other mental disorder that could explain the behavior, the diagnosis of factitious disorder by proxy is not appropriate.

In order to evaluate the results of Mrs. Smith's interview and psychological testing in light of these criteria, it is necessary to consider, first, whether Mrs. Smith's personality characteristics indicate that she might have the motive and inclination to deliberately fabricate or exaggerate symptoms in her children in order to assume the sick role by proxy.

Although some well-known experts who specialize in the diagnosis of Munchausen syndrome by proxy contend that there is a characteristic psychological profile, this has not been established by scientific research. However, assuming that the FDBP behavioral profile has some validity, Mrs. Smith's profile does not fit this "characteristic" pattern. The scientific literature that exists on the subject theorizes that the personality characteristics of Munchausen mothers place them in the "Cluster B" group of personality disorders, that is, individuals with antisocial, narcissistic, or histrionic personality styles. Mrs. Smith's personality disorder falls in the "Cluster C" group, which includes avoidant, dependent, and obsessive-compulsive disorders. Her valid MMPI-2 results indicate that she is a shy person who has difficulty in interactions with authority figures. I observed some of this apprehension in my own interview with her, although she became more relaxed as the evaluation went on. Logic suggests that a shy person who finds interactions with unfamiliar persons aversive would not actively seek attention by fabricating illnesses in children under her care.

The results of the parenting instruments I administered also do not support a factitious disorder by proxy diagnosis. A parent who would consciously and knowingly subject her child to painful, invasive, and possibly dangerous medical procedures for her own gratification could be expected to have deficits in empathy for their child. Mrs. Smith's scores on the AAPI, however, indicate that she has above-average levels of empathy. Nor is her role reversal score unusual.

Mrs. Smith's intelligence screening suggests that she has difficulties with certain types of information processing and low average verbal intellectual abilities. These results support the hypothesis that the inconsistencies between her accounts of the children's medical conditions and others' accounts were the result of misunderstandings.

In examining the medical records and other collateral data in light of the criteria for Munchausen syndrome by proxy, it is necessary to consider whether there is proof that symptoms were either feigned, exaggerated, or induced. In cases of suspected symptom induction, this proof would consist of videotapes of symptom induction by the caretaker or other physical evidence. In this case, it appears that Mrs. Smith is primarily suspected of feigning and exaggerating symptoms rather than inducing them. The diagnosis of FDBP that CPS has put forward appears to have been made in this case primarily on the basis of this aspect of the first diagnostic criterion, that is, that they believe there is evidence that symptoms were feigned. My review of this evidence (medical records provided by CPS), however, indicates that the diagnosis may have been based in part on inaccurate, misleading, or incomplete representations made by CPS personnel about the children. In addition, confirmatory bias (the tendency to interpret data in a way that confirms an already drawn conclusion) appears to have played a role in this investigation.

In their report dated April 13, 1998, Dr. C. and Dr. H. state: "In addition, there is repeated mention in the medical records that Mrs. Smith had told various physicians that the children were treated with paregoric during their newborn course, and that they were intubated and ventilated one week during that time." This fact is mentioned as part of the basis for the diagnosis of Munchausen syndrome by proxy; however, the report does not mention that the transfer summary completed by Dr. G., dictated December 5, 1996, states that Baby A was "found to be tachypneic with saturation of less than 90 percent and cyanotic. Suctioning was done and the baby improved." In view of the fact that one of the infants had breathing difficulties as a newborn, and since Mrs. Smith lacks a background in medicine and has difficulties with information processing, it is reasonable to consider the possibility that Mrs. Smith's account may have been the result of a misunderstanding or imperfect memory rather than a deliberate fabrication.

In the same report, Drs. C. and H. mention that Mrs. Smith incorrectly told doctors that the children were administered paregoric as newborns. Although the report states, "I don't know whether Mrs. Smith was given misinformation regarding this, or whether it was a deliberate fabrication," the implication appears to be that it was fabricated, since this possibility was cited as part of the justification for the diagnosis. When I discussed the matter of the paregoric with Mrs. Smith in our interview, she told me that she did believe the children were given paregoric subsequent to their delivery. She reported to me that a nurse told her this while she was visiting the neonatal ward. According to Mrs. Smith, when she asked the nurse why the ward was so quiet, the nurse replied that it was quiet because the newborns were all on paregoric. Mrs. Smith said she interpreted this statement to mean that literally all of the babies in the ward were on paregoric, including the twins. This account, assuming it is accurate, suggests that Mrs. Smith may be overly concrete and literal in her thinking, and may have misinterpreted a remark that the nurse more likely intended as a casual generalization. Such a tendency would be characteristic of someone with Mrs. Smith's information processing difficulties, and it is a plausible alternative explanation.

It should also be pointed out that the literature on FDBP makes it clear that bona fide cases are characterized by substantial misrepresentation of the medical histories of the alleged victims and often of the alleged perpetrator. In this case, I can find evidence of only minor inaccuracies in Mrs. Smith's relating of the twin's medical histories, and these do not appear to have made any difference in their treatment. There appears to have been no effort made by CPS to explore Mrs. Smith's medical history for evidence of a somatization disorder or adult Munchausen syndrome.

Drs. C. and H. also question the diagnosis of gastroesophageal reflux, noting: "The only independent observation that I see in the medical records on vomiting was from L.S., RN, a CPS nurse who made a home visit on August 28, 1997, and during the observation period of 1.5 hours did not observe either child to vomit." However, this statement appears to be factually incorrect, as it is contradicted by the CPS nurse's own report on the observation in question. The report states: "During the visit, Baby A had a few small amounts of emesis." Other sources of potentially exculpating information were also either ignored or not supplied to Drs. C. and H., and it is of great concern that only limited attempts were made to verify the vomiting, the seizures or tremors, and the developmental delays that Mrs. Smith reported. The physicians who treated the children at the times the symptoms were reported did not observe any of these symptoms firsthand, and the results of repeated electroencephalograms were negative. However, the records provided by CPS contains accounts from neighbors, friends, and disinterested parties who report that they witnessed either vomiting, spasms, and tremors, including D.S., a physical therapist who worked with the children on behalf of the local Visiting Nurse Association (VNA). I telephoned several of these sources. K.M., who had babysat for the children, told me that she saw the children vomiting "all of the time." She also said she had seen them shaking and asked Mrs. Smith questions about it, as she had seen children with similar conditions at a women's shelter where she worked. I also telephoned the Smiths' neighbor, J.K. Mrs. K. told me that she had seen the children throw up many times, and that she had reported this to a CPS worker who came to her house. There are similar accounts from other neighbors. This information from eyewitnesses who spent much more time with the children than any of the physicians' nurses or caseworkers involved appears to have been completely discounted by CPS, and the information either was not provided to Drs. C. and H. or was discounted by them as well.

In addition to the fact that witnesses can corroborate the reported spasms and tremors, according to scientific literature symptoms of this nature are common in cocaine-addicted babies. Further, my research and conversations with pediatric neurologists indicate that many non-addicted children with normal birth and delivery show transient spasms and seizures, that such symptoms are a frequent cause of referral to neuropediatric clinics, and that they are a major cause of distress and concern to parents, despite the fact that they are usually harmless.

In regard to the twins' reported developmental delays, it is not entirely clear whether Mrs. Smith is accused of fabricating or inducing the reported delays. However, the bulk of the material from the medical records supports the diagnosis of developmental delay, and the prenatal conditions of these children put them at high risk for developmental delay. If the symptoms had been fabricated, observation and testing of the twins upon their removal from the home could have established this. The assessments done while the twins were in the Smith household all support the existence of developmental delay. In order to place the blame for these delays on Mrs. Smith, several factors would need to be established. First, there would need to be evidence of rapid developmental improvement after the twins left the Smith household; moderate improvement would not be probative because the twins were progressing at the Smith household before their removal. The appropriate way to assess developmental delay is through the use of objective infant development tests, such as the Bailey, that have known reliability and validity. Unfortunately, despite repeated requests to

CPS through Mrs. Smith's attorney, I have been unable to obtain information about the twin's progress subsequent to their removal from the Smith household or even to ascertain whether any developmental assessment was undertaken.

In conclusion, I will refer the reader of this report to my paper, "Munchausen's Syndrome by Proxy: Psycho-Legal Issues." It is well established in medical science that when a particular diagnosis is very rare in the general population, and when the methods for diagnosing it are not extremely rigorous, there is a very high risk for a false positive diagnosis. This is certainly the case for factitious disorder by proxy. What scientific studies have been performed on the epidemiology of the disorder indicate that it is extremely rare. In this case the evidence that Mrs. Smith fabricated symptoms in the cases of the twins is very weak and subjective, and the eyewitness evidence that the twins did have the symptoms described by Mrs. Smith is far more robust. Given this situation, Bayes' theorem makes it clear that this diagnosis of Munchausen syndrome by proxy is much more likely to be incorrect than correct.

Taking all of this information into consideration—the results of Mrs. Smith's psychological evaluation, my review of the medical records, and information gathered from collateral sources—it is my professional opinion that Mrs. Smith does not suffer from Munchausen syndrome by proxy (factitious Disorder by Proxy).

Eric Mart, Ph.D.

Eric Mart, Ph.D.
Certified Psychologist

The Concise Child Custody Evaluation

ERIC G. MART, PH.D., ABPP

One of the most common functions in which mental health practitioners interact with the courts, the child custody evaluation, is also arguably one of the most poorly researched and developed specialties of forensic psychology. To quote Melton et al.,[1] "Indeed, there is probably no forensic question on which over-reaching by mental health experts has been so common and so egregious. Besides lacking scientific validity, such opinions have often been based on clinical data which are, on their face, irrelevant to the legal question in dispute."

In comparison, other forensic psychology specialties, such as the evaluation of criminal competency, are better developed and more rigorous. This discrepancy can be explained, in part, by the fact that criminal competency evaluations are undertaken in courts where higher standards of evidence are required. This places a higher demand for precision on the clinician and also limits the extent to which the clinician can rely on inferences and conjectures that are not based on reasonably reliable and valid data. In contrast, the laxer rules of evidence in divorce courts allow the clinician much more leeway in introducing information of limited or unknown reliability and validity, based on experience and conjecture. In such cases, objections about the scientific nature of the evaluator's conclusions go to the weight of the material rather than the admissibility.

Reprinted from *Trial Bar News*, Volume 21, Fall 1999.

A related contributing factor to the lack of rigor in custody evaluations is the vagueness in most states of the statutes governing child custody cases. The "child's best interest doctrine," which began in the 1920s to supplant the "tender years doctrine" that preceded it, was well intentioned but vague. Past attempts to clarify the meaning of "best interest" have included the Uniform Marriage and Divorce Act of 1979. However, while this standard clarified some elements of the term, it was also vague and was not based on empirical research about the relationship between the factors delineated and the outcomes for children.

PREVAILING METHODOLOGIES, INSTRUMENTS, AND TECHNIQUES

Perhaps in part because of the unusual discretion and power that have been accorded to custody evaluators, many mental health professionals use no explicit methodology for custody evaluations, instead relying heavily on experience and clinical judgment. This approach runs counter to a formidable body of scientific literature that indicates that clinical judgment is unreliable and that experience does not necessarily add validity to a clinician's conclusions.[2]

Nevertheless, those evaluators who rely on clinical judgment are not necessarily less accurate in their conclusions than those who use the various methodologies which have been developed for conducting custody evaluations. This is because most of the methodologies used most frequently either lack empirical support or are predicated on explicit theories that have not been empirically tested, such as family systems or psychodynamic personality theory. Many of these theories, although they may have utility in a clinical setting, cannot be falsified or empirically tested. This fact was noted by the U.S. Supreme Court in *Daubert v. Merrell Dow Pharmaceuticals*,[3] which specifically referenced Karl Popper's[4] description of psychoanalytic theory as unscientific because its assumptions could not be empirically tested.

Further, not only are many child custody evaluation methodologies based on shaky or nonexistent theoretical foundations, but many of the evaluation techniques that they employ are seriously flawed. In a recent article, Michaela Heinze and Thomas Grisso[5] reviewed a number of the commonly used custody assessment instruments in terms of their psychometric properties. According to their analysis, many of the instruments that are used frequently by mental health professionals have serious psychometric flaws, including low reliability and very questionable validity.

The practice of observing parent and child interactions either in the home or in the office, for example, is recommended by many psychology texts and articles.[6] Further, some authorities suggest a methodology for these observations, such as the Uniform Child Custody Evaluation System developed by Munsinger and Karlson.[7] This system is fairly typical in suggesting that the evaluator observe parent and child in a free play situation and then have the parent and child engage in a structured problem-solving situation such as assembling a puzzle or playing checkers. While this technique has a certain amount of face validity, no research exists regarding its reliability or validity in elucidating anything about the parent-child relationship.

THE ISSUE OF COMPREHENSIVENESS

Many professional writers on the subject of custody evaluations call for far-reaching data collection, including observations, home visits, and multiple interviews with family members; interviews of relatives, neighbors, and teachers; and record review. As a result, the expense of custody evaluations, always high, has increased in recent years. A study by Ackerman and Ackerman[8] surveying the custody evaluation practices of 201 experienced mental health professionals across the country found that the average price of a custody evaluation was $2,645.96, and prices ranged as high as $15,000. This expense creates a situation in which custody evaluations are often out of the reach of divorcing parties, and information that would assist the fact finder is not elicited due to the expense.

Further, more information is not necessarily better. While many evaluators claim to rely on the totality of the data, a substantial body of research indicates that most, if not all, practitioners rely and base their conclusions on a few salient pieces of data.[9] While it is certainly important to gather and confirm relevant information when performing child custody evaluations, there should be a rationale for data collection and a prioritization of issues to be explored. This approach helps to spare the family unnecessary expense and intrusions into their private lives.

Excess information may also make the evaluator's report more difficult for the court to decipher. Clinicians' evaluations and testimony in custody cases are often a melange of data derived from tests, observations of parents and children, interview data, and conclusions drawn from clinical judgment. Consequently, it is frequently difficult for the fact finder to discern a connection between the mental health professional's opinion and the basis for that opinion.

It is not clear whether the conclusions of expert witnesses in child custody cases are required to have an explicit logical connection to the data upon which they are based. However, in *State of New Hampshire v. Wayne Cressy*[10] and *State of New Hampshire in re Gina D.*,[11] the New Hampshire Supreme Court ruled that this logical nexus was required. Specifically, in *Gina D.* the court stated:

> An opinion that is impenetrable on cross-examination due to the unveri-fiable methodology of the expert witness in arriving at the conclusion is not helpful to the court in its search for the truth. . . . If the court, as the trier of fact, cannot determine and assess the bases for the expert's opin-ion, it also cannot accord the proper weight, if any, to the testimony.

While the strict rules of evidence do not apply in divorce cases, the New Hampshire Supreme Court makes it clear that the formal rules of evidence should be used to direct and inform marital courts in regard to the admissibility of different forms of testimony, including testimony from psychological experts. It is reasonable to suggest that the same re-quirement for a logical connection between conclusions reached and data relied upon be applied to custody evaluations.

ETHICAL AND LEGAL BASES FOR A CONCISE APPROACH

These rulings (*Cressy* and *Gina D.*), together with the American Psy-chological Association (APA)'s Ethical Principles of Psychologists and Code of Conduct[12] and the Specialty Guidelines for Forensic Psycholo-gists,[13] provide the basis for the Concise Child Custody Evaluation guidelines.

To quote section 2.04 of the APA Ethical Principles ("Use of Assess-ment in General and with Special Populations"):

> (a) Psychologists who perform interventions or administer, score, inter-pret, or use assessment techniques are familiar with the reliability, vali-dation, and related standardization or outcome studies of, and proper applications and uses of, the techniques they use.

306

Section 7.02 ("Forensic Activities") of the APA Ethical Principles states:

> (a) Psychologists' forensic assessments, recommendations, and reports are based on information and techniques (including personal interviews of the individual, when appropriate) sufficient to provide substantiation for their findings.
>
> (b) Except as noted . . . psychologists provide written or oral forensic reports or testimony about the characteristics of an individual only after they have conducted an examination of the individual adequate to support their conclusions.

Finally, the Specialty Guidelines for Forensic Psychologists, Section VII (F), states:

> Forensic psychologists are aware that their essential role as expert to the court is to assist the trier of fact to understand the evidence or to determine a fact in issue. In offering expert evidence, they are aware that their own professional observations, inferences, and conclusions must be distinguished from legal facts, opinions, and conclusions. Forensic psychologists are prepared to explain the relationship between their expert testimony and the legal issues and facts of an instant case.

These ethical standards and guidelines strongly suggest that psychologists and other mental health professionals performing custody evaluations have an obligation to use assessment techniques with the best reliability and validity available.

In addition, the evaluator must be able to inform the court regarding the reliability and validity of the techniques utilized in the evaluation, and to explain the relationship between the data elicited and the conclusions proffered. Cantner et al.'s *Ethics for Psychologists: A Commentary on the APA Ethics Code*[14] makes it clear that this duty to inform the court is an affirmative obligation. This means that the ethical custody evaluator does not wait to have limitations in the data brought out through clever cross-examination, but rather is obligated to present these limitations as part of the report or testimony.

OVERVIEW OF THE CONCISE MODEL

A number of changes in focus and emphasis would characterize this alternative custody evaluation methodology. It is an axiom of this custody methodology that the child custody evaluation should closely follow the applicable state statute or standard. In cases where the issue is a legal or factual rather than a psychological concept, the evaluator either should refrain from giving an opinion about the issue or should set measurable criteria by which to evaluate the issue and explicitly state the rationale behind the choice of criteria.

Evaluations should be concise and circumscribed rather than comprehensive. Evaluators should not volunteer opinions that are not specifically related to the questions being asked by the court, but should focus on issues and questions that are relevant to the purpose of the evaluation. Volunteering opinions constitutes overreaching and runs the risk of usurping the role of the fact finder. Evaluation techniques and conclusions should, to the extent possible, correspond to the questions posed by the court. While important data needs to be confirmed from another source where possible, there should be an explicit rationale for the collection of data.

The evaluator's conclusions, stated in reports and testimony, should be based on objective data gathered in the evaluation, and should have an explicit logical connection to this data. While clinical impressions and other data drawn from nonobjective methods have a role in child custody evaluations, such data should generally be used only to generate hypotheses that can be scientifically tested.

Issues in child custody that do not lend themselves to assessment with known reliability and validity should generally not be part of a child custody evaluation. If the guardian *ad litem* (GAL) or fact finder can assess a particular issue as well as the evaluator (e.g., cleanliness of the family home), then the assessment of that issue should be left to those parties. To do otherwise can be misleading to the court, since it gives the illusion that the conclusion being rendered is an expert opinion.

Conclusions in child custody evaluations should be made at the lowest inferential level possible.

THE CONCISE MODEL AS APPLIED TO THE NEW HAMPSHIRE ORDER ON APPOINTMENT OF THE GUARDIAN *AD LITEM*

In New Hampshire custody cases, the presiding justice issues a document called the "Order on Appointment of the Guardian *Ad Litem*," which includes a list of custody-related issues. The justice indicates which of these issues the GAL is to investigate in order to make recommendations to the court. Mental health professionals frequently assist the GAL by assessing those areas that lend themselves to psychological testing and evaluation.

The following table lists each of the potential evaluation issues listed on this document, along with a suggested method of evaluating each issue if it falls within the evaluator's sphere. As indicated in the table, mental health professionals using the concise model of child custody evaluation would evaluate only those issues ordered by the court, and would make maximal use of those instruments with the highest reliability and validity for assessing each issue. In states other than New Hampshire, evaluators would refer to their state's controlling statute.

Legal Issue	Recommended Method of Psychological Assessment
Legal custody	Best evaluated by the GAL or fact finder.
Primary physical custody/shared custody	Assess family for characteristics associated with various adjustments to physical custody versus shared custody arrangements.
Visitation/custodial time	Assess family for characteristics associated with various adjustments to visitation versus custodial time arrangements.
Special needs of the child(ren)	Assess children for psychological disorders or cognitive limitations requiring special attention.
Counseling for family/individual counseling for plaintiff/defendant/child(ren)	If family assessment reveals clinical-level symptomatology, recommend therapeutic method with demonstrated efficacy.
Psychological evaluations of plaintiff/defendant/child(ren)	Assess indicated individuals for general psychological profile using interviews, objective testing, and collateral data.
Parenting skills of plaintiff/defendant/both parties	Evaluate parents for skill deficiency or gross incapacity; assess ability to articulate appropriate parenting knowledge and attitudes.
Appropriateness of the home environment of plaintiff/defendant/both parties	This is equally well assessed by the GAL. However, if so directed the evaluator may assess, through home visits and collateral data, whether the home environment is safe and supports normal child development.
Substance abuse: alcohol/drugs/both/other	Assess contemporaneous use of alcohol or drugs at levels consistent with *DSM-IV* diagnosis of substance abuse or dependency.
Violence, physical abuse, emotional abuse	Assess parent for psychological disorders causally related to abuse; assess documented or founded violence or abuse. Evaluate children for trauma-related symptoms and collateral information.

(Continued)

Legal Issue	Recommended Method of Psychological Assessment
Sexual abuse	Usually investigated separately by law enforcement or child protective personnel, but if so directed the evaluator may conduct a comprehensive child sexual abuse evaluation. Videotaping or audiotaping is essential.
Supervision of visitation	Best evaluated by the GAL or fact finder unless there is evidence of danger, incapacity, or harmful behavior.
Rights of grandparents to visit	The issue of rights is best evaluated by the GAL or fact finder. However, the evaluator may assess the psychological stability and appropriateness of the grandparents' behavior with the children.
Influence of companions of either party on the child(ren)	Assess psychological state, skill deficiency or incapacity, ability to articulate appropriate parenting knowledge and attitudes, and substance abuse. Scope is determined by issues of concern to the court.
Maturity of child(ren) stating a preference	Evaluate intelligence and other cognitive or emotional characteristics that might affect choice related to custody arrangements.
Travel arrangements	Best evaluated by the GAL or fact finder.
Time, place, and manner of exchange for visits	Best evaluated by the GAL or fact finder.
Assessment of bond between child and each parent and/or between siblings	Although "bond" is not an empirically derived or scientific concept, attitudes and feelings can be assessed through child and parent interviews and through psychological testing of parents.

BENEFITS OF THE CONCISE MODEL

The concise model has several advantages over what might be called comprehensive methodologies. Custody evaluations performed in this manner would contain less information, but this information would be more reliable. The concise evaluation would produce conclusions about fewer issues related to child custody compared to the comprehensive evaluation model. However, these conclusions would have a much greater probability of being correct than those produced by many of the methods advocated in comprehensive methodologies, such as projective drawings and parent-child observations, which have a low or unknown probability of being correct.

Psychological assessment techniques should conform to recognized methodology and to American Professional Society on the Abuse of Children (APSAC) or American Academy of Child & Adolescent Psychiatry (AACAP) guidelines, and should employ standardized psychological instruments with known reliability and validity.

Strict adherence to standards set by professional and legal authorities would help to reduce the problem of expert overreaching in custody matters. An expert who employed the common technique of observing a parent and child in a free play situation and in a structured problem-solving situation, for example, would be obligated under the APA ethical standards to disclose in direct examination that the technique has no known reliability.

The concise model of custody evaluation is designed to assist the fact finder by specifically defining the scope of the issues being examined, addressing the probability that the conclusions being drawn are actually correct, and explicitly mapping the path between the data and conclusions. This provides the fact finder with more and clearer information about the evaluator's methodology and thought process, and allows the fact finder to draw his or her own conclusions about the weight that should be accorded to the evaluator's report or testimony.

The concise model saves the involved parties a substantial sum in expert fees. Since the courts generally do not pay for custody evaluations, the high price of comprehensive custody evaluations puts them out of reach for many divorcing couples, and as a result the potentially valuable information that would be elicited by a child custody evaluation is not available to the court. By reducing the time and expense involved in the evaluation, the concise model makes the service available to more couples, while actually increasing the quality of the data.

In conclusion, it appears that a closer adherence to the APA's Ethical Principles of Psychologists, along with purposeful efforts to make custody evaluation practices maximally scientific, suggests an alternative model for custody evaluations that is "leaner and meaner" than those currently in general use. The use of this alternative methodology has the potential of increasing the quality and utility of custody evaluations while bringing child custody evaluation practices more in line with the forensic expert's essential role in assisting the court.

NOTES

1. Melton, G. B., Petrila, J., Poythress, N. G., Jr., & Slobogin, C. (1987). *Psychological evaluations for the courts: A handbook for mental health professionals and lawyers.* New York: Guilford Press.
2. Dawes, R. M., Faust, D., & Meehl, P. E. (1989). Clinical versus actuarial judgement. *Science, 243*(4899), 1668–1674.

3. Daubert v. Merrell Dow Pharmaceuticals, Supreme Court of the United States (509 U.S. 579), June 28, 1993.

4. Popper, K. (1992). *Realism and the aim of science* (Postscript to *The logic of scientific discovery*). London: Routledge.

5. Heinze, M. C., & Grisso, T. (1996). Review of instruments assessing parenting competencies used in child custody evaluations. *Behavioral Sciences and the Law, 14*(3), 293–313.

6. Schultz, B., Dixon, E., Lindenberger, J., & Ruther, N. (1989). *Solomon's sword: A practical guide to conducting child custody evaluations.* San Francisco: Jossey-Bass.

7. Munsinger, H., & Karlson, K. (1994). *Uniform child custody evaluation system.* Odessa, FL: Psychological Assessment Resources, Inc.

8. Ackerman, M. J., & Ackerman, M. C. (1997). Custody evaluation practices: A survey of experienced professionals (revisited). *Professional Psychology: Research and Practice, 28*(2), 137–145.

9. Oskamp, S. (1965). Overconfidence in case-study judgements. *Journal of Consulting Psychology, 29*, 261–265; Wedding, D. (1983). Clinical and statistical prediction in neuropsychology. *Clinical Neuropsychology, 5*, 49–55.

10. State of New Hampshire v. Wayne Cressey, Supreme Court of New Hampshire, July 15, 1993.

11. State of New Hampshire in re Gina D., Supreme Court of New Hampshire, July 22, 1994.

12. American Psychological Association. (1992). Ethical principles of psychologists and code of conduct. *American Psychologist, 47*, 1597–1611.

13. Committee on Ethical Guidelines for Forensic Psychologists. (1991). Specialty guidelines for forensic psychologists. *Law and Human Behavior, 15*, 655–665.

14. Cantner, M., Bennett, B., Jones, S., & Nagy, T. (1994). *Ethics for psychologists: A commentary on the APA ethics code.* Washington, DC: American Psychological Association.

The Concise Approach to Child Custody Assessment

ERIC G. MART, PH.D., ABPP

One of the most common functions in which mental health practitioners interact with the courts, the child custody evaluation, is also arguably one of the most poorly researched and developed specialties of forensic psychology. To quote Melton et al.,[1] "Indeed, there is probably no forensic question on which over-reaching by mental health experts has been so common and so egregious." This article will examine a number of issues related to the practice of child custody evaluations. These will including an overview of the ethical and practice guidelines promulgated by the American Psychological Association (APA) in relation to custody evaluations, as well as other ethical standards related to forensic assessment in general that relate to such evaluations. A discussion of concerns that have been raised regarding the reliability and validity of custody assessments will be included. Finally, suggestions will be made for a model of custody-related assessment that addresses these concerns and assists the courts without the risk of usurping their function and prerogatives.

There can be little doubt that child custody evaluations are a type of forensic assessment. The Specialty Guidelines for Forensic Psychologists,[2] developed by the American Psychology–Law Society and the American Academy of Forensic Psychology, define forensic psychology as "all forms of professional psychological conduct when acting,

Reprinted from Eric G. Mart, "The Concise Approach to Child Custody Assessment," *Journal of Psychiatry and the Law*, *31*(4) (2003), 461; © 2004 by Federal Legal Publications, Inc.

with definable foreknowledge, as a psychological expert on explicitly psycholegal issues, in direct assistance to courts, parties to legal proceedings, correctional and forensic mental health facilities, and administrative, judicial, and legislative agencies acting in an adjudicative capacity" (p. 657). Clearly, psychologists who perform custody evaluations are acting as expert witnesses to provide technical information and opinions to divorce courts.

As a consequence, those provisions of the Ethical Principles of Psychologists and Code of Conduct[3] that relate to forensic work, both generally and specifically, are enforceable for psychologists performing custody assessments. In addition, the Specialty Guidelines for Forensic Psychologists, which are aspirational, indicate that psychologists engaging in forensic activities are held to high standards with regard to their knowledge of scientific, professional, and legal developments within the area of their claimed competence, and are obligated to use that knowledge to select data collection methods and procedures for activities due to their "special status as persons qualified as experts to the court" (p. 661).

The Specialty Guidelines for Forensic Psychologists state: "Forensic psychologists are aware that their essential role as expert to the court is to assist the trier of fact to understand the evidence or to determine a fact in issue. In offering expert evidence, they are aware that their own professional observations, inferences, and conclusions must be distinguished from legal facts, opinions, and conclusions. Forensic psychologists are prepared to explain the relationship between their expert testimony and the legal issues and facts of an instant case" (p. 665). This provision of the Specialty Guidelines suggests that forensic psychologists performing forensic evaluations generally, and custody evaluations specifically, should structure their evaluations and reports so as to make the basis for their conclusions understandable to the fact finder. Making these relationships clear and distinguishing between those aspects of the custody report that are based on clinical judgment, objective test scores, and observations also allows the finder of fact to decide what weight to give each conclusion offered. The Specialty Guidelines also strongly recommend that psychologists performing forensic evaluations generally have an obligation to use assessment techniques with the best reliability and validity available (p. 661). In addition, it has been suggested[4] that the forensic psychologist has an affirmative obligation to inform the court of any factors that might place limitations on the reliability and validity of the data elicited and relied upon. This means that the ethical custody evaluator does not wait to have limitations in the data brought out through clever cross-examination, but rather is obligated to present these limitations as part of the report or testimony.

A number of organizations have developed guidelines specifically related to custody evaluations, such as the American Psychological Association (APA) Guidelines for Child Custody Evaluations in Divorce Proceedings[5] and the Association of Family and Conciliation Courts (AFCC) Model Standards of Practice for Child Custody Evaluation.[6] Both organizations appear to view the purpose of custody evaluations as providing information to the courts about the best interest of the child or children involved in the divorce. The APA Guidelines for Child Custody Evaluations in Divorce Proceedings explicitly delineate the purpose of custody evaluations as follows:

1. The primary purpose of the evaluation is to assess the best psychological interests of the child.
2. The child's interests and well-being are paramount.
3. The focus of the evaluation is on parenting capacity, the psychological and development needs of the child, and resulting fit.

However, the stated purpose of the custody evaluations as outlined is problematic. A growing number of authors have raised concerns about the extent to which issues such as "best interest of the child" and "fit" can be reliably and validly measured given the current state of the research available on the relationship between parent variables, child variables, custody arrangements, and visitation schedules as they relate to outcome for the children involved. For example, O'Donohue and Bradley[7] suggest that custody evaluations as currently undertaken are based as much on the unstated value judgments of psychologists as on any scientific data, and that the current state of the science in this field does not allow for empirically defensible conclusions to be drawn with any degree of scientific certainty. Others, such as Grisso,[8] have raised similar concerns about both the scientific underpinnings of custody evaluations and the methods used specifically in such assessments. The laws of many states outline areas to be considered in determining the best interest of the child and can be used for guidance by professionals in orienting and conducting custody evaluations, but these statutes often raise more issues than they resolve. For example, the Michigan Child Custody Act of 1970 provided standards for custody decisions that have been very influential throughout the country. These standards dictate that child custody decisions by the courts take into account 10 factors:

1. Love, affection, and emotional ties between the child and competing parties.
2. Ability of competing parties to provide the child with love, affection, guidance, education, and, if necessary, continued religious education.
3. Ability of competing parties to provide the child with material needs such as clothing and medical care.
4. Length of the child's residence in a stable, satisfactory environment, and the desirability of continuity.
5. Permanence of the existing or proposed custodial family unit.
6. Moral fitness of competing parties.
7. Mental and physical health of competing parties.
8. The child's home, school, and community records.
9. Preference of the child, if the court deems the child to be of sufficient age.
10. Any other factors the court considers relevant to a particular case.

All of these factors have obvious face validity, and it would be difficult to imagine how a reasonable decision about child custody could be made without considering some or all of these factors. But as Grisso points out, these factors are difficult to measure with any degree of precision. In addition, it is not clear what weight should be given to each factor in relation to the others, and the court has broad discretion in determining which of these factors to consider and how to prioritize them. Consequently, any attempt to derive a reliable methodology for determining the best interest of the child based on these factors is likely to be inadequate. In the same way, the general idea behind an attempt to assess fit between the particular strengths, weaknesses, and psychological adjustment of a particular parent and similar factors in a child can involve a large number of ill-defined and dynamic variables. Since there is no scientific method of determining the relationship between these variables and a concept as nebulous as fit, the most likely outcome of any attempt to assess such an issue will be a melange of scientific data, clinical judgment, and personal opinions. Further, the relationship between the information elicited and relied on and the conclusions rendered is likely to remain obscure.

One of the major issues that contributes to this unfortunate state of affairs in performing custody assessments may be related to the way in which the purpose of such evaluations is formulated. In most other areas of forensic psychology, the purpose of an evaluation is much more technical and circumscribed than in custody assessments. The assessment of an individual's competence to stand trial is generally quite focused and closely informed by the controlling statute in the jurisdiction in which the evaluation is performed. For example, in New Hampshire the purpose of a competency assessment is to assist the court by providing information about the defendant's rational and factual understanding of the issues related to standing trial, as well as his or her ability to appropriately assist his or her lawyer. While the psychologist has considerable latitude in determining how to approach these issues, the scope of the evaluation as well as what would be considered relevant information by the court is relatively circumscribed. In contrast, under the heading "Orienting Guidelines: Purpose of a Child Custody Evaluation" the APA Guidelines for Child Custody Evaluations in Divorce Proceedings states: "The primary purpose of evaluation is to assess the best psychological interests of the child" and "The child's best interests and well-being are paramount." Further, under "Procedural Guidelines: Conducting a Child Custody Evaluation," it is stated that "The scope of the evaluation is determined by the evaluator, based on the nature of the referral question." These guidelines clearly define the role of the psychologist in custody assessments in a much broader, albeit more vague way than is the case in any other area of forensic practice. For example, the role of the psychologist in performing a not guilty by reason of insanity (NGRI) assessment is not defined in professional guidelines as "supporting the American system of jurisprudence." Forensic psychologists define their roles much more narrowly in other types of evaluations. The APA custody guidelines are characterized by O'Donohue and Bradley as "vague, quite general, and do not indicate specific practices or techniques to be used in evaluations." They rightly suggest that these guidelines are actually a collection of ethical standards and are "largely truisms" (pp. 316–317). This pervasive lack of focus and rigor contributes to the likelihood that psychologists will overreach in custody assessments and usurp the role of the fact finder.

The problem of assessing the best interest of the child is further complicated by the paucity of longitudinal research regarding the outcomes of various custody and visitation arrangements. Those studies that have been done have not demonstrated robust effects for any particular arrangement, even when factors such as conflict level between parents are considered, and the results of studies run in different directions. There is research that suggests that more extreme maladaptive behaviors on the part of parents, either individually or as a dyad, contribute to poorer outcomes.[9] However, findings indicating that poorer outcomes result from exposure of children to ongoing high conflict between divorced parents and witnessing or being the victim of domestic violence, while important, are hardly counterintuitive.

Prevailing Methodologies, Instruments, and Techniques

Problems also exist in relation to the actual methods used by psychologists in performing custody evaluations. Many mental health professionals use no explicit methodology for custody evaluations, but instead rely heavily on experience and clinical judgment. This approach runs counter to a formidable body of scientific literature, which indicates that clinical judgment is often unreliable and that experience does not necessarily add validity to a clinician's conclusions.[10] Nevertheless, those evaluators who rely on clinical judgment are not necessarily less accurate in their conclusions than those who use the various methodologies that have been developed for conducting custody evaluations. This is because most of the prevailing methodologies either lack empirical support or are predicated on explicit theories that have not been empirically tested, such as family systems or psychodynamic personality theory. Many of these theories, although they may have some utility in a clinical setting, cannot be falsified or empirically tested. In *Daubert v. Merrell Dow Pharmaceuticals*,[11] the U.S. Supreme Court specifically referenced Karl Popper's[12] citation of psychoanalytic theory as an unscientific theory because its assumptions could not be empirically tested. And, while the five-point test outlined in *Daubert* for determining whether expert testimony is scientific and thus admissible has been very influential in criminal proceedings, it has not appeared to have exerted much influence on custody evaluators.

Further, not only are many child custody evaluation methodologies based on shaky or nonexistent theoretical foundations, but many of the evaluation techniques which they employ are seriously flawed. In an article, Michaela Heinze and Thomas Grisso[13] reviewed a number of the commonly used custody assessment instruments in terms of their psychometric properties. According to the authors' analysis, many of the instruments that are used frequently by mental health professionals have serious psychometric flaws, including low reliability and very questionable validity.

It is helpful to use an example of how many widely accepted and utilized custody assessment methods are employed without established reliability and validity. The practice of observing parent and child interactions either in the home or in the office, for example, is recommended by many psychology texts and articles.[14] Ackerman and Ackerman[15] surveyed 201 psychologists in the United States in regard to child custody evaluation practices. They found that a high number of the psychologists included observations of parent-child interaction as a component of their evaluations. Different authors suggest different methods for conducting parent/child observations. The Uniform Child Custody Evaluation System developed by Munsinger and Karlson[16] is fairly typical in suggesting that the evaluator observe parent and child in a free play situation and then have the parent and child engage in a structured problem-solving situation such as assembling a puzzle or playing checkers. Clearly, it makes sense that a psychologist who bases custody and visitation recommendations, at least in part, on the quality of parent-child interactions would include observations of these interactions in determining the best interest of the child. However, a review of the PsychLit database found no research that examined conclusions derived from observations of parent-child interaction in custody assessments and outcomes for children involved. It is of concern that an assessment technique so widely utilized by professionals in contributing to custody decisions should rest on what is at best extremely tenuous methodological ground. Similar problems exist with virtually all techniques utilized in custody assessment.

THE ISSUE OF COMPREHENSIVENESS: IS LESS MORE?

Many professional writers on the subject of custody evaluations call for far-reaching data collection, including observations, home visits, and multiple interviews with family members; interviews of relatives, neighbors, and teachers; and record review. As a result, the expense of custody evaluations, always high, has increased in recent years. Ackerman and Ackerman's study surveying the custody evaluation practices of 201 experienced mental health professionals across the country found that the average price of a custody evaluation was $2,645.96, and prices ranged as high as $15,000.[17] This expense creates a situation in which custody evaluations are often out of the reach of divorcing parties, and information that would assist the fact finder is not elicited due to the expense.

Further, more information is not necessarily better. Although many evaluators claim to rely on the totality of the data, a substantial body of research indicates that most, if not all, practitioners rely and base their conclusions on a few salient pieces of data.[18] While it is certainly important to gather and confirm relevant information when performing child custody evaluations, in general practice there often appears to be no rationale for data collection and/or prioritization of issues to be explored. This type of freewheeling data collection raises ethical issues above and beyond its impact on the validity of conclusions based on such data. The Specialty Guidelines point out (VI, F. 2), "With respect to evidence of any type, forensic psychologists avoid offering information from their investigations or evaluations that does not bear directly upon the purpose of their professional services and that is not critical as support for their product, evidence, or testimony, except where such disclosure is required by law." Although this is not stated explicitly in this standard, it appears to indicate that there is a requirement that there must be respect for the privacy of those being evaluated, and that only information likely to bear directly on the legal issue at hand should be elicited from the client. Unfortunately, there are pressures that motivate psychologists to gather more and more information about families in custody evaluations. In this regard, Amundson et al. have stated that "in their desire to be helpful, psychologists may, in their inquiry regarding 'children's best interests,' conduct quasi-experimental procedures, invade privacy, and induce patients to abandon constitutional rights in the service of obtaining 'good data' and evidence for the court."[19]

The absence of an explicit methodology and rationale for data collection can create a situation in which custody evaluators collect information in ways that can be very intrusive for families and children without adequate justification for this violation of privacy. In addition, parents sometimes reveal information that becomes part of the court record and has the effect of increasing emotional tensions and conflict. It is not clear how the risk of such intrusive data collection is counterbalanced against the need for comprehensive assessment.

It is possible that continued research regarding custody assessment, custody and visitation arrangements, and outcomes for children may eventually improve the reliability and validity of comprehensive child custody assessments. In the opinion of this author, the current state of the science in this area at present is not sufficiently developed to provide reliable and valid conclusions about the best interests of children before the court in custody matters. As previously noted, O'Donohue and Bradley and others have suggested that child custody evaluations in their present form are not reliable or valid enough to be given serious consideration by the courts. Following these conclusions, it would seem logical that psychologists should cease performing such evaluations and testifying about custody and visitation in divorces. It would also follow that the presentation of expert reports and testimony in custody matters by psychologists is counterproductive, in that rather than assisting the trier of fact by providing reliable technical information, custody assessments and testimony as practiced at present actually usurp the role of the court. As matters presently stand, psychologists are actually substituting judgments about lifestyles and their personal preferences for scientific data, and while judges and guardians *ad litem* clearly make their decisions based in part on moral beliefs and personal preferences, they are empowered by our society to make such decisions while psychologists as experts to the court are not.

Despite these problems, it appears unlikely that divorce courts will dispense with the services of psychologists and other mental health professionals in the foreseeable future. If anything, there appears to be an ongoing expansion of the role of mental health professionals in areas associated with child custody. This raises the question of whether it is possible to perform child custody evaluations in a manner which is ethical, scientifically defensible, and of assistance to the court. The remainder of this article will suggest a model for psychological evaluations designed to assist the court in such a manner. It is suggested that by focusing attention on circumscribed issues specifically suggested by the court and being conscious of the limitations of data and conclusions arrived at by these methods, valuable technical information can be supplied to the court with less risk of overreaching and less dependence on unreliable data. I will refer to this method of performing psychological evaluations for the courts in custody-related matters as the concise model of custody assessment.

OVERVIEW OF THE CONCISE MODEL

A number of changes in focus and emphasis would characterize this alternative custody evaluation methodology.

1. It is an axiom of this methodology that the child custody evaluation should closely follow the applicable state statutes or standard. In cases where the standard is nebulous or when there is no closely corresponding psycholegal equivalent, the evaluator should either refrain from giving an opinion about the issue or attempt to operationalize the issue and explicitly state the rationale behind the operationalization.

2. Evaluations should be concise and circumscribed rather than comprehensive. Evaluators should not volunteer opinions that are not specifically related to the questions being asked, but should focus on issues and questions relevant to the purpose of the evaluation. To do so constitutes overreaching and runs the risk of usurping the role of the fact finder. Evaluation techniques and conclusions should, to the extent possible, correspond to the hypothetical questions posed by the court or guardian *ad litem* (GAL). Although important data needs to be confirmed from other sources where possible, there should be an explicit rationale for the collection of data.

3. The evaluator's conclusions, stated in reports and testimony, should be based on objective data gathered in the evaluation, and should have an explicit logical connection to this data. Although clinical impressions and other data drawn from nonobjective methods have a role in child custody evaluations, such data should generally be used only to generate hypotheses that can be scientifically tested.

4. Issues in child custody that do not lend themselves to assessment with known reliability and validity should generally not be part of a child custody evaluation. If the guardian *ad litem* or fact finder can assess a particular issue as well as the evaluator (i.e., cleanliness of the family home), then the assessment of that issue should be left to those parties. To do otherwise can be misleading to the court, since it gives the illusion that the conclusion being rendered is an expert opinion.

5. Conclusions in child custody evaluations should be made at the lowest inferential level possible.

322

THE CONCISE MODEL AS APPLIED TO THE NEW HAMPSHIRE CUSTODY EVALUATION

In New Hampshire custody cases, the presiding justice issues a document called the Order on Appointment of the Guardian *Ad Litem*, which includes a list of custody-related issues. The justice indicates which of these issues the GAL is to investigate in order to make recommendations to the court. Mental health professionals frequently assist the GAL by assessing those areas that lend themselves to psychological testing and evaluation.

The New Hampshire Order on Appointment of the Guardian *Ad Litem* parallels the factors that have generally been considered to reflect the consensus of jurisdictions throughout the United States regarding the components of best interest considerations in child custody. Schultz et al. reviewed the laws in all 50 states to determine which custody-related factors reflected a high degree of consensus.[20] They listed 19 high-consensus factors:

1. Presence of child or spousal abuse.
2. Age and sex of the child.
3. Adjustment of the child to current environment.
4. Length of time in present environment.
5. The child's need for special emotional or physical care.
6. Economic position of the parties.
7. The child's wishes, if a sufficient age.
8. Parents' desires.
9. Educational needs of the child.
10. Agreement between the parents.
11. Separation of the siblings.
12. Mental and physical health of the parents.
13. Prior custody determinations.
14. Hostility levels between parents.
15. Flexibility on the part of either parent.
16. General parenting skills.
17. Religious concerns.
18. Caretaking arrangements prior to and after separation.
19. Likelihood that custodial parent will move child from jurisdiction or alienate the affections of the child for the other parent.

It should be noted that virtually all jurisdictions allow the courts the discretion to consider other factors in making custody determinations.

However, the framework provided by the New Hampshire Order on Appointment of the Guardian *Ad Litem* conforms closely to the factors outlined by Schultz et al. The following table lists each of the potential evaluation issues that appear in New Hampshire's Order on Appointment of the Guardian *Ad Litem* and a suggested method of evaluating each issue that falls within the evaluator's sphere. Mental health professionals following the concise model of child custody evaluation would evaluate only those issues ordered by the court. In addition, practitioners of this model would make maximal use of those instruments with the highest reliability and validity for assessing a particular issue indicated by the Order on Appointment of the Guardian *Ad Litem*. In other states, custody evaluators would refer to their own states' controlling statutes or work out an explicit plan for determining the issues to be assessed with the court or GAL.

Legal Issue	Recommended Method of Psychological Assessment
Legal custody	Best evaluated by the GAL or fact finder.
Primary physical custody/shared custody	Assess family for characteristics associated with various adjustments to physical custody versus shared custody arrangements.
Visitation/custodial time	Assess family for characteristics associated with various adjustments to visitation versus custodial time arrangements.
Special needs of the child(ren)	Assess children for psychological disorders or cognitive limitations requiring special attention.
Counseling for family/individual counseling for plaintiff/defendant/child(ren)	If family assessment reveals clinical-level symptomatology, recommend therapeutic method with demonstrated efficacy.
Psychological evaluations of plaintiff/defendant/ child(ren)	Assess indicated individuals for general psychological profile using interviews, objective testing, and collateral data.
Parenting skills of plaintiff/defendant/both parties	Evaluate parents for skill deficiency or gross incapacity; assess ability to articulate appropriate parenting knowledge and attitudes.
Appropriateness of the home environment of plaintiff/defendant/both parties	This is equally well assessed by the GAL. However, if so directed the evaluator may assess, through home visits and collateral data, whether the home environment is safe and supports normal child development.
Substance abuse: alcohol/drugs/both/other	Assess contemporaneous use of alcohol or drugs at levels consistent with *DSM-IV* diagnosis of substance abuse or dependency.
Violence, physical abuse, emotional abuse	Assess parent for psychological disorders causally related to abuse; assess documented or founded violence or abuse. Evaluate children for trauma-related symptoms and collateral information.

Legal Issue	Recommended Method of Psychological Assessment
Sexual abuse	Usually investigated separately by law enforcement or child protective personnel, but if so directed the evaluator may conduct a comprehensive child sexual abuse evaluation. Videotaping or audiotaping is essential.
Supervision of visitation	Best evaluated by the GAL or fact finder unless there is evidence of danger, incapacity, or harmful behavior.
Rights of grandparents to visit	The issue of rights is best evaluated by the GAL or fact finder. However, the evaluator may assess the psychological stability and appropriateness of the grandparents' behavior with the children.
Influence of companions of either party on the child(ren)	Assess psychological state, skill deficiency or incapacity, ability to articulate appropriate parenting knowledge and attitudes, and substance abuse. Scope is determined by issues of concern to the court.
Maturity of child(ren) stating a preference	Evaluate intelligence and other cognitive or emotional characteristics that might affect choice related to custody arrangements.
Travel arrangements	Best evaluated by the GAL or fact finder.
Time, place, and manner of exchange for visits	Best evaluated by the GAL or fact finder.
Assessment of bond between child and each parent and/or between siblings	Although "bond" is not an empirically derived or scientific concept, attitudes and feelings can be assessed through child and parent interviews and through psychological testing of parents.

ADVANTAGES OF THE CONCISE MODEL

This concise model has a number of advantages over what might be called comprehensive methodologies. Custody evaluations performed in this manner would contain less, but more reliable, information. The concise evaluation would produce conclusions about fewer issues related to child custody compared to the comprehensive evaluation model. However, these conclusions would have a much greater probability of being correct than those produced by many of the methods advocated in comprehensive methodologies, such as projective drawings and parent-child observations, which have a low or unknown probability of being correct. Strict adherence to standards set by professional and legal authorities would help to reduce the problem of expert overreaching in custody matters. An expert who employed the common technique of observing a parent and child in a free play situation and in a structured problem-solving situation, for example, would be obligated under the APA ethical standards to disclose in direct examination that the technique has no known reliability.

Another advantage of the concise model of custody evaluation is that it is designed to assist the fact finder by specifically defining the scope of the issues being examined, addressing the probability that the conclusions being drawn are actually correct, and explicitly mapping the path between the data and conclusions. This assists the fact finder by providing more and clearer information about the evaluator's methodology and thought process, and allowing the fact finder to draw his or her own conclusions about the weight that should be accorded to the evaluator's report or testimony. For example, it is not uncommon for allegations of mental instability on the part of one or both parents to become an issue in a divorce and custody proceeding. In such a situation, the judge or guardian *ad litem* may wish to have a psychologist assess the mental health and level of psychopathology of the parents and the potential impact of any detected psychological conditions on the parents' ability to rear their children.

Finally, the concise model has the concrete advantage of saving the involved parties a substantial sum in expert fees. Since courts generally do not pay for custody evaluations, the high price of comprehensive custody evaluations puts them out of reach for many divorcing couples, and as a result the potentially valuable information that would be elicited by a child custody evaluation is not available to the court. By reducing the time and expense involved in the evaluation, the concise model makes the service available to more couples, while actually increasing the quality of the data.

In conclusion, it is the opinion of this author that a closer adherence to the APA's Ethical Principles of Psychologists, along with an emphasis on custody evaluation practices that are maximally scientific, would provide an alternative model for custody evaluations that is "leaner and meaner." The use of this alternative methodology has the potential to increase the quality and utility of custody evaluations while at the same time bringing child custody evaluation practices more in line with the forensic expert's essential role in assisting courts.

NOTES

1. Melton, G. B., Petrila, J., Poythress, N. G., Jr., & Slobogin, C. (1987). *Psychological evaluations for the courts: A handbook for mental health professionals and lawyers.* New York: Guilford Press.
2. Committee on Ethical Guidelines for Forensic Psychologists. (1991). Specialty guidelines for forensic psychologists. *Law and Human Behavior, 15,* 655–665.

3. American Psychological Association. (1992). Ethical principles of psychologists and code of conduct. *American Psychologist, 47,* 1597–1611.

4. Cantner, M., Bennett, B., Jones, S., & Nagy, T. (1994). *Ethics for psychologists: A commentary on the APA ethics code.* Washington, DC: American Psychological Association.

5. American Psychological Association. (1994). Guidelines for Child Custody Evaluations in Divorce Proceedings. *American Psychologist, 49,* 677–680.

6. Association of Family and Conciliation Courts. (1995). *AFCC model standards of practice for child custody evaluation.* Madison, WI: Association of Family and Conciliation Courts.

7. O'Donohue, W., & Bradley, A. R. (1999). Commentary: Conceptual and empirical issues in child custody evaluations. *Clinical Psychology: Science and Practice, 6*(3), 310–322.

8. Grisso, T. (2003). *Evaluating competencies: Forensic assessments and instruments* (2nd ed.). New York: Kluwer Academic/Plenum.

9. Wallerstein, J. S., Corbin, S. B., & Lewis, J. M. (1988). Children of divorce: A 10-year study. In E. M. Hetherington & J. D. Arasteh (Eds.), *Impact of divorce, single parenting and stepparenting on children* (pp. 198–214). Hillsdale, NJ: Lawrence Erlbaum.

10. Dawes, R. M., Faust, D., & Meehl, P. E. (1989). Clinical versus actuarial judgement. *Science, 243*(4899), 1668–1674.

11. Daubert v. Merrell Dow Pharmaceuticals, Supreme Court of the United States (509 US 579), June 28, 1993.

12. Popper, K. (1992). *Realism and the aim of science* (Postscript to *The Logic of Scientific Discovery*). London: Routledge.

13. Heinze, M. C., & Grisso, T. (1996). Review of instruments assessing parenting competencies used in child custody evaluations. *Behavioral Sciences and the Law, 14*(3), 293–313.

14. Schultz, B., Dixon, E., Lindenberger, J., & Ruther, N. (1989). *Solomon's sword: A practical guide to conducting child custody evaluations.* San Francisco: Jossey-Bass.

15. Ackerman, M. J., & Ackerman, M. C. (1997). Custody evaluation practices: A survey of experienced professionals (revisited). *Professional Psychology: Research and Practice, 28*(2), 137–145.

16. Munsinger, H., & Karlson, K. (1994). *Uniform child custody evaluation system.* Odessa, FL: Psychological Assessment Resources, Inc.

17. Ackerman & Ackerman. Custody evaluation practices.

18. Garb, H. N. (1998). *Studying the clinician: Judgment research and psychological assessment.* Washington, DC: American Psychological Association.

19. Amundson, J. K., Daya, R., & Gill, E. (2000). A minimalist approach to child custody evaluation. *American Journal of Forensic Psychology, 18*(3), 63–87.

20. Schultz et al. *Solomon's sword.*

The Niche Practice in Forensic Psychology

STANLEY L. BRODSKY

ABSTRACT

Practice within forensic psychology may be differentiated into primary, secondary, and niche areas. A niche practice is defined as a specialized and limited scope of professional activity designed to meet a geographical or particular client need or as a new practice application within an emerging field of knowledge. The present paper explores the conceptualization and development of the niche practice. Special emphasis is placed on identification of niches and competencies and ethics within one's niche.

THE NICHE PRACTICE IN FORENSIC PSYCHOLOGY

If one examines the divisions of the American Psychological Association (APA) that have been approved over the past three decades, a pattern emerges of specialized fields of knowledge and practice becoming mainstream and central. The applied areas of health psychology, psychology and law, gay and lesbian psychology, and psychology of men and of women, all started as small and specialized, either practiced part-time or as a secondary practice by a modest number of individuals or full-time by a small number of psychologists. It is possible to

Stanley L. Brodsky teaches in the Department of Psychology, University of Alabama, Tuscaloosa. He may be contacted at sbrodsky@bama.ua.edu.

conceptualize professional practice and specializations as falling into categories of primary, secondary, and niche. In the early days of clinical psychology there were only clinical psychologists. The occasional and more limited practice areas played a secondary role within one clear and solidified professional identity. Influenced by scholarly foundations and societal changes, these secondary roles have morphed into primary areas of substantive research and practice.

The history of development of divisions of the APA illustrates this process of differentiation, in which a broad psychological umbrella encompassed increasing numbers of diverse and growing specializations. The American Psychology–Law Society, Division 41 of the APA, is a good example. When the first organizing meeting was held at an APA convention in 1969, about 40 psychologists were present. Over the next dozen years the markers of a main area of practice and knowledge emerged, in the form of larger numbers, a newsletter followed by a journal, and membership as a division in APA (Grisso, 1991). After this initial process of establishment, secondary specialties became developed, full-time areas for practice and research. Following these secondary areas are the more narrow and focused, usually part-time practices that will be referred to as niches.

Attention to a focused and niche practice area extends beyond the field of psychology, as well as beyond the United States context. One may look to law and business practices for parallel examples. Chanen (2001) has described the development of gay and lesbian legal practice as an important and needed niche. Within the field of accounting, niche practices with a focus on franchise specialization have been presented as promising, particularly in Australia. In a discussion of practice niches in educational psychology in the United Kingdom, psychologist Lesley Thompson (1996) has argued that three components should be included: (1) a consultancy model, (2) the psychologist engaging in problem-solving activities, and (3) an interactionist frame of reference.

As a departure point in the present discussion of niche practices in forensic psychology, the nature of "niche" should be defined. The Oxford English Dictionary (OED) 2nd edition offers two definitions, the first of which is: "A place or position suited to or intended for the character, capabilities, status, etc., of a person or thing." However, the second OED definition brings us closer to niche practice in forensic psychology: "A position from which an entrepreneur seeks to exploit a shortcoming or an opportunity in an economy, market, etc.; a specialized market for a product or service." Niche practitioners often begin with the awareness of possible gaps in professional services that have not been sufficiently pursued or locally developed.

FROM DILETTANTE TO NICHE

For many forensic professionals, a supplemental career pattern is to move from personal interests as a dilettante to professional interests as a niche practitioner. As a dilettante, one pursues a topic as an amateur out of interest or affection. As a practitioner, the work encompasses an area that was formerly a personal interest or avocation.

An illustrative general example is a psychologist who had a long-standing involvement in musical performance. Her early career choices included the possibility of becoming a flute instructor or performer. A friend who taught music at the nearby university asked her about assistance in preparing students to deal with performance anxiety in forthcoming senior recitals. After agreeing to assist, the psychologist studied the literature on performance anxiety, consulted with colleagues, and then aided a few students on a pro bono basis. This initial work turned into a small and episodic practice in which wind instrument students and performers would seek assistance in anxiety reduction prior to and during recitals. The psychologist's own interest in music led to her becoming a consultant to a few musicians about their performance anxiety.

The dilettante to niche transition sometimes occurs with mental health professionals who have sports skills or interests. These practitioners are typically involved with the so-called minor sports because professional and collegiate football and basketball produce considerable income and have access to full-time sports consultants. Competitive sports as diverse as fencing, swimming, track and field, lacrosse, and chess all have major psychological components. One can reasonably argue that the outcome of every athletic and sports endeavor is influenced by psychological elements. Former athletes and current dilettantes can combine their specific sports knowledge with psychological concepts and treatments to develop a niche practice, and the substantive knowledge can make a difference in athletic confidence and performance. This area of work has the further advantages of work with healthy clients in an atmosphere free of managed care paperwork and constraints (LoPresti and Zuckerman, 2004).

In forensic psychology the dilettantes are often involved in some aspects of court of justice work. In several instances, psychologists have

331

begun with their personal interests in law enforcement, either from brief careers or from some transient professional role. These psychologists then carve out a part-time role as a training consultant or in police selection or promotion. Aside from a few large urban areas, only consultants perform testing for police selection or promotion. Furthermore, this entrée is commonly followed by counseling of officers who have had to shoot suspects, who have substance abuse problems, or whose family situations interfere with effectiveness at work. A few psychologists who fall into this niche also train officers in hostage negotiations or do such negotiations themselves. Almost none of these psychologists begin with the objective of being a law enforcement psychologist; rather, they move from having interests to offering services.

THE OPPORTUNISTIC NICHE

In contrast to the practice work that arises out of existing skills or knowledge, a second category of work may be described as the opportunistic niche. LoPresti and Zuckerman (2004) have observed that small and rural communities are greatly underserved and that forensic practitioners in residence may need to be generalists who add to their existing knowledge base. Rural practice may be thought of as either the outsiders in—that is, urban practitioners spending limited time in rural areas—or as insiders—rural practitioners with expanding reach.

For urban practitioners, rural forensic consulting and services may yield a useful niche, parallel to the large urban medical and mental health practices that maintain a once-a-week office practice in underserved communities. The urban forensic consultant may be sought out for specialized issues as diverse as threats of family violence, jail management difficulties, disordered citizens who are repeatedly arrested and brought before the courts, and management of youth behavior problems. As some of these referrals are accepted, a choice often must be made about how much additional effort and training should be invested to develop a particular subject as an expanded niche.

In contrast, the "insider" psychologist living in rural areas already has a variety of secondary forensic practices. This professional has to make decisions about balancing local demands for forensic evaluations and treatment and professional interests with the levels of training and competencies necessary to add to the existing breadth of activity. Although these competing demands are always present, the marginal payoff of still another specialization, such as trial consultation, makes such decisions difficult. Nevertheless, a sharp awareness sometimes does arise in a rural practice of a niche that serves the psychologist and community equally well. For some forensic psychologists, addressing bullying and violence prevention in the public schools may represent such a productive niche.

Other opportunistic niches may be found by expanding on an area within existing direct client services. Here are two examples. First, a clinician found that much time with one client was devoted to treatment of an Internet addiction to gambling. He went through a self-directed program of further study that eventually allowed him to treat and assess others in trouble with the law because of Internet-related addictions to pornography and gambling. In a second example, substance abuse in a small religious community led to break-ins, assaults, and suicide attempts. The local psychologist studied this process and become a treatment resource for some of the defendants and their families.

LEARNING NICHE SKILLS

Although many psychological skills are generalizable, responsible clinicians should not automatically assume that approaches they already know and use are transferable as a whole to a niche practice. In different contexts, Garb (1989) and Dawes, Faust, and Meehl (1989) have concluded that experience does not assure competence. The explanation for these conclusions, based in part on examination of the research literature, is that many professionals learn only from directed feedback and from structured experiences; doing does not ensure knowing. Four niche-related learning steps should be considered for the forensic psychologist.

First, a systematic analysis of the niche-related behaviors and problems at hand can clarify the nature of additional needed skills. If the clinical issue is job performance lapses at work-release centers, then the learning process would include observations at the centers, interviews with parolees, understanding of the influences of behaviors following institutional release, and time spent in reviewing the literature.

Second, periods of shadowing or otherwise learning from other practitioners and consulting experts are good options. In this process, psychologists with major practice commitments to the prospective niche permit the forensic novice to accompany them in their practices. In my own forensic work, I occasionally agree to offer consultation to practitioners seeking forensic skills. They send me drafts of reports, transcripts of court testimony and depositions, and details of forthcoming cases, often with identifying information removed. We speak by telephone once a week and work with much intensity on the essential issues, skills, and practices that improve the competence of the psychologist.

Pro bono work also provides an aid to learning. Giving away services initially (with the caveat that one is learning) can provide good direct experience. Once the foot is in the door for, say, counseling spouses as they fight over divorce and custody issues, then the referring attorneys become regular referral sources and sometimes clients themselves.

Finally, a common way of the mastering the niche is to attend workshops and short courses. As part of licensing renewal requirements, practitioners are seeking continuing education unit (CEU) courses, anyway. With a modest amount of searching, one can find coverage of most topics within psychology. One neuropsychologist I know who wanted to expand into forensic neuropsychology attended a few days of workshops offered by the American Academy of Forensic Psychology, and felt reassured and more comfortable in her new venture.

PROMOTING THE NICHE

As a general rule, indirection should be the preferred marketing modality. Pushing and promoting may offend. One forensic psychologist of my acquaintance went from one law office to another, dropping off his business card and a self-promotional brochure. He quickly became a target of ridicule.

How does one develop indirection? Three steps are often productive.

1. *Giving talks to target audiences about the niche issues and interventions.* Sometimes the niche audiences will have annual or local meetings, and an intermediary can facilitate an invitation to speak. At their best, these opportunities call for dynamic and engaging presentations of meaningful knowledge and practices; however, matter-of-fact presentations do not necessarily shut down a possible niche. Being visible and having word-of-mouth awareness by others by itself seems to help. The most referral-promoting talk I ever gave was to a semiannual meeting of the state association of trial attorneys. Nobody called me for two

months; however, within a year dozens of attorneys had called inquiring about my availability and services.

2. *A few clinicians have used the concept of the gratis newsletter.* As one learns, one can produce a niche newsletter that shares practical applications, research findings, and professional observations. Sent electronically or by regular mail, and kept short, pointed, visually attractive, and readable, they can create an audience. A few forensic psychologists write brief summaries of what they have done, do, and can do, along with personally abstracted articles, to law firms that specialize in trial work.

3. *A more subtle and nuanced promotion is to use the media.* One can become known by letting newspaper and TV reporters know of interest and expertise, as long as there is an issue of clear relevance and content. At the same time, I am cautious about making any public comment about high-publicity trials in which I play a role. Such comments are close to testifying out of court.

The Master of Multiple Skills

A hazard exists of trying to do too much and stretch oneself too thin. Many clinicians are suspicious of the person who lists a dozen or more specializations. As secondary and niche practices are developed, two rules of thumb may assist.

1. *Keep multiple skills to a manageable number.* Some forensic clinicians divert so much of their effort into developing specializations that the careful and accountable maintenance of their practices suffers.

2. *Be willing to expand skills slowly.* A colleague who had never done or studied custody assessments rushed into the field with a burst of study and elicitation of referrals. As experienced custody assessors would anticipate, the unexpected demands and stressors made the process uncomfortable.

Becoming the Niche Consultant: Some Conclusions

Some niche practice in forensic psychology comes directly from reading and searching the literature. Psychologists may see an article, decide they wish to pursue this work, and then generate business. This journal-driven practice is difficult to mobilize. Word of mouth among attorneys is amazingly effective. Once a practitioner does one thing really well, just once, the word spreads. When I ask attorneys why they have called me, most of the time the answer is that an attorney recommended me.

Practitioners with time of their hands should not rush out pell-mell to develop niches. A careful process of self-assessment is in order. They should consider what they truly want to do. A systematic inventory needs to be taken of what they want to do, and what they can manage personally. The strains of work should be judged by checking with experienced practitioners, and then reviewed in terms of the personal level of tolerance.

References

Ackerman, M. (1999). *Essentials of forensic psychological assessment*. New York: John Wiley & Sons.

————. (2006). *Clinician's guide to child custody evaluations, 2006 edition*. Hoboken, NJ: John Wiley & Sons.

Alberts, F. L., & Blau, T. H. (1993). Psychological Seminars Press.

American Psychiatric Association. (2000). *Diagnostic and statistical manual of mental disorders* (4th ed., Text revision). Washington, DC: Author.

American Psychological Association. (2002). Ethical principles of psychologists and code of conduct. *American Psychologist, 47*, 1597–1611.

Atkins v. Virginia, 536 U.S. 304 (2002).

Blau, T. H. (2001). *The psychologist as expert witness* (2nd ed.). New York: John Wiley & Sons.

Blau, T. H., & Alberts, F. L., Jr. (2004). *The forensic documentation sourcebook: The complete paperwork resource for forensic mental health practice* (2nd ed.). Hoboken, NJ: John Wiley & Sons.

Brodsky, S., & McKinzey, R. K. (2002, June). The ethical confrontation of the unethical forensic colleague. *Professional Psychology: Research and Practice, 33*(3), 307–309.

Campbell, T. W. (2004). Assessing sex offenders: Problems and pitfalls. Springfield, IL: Charles C Thomas Publishers.

Chanen, J. S. (2001). Building a niche from scratch. *ABA Journal, 87*(10), 36–41.

337

Condie, L. O. (2003, June). *Parenting evaluations for the court.* (Perspectives in Law and Psychology, Vol. 18). Springer.

Daubert v. Merrell Dow Pharmaceuticals, 509 U.S. 579 (1993).

Dawes, R. M., Faust, D., & Meehl, P. E. (1989, March). Clinical versus actuarial judgment. *Science New Series, 243*(4899).

DeClue, G. (2005). *Interrogations and disputed confessions: A manual for forensic psychological practice.* Sarasota, FL: Professional Resource Press.

Doren, D. M. (2002). *Evaluating sex offenders: A manual for civil commitments and beyond.* Thousand Oaks, CA: Sage Publications.

Durham v. United States, 214 F. 2d 862 (D.C. Cir., 1954).

Dusky v. United States, 362 U.S. 402 (1960).

Dyer, F. J. (1999). *Psychological consultation in parental rights cases.* New York: Guilford Press.

Frye v. United States, 293 F.1013 (D.C. Cir., 1923).

Galatzer-Levy, R. M., & Kraus, L. (eds.) (1999). The scientific basis of child custody decisions. New York: John Wiley & Sons.

Garb, H. N. (1989, May). Clinical judgment, clinical training, and professional experience. *Psychological Bulletin, 105*(3), 387–396.

Godinez v. Moran, 113 S. Ct. 2680 (1993).

Gould, J. W. (2006). *Conducting scientifically crafted child custody evaluations* (2nd ed.). Sarasota, FL: Professional Resource Press.

Greenberg, S., & Shuman, D. (1997, February). Irreconcilable conflict between therapeutic and forensic roles. *Professional psychology: Research and practice, 28*(1), 50–57.

Grisso, T. (1988). *Competency to stand trial evaluation: A manual for practice.* Sarasota, FL: Professional Resource Press.

———. (1991). A developmental history of the American Psychology–Law Society. *Law and Human Behavior, 15*, 213–231.

———. (1998). *Forensic evaluation of juveniles.* Sarasota, FL: Professional Resource Press.

———. (2002). *Evaluating competencies: Forensic assessments and instruments* (2nd ed.). (Perspectives in Law and Psychology, 16.) Springer.

Gudjonsson, G. H. (2003). *The psychology of interrogations and confessions: A handbook.* Hoboken, NJ: John Wiley & Sons.

Hagen, M. A. (1997). *Whores of the court: The fraud of psychiatric testimony in the rape of American justice.* New York: ReganBooks.

Hess, A., & Weiner, I. (Eds.). (2005). *The handbook of forensic psychology* (3rd ed.). Hoboken, NJ: John Wiley & Sons.

Kansas v. Hendricks, 117 S. Ct. 2072 (1997).

Kirkland, K., & Kirkland, K. L. (2001). Frequency of child custody evaluation complaints and related disciplinary action: A survey of the Association of State and Provincial Psychology Boards. *Professional Psychology: Research and Practice, 32*(2), 171–174.

References

Lally, S. J. (2003, October). What tests are acceptable for use in forensic evaluations? A survey of experts. *Professional Psychology: Research and Practice*, *34*(5), 491–498.

Lipsitt, P., Lelos, D., & McGarry, A. L. (1971). Competency for trial: A screening instrument. *American Journal of Psychiatry*, *128*, 105–109.

LoPresti, R. L., & Zuckerman, E. L. (2004). *Rewarding specialties for mental health clinicians: Developing your practice niche.* New York: Guilford.

Mart, E. G. (1998). Problems with the diagnosis of factitious disorder by proxy in forensic settings. Presented at the Eastern Psychological Association, Boston, Massachusetts.

———. (1998, February). Munchausen's syndrome by proxy: Psycho-legal issues. (Paper presentation). Eastern Psychological Association Annual Meeting, Boston, Massachusetts, February 28, 1998.

———. (1999, January). Problems with the diagnosis of factitious disorder by proxy in forensic settings. *American Journal of Forensic Psychology*, *17*(1).

———. (1999, October). Factitious disorder by proxy and the federal rules of evidence (Poster session). American Bar Association/American Psychological Association Conference, "Psychological Expertise and Criminal Justice," Washington, D.C.

———. (2002). *Munchausen syndrome by proxy reconsidered.* Manchester, NH: Bally Vaughan Pub.

Melton, G. B., Petrila, J., Poythress, N. G., & Slobogin, C. (1997). *Psychological evaluations for the courts* (2nd ed.). New York: Guilford Press.

Price, J. R. (1991). *Deception and malingering.* Continuing Education Workshop, Psychological Seminars.

Rogers, R. (2001). *Handbook of diagnostic and structured interviewing: A guide for psychologists.* New York: Guilford Press.

Rogers, R. (ed.). (1997). *Clinical assessment of malingering and deception* (2nd ed.). New York : Guilford Press.

Rogers, R., & Shuman, D. (2000). *Conducting insanity evaluations* (2nd ed.). New York: Guilford Press.

Schreier, H., & Libow, J. (1993). *Hurting for love: Munchausen by Proxy Syndrome.* New York: Guilford Press.

State v. Champagne, 127 N.H. 266, 270 (1985).

Stout, C. E., & Grand, L. C. (2005). *Getting started in private practice.* Hoboken, NJ: John Wiley & Sons.

Sullivan, H. S., & Perry, H. S. (1972). *The psychiatric interview.* New York: W. W. Norton.

Sun Tzu. (1991). *The art of war* (T. Cleary, Trans.). Boston: Shambala.

Thompson, L. (1996). Search for a niche: Future directions for educational psychologists. *Educational Psychology in Practice*, *12*, 99–106.

Van Horne, B. A. (2004). Psychology licensing board disciplinary actions: The realities. *Professional Psychology: Research and Practice*, *35*(2), 170–178.

Weiner, I., & Hess, A. (Eds.). (2006). *The handbook of forensic psychology.* Hoboken, NJ: John Wiley & Sons.

Younggren, J. N., & Gottlieb, M. C. Managing risk when contemplating multiple relationships. *Professional Psychology: Research and Practice, 35*(3), 255–260.

Ziskin, J., & Faust, D. (1995). *Coping with psychiatric and psychological testimony.* Los Angeles: Law and Psychology Press.

Index